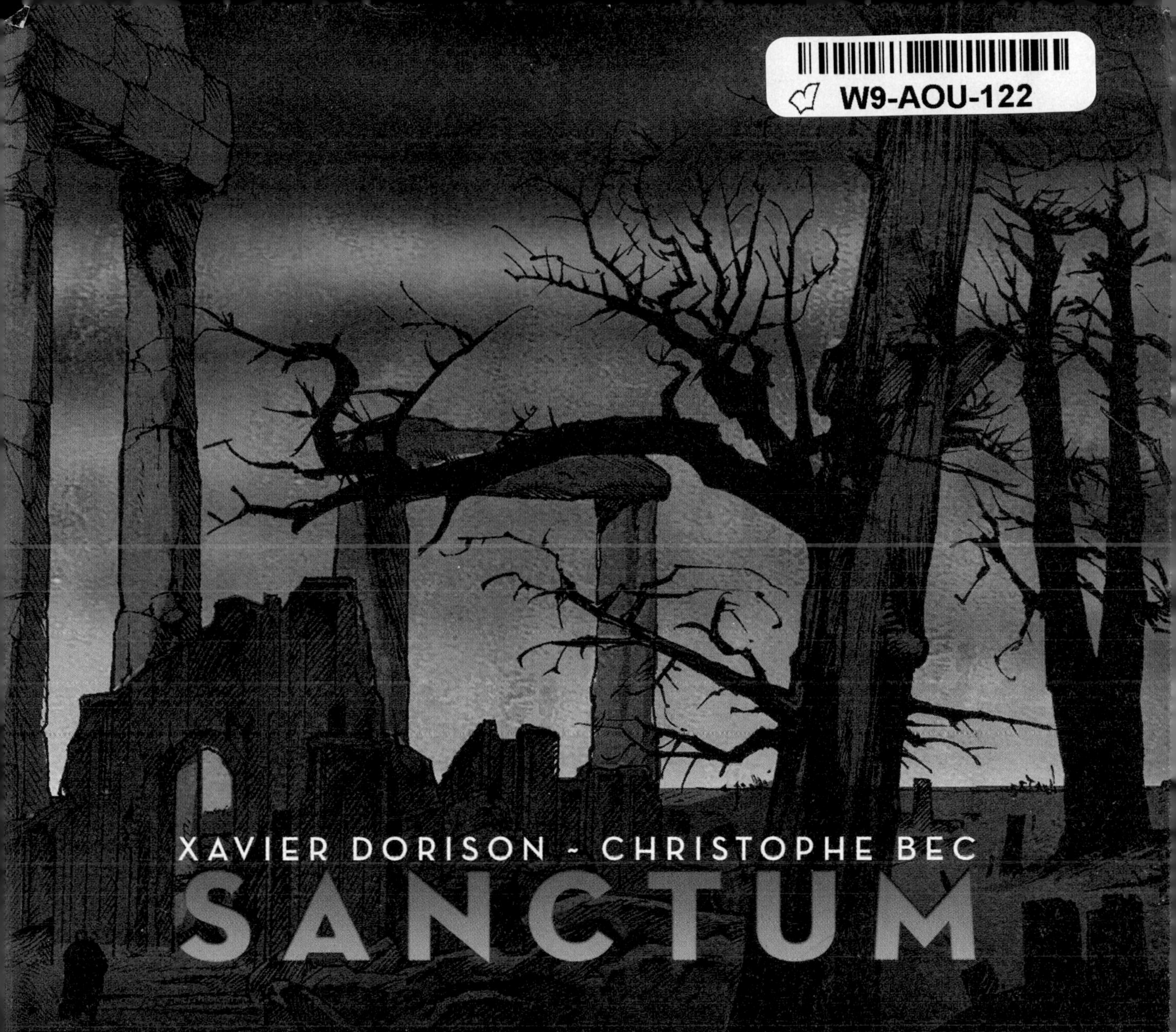

XAVIER DORISON - CHRISTOPHE BEC

SANCTUM

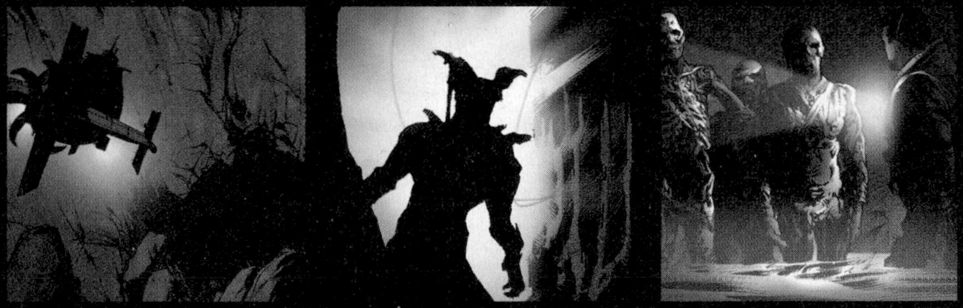

Humanoids / DC Comics

SANCTUM

XAVIER DORISON, *Writer* **CHRISTOPHE BEC,** *Artist* **HOMER REYES,** *Colorist* **JUSTIN KELLY & SASHA WATSON,** *Translators*

THIERRY FRISSEN, *Book Designer*
PATRICK LEHANCE, *Letterer*
FRANCIS LOMBARD, *Editor, Collected Edition*
PHILIPPE HAURI & FABRICE GIGER, *Editors, Original Edition*

SANCTUM, Humanoids Publishing, PO Box 931658, Hollywood, CA 90094. This is a publication of DC Comics, 1700 Broadway, New York, NY 10019.

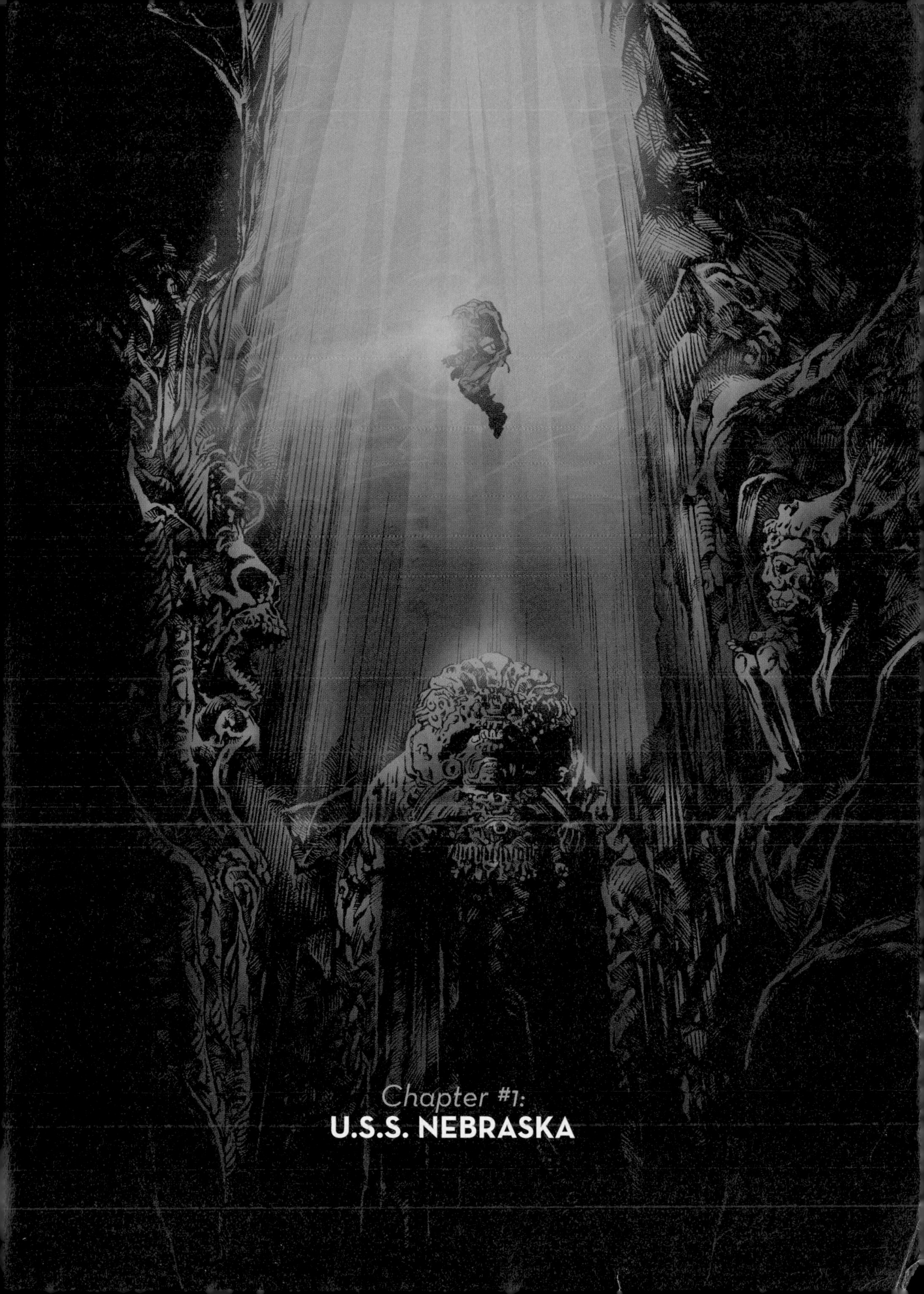

Chapter #1:
U.S.S. NEBRASKA

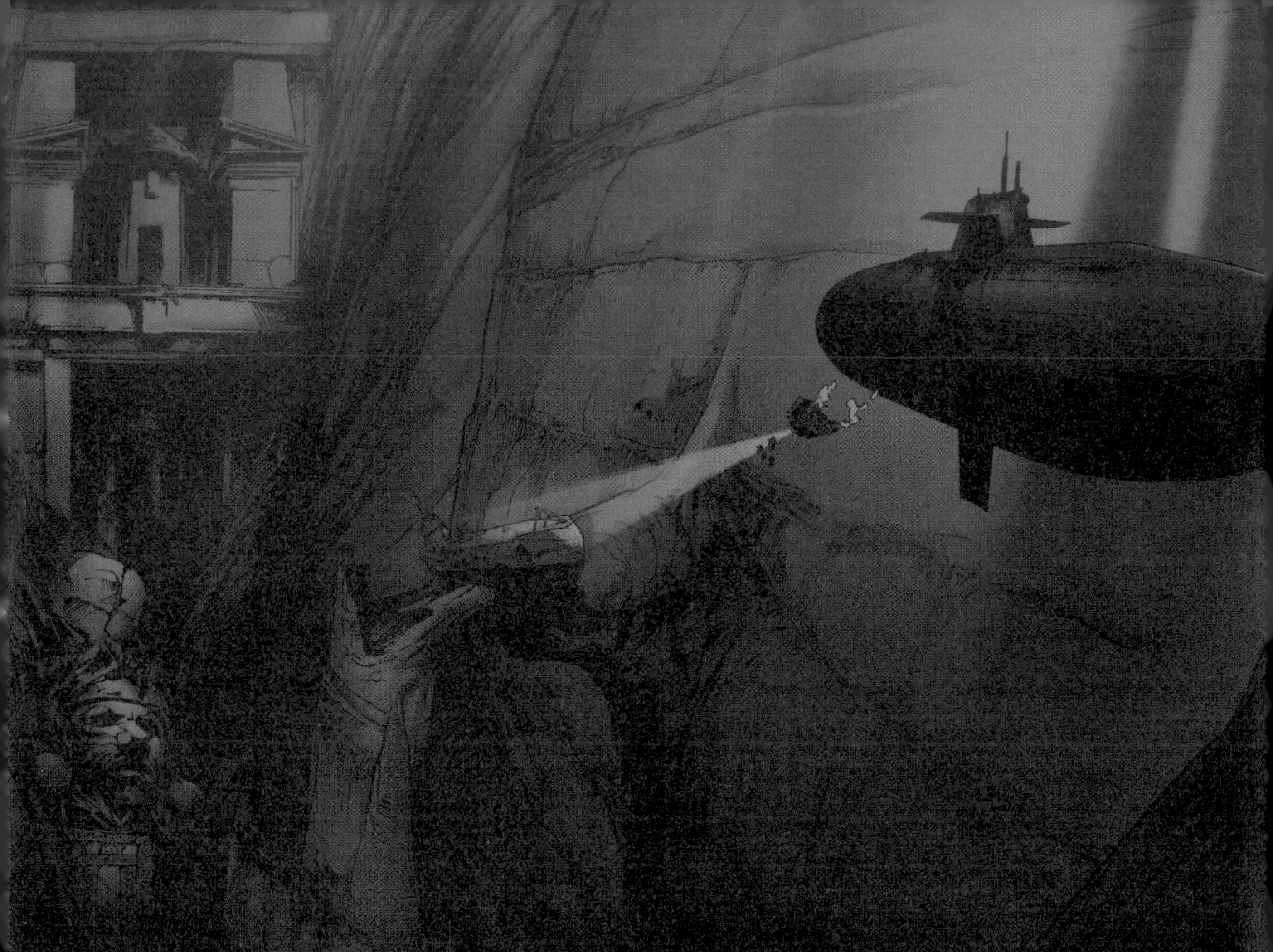

Ba'al, seated in his palace,
will it be king or commoner
who conquers the earth, My domain?
To the god Môt I send My envoy,
who will speak to
the warrior El,
His champion.
In silence, Môt shrieks.
In silence, El plots.
Only I rule the gods.
I nourish gods and
humans, satisfying
the throngs who dwell on earth.

- Ugarit poem

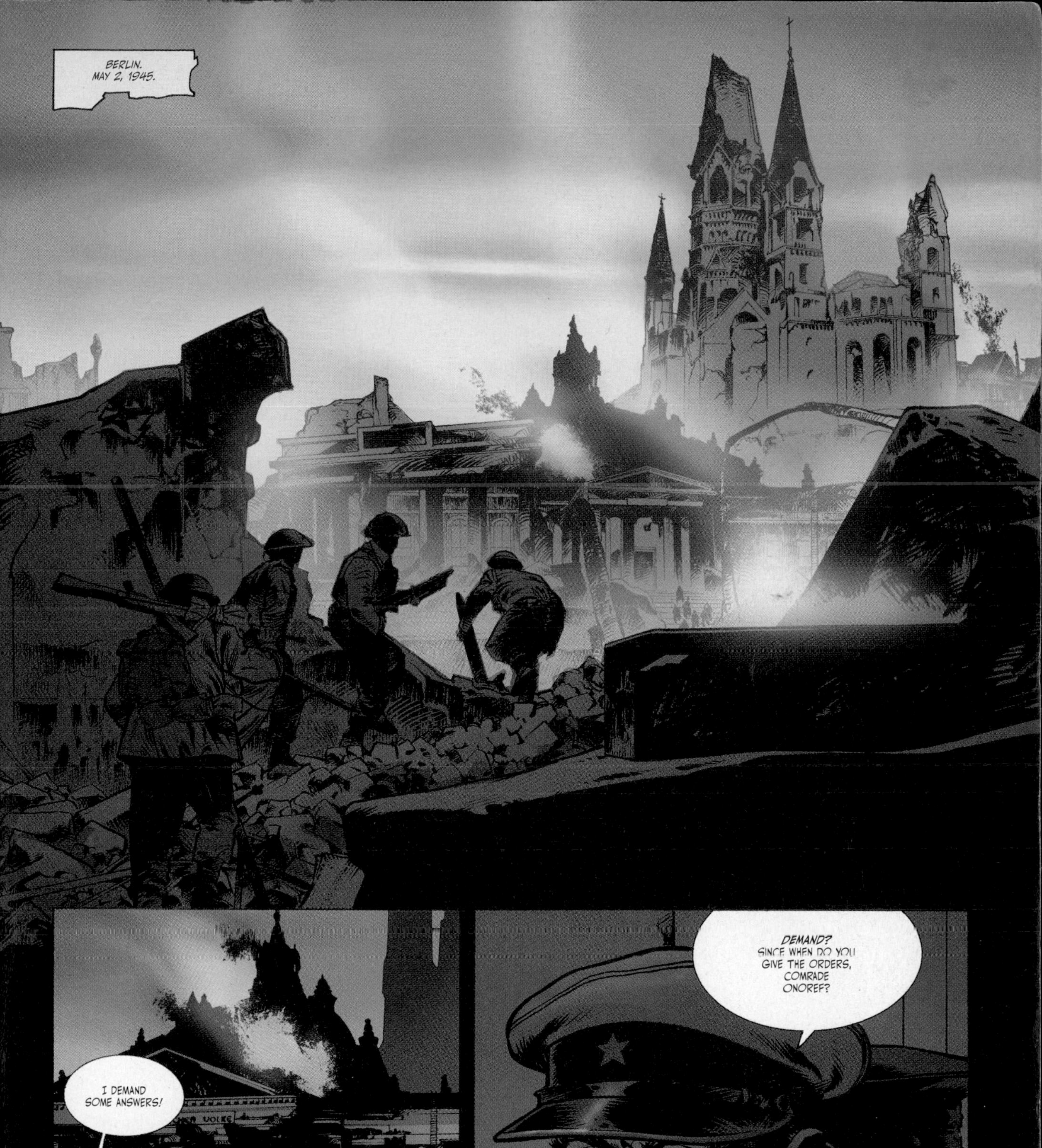
BERLIN. MAY 2, 1945.
I DEMAND SOME ANSWERS!
DEMAND? SINCE WHEN DO YOU GIVE THE ORDERS, COMRADE ONOREF?

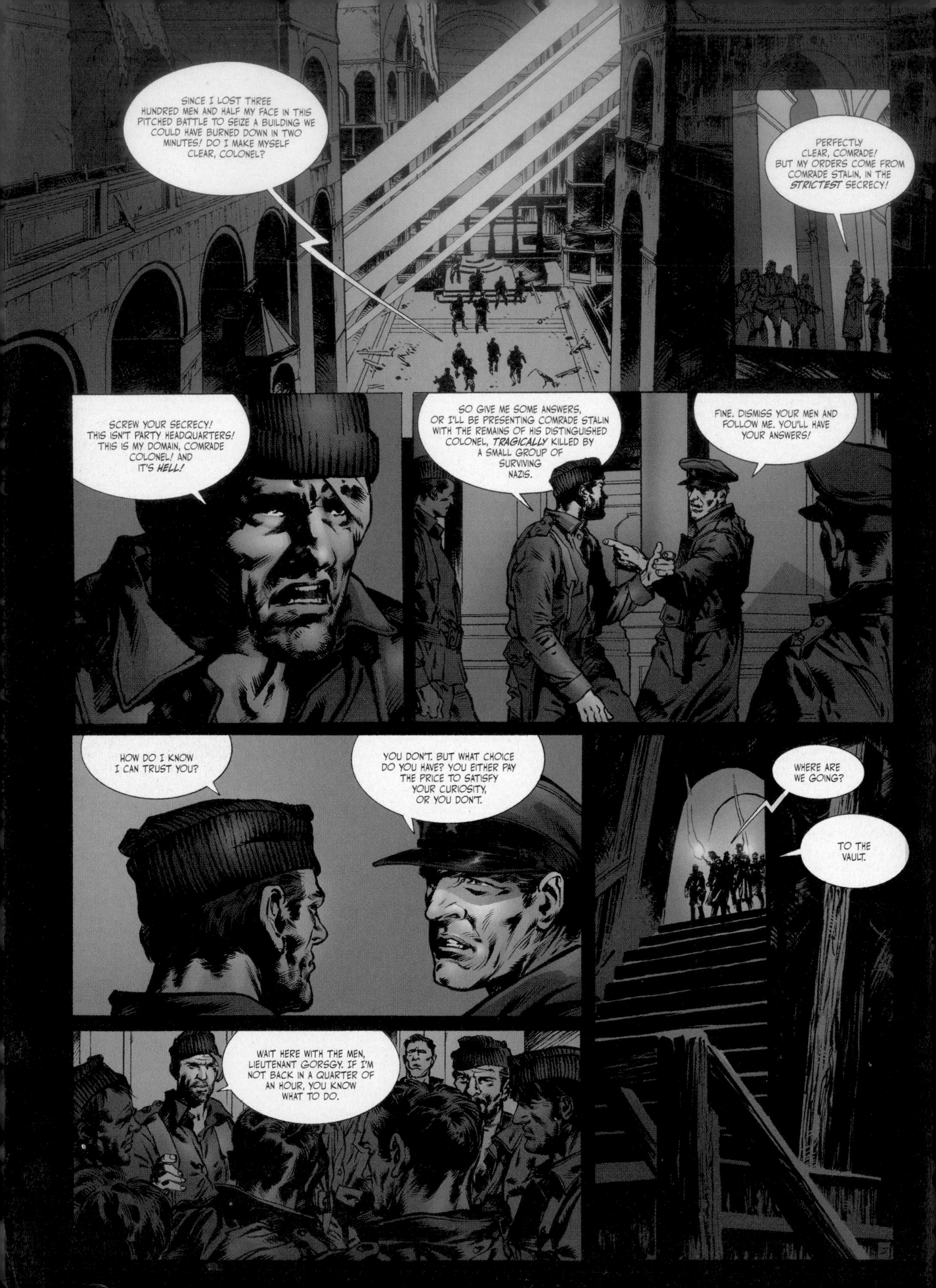
SINCE I LOST THREE HUNDRED MEN AND HALF MY FACE IN THIS PITCHED BATTLE TO SEIZE A BUILDING WE COULD HAVE BURNED DOWN IN TWO MINUTES! DO I MAKE MYSELF CLEAR, COLONEL?
PERFECTLY CLEAR, COMRADE! BUT MY ORDERS COME FROM COMRADE STALIN, IN THE *STRICTEST* SECRECY!
SCREW YOUR SECRECY! THIS ISN'T PARTY HEADQUARTERS! THIS IS MY DOMAIN, COMRADE COLONEL! AND IT'S *HELL!*
SO GIVE ME SOME ANSWERS, OR I'LL BE PRESENTING COMRADE STALIN WITH THE REMAINS OF HIS DISTINGUISHED COLONEL, *TRAGICALLY* KILLED BY A SMALL GROUP OF SURVIVING NAZIS.
FINE. DISMISS YOUR MEN AND FOLLOW ME. YOU'LL HAVE YOUR ANSWERS!
HOW DO I KNOW I CAN TRUST YOU?
YOU DON'T. BUT WHAT CHOICE DO YOU HAVE? YOU EITHER PAY THE PRICE TO SATISFY YOUR CURIOSITY, OR YOU DON'T.
WAIT HERE WITH THE MEN, LIEUTENANT GORSGY. IF I'M NOT BACK IN A QUARTER OF AN HOUR, YOU KNOW WHAT TO DO.
WHERE ARE WE GOING?
TO THE VAULT.

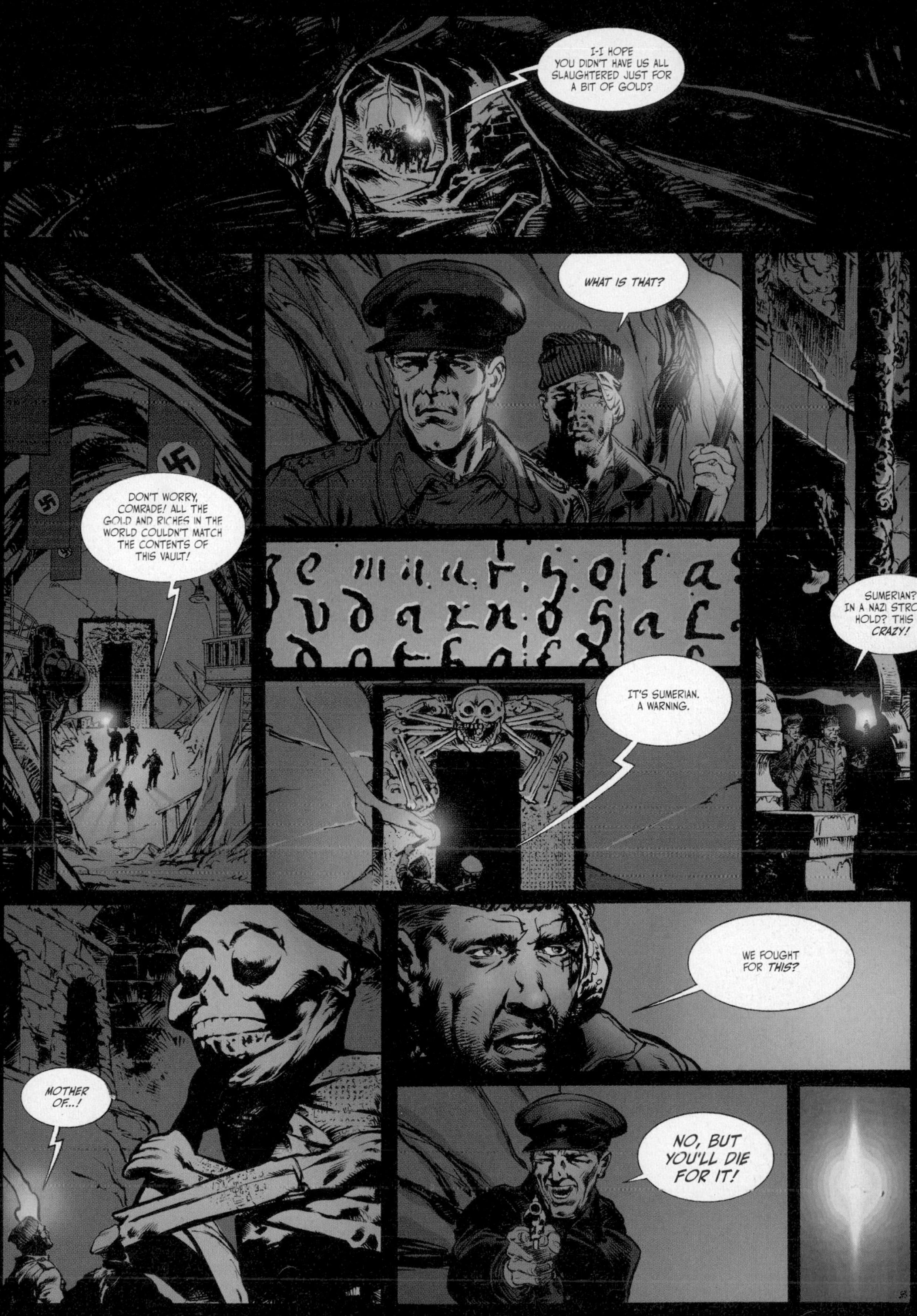
I-I HOPE YOU DIDN'T HAVE US ALL SLAUGHTERED JUST FOR A BIT OF GOLD?
WHAT IS THAT?
DON'T WORRY, COMRADE! ALL THE GOLD AND RICHES IN THE WORLD COULDN'T MATCH THE CONTENTS OF THIS VAULT!
IT'S SUMERIAN. A WARNING.
SUMERIAN? IN A NAZI STRONG-HOLD? THIS IS CRAZY!
MOTHER OF...!
WE FOUGHT FOR THIS?
NO, BUT YOU'LL DIE FOR IT!

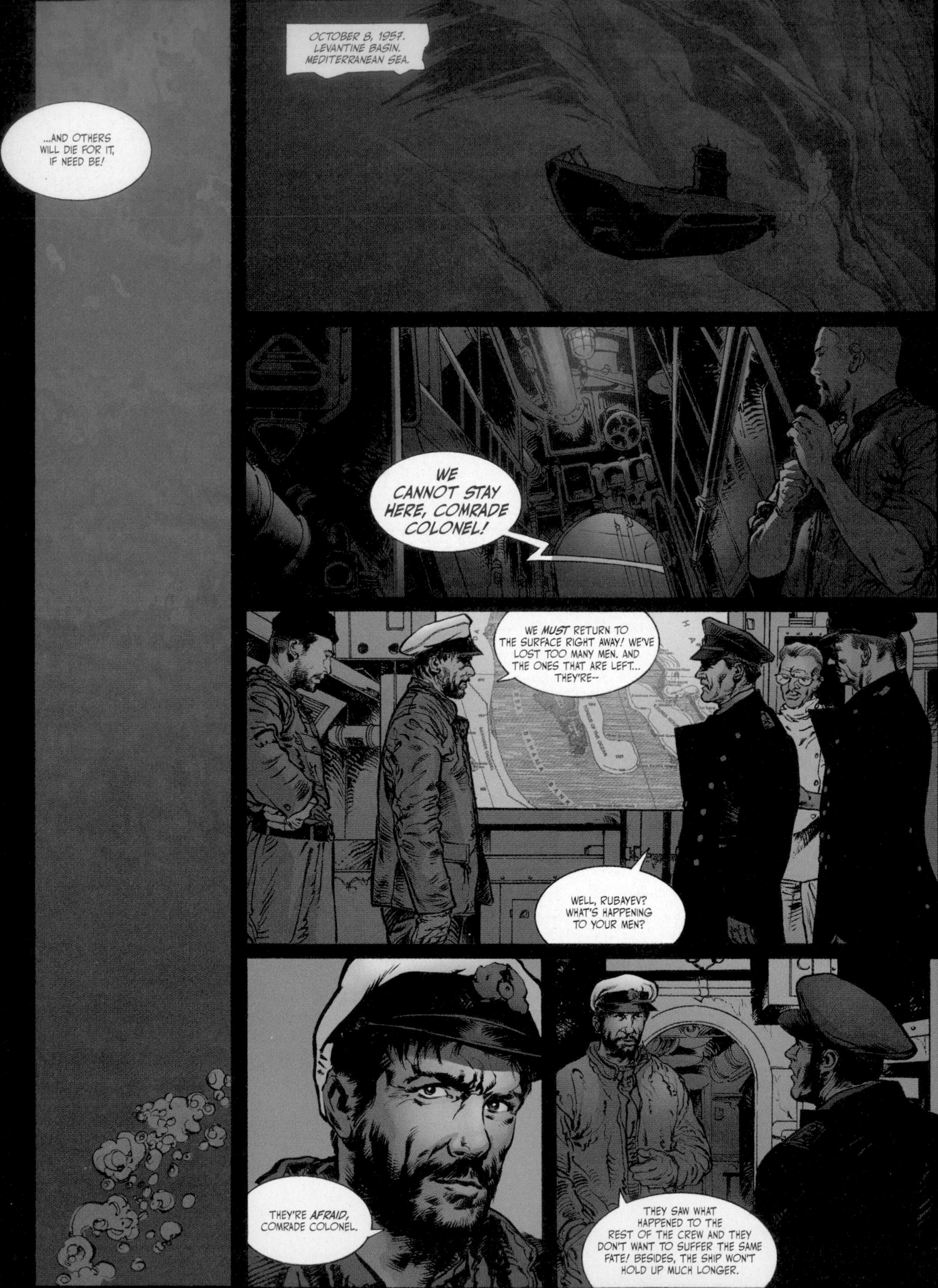

...AND OTHERS WILL DIE FOR IT, IF NEED BE!
OCTOBER 8, 1957. LEVANTINE BASIN. MEDITERRANEAN SEA.
WE CANNOT STAY HERE, COMRADE COLONEL!
WE MUST RETURN TO THE SURFACE RIGHT AWAY! WE'VE LOST TOO MANY MEN. AND THE ONES THAT ARE LEFT... THEY'RE--
WELL, RUBAYEV? WHAT'S HAPPENING TO YOUR MEN?
THEY'RE AFRAID, COMRADE COLONEL.
THEY SAW WHAT HAPPENED TO THE REST OF THE CREW AND THEY DON'T WANT TO SUFFER THE SAME FATE! BESIDES, THE SHIP WON'T HOLD UP MUCH LONGER.

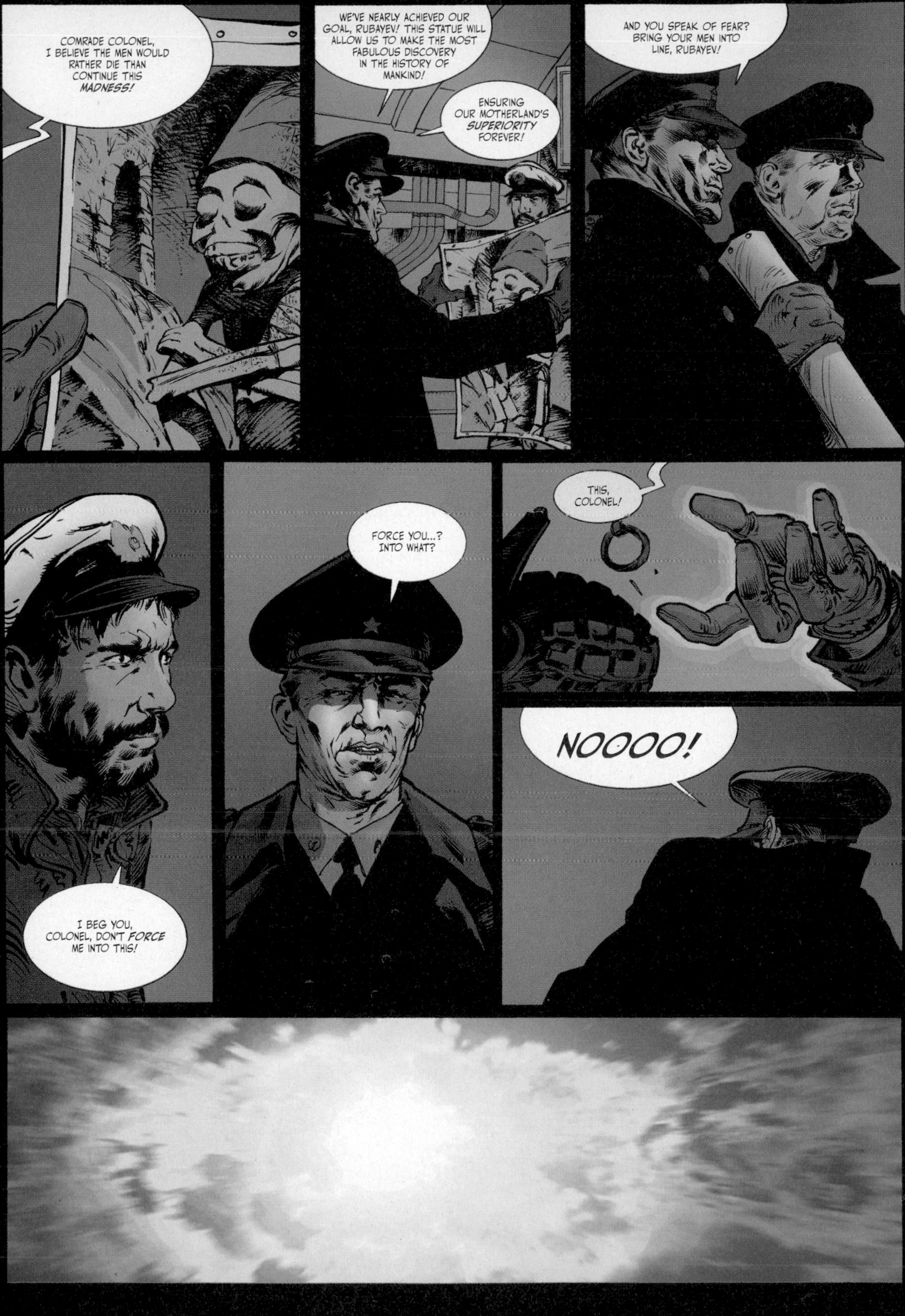
COMRADE COLONEL, I BELIEVE THE MEN WOULD RATHER DIE THAN CONTINUE THIS MADNESS!
WE'VE NEARLY ACHIEVED OUR GOAL, RUBAYEV! THIS STATUE WILL ALLOW US TO MAKE THE MOST FABULOUS DISCOVERY IN THE HISTORY OF MANKIND!
ENSURING OUR MOTHERLAND'S SUPERIORITY FOREVER!
AND YOU SPEAK OF FEAR? BRING YOUR MEN INTO LINE, RUBAYEV!
I BEG YOU, COLONEL, DON'T FORCE ME INTO THIS!
FORCE YOU...? INTO WHAT?
THIS, COLONEL!
NOOOO!

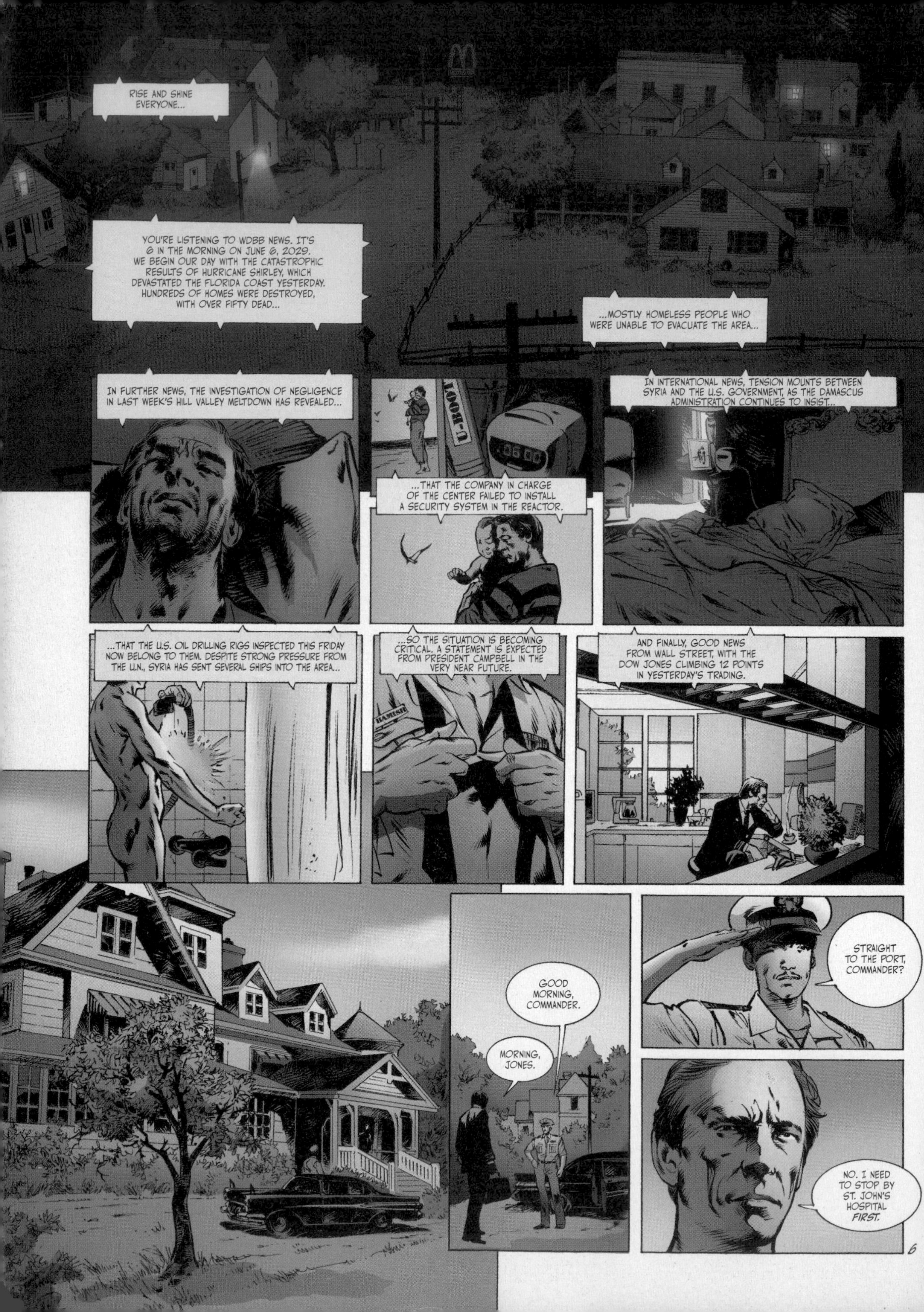
RISE AND SHINE EVERYONE...
YOU'RE LISTENING TO WDBB NEWS. IT'S 6 IN THE MORNING ON JUNE 6, 2029. WE BEGIN OUR DAY WITH THE CATASTROPHIC RESULTS OF HURRICANE SHIRLEY, WHICH DEVASTATED THE FLORIDA COAST YESTERDAY. HUNDREDS OF HOMES WERE DESTROYED, WITH OVER FIFTY DEAD...
...MOSTLY HOMELESS PEOPLE WHO WERE UNABLE TO EVACUATE THE AREA...
IN FURTHER NEWS, THE INVESTIGATION OF NEGLIGENCE IN LAST WEEK'S HILL VALLEY MELTDOWN HAS REVEALED...
U-BOOT
06:00
...THAT THE COMPANY IN CHARGE OF THE CENTER FAILED TO INSTALL A SECURITY SYSTEM IN THE REACTOR.
IN INTERNATIONAL NEWS, TENSION MOUNTS BETWEEN SYRIA AND THE U.S. GOVERNMENT, AS THE DAMASCUS ADMINISTRATION CONTINUES TO INSIST...
...THAT THE U.S. OIL DRILLING RIGS INSPECTED THIS FRIDAY NOW BELONG TO THEM. DESPITE STRONG PRESSURE FROM THE U.N., SYRIA HAS SENT SEVERAL SHIPS INTO THE AREA...
...SO THE SITUATION IS BECOMING CRITICAL. A STATEMENT IS EXPECTED FROM PRESIDENT CAMPBELL IN THE VERY NEAR FUTURE.
HAMISH
AND FINALLY, GOOD NEWS FROM WALL STREET, WITH THE DOW JONES CLIMBING 12 POINTS IN YESTERDAY'S TRADING.
GOOD MORNING, COMMANDER.
MORNING, JONES.
STRAIGHT TO THE PORT, COMMANDER?
NO. I NEED TO STOP BY ST. JOHN'S HOSPITAL *FIRST*.

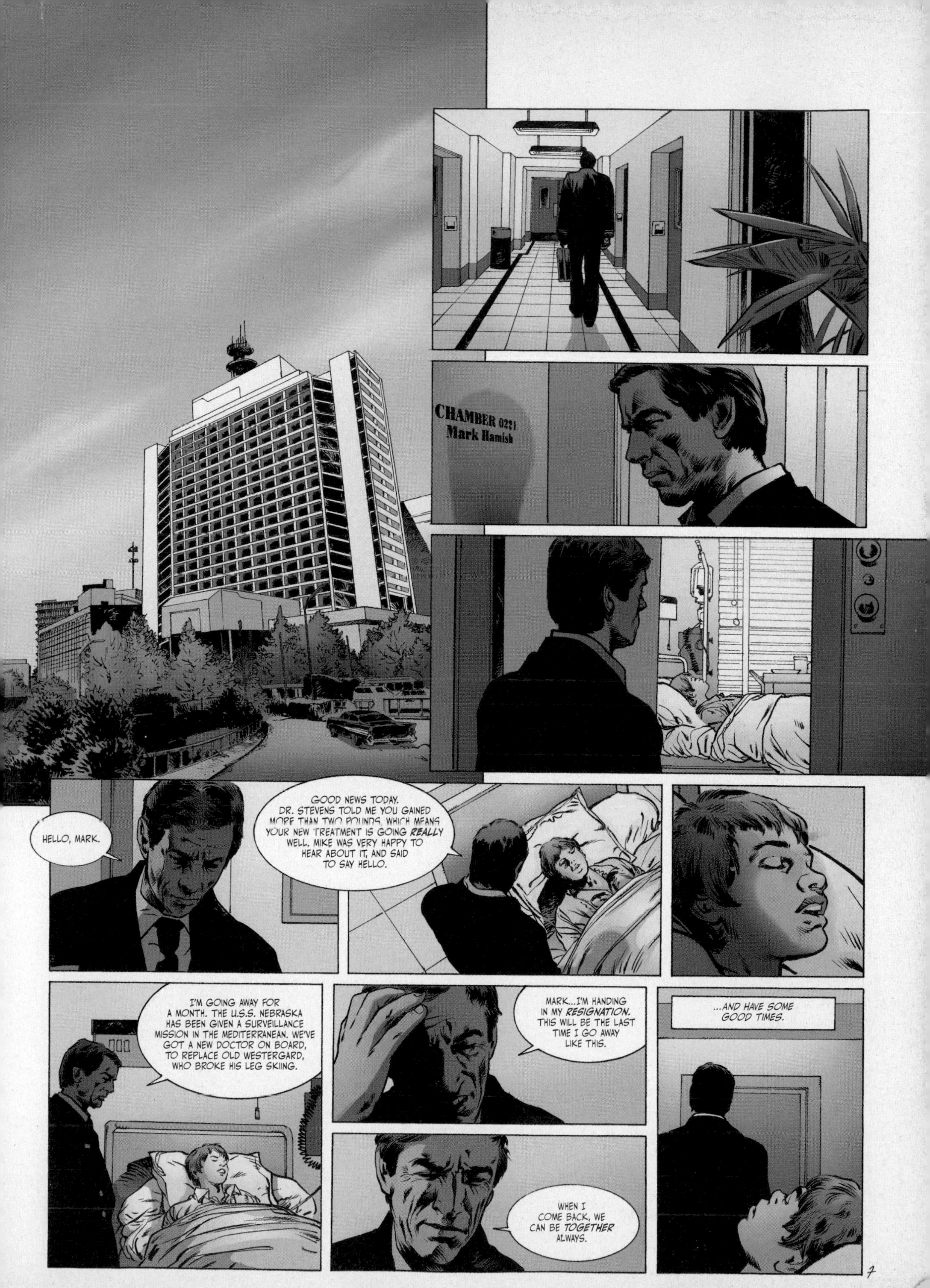
CHAMBER 0221
Mark Hamish
HELLO, MARK.
GOOD NEWS TODAY. DR. STEVENS TOLD ME YOU GAINED MORE THAN TWO POUNDS, WHICH MEANS YOUR NEW TREATMENT IS GOING REALLY WELL. MIKE WAS VERY HAPPY TO HEAR ABOUT IT, AND SAID TO SAY HELLO.
I'M GOING AWAY FOR A MONTH. THE U.S.S. NEBRASKA HAS BEEN GIVEN A SURVEILLANCE MISSION IN THE MEDITERRANEAN. WE'VE GOT A NEW DOCTOR ON BOARD, TO REPLACE OLD WESTERGARD, WHO BROKE HIS LEG SKIING.
MARK...I'M HANDING IN MY RESIGNATION. THIS WILL BE THE LAST TIME I GO AWAY LIKE THIS.
WHEN I COME BACK, WE CAN BE TOGETHER ALWAYS.
...AND HAVE SOME GOOD TIMES.

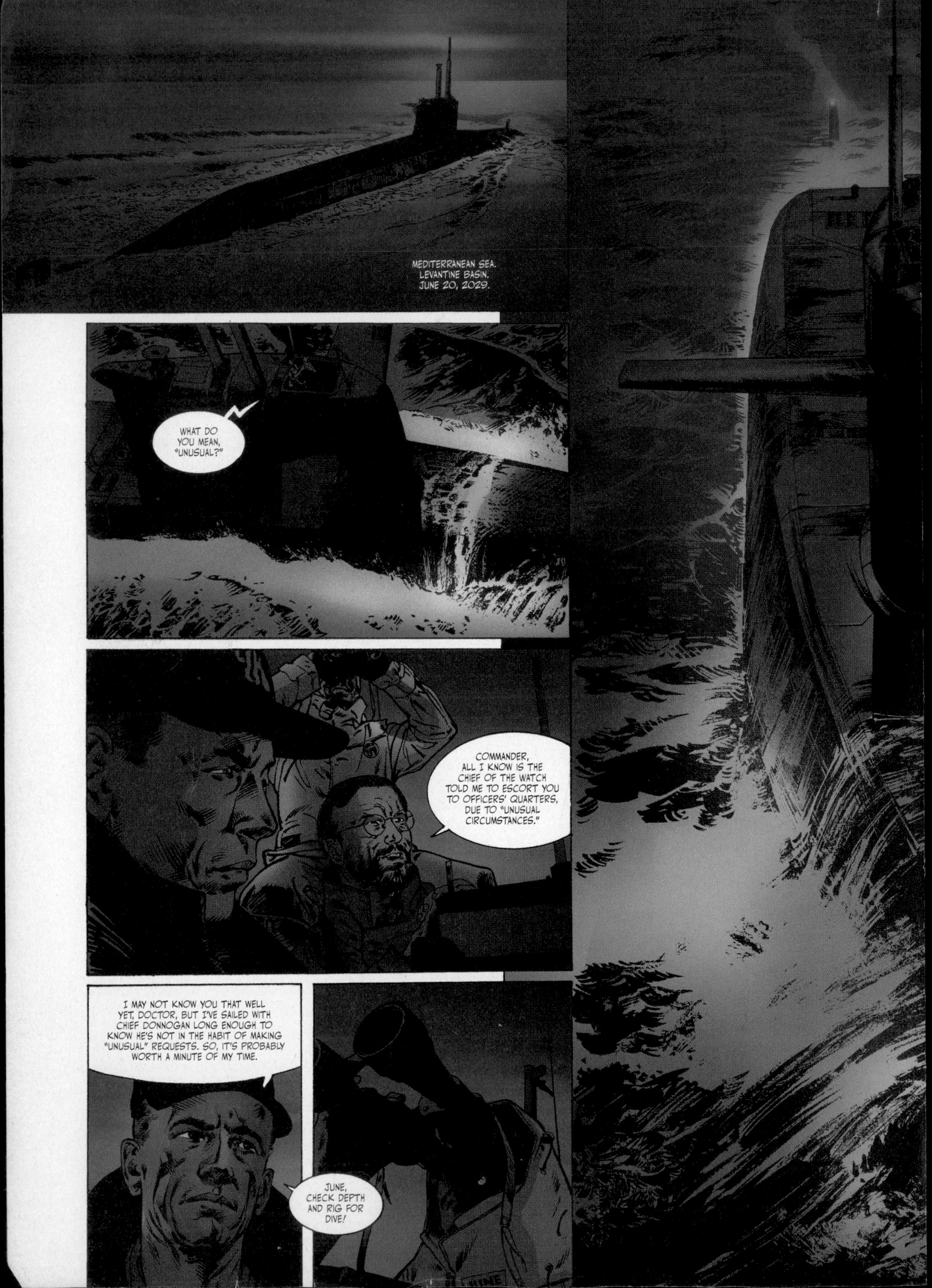
MEDITERRANEAN SEA. LEVANTINE BASIN. JUNE 20, 2029.
WHAT DO YOU MEAN, "UNUSUAL?"
COMMANDER, ALL I KNOW IS THE CHIEF OF THE WATCH TOLD ME TO ESCORT YOU TO OFFICERS' QUARTERS, DUE TO "UNUSUAL CIRCUMSTANCES."
I MAY NOT KNOW YOU THAT WELL YET, DOCTOR, BUT I'VE SAILED WITH CHIEF DONNOGAN LONG ENOUGH TO KNOW HE'S NOT IN THE HABIT OF MAKING "UNUSUAL" REQUESTS. SO, IT'S PROBABLY WORTH A MINUTE OF MY TIME.
JUNE, CHECK DEPTH AND RIG FOR DIVE!

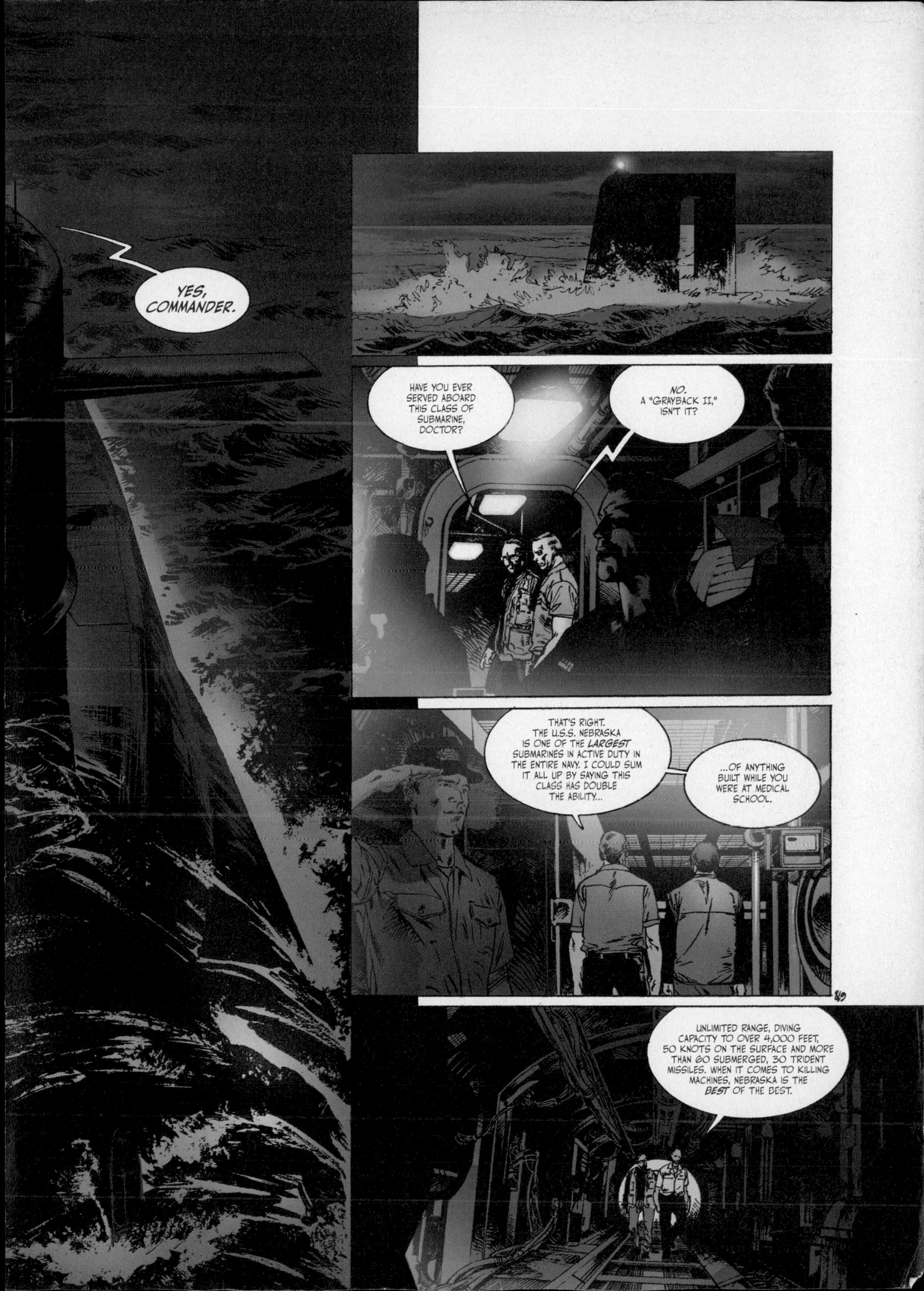
YES, COMMANDER.
HAVE YOU EVER SERVED ABOARD THIS CLASS OF SUBMARINE, DOCTOR?
NO. A "GRAYBACK II," ISN'T IT?
THAT'S RIGHT. THE U.S.S. NEBRASKA IS ONE OF THE LARGEST SUBMARINES IN ACTIVE DUTY IN THE ENTIRE NAVY. I COULD SUM IT ALL UP BY SAYING THIS CLASS HAS DOUBLE THE ABILITY...
...OF ANYTHING BUILT WHILE YOU WERE AT MEDICAL SCHOOL.
UNLIMITED RANGE, DIVING CAPACITY TO OVER 4,000 FEET, 50 KNOTS ON THE SURFACE AND MORE THAN 60 SUBMERGED, 30 TRIDENT MISSILES. WHEN IT COMES TO KILLING MACHINES, NEBRASKA IS THE BEST OF THE BEST.

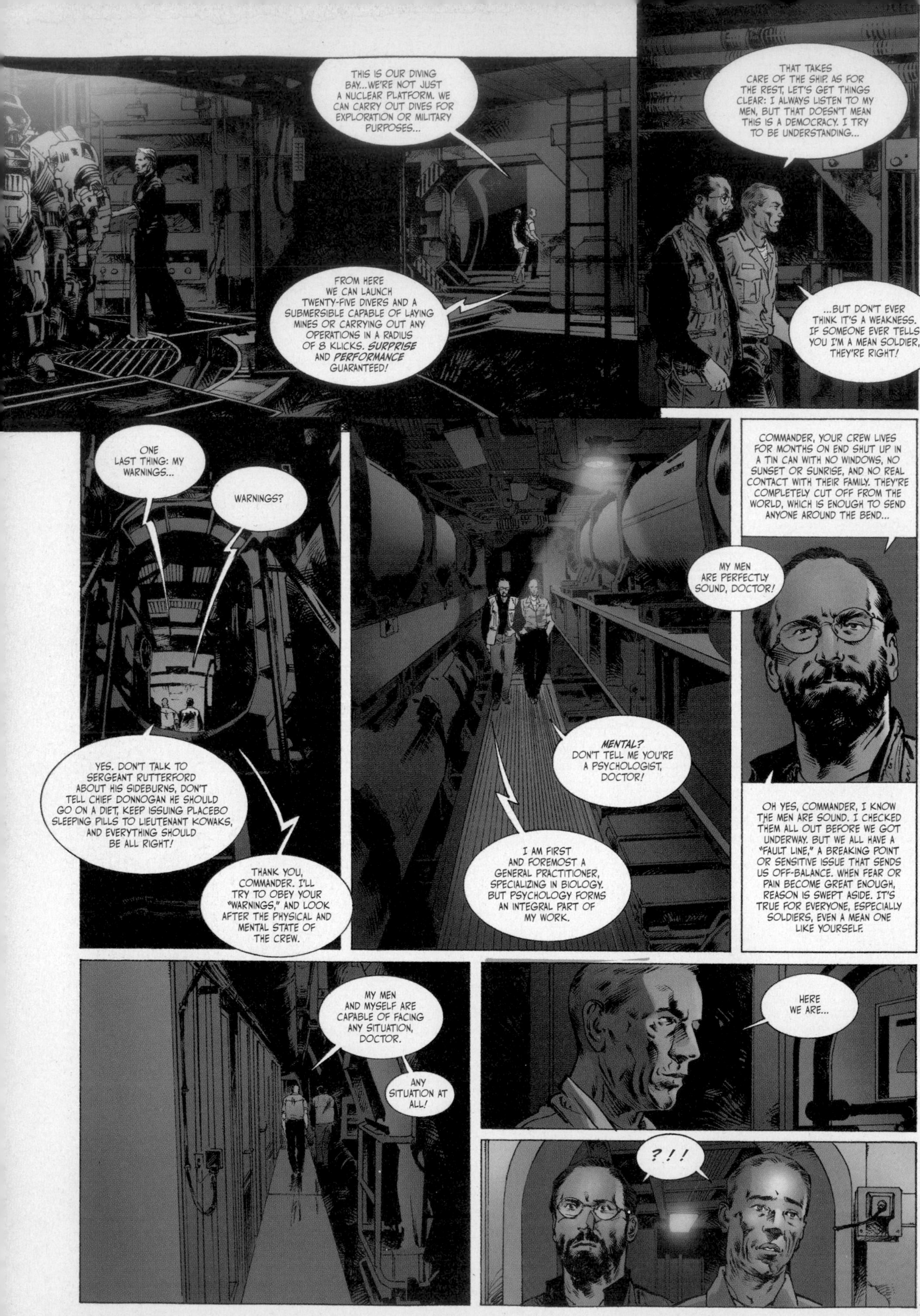
THIS IS OUR DIVING BAY...WE'RE NOT JUST A NUCLEAR PLATFORM. WE CAN CARRY OUT DIVES FOR EXPLORATION OR MILITARY PURPOSES...
FROM HERE WE CAN LAUNCH TWENTY-FIVE DIVERS AND A SUBMERSIBLE CAPABLE OF LAYING MINES OR CARRYING OUT ANY OPERATIONS IN A RADIUS OF 8 KLICKS. SURPRISE AND PERFORMANCE GUARANTEED!
THAT TAKES CARE OF THE SHIP. AS FOR THE REST, LET'S GET THINGS CLEAR: I ALWAYS LISTEN TO MY MEN, BUT THAT DOESN'T MEAN THIS IS A DEMOCRACY. I TRY TO BE UNDERSTANDING...
...BUT DON'T EVER THINK IT'S A WEAKNESS. IF SOMEONE EVER TELLS YOU I'M A MEAN SOLDIER, THEY'RE RIGHT!
ONE LAST THING: MY WARNINGS...
WARNINGS?
YES. DON'T TALK TO SERGEANT RUTTERFORD ABOUT HIS SIDEBURNS, DON'T TELL CHIEF DONNOGAN HE SHOULD GO ON A DIET, KEEP ISSUING PLACEBO SLEEPING PILLS TO LIEUTENANT KOWAKS, AND EVERYTHING SHOULD BE ALL RIGHT!
THANK YOU, COMMANDER. I'LL TRY TO OBEY YOUR "WARNINGS," AND LOOK AFTER THE PHYSICAL AND MENTAL STATE OF THE CREW.
MENTAL? DON'T TELL ME YOU'RE A PSYCHOLOGIST, DOCTOR!
I AM FIRST AND FOREMOST A GENERAL PRACTITIONER, SPECIALIZING IN BIOLOGY. BUT PSYCHOLOGY FORMS AN INTEGRAL PART OF MY WORK.
COMMANDER, YOUR CREW LIVES FOR MONTHS ON END SHUT UP IN A TIN CAN WITH NO WINDOWS, NO SUNSET OR SUNRISE, AND NO REAL CONTACT WITH THEIR FAMILY. THEY'RE COMPLETELY CUT OFF FROM THE WORLD, WHICH IS ENOUGH TO SEND ANYONE AROUND THE BEND...
MY MEN ARE PERFECTLY SOUND, DOCTOR!
OH YES, COMMANDER, I KNOW THE MEN ARE SOUND. I CHECKED THEM ALL OUT BEFORE WE GOT UNDERWAY. BUT WE ALL HAVE A "FAULT LINE," A BREAKING POINT OR SENSITIVE ISSUE THAT SENDS US OFF-BALANCE. WHEN FEAR OR PAIN BECOME GREAT ENOUGH, REASON IS SWEPT ASIDE. IT'S TRUE FOR EVERYONE, ESPECIALLY SOLDIERS, EVEN A MEAN ONE LIKE YOURSELF.
MY MEN AND MYSELF ARE CAPABLE OF FACING ANY SITUATION, DOCTOR.
ANY SITUATION AT ALL!
HERE WE ARE...
?!!

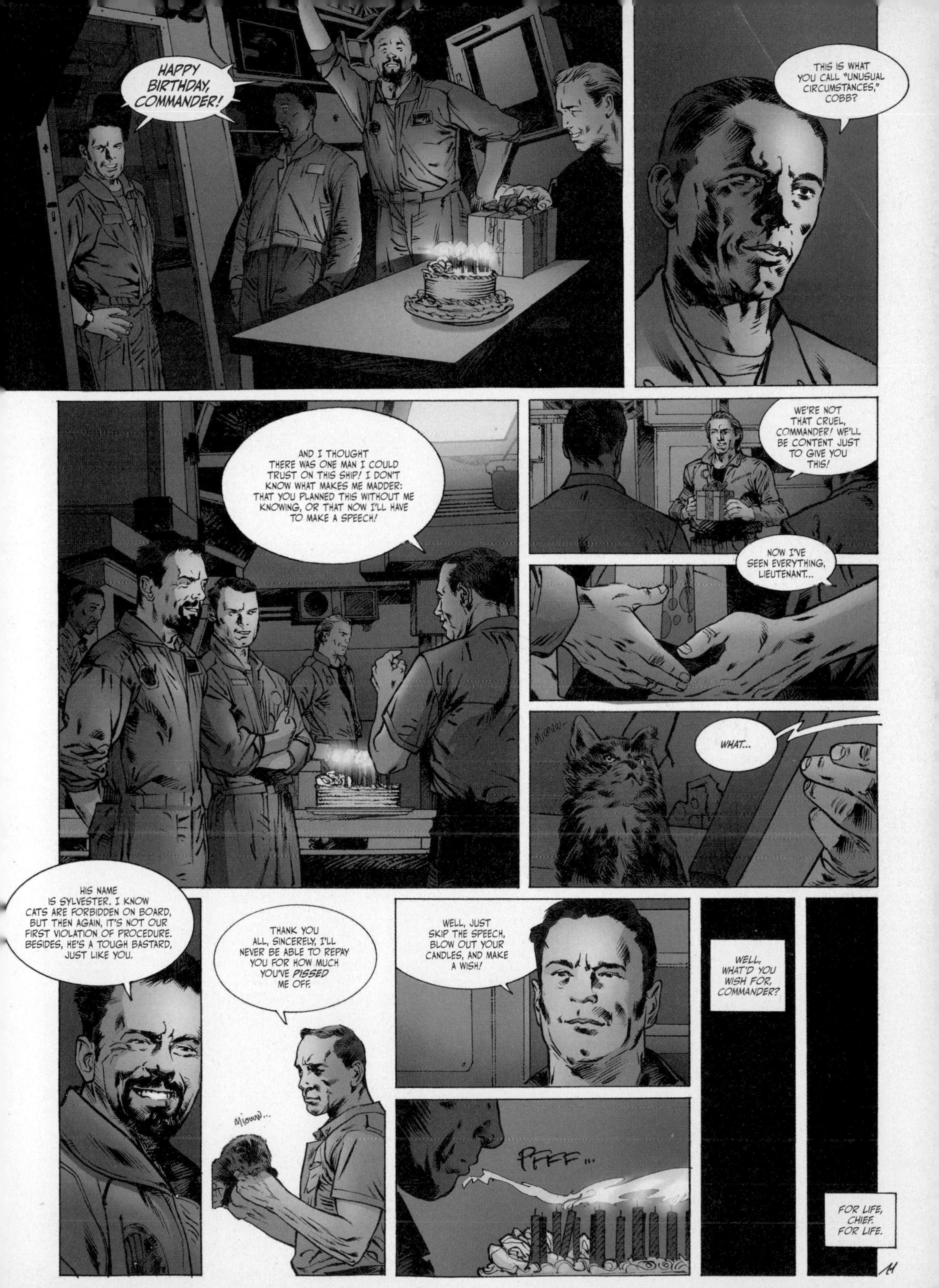
HAPPY BIRTHDAY, COMMANDER!
THIS IS WHAT YOU CALL "UNUSUAL CIRCUMSTANCES," COBB?
AND I THOUGHT THERE WAS ONE MAN I COULD TRUST ON THIS SHIP! I DON'T KNOW WHAT MAKES ME MADDER: THAT YOU PLANNED THIS WITHOUT ME KNOWING, OR THAT NOW I'LL HAVE TO MAKE A SPEECH!
WE'RE NOT THAT CRUEL, COMMANDER! WE'LL BE CONTENT JUST TO GIVE YOU THIS!
NOW I'VE SEEN EVERYTHING, LIEUTENANT...
WHAT...
HIS NAME IS SYLVESTER. I KNOW CATS ARE FORBIDDEN ON BOARD, BUT THEN AGAIN, IT'S NOT OUR FIRST VIOLATION OF PROCEDURE. BESIDES, HE'S A TOUGH BASTARD, JUST LIKE YOU.
THANK YOU ALL, SINCERELY, I'LL NEVER BE ABLE TO REPAY YOU FOR HOW MUCH YOU'VE *PISSED* ME OFF.
MIOUW...
WELL, JUST SKIP THE SPEECH, BLOW OUT YOUR CANDLES, AND MAKE A WISH!
PFFF...
WELL, WHAT'D YOU WISH FOR, COMMANDER?
FOR LIFE, CHIEF. FOR LIFE.

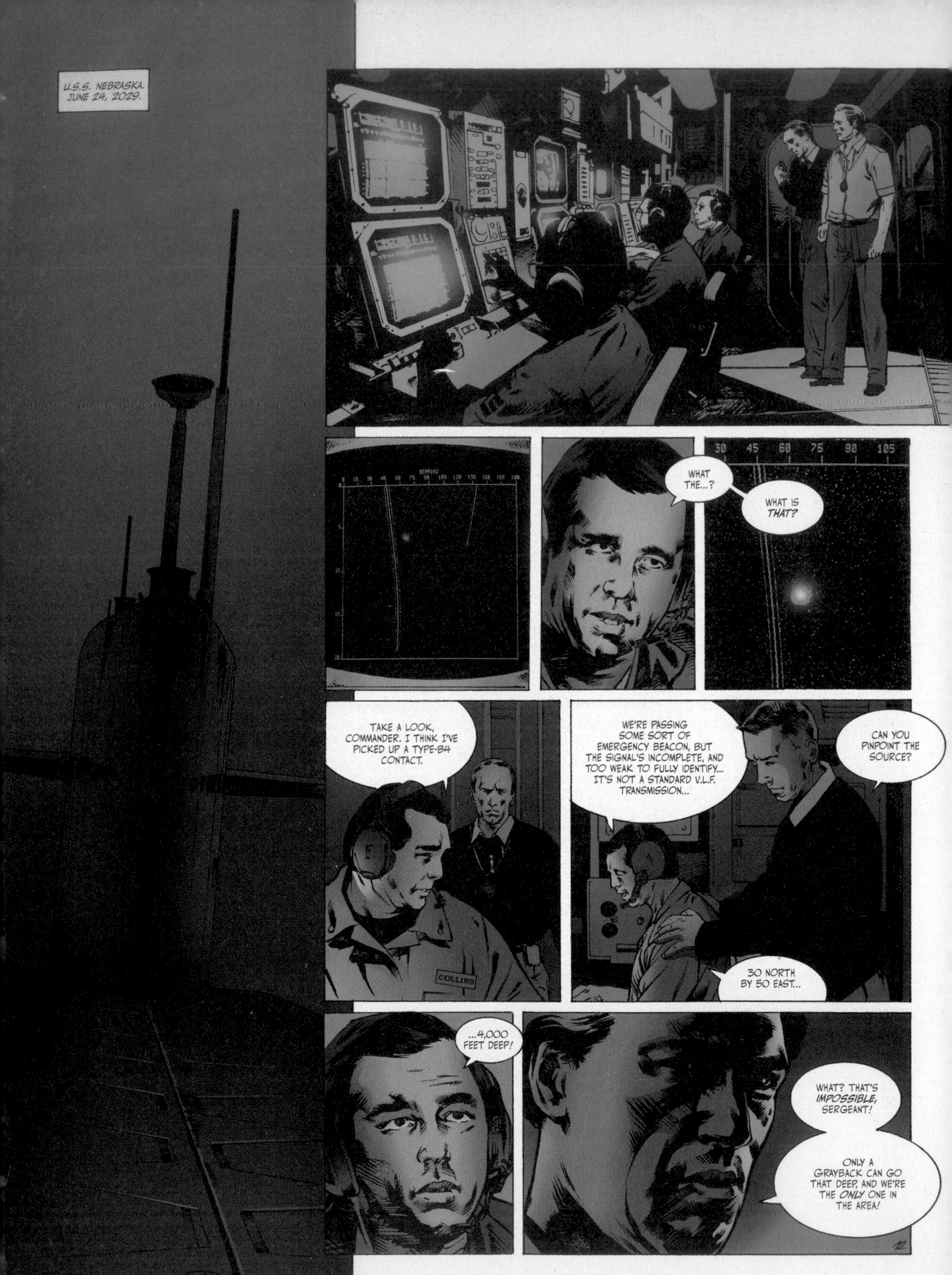
U.S.S. NEBRASKA.
JUNE 24, 2029.
WHAT THE...?
30 45 60 75 90 105
WHAT IS *THAT?*
TAKE A LOOK, COMMANDER. I THINK I'VE PICKED UP A TYPE-B4 CONTACT.
COLLINS
WE'RE PASSING SOME SORT OF EMERGENCY BEACON, BUT THE SIGNAL'S INCOMPLETE, AND TOO WEAK TO FULLY IDENTIFY... IT'S NOT A STANDARD V.L.F. TRANSMISSION...
CAN YOU PINPOINT THE SOURCE?
30 NORTH BY 50 EAST...
...4,000 FEET DEEP!
WHAT? THAT'S *IMPOSSIBLE,* SERGEANT!
ONLY A GRAYBACK CAN GO THAT DEEP, AND WE'RE THE *ONLY* ONE IN THE AREA!

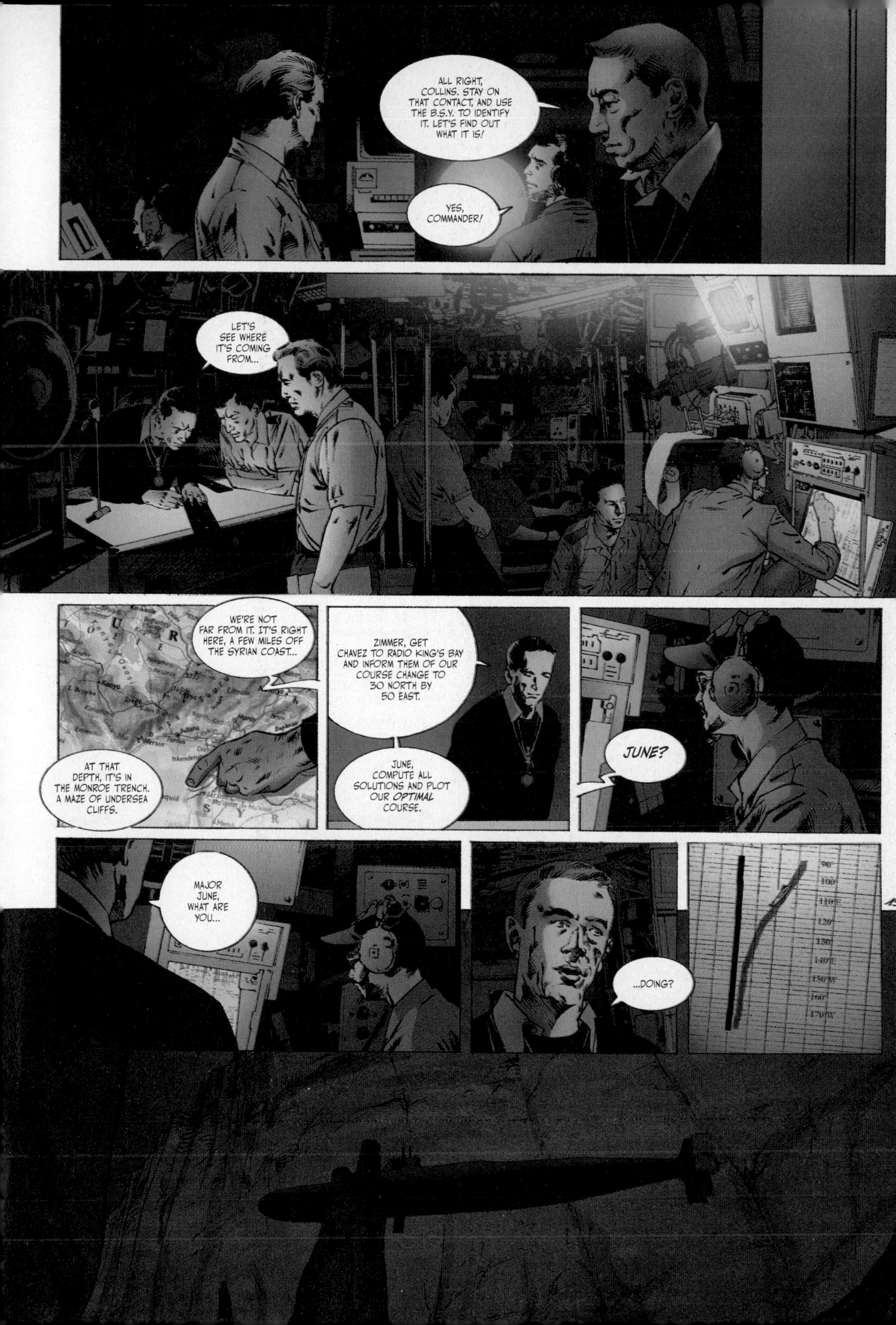
ALL RIGHT, COLLINS. STAY ON THAT CONTACT, AND USE THE B.S.Y. TO IDENTIFY IT. LET'S FIND OUT WHAT IT IS!
YES, COMMANDER!
LET'S SEE WHERE IT'S COMING FROM...
WE'RE NOT FAR FROM IT. IT'S RIGHT HERE, A FEW MILES OFF THE SYRIAN COAST...
AT THAT DEPTH, IT'S IN THE MONROE TRENCH. A MAZE OF UNDERSEA CLIFFS.
ZIMMER, GET CHAVEZ TO RADIO KING'S BAY AND INFORM THEM OF OUR COURSE CHANGE TO 30 NORTH BY 50 EAST.
JUNE, COMPUTE ALL SOLUTIONS AND PLOT OUR *OPTIMAL* COURSE.
JUNE?
MAJOR JUNE, WHAT ARE YOU...
...DOING?

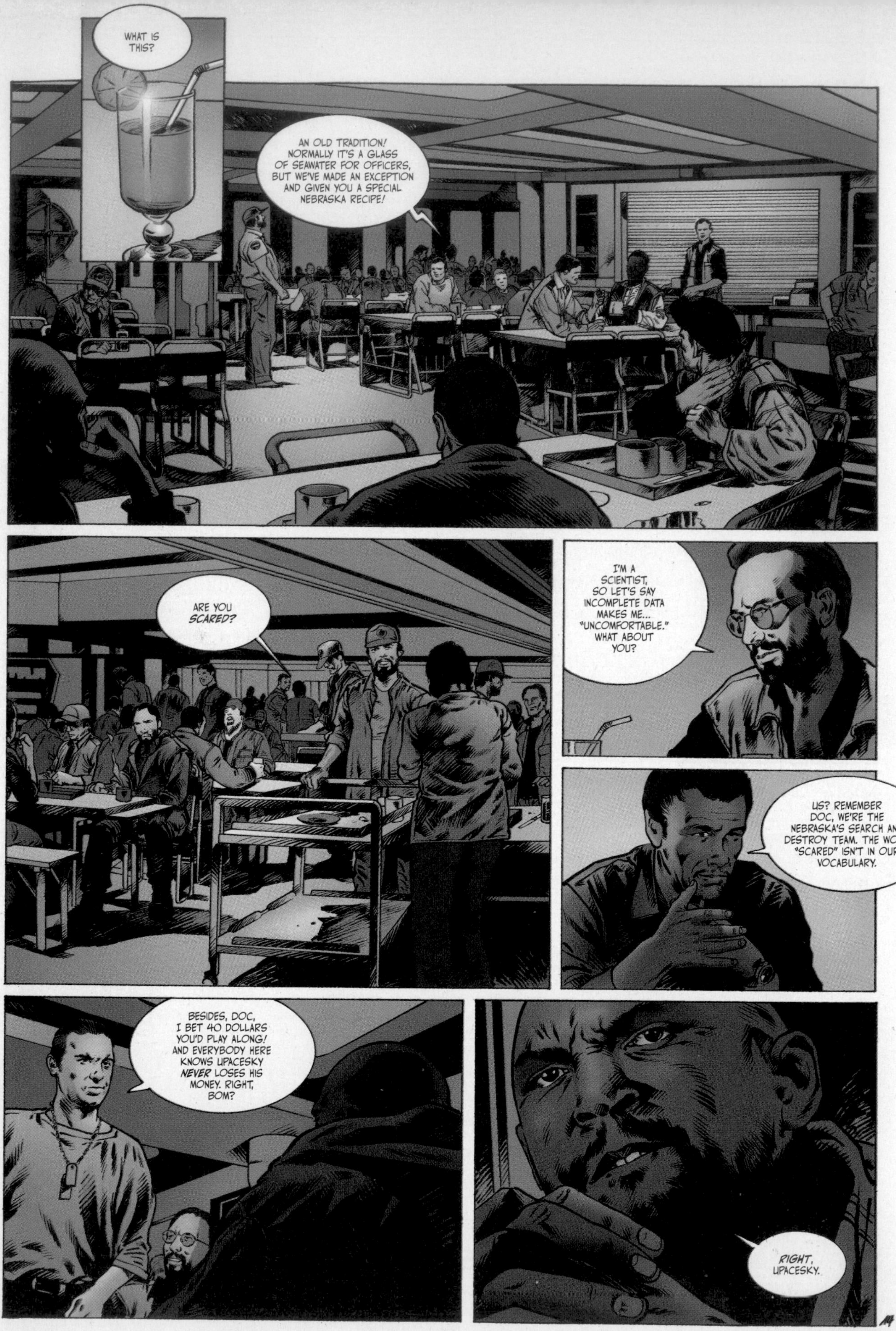
WHAT IS THIS?
AN OLD TRADITION! NORMALLY IT'S A GLASS OF SEAWATER FOR OFFICERS, BUT WE'VE MADE AN EXCEPTION AND GIVEN YOU A SPECIAL NEBRASKA RECIPE!
ARE YOU *SCARED?*
I'M A SCIENTIST, SO LET'S SAY INCOMPLETE DATA MAKES ME... "UNCOMFORTABLE." WHAT ABOUT YOU?
US? REMEMBER DOC, WE'RE THE NEBRASKA'S SEARCH AND DESTROY TEAM. THE WORD "SCARED" ISN'T IN OUR VOCABULARY.
BESIDES, DOC, I BET 40 DOLLARS YOU'D PLAY ALONG! AND EVERYBODY HERE KNOWS UPACESKY ***NEVER*** LOSES HIS MONEY. RIGHT, BOM?
RIGHT, UPACESKY.

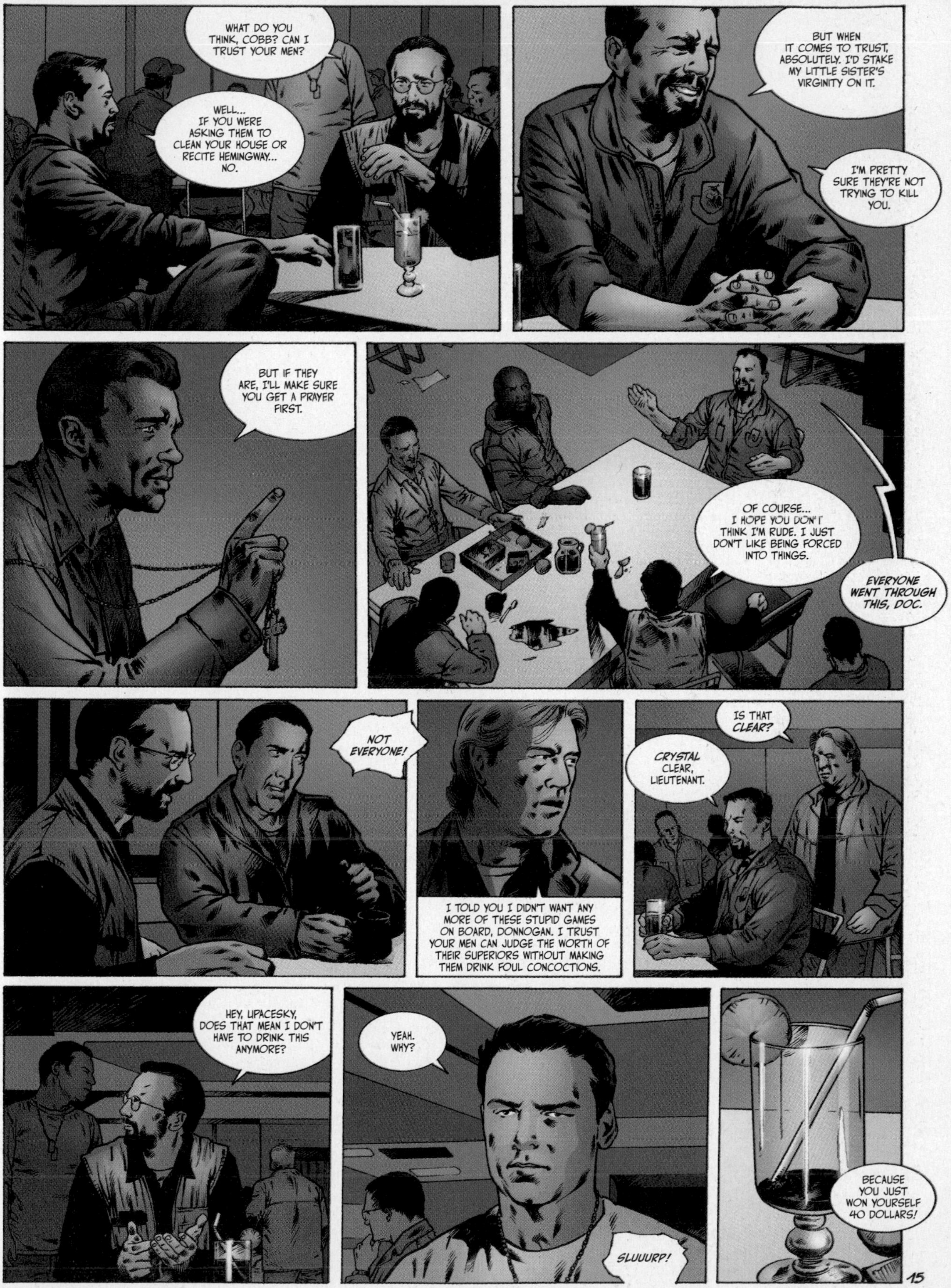
WHAT DO YOU THINK, COBB? CAN I TRUST YOUR MEN?
WELL... IF YOU WERE ASKING THEM TO CLEAN YOUR HOUSE OR RECITE HEMINGWAY... NO.
BUT WHEN IT COMES TO TRUST, ABSOLUTELY. I'D STAKE MY LITTLE SISTER'S VIRGINITY ON IT.
I'M PRETTY SURE THEY'RE NOT TRYING TO KILL YOU.
BUT IF THEY ARE, I'LL MAKE SURE YOU GET A PRAYER FIRST.
OF COURSE... I HOPE YOU DON'T THINK I'M RUDE. I JUST DON'T LIKE BEING FORCED INTO THINGS.
EVERYONE WENT THROUGH THIS, DOC.
NOT EVERYONE!
I TOLD YOU I DIDN'T WANT ANY MORE OF THESE STUPID GAMES ON BOARD, DONNOGAN. I TRUST YOUR MEN CAN JUDGE THE WORTH OF THEIR SUPERIORS WITHOUT MAKING THEM DRINK FOUL CONCOCTIONS.
IS THAT CLEAR?
CRYSTAL CLEAR, LIEUTENANT.
HEY, LIPACESKY, DOES THAT MEAN I DON'T HAVE TO DRINK THIS ANYMORE?
YEAH. WHY?
SLUUURP!
BECAUSE YOU JUST WON YOURSELF 40 DOLLARS!
15

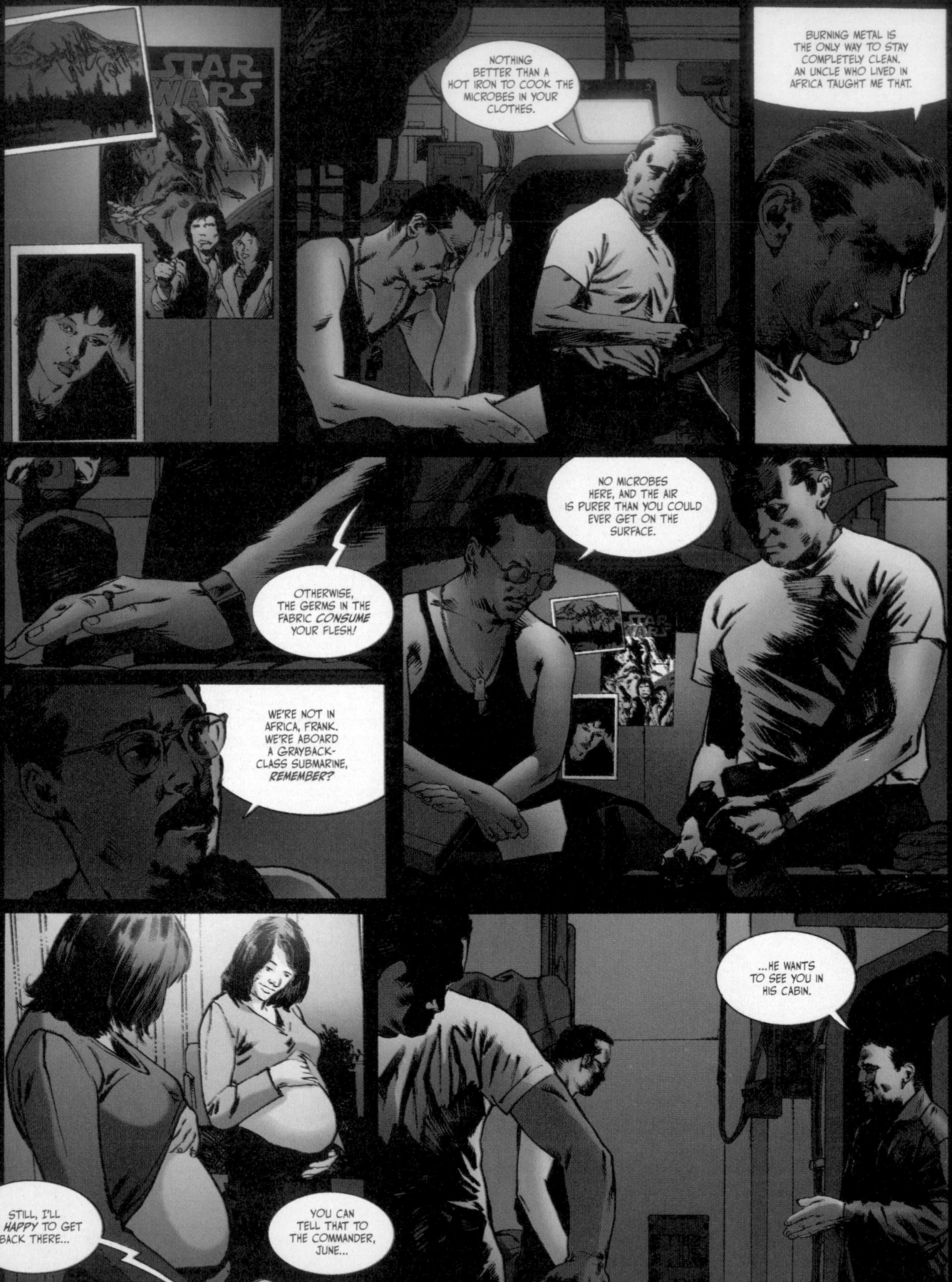
NOTHING BETTER THAN A HOT IRON TO COOK THE MICROBES IN YOUR CLOTHES.
BURNING METAL IS THE ONLY WAY TO STAY COMPLETELY CLEAN. AN UNCLE WHO LIVED IN AFRICA TAUGHT ME THAT.
OTHERWISE, THE GERMS IN THE FABRIC CONSUME YOUR FLESH!
NO MICROBES HERE, AND THE AIR IS PURER THAN YOU COULD EVER GET ON THE SURFACE.
WE'RE NOT IN AFRICA, FRANK. WE'RE ABOARD A GRAYBACK-CLASS SUBMARINE, REMEMBER?
STILL, I'LL BE HAPPY TO GET BACK THERE...
YOU CAN TELL THAT TO THE COMMANDER, JUNE...
...HE WANTS TO SEE YOU IN HIS CABIN.

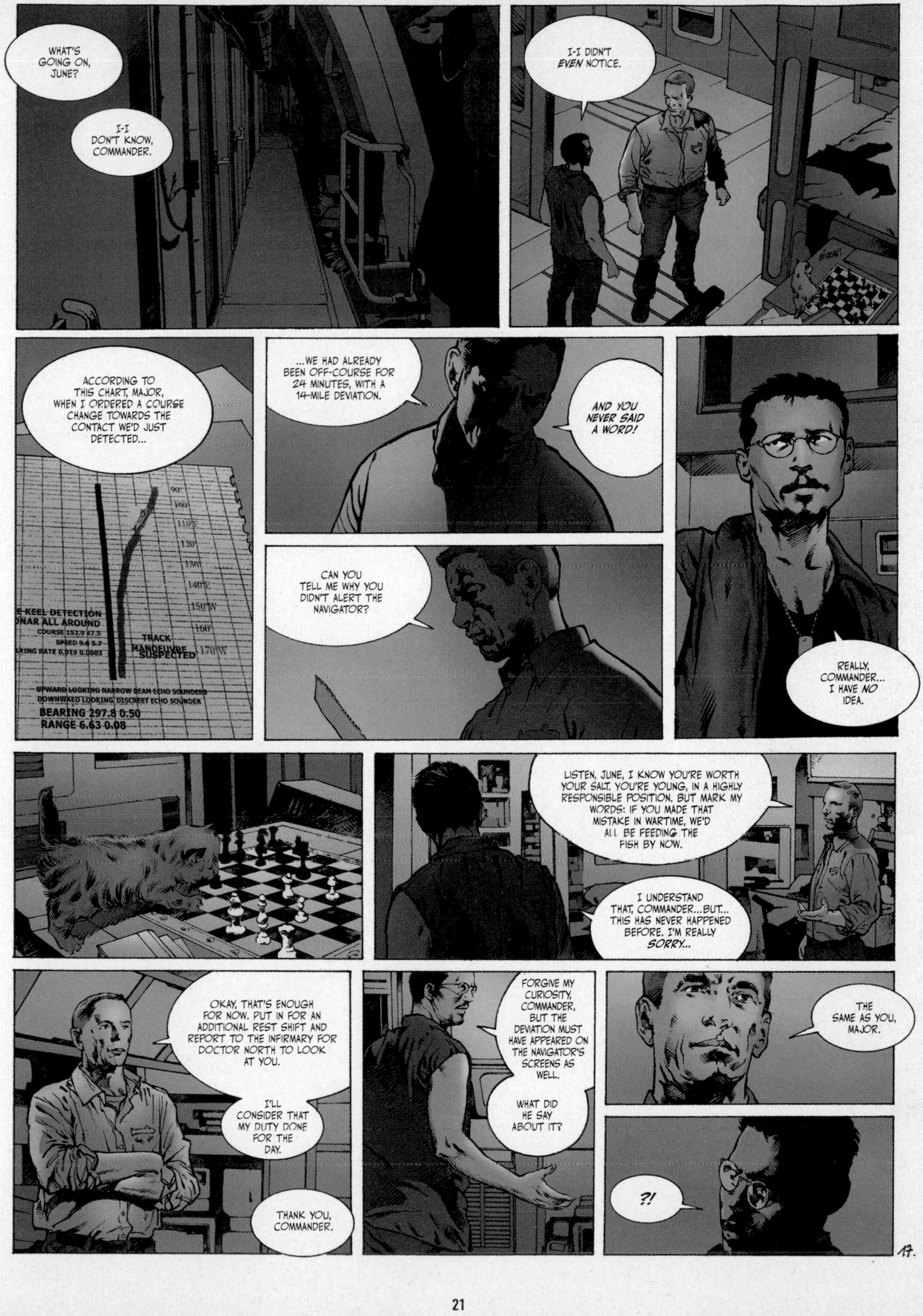
WHAT'S GOING ON, JUNE?
I-I DON'T KNOW, COMMANDER.
I-I DIDN'T *EVEN* NOTICE.
ACCORDING TO THIS CHART, MAJOR, WHEN I ORDERED A COURSE CHANGE TOWARDS THE CONTACT WE'D JUST DETECTED...
E KEEL DETECTION
ONAR ALL AROUND
COURSE 152.9 47.5
SPEED 9.8 5.7
ARING RATE 0.019 0.0003
TRACK
MANOEUVRE
SUSPECTED
UPWARD LOOKING NARROW BEAM ECHO SOUNDERS
DOWNWARD LOOKING DISCREET ECHO SOUNDER
BEARING 297.8 0.50
RANGE 6.63 0.08
...WE HAD ALREADY BEEN OFF-COURSE FOR 24 MINUTES, WITH A 14-MILE DEVIATION.
AND YOU NEVER SAID A WORD!
CAN YOU TELL ME WHY YOU DIDN'T ALERT THE NAVIGATOR?
REALLY, COMMANDER... I HAVE *NO* IDEA.
LISTEN, JUNE, I KNOW YOU'RE WORTH YOUR SALT. YOU'RE YOUNG, IN A HIGHLY RESPONSIBLE POSITION. BUT MARK MY WORDS: IF YOU MADE THAT MISTAKE IN WARTIME, WE'D ALL BE FEEDING THE FISH BY NOW.
I UNDERSTAND THAT, COMMANDER...BUT... THIS HAS NEVER HAPPENED BEFORE. I'M REALLY *SORRY...*
OKAY, THAT'S ENOUGH FOR NOW. PUT IN FOR AN ADDITIONAL REST SHIFT AND REPORT TO THE INFIRMARY FOR DOCTOR NORTH TO LOOK AT YOU.
I'LL CONSIDER THAT MY DUTY DONE FOR THE DAY.
THANK YOU, COMMANDER.
FORGIVE MY CURIOSITY, COMMANDER, BUT THE DEVIATION MUST HAVE APPEARED ON THE NAVIGATOR'S SCREENS AS WELL.
WHAT DID HE SAY ABOUT IT?
THE SAME AS YOU, MAJOR.
?!
17.

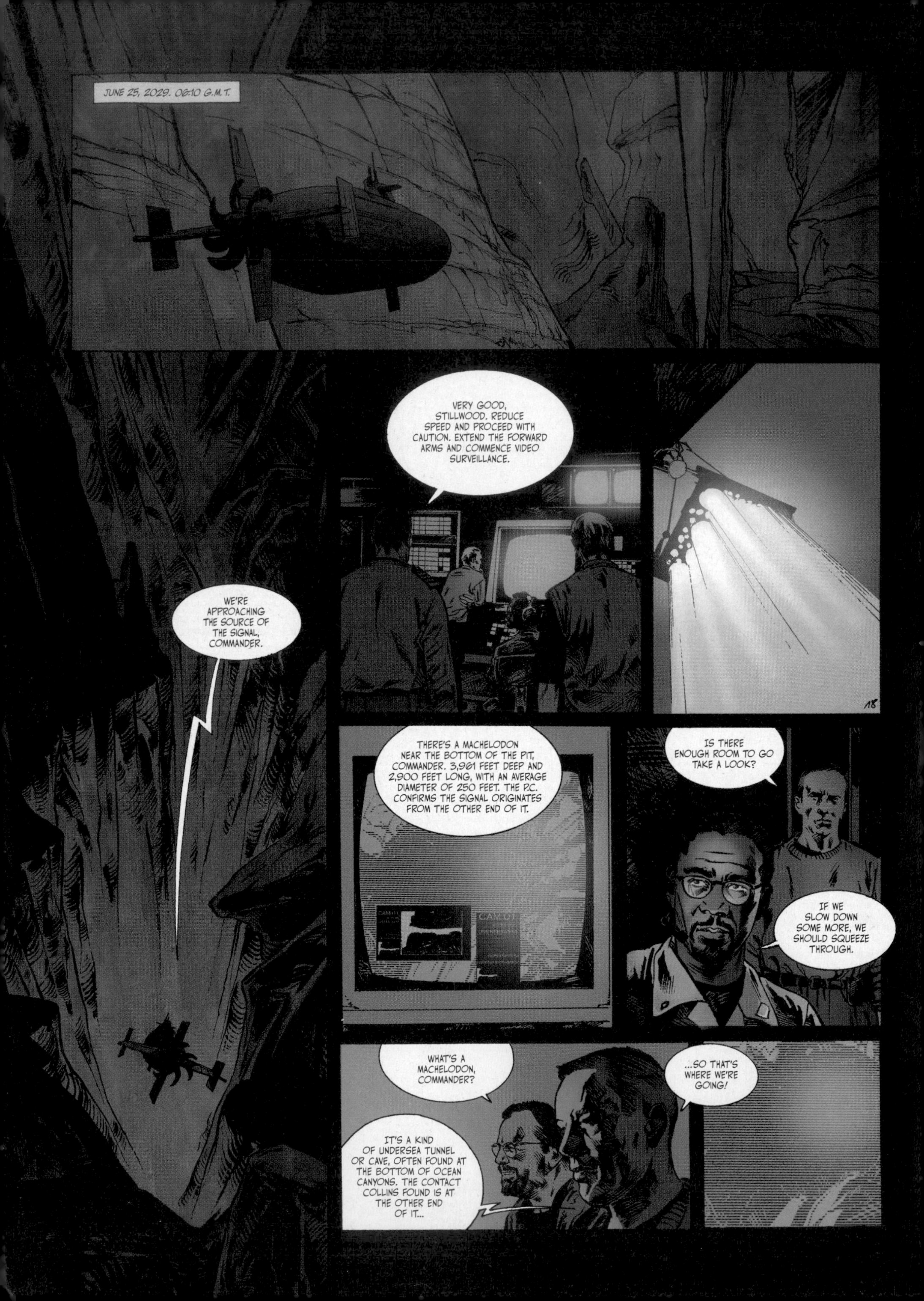
JUNE 25, 2029. 06:10 G.M.T.
WE'RE APPROACHING THE SOURCE OF THE SIGNAL, COMMANDER.
VERY GOOD, STILLWOOD. REDUCE SPEED AND PROCEED WITH CAUTION. EXTEND THE FORWARD ARMS AND COMMENCE VIDEO SURVEILLANCE.
THERE'S A MACHELODON NEAR THE BOTTOM OF THE PIT, COMMANDER. 3,961 FEET DEEP AND 2,900 FEET LONG, WITH AN AVERAGE DIAMETER OF 250 FEET. THE P.C. CONFIRMS THE SIGNAL ORIGINATES FROM THE OTHER END OF IT.
IS THERE ENOUGH ROOM TO GO TAKE A LOOK?
IF WE SLOW DOWN SOME MORE, WE SHOULD SQUEEZE THROUGH.
WHAT'S A MACHELODON, COMMANDER?
IT'S A KIND OF UNDERSEA TUNNEL OR CAVE, OFTEN FOUND AT THE BOTTOM OF OCEAN CANYONS. THE CONTACT COLLINS FOUND IS AT THE OTHER END OF IT...
...SO THAT'S WHERE WE'RE GOING!

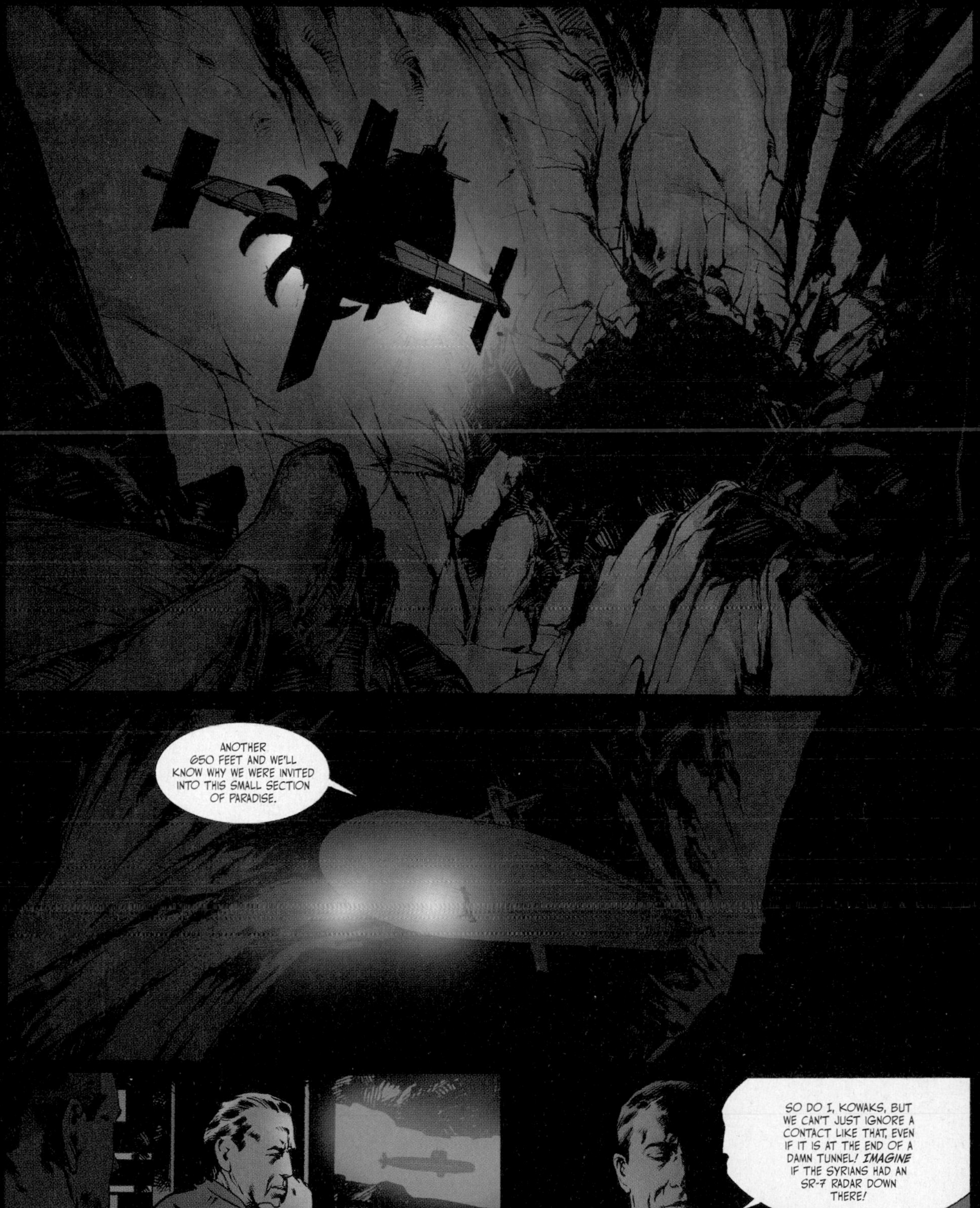
ANOTHER 650 FEET AND WE'LL KNOW WHY WE WERE INVITED INTO THIS SMALL SECTION OF PARADISE.
SEPARATE TWO PLANE ACTIVE SONAR ARRAY
I HOPE IT'S WORTH IT, BECAUSE WITH THE AMOUNT OF CLEARANCE BETWEEN US AND THE WALL, IT'S LIKE WALKING A TIGHTROPE. I WISH WE COULD BE SURE WE'RE NOT MAKING A BIG MISTAKE.
SO DO I, KOWAKS, BUT WE CAN'T JUST IGNORE A CONTACT LIKE THAT, EVEN IF IT IS AT THE END OF A DAMN TUNNEL! *IMAGINE* IF THE SYRIANS HAD AN SR-7 RADAR DOWN THERE!
ALL OUR MOVEMENTS IN THE AREA WOULD BE AS *DISCREET* AS A CALL GIRL IN A MOSQUE.

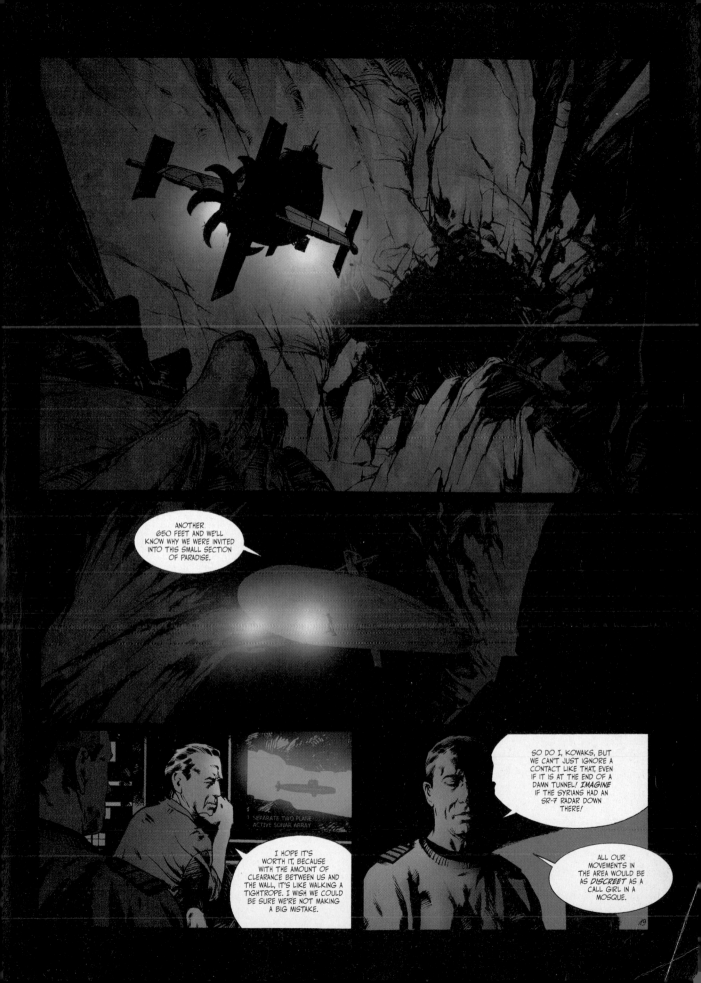

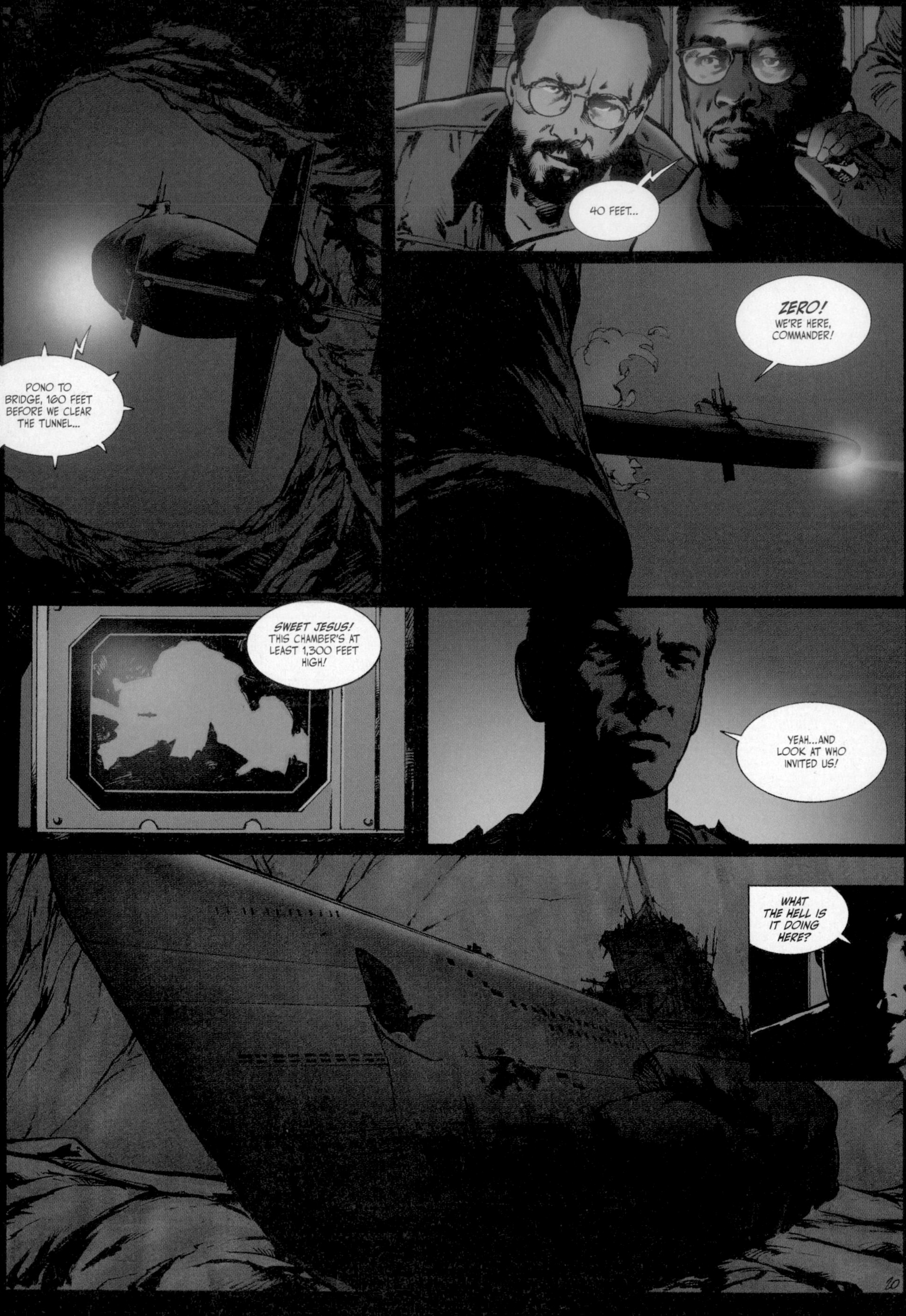
PONO TO BRIDGE, 160 FEET BEFORE WE CLEAR THE TUNNEL...
40 FEET...
ZERO! WE'RE HERE, COMMANDER!
SWEET JESUS! THIS CHAMBER'S AT LEAST 1,300 FEET HIGH!
YEAH...AND LOOK AT WHO INVITED US!
WHAT THE HELL IS IT DOING HERE?

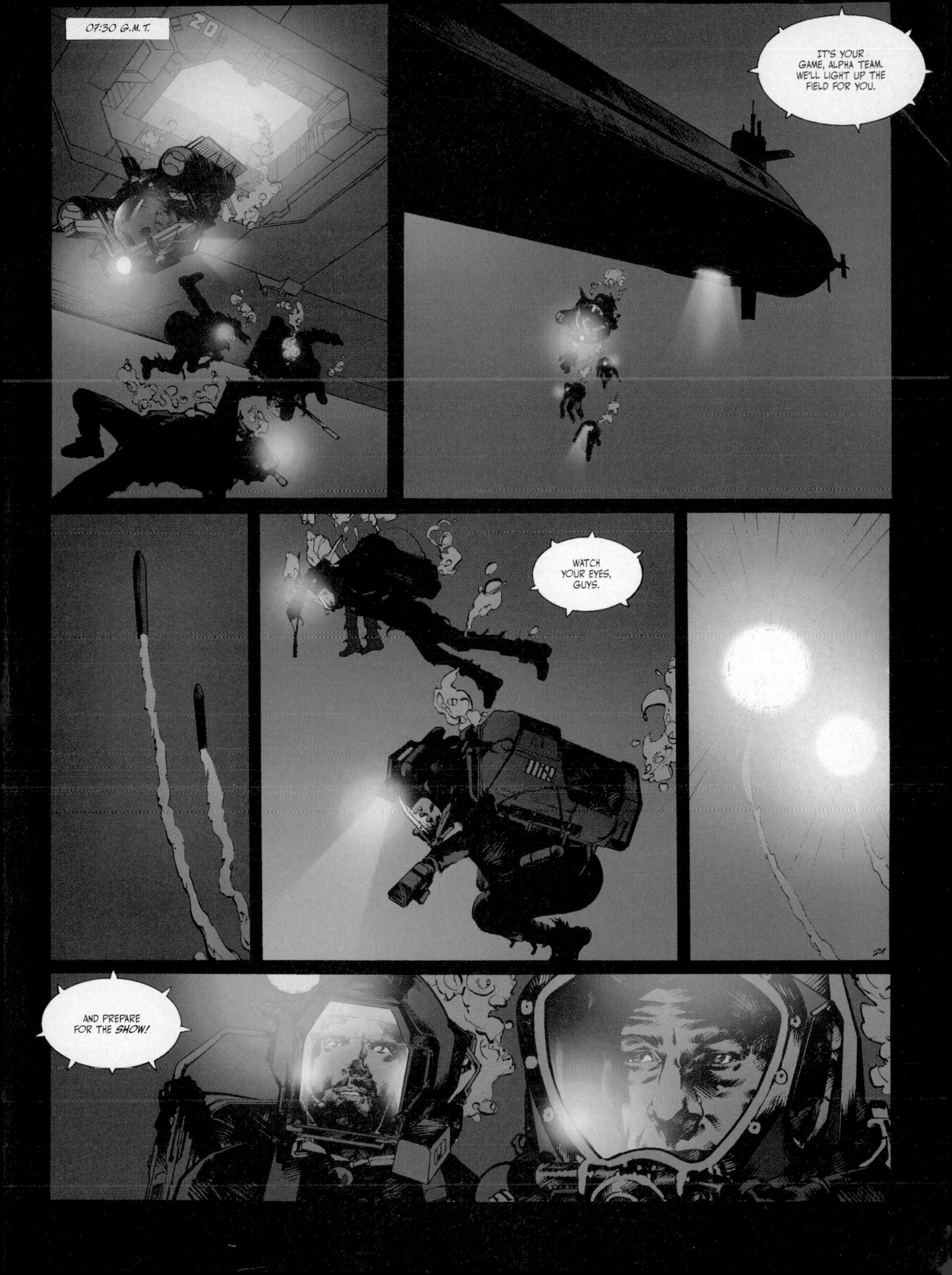
07:30 G.M.T.
IT'S YOUR GAME, ALPHA TEAM. WE'LL LIGHT UP THE FIELD FOR YOU.
WATCH YOUR EYES, GUYS.
AND PREPARE FOR THE SHOW!

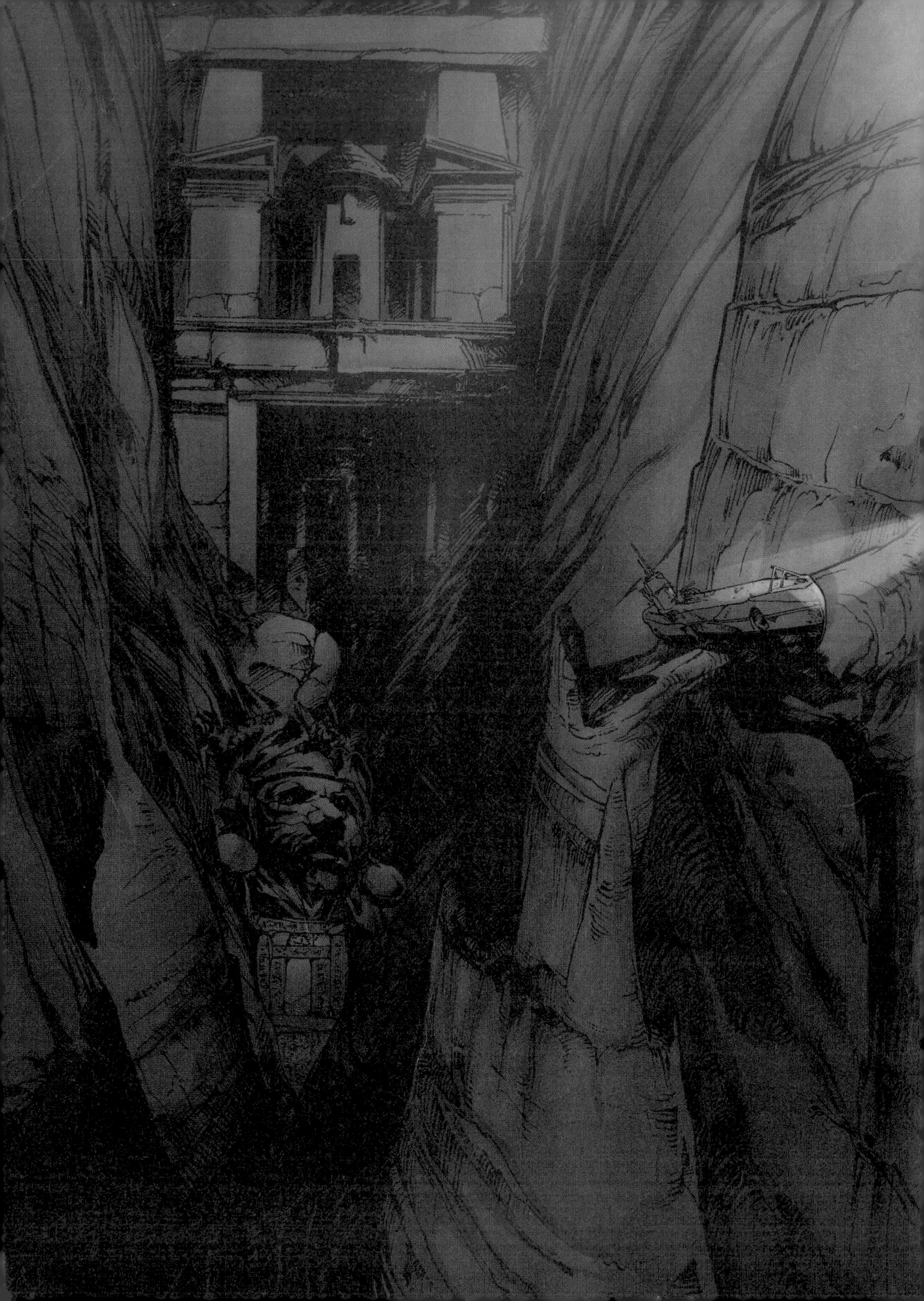

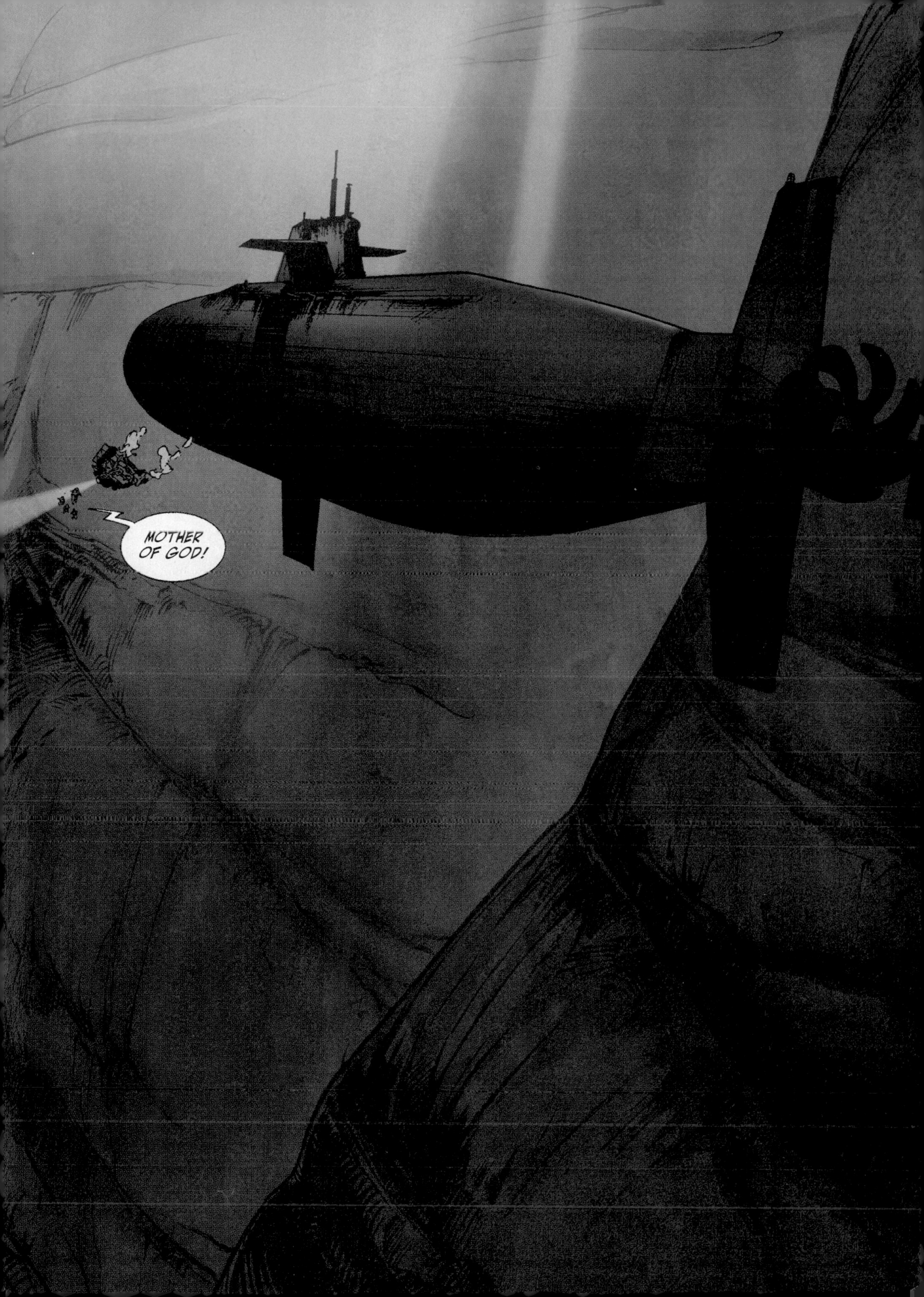
MOTHER OF GOD!

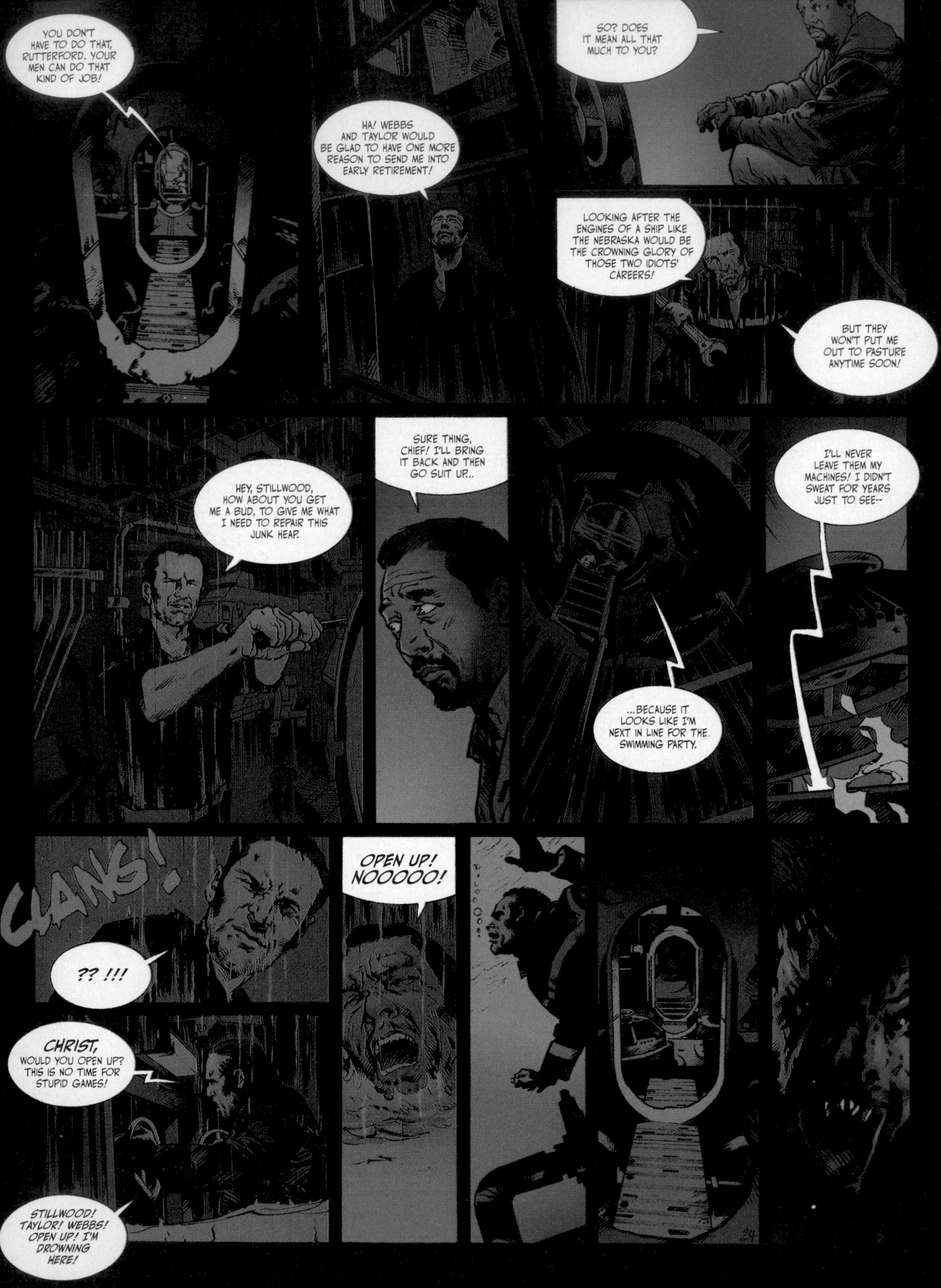
YOU DON'T HAVE TO DO THAT, RUTTERFORD. YOUR MEN CAN DO THAT KIND OF JOB!
HA! WEBBS AND TAYLOR WOULD BE GLAD TO HAVE ONE MORE REASON TO SEND ME INTO EARLY RETIREMENT!
SO? DOES IT MEAN ALL THAT MUCH TO YOU?
LOOKING AFTER THE ENGINES OF A SHIP LIKE THE NEBRASKA WOULD BE THE CROWNING GLORY OF THOSE TWO IDIOTS' CAREERS!
BUT THEY WON'T PUT ME OUT TO PASTURE ANYTIME SOON!
HEY, STILLWOOD, HOW ABOUT YOU GET ME A BUD, TO GIVE ME WHAT I NEED TO REPAIR THIS JUNK HEAP.
SURE THING, CHIEF! I'LL BRING IT BACK AND THEN GO SUIT UP...
...BECAUSE IT LOOKS LIKE I'M NEXT IN LINE FOR THE SWIMMING PARTY.
I'LL NEVER LEAVE THEM MY MACHINES! I DIDN'T SWEAT FOR YEARS JUST TO SEE--
CLANG!
?? !!!
CHRIST, WOULD YOU OPEN UP? THIS IS NO TIME FOR STUPID GAMES!
STILLWOOD! TAYLOR! WEBBS! OPEN UP! I'M DROWNING HERE!
OPEN UP! NOOOOO!
24

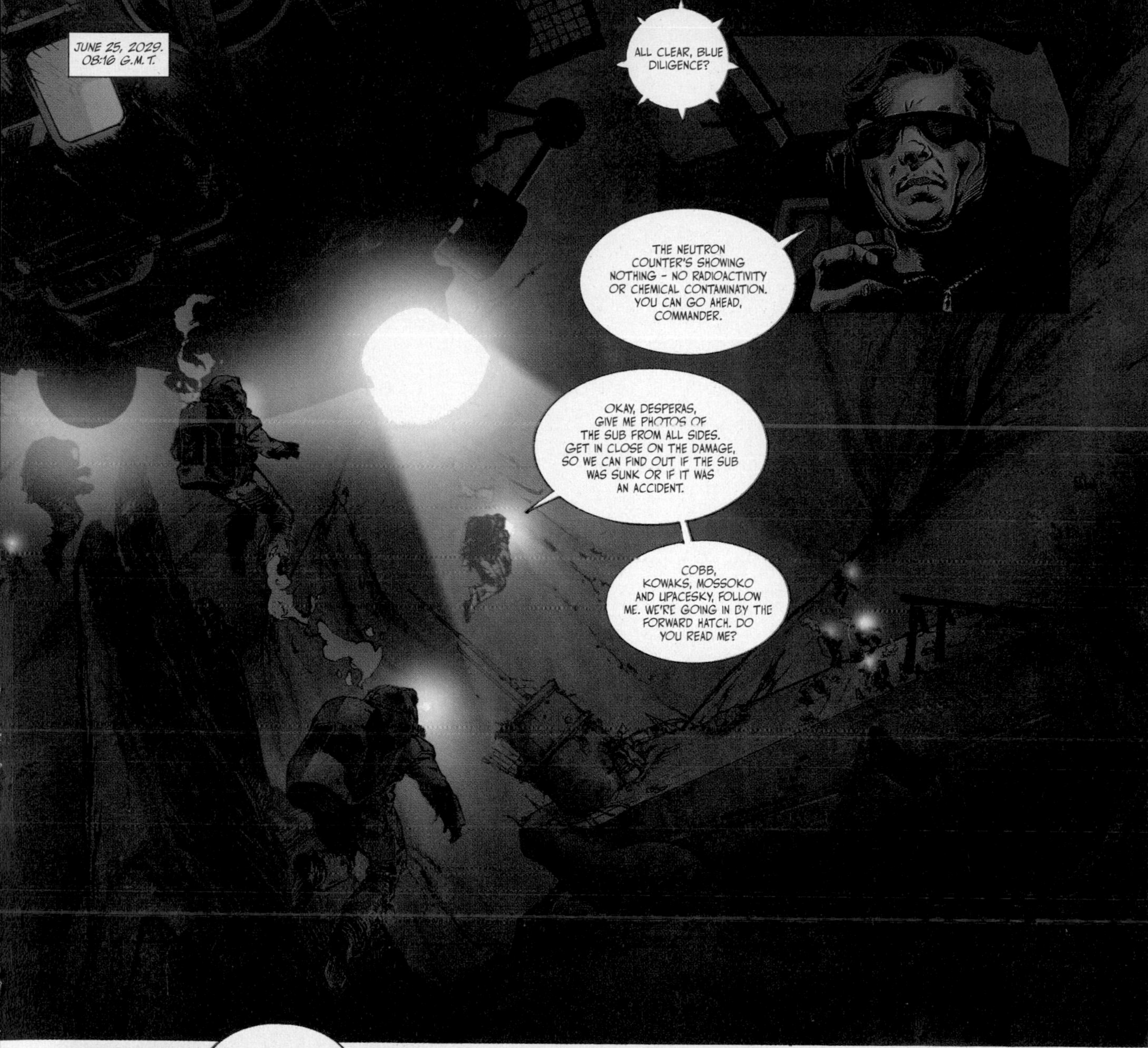
JUNE 25, 2029.
08:16 G.M.T.
ALL CLEAR, BLUE DILIGENCE?
THE NEUTRON COUNTER'S SHOWING NOTHING - NO RADIOACTIVITY OR CHEMICAL CONTAMINATION. YOU CAN GO AHEAD, COMMANDER.
OKAY, DESPERAS, GIVE ME PHOTOS OF THE SUB FROM ALL SIDES. GET IN CLOSE ON THE DAMAGE, SO WE CAN FIND OUT IF THE SUB WAS SUNK OR IF IT WAS AN ACCIDENT.
COBB, KOWAKS, MOSSOKO AND UPACESKY, FOLLOW ME. WE'RE GOING IN BY THE FORWARD HATCH. DO YOU READ ME?

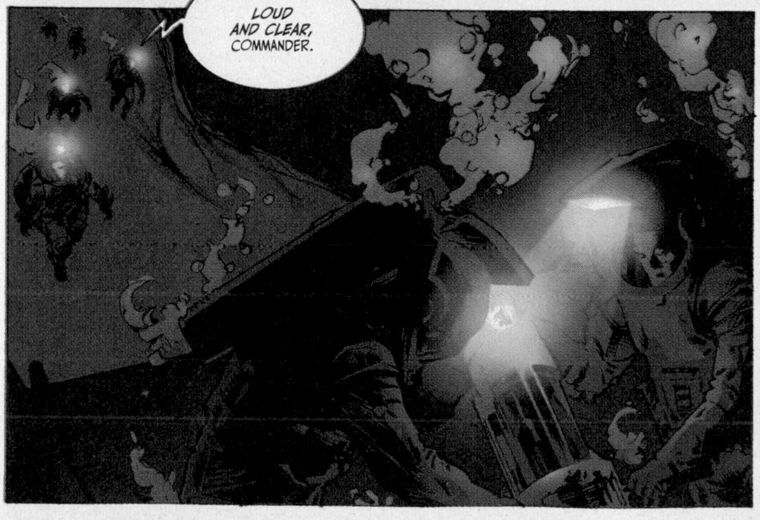
LOUD AND CLEAR, COMMANDER.

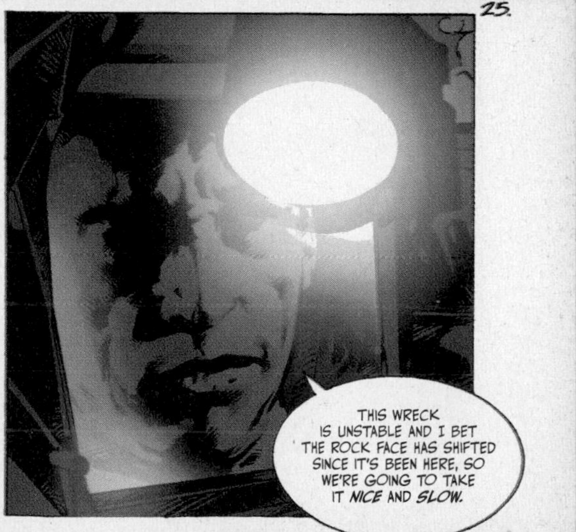
THIS WRECK IS UNSTABLE AND I BET THE ROCK FACE HAS SHIFTED SINCE IT'S BEEN HERE, SO WE'RE GOING TO TAKE IT NICE AND SLOW.

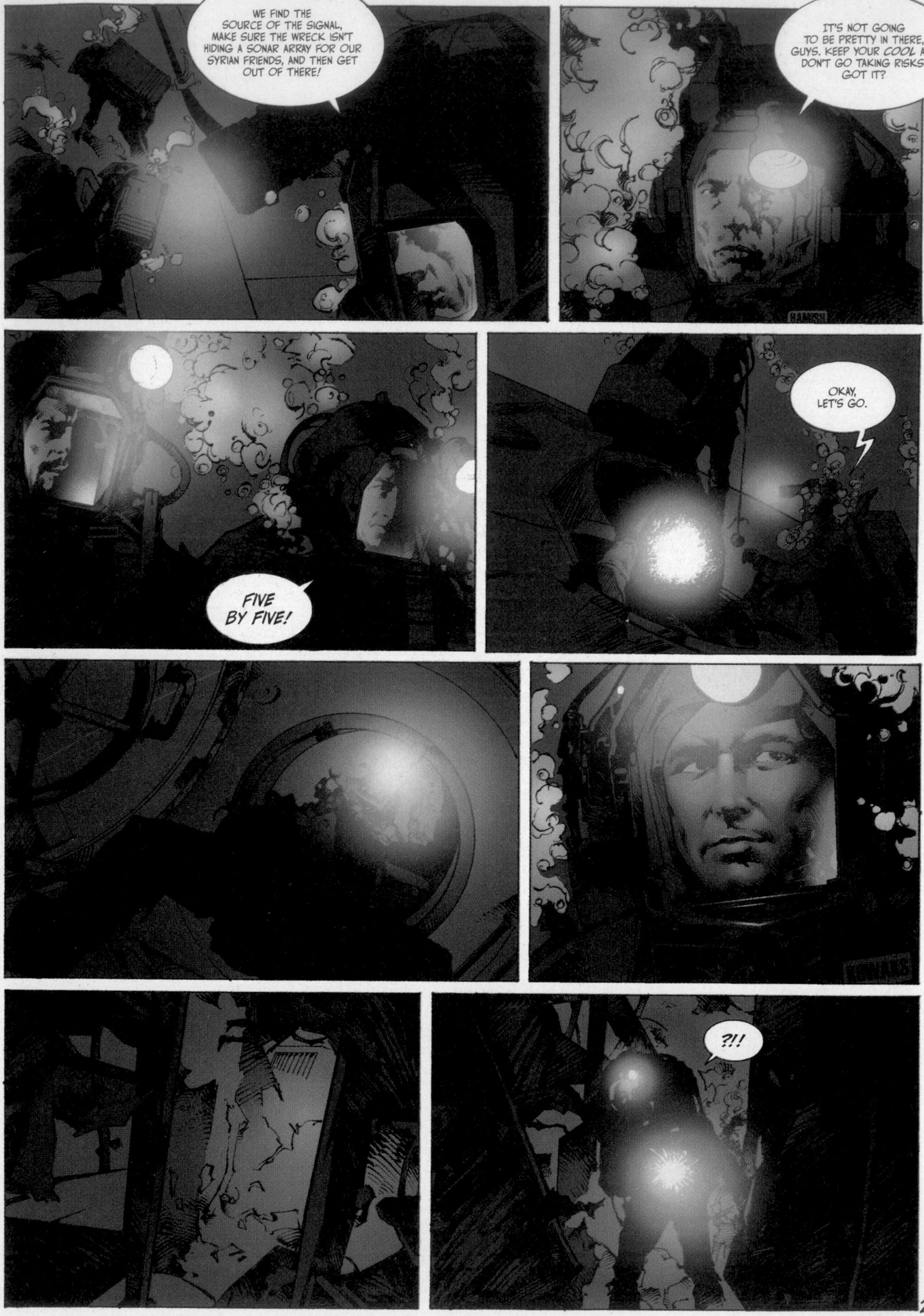
WE FIND THE SOURCE OF THE SIGNAL, MAKE SURE THE WRECK ISN'T HIDING A SONAR ARRAY FOR OUR SYRIAN FRIENDS, AND THEN GET OUT OF THERE!
IT'S NOT GOING TO BE PRETTY IN THERE, GUYS. KEEP YOUR COOL AND DON'T GO TAKING RISKS. GOT IT?
FIVE BY FIVE!
OKAY, LET'S GO.
?!!
26

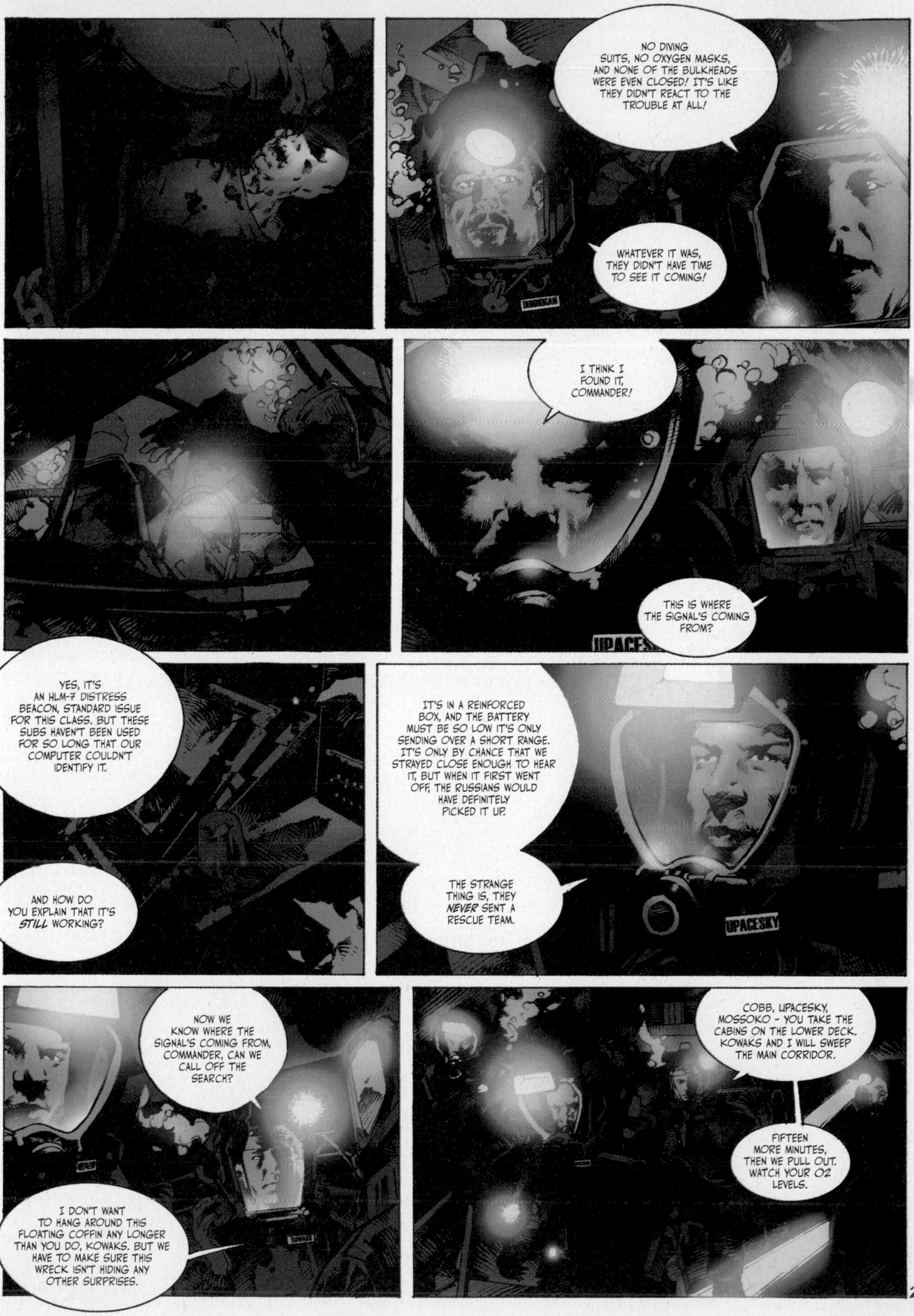

NO DIVING SUITS, NO OXYGEN MASKS, AND NONE OF THE BULKHEADS WERE EVEN CLOSED! IT'S LIKE THEY DIDN'T REACT TO THE TROUBLE AT ALL!
WHATEVER IT WAS, THEY DIDN'T HAVE TIME TO SEE IT COMING!
I THINK I FOUND IT, COMMANDER!
THIS IS WHERE THE SIGNAL'S COMING FROM?
UPACESKY
YES, IT'S AN HLM-7 DISTRESS BEACON, STANDARD ISSUE FOR THIS CLASS. BUT THESE SUBS HAVEN'T BEEN USED FOR SO LONG THAT OUR COMPUTER COULDN'T IDENTIFY IT.
AND HOW DO YOU EXPLAIN THAT IT'S *STILL* WORKING?
IT'S IN A REINFORCED BOX, AND THE BATTERY MUST BE SO LOW IT'S ONLY SENDING OVER A SHORT RANGE. IT'S ONLY BY CHANCE THAT WE STRAYED CLOSE ENOUGH TO HEAR IT, BUT WHEN IT FIRST WENT OFF, THE RUSSIANS WOULD HAVE DEFINITELY PICKED IT UP.
THE STRANGE THING IS, THEY *NEVER* SENT A RESCUE TEAM.
UPACESKY
NOW WE KNOW WHERE THE SIGNAL'S COMING FROM, COMMANDER, CAN WE CALL OFF THE SEARCH?
I DON'T WANT TO HANG AROUND THIS FLOATING COFFIN ANY LONGER THAN YOU DO, KOWAKS. BUT WE HAVE TO MAKE SURE THIS WRECK ISN'T HIDING ANY OTHER SURPRISES.
COBB, UPACESKY, MOSSOKO - YOU TAKE THE CABINS ON THE LOWER DECK. KOWAKS AND I WILL SWEEP THE MAIN CORRIDOR.
FIFTEEN MORE MINUTES, THEN WE PULL OUT. WATCH YOUR O2 LEVELS.
27.

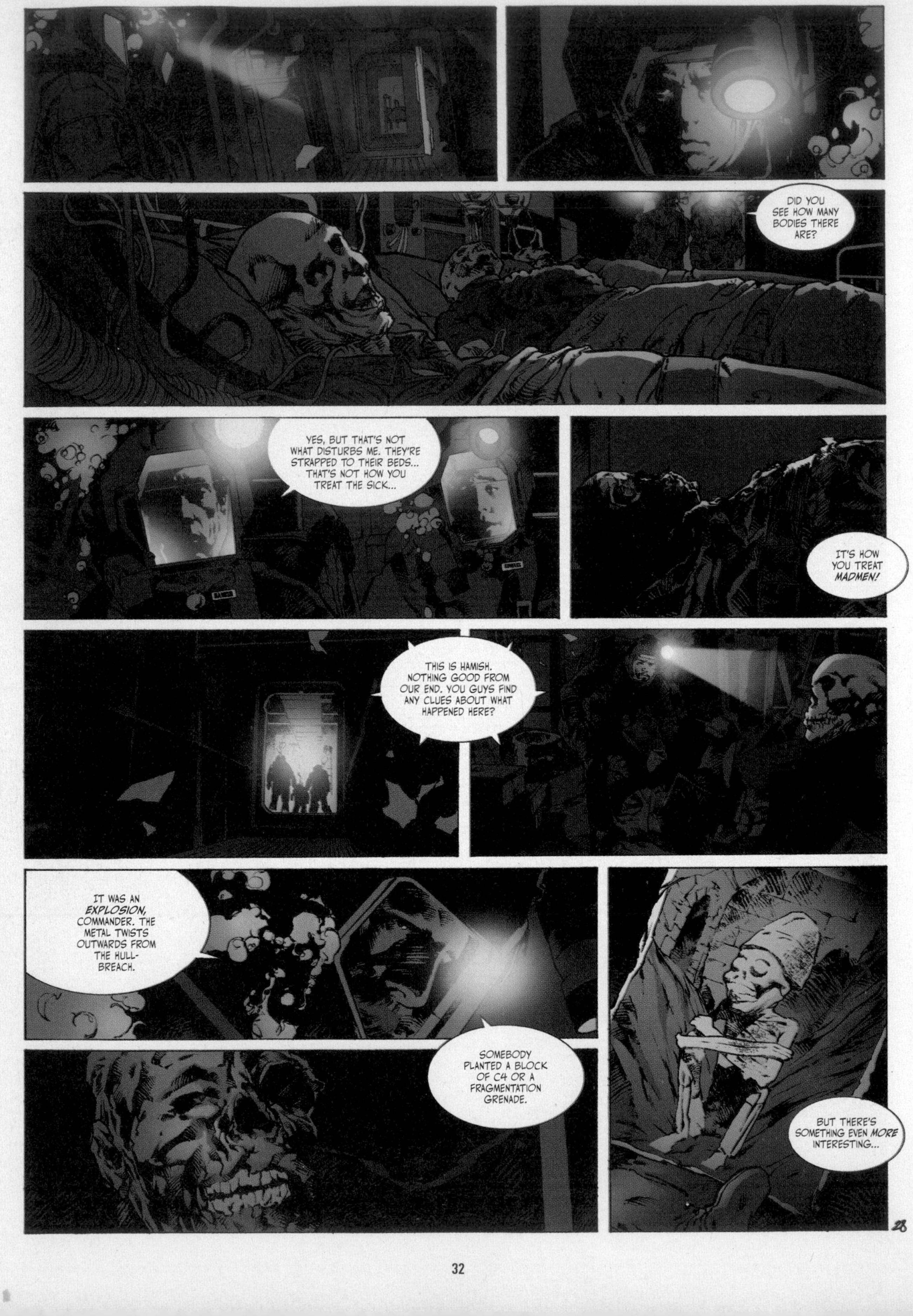
DID YOU SEE HOW MANY BODIES THERE ARE?
YES, BUT THAT'S NOT WHAT DISTURBS ME. THEY'RE STRAPPED TO THEIR BEDS... THAT'S NOT HOW YOU TREAT THE SICK...
IT'S HOW YOU TREAT *MADMEN!*
THIS IS HAMISH. NOTHING GOOD FROM OUR END. YOU GUYS FIND ANY CLUES ABOUT WHAT HAPPENED HERE?
IT WAS AN *EXPLOSION,* COMMANDER. THE METAL TWISTS OUTWARDS FROM THE HULL-BREACH.
SOMEBODY PLANTED A BLOCK OF C4 OR A FRAGMENTATION GRENADE.
BUT THERE'S SOMETHING EVEN *MORE* INTERESTING...
28

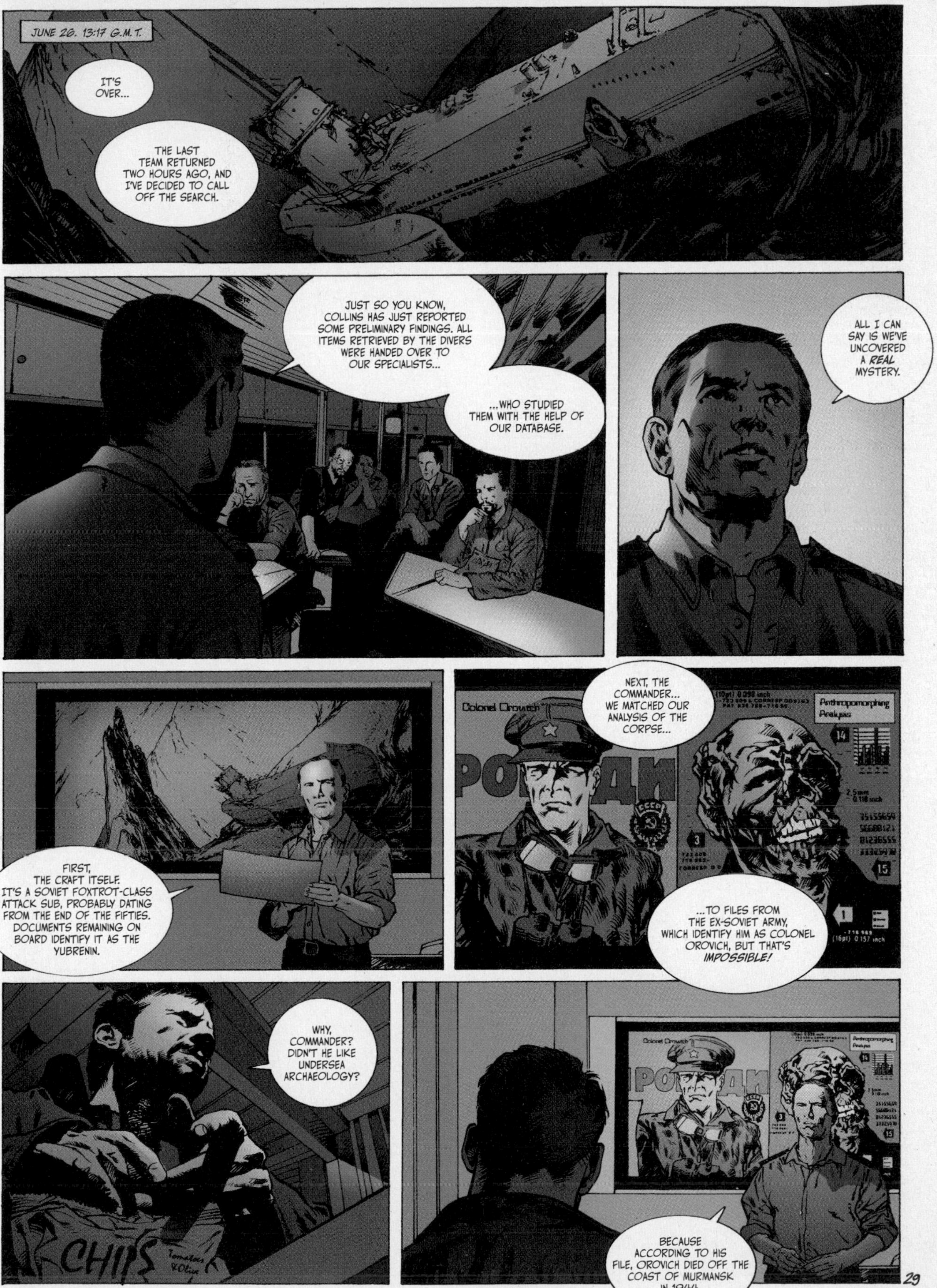

JUNE 26. 13:17 G.M.T.
IT'S OVER...
THE LAST TEAM RETURNED TWO HOURS AGO, AND I'VE DECIDED TO CALL OFF THE SEARCH.
JUST SO YOU KNOW, COLLINS HAS JUST REPORTED SOME PRELIMINARY FINDINGS. ALL ITEMS RETRIEVED BY THE DIVERS WERE HANDED OVER TO OUR SPECIALISTS...
...WHO STUDIED THEM WITH THE HELP OF OUR DATABASE.
ALL I CAN SAY IS WE'VE UNCOVERED A *REAL* MYSTERY.
FIRST, THE CRAFT ITSELF. IT'S A SOVIET FOXTROT-CLASS ATTACK SUB, PROBABLY DATING FROM THE END OF THE FIFTIES. DOCUMENTS REMAINING ON BOARD IDENTIFY IT AS THE YUBRENIN.
NEXT, THE COMMANDER... WE MATCHED OUR ANALYSIS OF THE CORPSE...
...TO FILES FROM THE EX-SOVIET ARMY, WHICH IDENTIFY HIM AS COLONEL OROVICH, BUT THAT'S *IMPOSSIBLE!*
WHY, COMMANDER? DIDN'T HE LIKE UNDERSEA ARCHAEOLOGY?
BECAUSE ACCORDING TO HIS FILE, OROVICH DIED OFF THE COAST OF MURMANSK IN 1944.
29

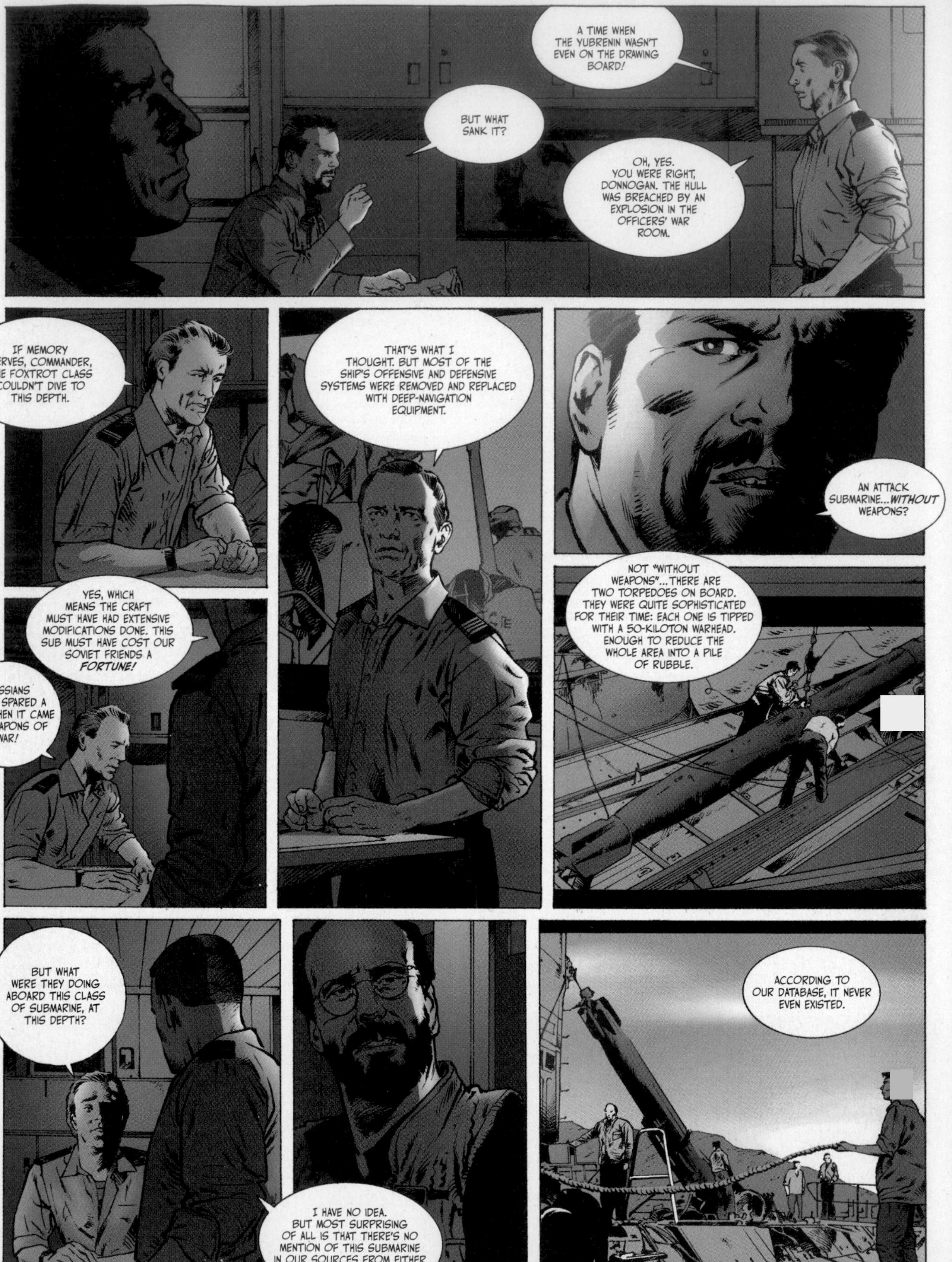
A TIME WHEN THE YUBRENIN WASN'T EVEN ON THE DRAWING BOARD!
BUT WHAT SANK IT?
OH, YES. YOU WERE RIGHT, DONNOGAN. THE HULL WAS BREACHED BY AN EXPLOSION IN THE OFFICERS' WAR ROOM.
IF MEMORY SERVES, COMMANDER, THE FOXTROT CLASS COULDN'T DIVE TO THIS DEPTH.
THAT'S WHAT I THOUGHT. BUT MOST OF THE SHIP'S OFFENSIVE AND DEFENSIVE SYSTEMS WERE REMOVED AND REPLACED WITH DEEP-NAVIGATION EQUIPMENT.
AN ATTACK SUBMARINE...WITHOUT WEAPONS?
YES, WHICH MEANS THE CRAFT MUST HAVE HAD EXTENSIVE MODIFICATIONS DONE. THIS SUB MUST HAVE COST OUR SOVIET FRIENDS A FORTUNE!
RUSSIANS NEVER SPARED A CENT WHEN IT CAME TO WEAPONS OF WAR!
NOT "WITHOUT WEAPONS"... THERE ARE TWO TORPEDOES ON BOARD. THEY WERE QUITE SOPHISTICATED FOR THEIR TIME: EACH ONE IS TIPPED WITH A 50-KILOTON WARHEAD. ENOUGH TO REDUCE THE WHOLE AREA INTO A PILE OF RUBBLE.
BUT WHAT WERE THEY DOING ABOARD THIS CLASS OF SUBMARINE, AT THIS DEPTH?
I HAVE NO IDEA. BUT MOST SURPRISING OF ALL IS THAT THERE'S NO MENTION OF THIS SUBMARINE IN OUR SOURCES FROM EITHER THE K.G.B. OR THE C.I.A.
ACCORDING TO OUR DATABASE, IT NEVER EVEN EXISTED.
30

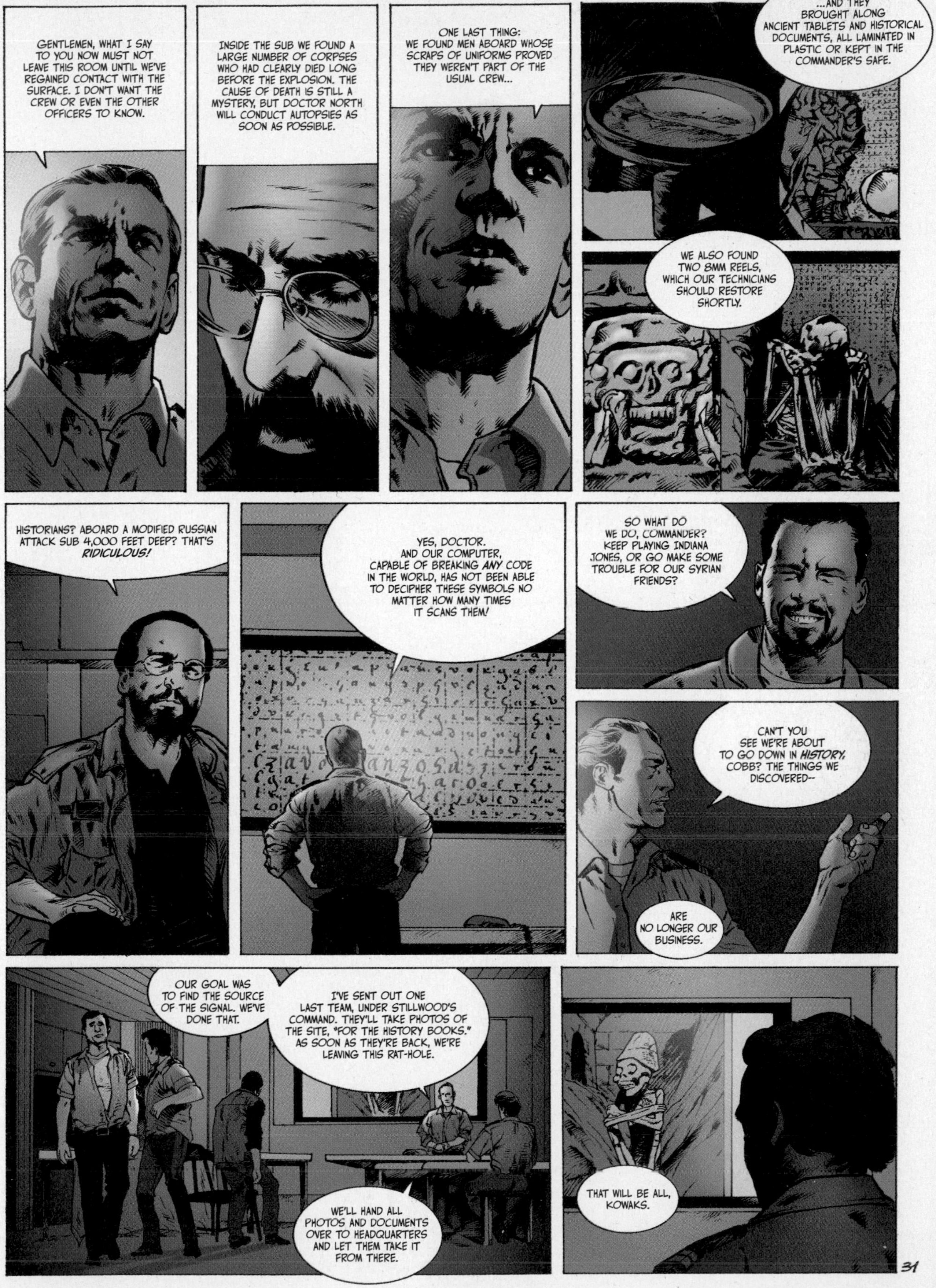
GENTLEMEN, WHAT I SAY TO YOU NOW MUST NOT LEAVE THIS ROOM UNTIL WE'VE REGAINED CONTACT WITH THE SURFACE. I DON'T WANT THE CREW OR EVEN THE OTHER OFFICERS TO KNOW.
INSIDE THE SUB WE FOUND A LARGE NUMBER OF CORPSES WHO HAD CLEARLY DIED LONG BEFORE THE EXPLOSION. THE CAUSE OF DEATH IS STILL A MYSTERY, BUT DOCTOR NORTH WILL CONDUCT AUTOPSIES AS SOON AS POSSIBLE.
ONE LAST THING: WE FOUND MEN ABOARD WHOSE SCRAPS OF UNIFORMS PROVED THEY WEREN'T PART OF THE USUAL CREW...
...AND THEY BROUGHT ALONG ANCIENT TABLETS AND HISTORICAL DOCUMENTS, ALL LAMINATED IN PLASTIC OR KEPT IN THE COMMANDER'S SAFE.
WE ALSO FOUND TWO 8MM REELS, WHICH OUR TECHNICIANS SHOULD RESTORE SHORTLY.
HISTORIANS? ABOARD A MODIFIED RUSSIAN ATTACK SUB 4,000 FEET DEEP? THAT'S *RIDICULOUS!*
YES, DOCTOR. AND OUR COMPUTER, CAPABLE OF BREAKING *ANY* CODE IN THE WORLD, HAS NOT BEEN ABLE TO DECIPHER THESE SYMBOLS NO MATTER HOW MANY TIMES IT SCANS THEM!
SO WHAT DO WE DO, COMMANDER? KEEP PLAYING INDIANA JONES, OR GO MAKE SOME TROUBLE FOR OUR SYRIAN FRIENDS?
CAN'T YOU SEE WE'RE ABOUT TO GO DOWN IN *HISTORY,* COBB? THE THINGS WE DISCOVERED--
ARE NO LONGER OUR BUSINESS.
OUR GOAL WAS TO FIND THE SOURCE OF THE SIGNAL. WE'VE DONE THAT.
I'VE SENT OUT ONE LAST TEAM, UNDER STILLWOOD'S COMMAND. THEY'LL TAKE PHOTOS OF THE SITE, "FOR THE HISTORY BOOKS." AS SOON AS THEY'RE BACK, WE'RE LEAVING THIS RAT-HOLE.
WE'LL HAND ALL PHOTOS AND DOCUMENTS OVER TO HEADQUARTERS AND LET THEM TAKE IT FROM THERE.
THAT WILL BE ALL, KOWAKS.
31

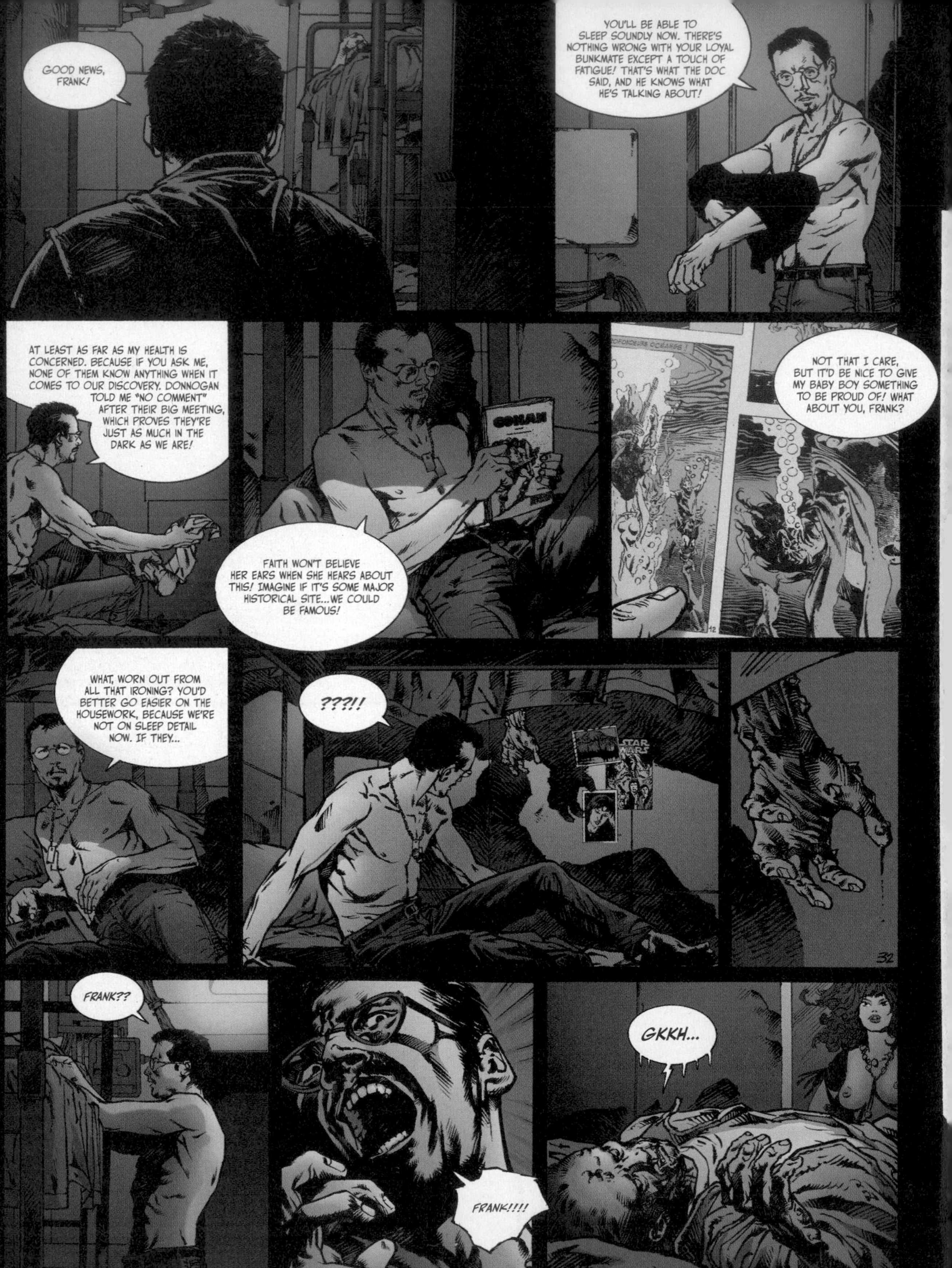
GOOD NEWS, FRANK!
YOU'LL BE ABLE TO SLEEP SOUNDLY NOW. THERE'S NOTHING WRONG WITH YOUR LOYAL BUNKMATE EXCEPT A TOUCH OF FATIGUE! THAT'S WHAT THE DOC SAID, AND HE KNOWS WHAT HE'S TALKING ABOUT!
AT LEAST AS FAR AS MY HEALTH IS CONCERNED. BECAUSE IF YOU ASK ME, NONE OF THEM KNOW ANYTHING WHEN IT COMES TO OUR DISCOVERY. DONNOGAN TOLD ME "NO COMMENT" AFTER THEIR BIG MEETING, WHICH PROVES THEY'RE JUST AS MUCH IN THE DARK AS WE ARE!
FAITH WON'T BELIEVE HER EARS WHEN SHE HEARS ABOUT THIS! IMAGINE IF IT'S SOME MAJOR HISTORICAL SITE...WE COULD BE FAMOUS!
CONAN
NOT THAT I CARE, BUT IT'D BE NICE TO GIVE MY BABY BOY SOMETHING TO BE PROUD OF! WHAT ABOUT YOU, FRANK?
WHAT, WORN OUT FROM ALL THAT IRONING? YOU'D BETTER GO EASIER ON THE HOUSEWORK, BECAUSE WE'RE NOT ON SLEEP DETAIL NOW. IF THEY...
???!!
STAR WARS
FRANK??
GKKH...
FRANK!!!!

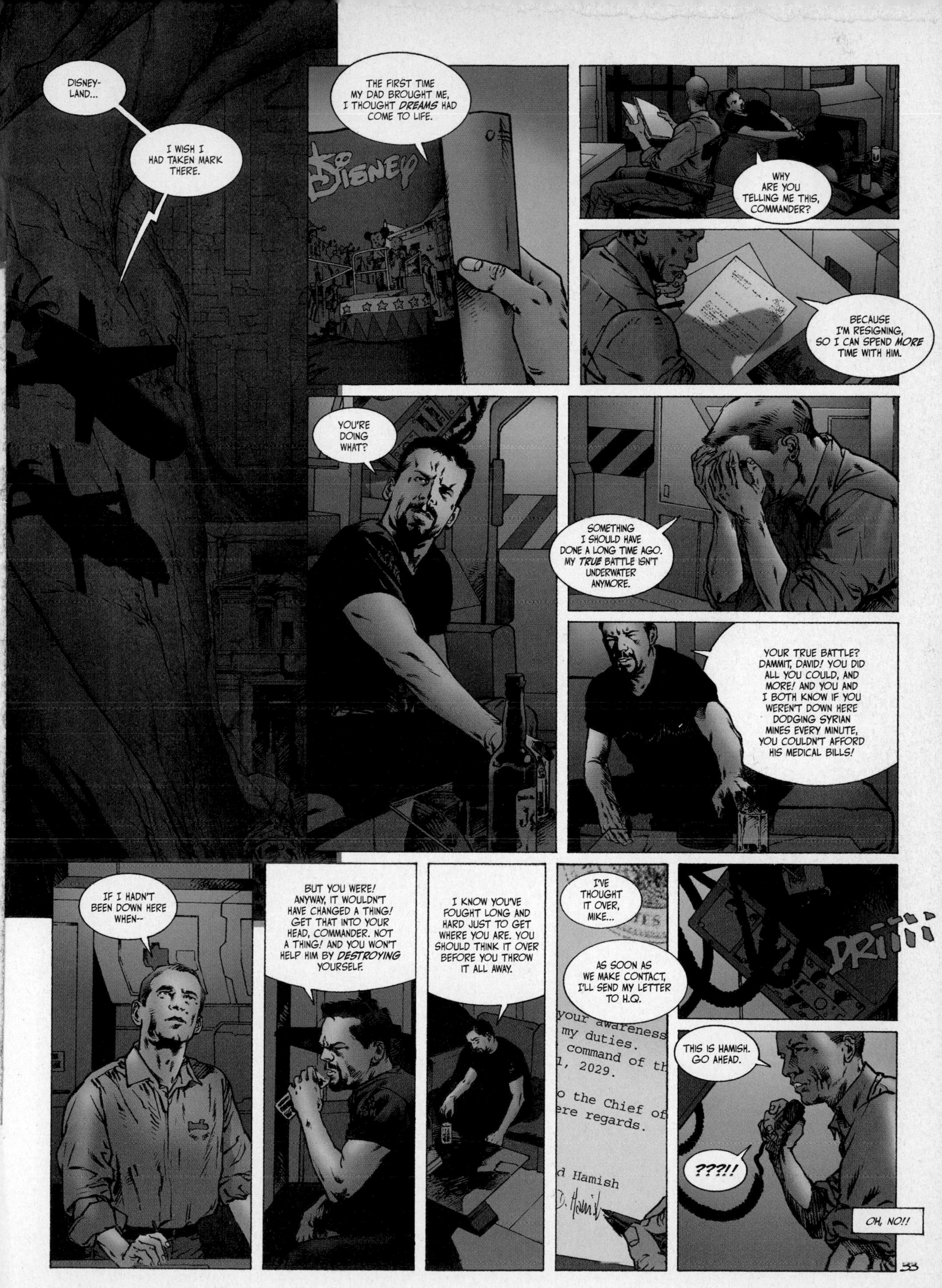
DISNEY-LAND...
I WISH I HAD TAKEN MARK THERE.
THE FIRST TIME MY DAD BROUGHT ME, I THOUGHT *DREAMS* HAD COME TO LIFE.
DISNEY
WHY ARE YOU TELLING ME THIS, COMMANDER?
BECAUSE I'M RESIGNING, SO I CAN SPEND *MORE* TIME WITH HIM.
YOU'RE DOING WHAT?
SOMETHING I SHOULD HAVE DONE A LONG TIME AGO. MY *TRUE* BATTLE ISN'T UNDERWATER ANYMORE.
YOUR TRUE BATTLE? DAMMIT, DAVID! YOU DID ALL YOU COULD, AND MORE! AND YOU AND I BOTH KNOW IF YOU WEREN'T DOWN HERE DODGING SYRIAN MINES EVERY MINUTE, YOU COULDN'T AFFORD HIS MEDICAL BILLS!
IF I HADN'T BEEN DOWN HERE WHEN--
BUT YOU WERE! ANYWAY, IT WOULDN'T HAVE CHANGED A THING! GET THAT INTO YOUR HEAD, COMMANDER. NOT A THING! AND YOU WON'T HELP HIM BY *DESTROYING* YOURSELF.
I KNOW YOU'VE FOUGHT LONG AND HARD JUST TO GET WHERE YOU ARE. YOU SHOULD THINK IT OVER BEFORE YOU THROW IT ALL AWAY.
I'VE THOUGHT IT OVER, MIKE...
AS SOON AS WE MAKE CONTACT, I'LL SEND MY LETTER TO H.Q.
your awareness
my duties.
command of th
l, 2029.
o the Chief of
ere regards.
d Hamish
DRIIIII
THIS IS HAMISH. GO AHEAD.
???!!
OH, NO!!

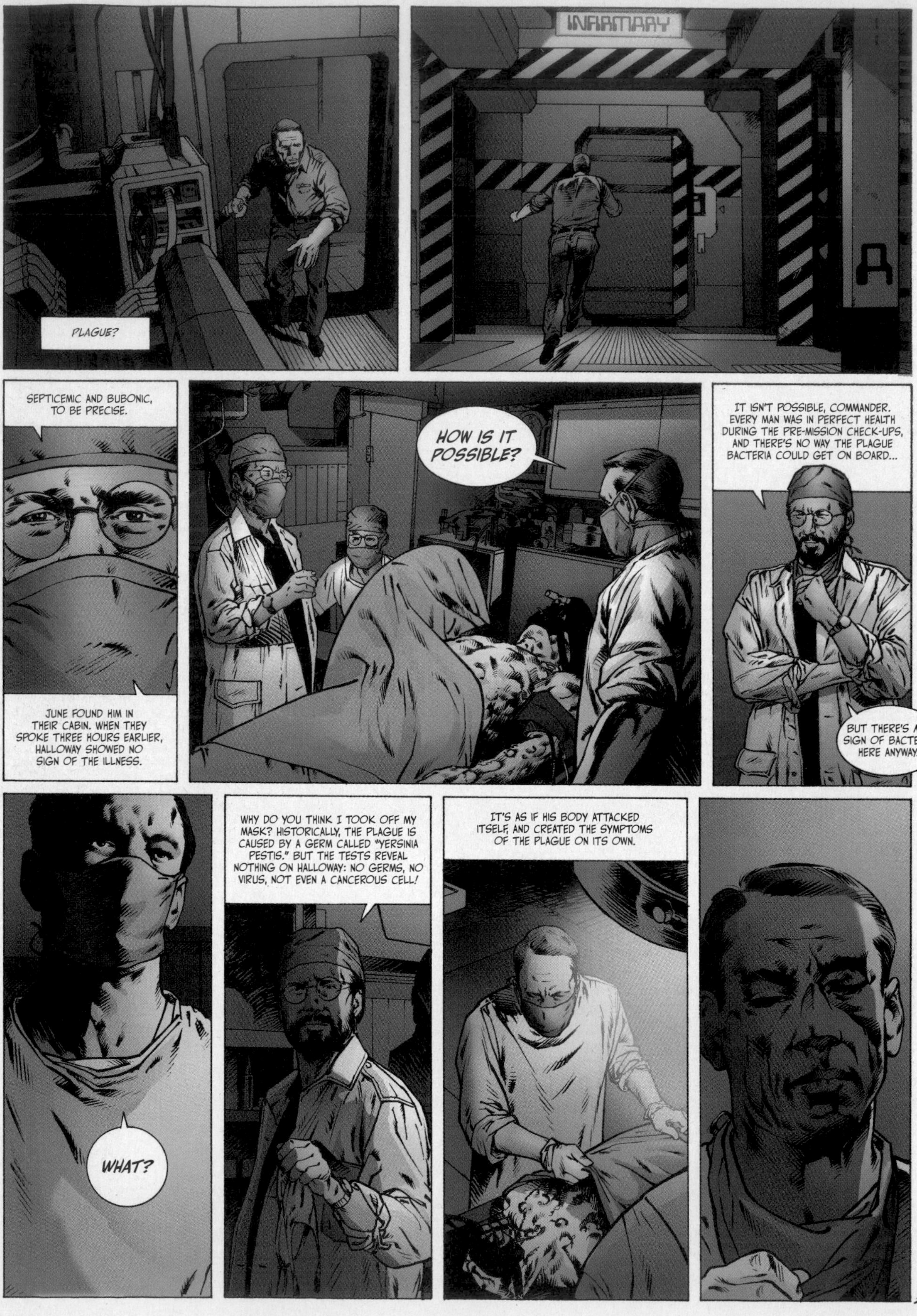
PLAGUE?
INFIRMARY
SEPTICEMIC AND BUBONIC, TO BE PRECISE.
JUNE FOUND HIM IN THEIR CABIN. WHEN THEY SPOKE THREE HOURS EARLIER, HALLOWAY SHOWED NO SIGN OF THE ILLNESS.
HOW IS IT POSSIBLE?
IT ISN'T POSSIBLE, COMMANDER. EVERY MAN WAS IN PERFECT HEALTH DURING THE PRE-MISSION CHECK-UPS, AND THERE'S NO WAY THE PLAGUE BACTERIA COULD GET ON BOARD...
BUT THERE'S NO SIGN OF BACTERIA HERE ANYWAY.
WHAT?
WHY DO YOU THINK I TOOK OFF MY MASK? HISTORICALLY, THE PLAGUE IS CAUSED BY A GERM CALLED "YERSINIA PESTIS." BUT THE TESTS REVEAL NOTHING ON HALLOWAY: NO GERMS, NO VIRUS, NOT EVEN A CANCEROUS CELL!
IT'S AS IF HIS BODY ATTACKED ITSELF, AND CREATED THE SYMPTOMS OF THE PLAGUE ON ITS OWN.
34

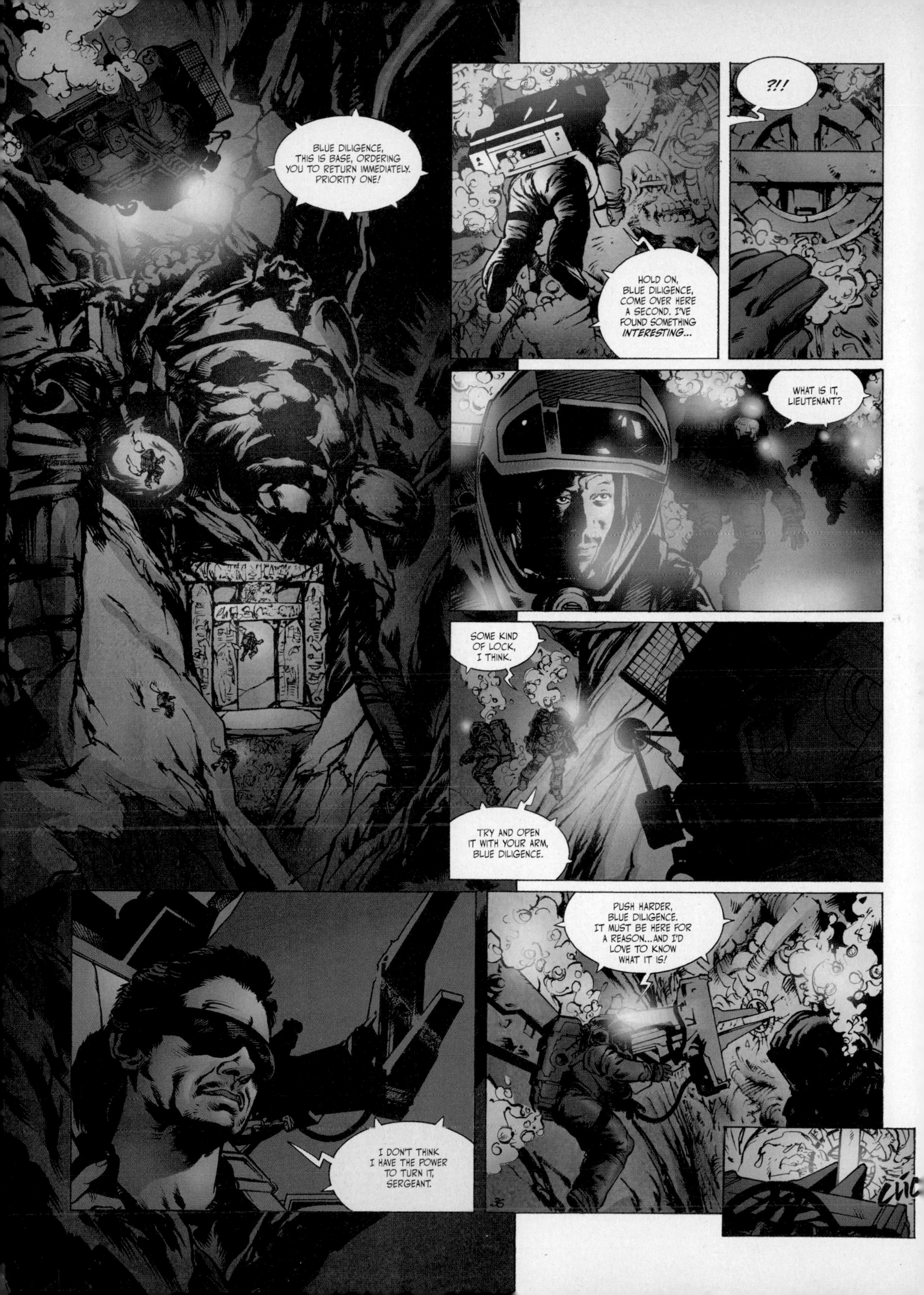
BLUE DILIGENCE, THIS IS BASE, ORDERING YOU TO RETURN IMMEDIATELY. PRIORITY ONE!
HOLD ON, BLUE DILIGENCE, COME OVER HERE A SECOND. I'VE FOUND SOMETHING *INTERESTING*...
?!!
WHAT IS IT, LIEUTENANT?
SOME KIND OF LOCK, I THINK.
TRY AND OPEN IT WITH YOUR ARM, BLUE DILIGENCE.
I DON'T THINK I HAVE THE POWER TO TURN IT, SERGEANT.
PUSH HARDER, BLUE DILIGENCE. IT MUST BE HERE FOR A REASON...AND I'D LOVE TO KNOW WHAT IT IS!
CLIC

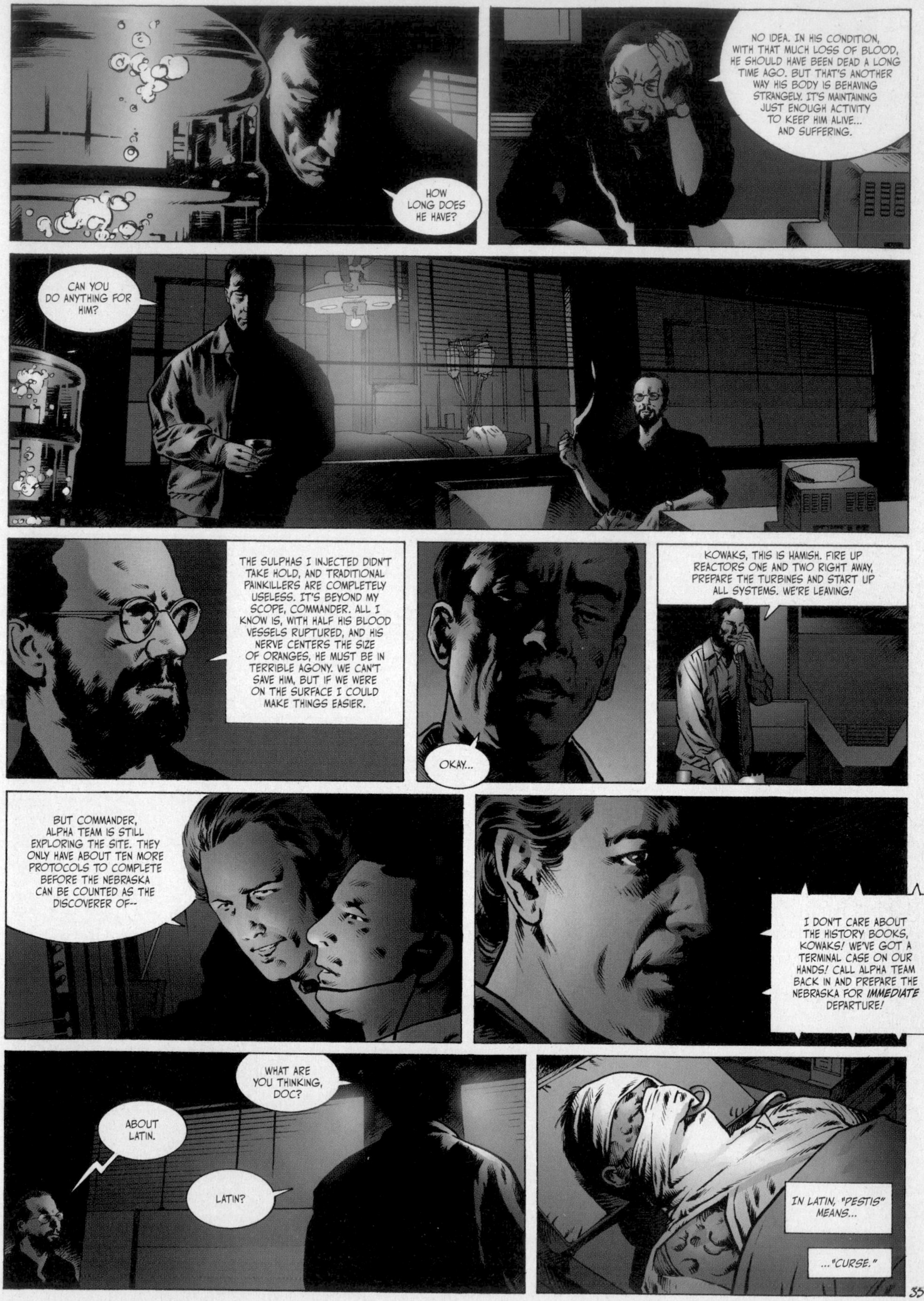
HOW LONG DOES HE HAVE?
NO IDEA. IN HIS CONDITION, WITH THAT MUCH LOSS OF BLOOD, HE SHOULD HAVE BEEN DEAD A LONG TIME AGO. BUT THAT'S ANOTHER WAY HIS BODY IS BEHAVING STRANGELY. IT'S MAINTAINING JUST ENOUGH ACTIVITY TO KEEP HIM ALIVE... AND SUFFERING.
CAN YOU DO ANYTHING FOR HIM?
THE SULPHAS I INJECTED DIDN'T TAKE HOLD, AND TRADITIONAL PAINKILLERS ARE COMPLETELY USELESS. IT'S BEYOND MY SCOPE, COMMANDER. ALL I KNOW IS, WITH HALF HIS BLOOD VESSELS RUPTURED, AND HIS NERVE CENTERS THE SIZE OF ORANGES, HE MUST BE IN TERRIBLE AGONY. WE CAN'T SAVE HIM, BUT IF WE WERE ON THE SURFACE I COULD MAKE THINGS EASIER.
OKAY...
KOWAKS, THIS IS HAMISH. FIRE UP REACTORS ONE AND TWO RIGHT AWAY, PREPARE THE TURBINES AND START UP ALL SYSTEMS. WE'RE LEAVING!
BUT COMMANDER, ALPHA TEAM IS STILL EXPLORING THE SITE. THEY ONLY HAVE ABOUT TEN MORE PROTOCOLS TO COMPLETE BEFORE THE NEBRASKA CAN BE COUNTED AS THE DISCOVERER OF--
I DON'T CARE ABOUT THE HISTORY BOOKS, KOWAKS! WE'VE GOT A TERMINAL CASE ON OUR HANDS! CALL ALPHA TEAM BACK IN AND PREPARE THE NEBRASKA FOR IMMEDIATE DEPARTURE!
WHAT ARE YOU THINKING, DOC?
ABOUT LATIN.
LATIN?
IN LATIN, "PESTIS" MEANS...
..."CURSE."
35

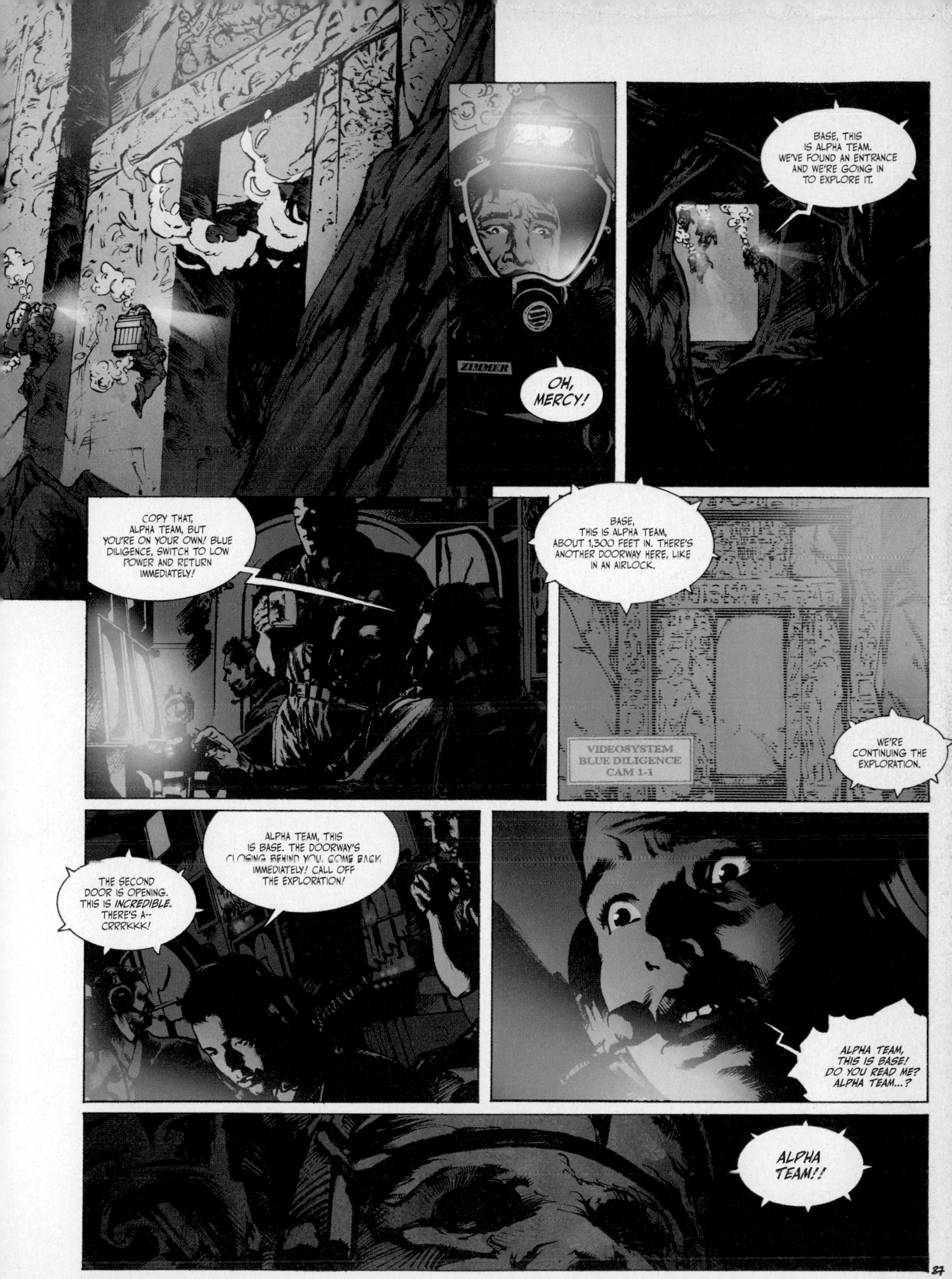
ZIMMER
OH, MERCY!
BASE, THIS IS ALPHA TEAM. WE'VE FOUND AN ENTRANCE AND WE'RE GOING IN TO EXPLORE IT.
COPY THAT, ALPHA TEAM, BUT YOU'RE ON YOUR OWN! BLUE DILIGENCE, SWITCH TO LOW POWER AND RETURN IMMEDIATELY!
BASE, THIS IS ALPHA TEAM, ABOUT 1,300 FEET IN. THERE'S ANOTHER DOORWAY HERE, LIKE IN AN AIRLOCK.
VIDEOSYSTEM BLUE DILIGENCE CAM 1-1
WE'RE CONTINUING THE EXPLORATION.
THE SECOND DOOR IS OPENING. THIS IS *INCREDIBLE*. THERE'S A-- CRRRKKK!
ALPHA TEAM, THIS IS BASE. THE DOORWAY'S CLOSING BEHIND YOU. COME BACK IMMEDIATELY! CALL OFF THE EXPLORATION!
ALPHA TEAM, THIS IS BASE! DO YOU READ ME? ALPHA TEAM...?
ALPHA TEAM!!

37

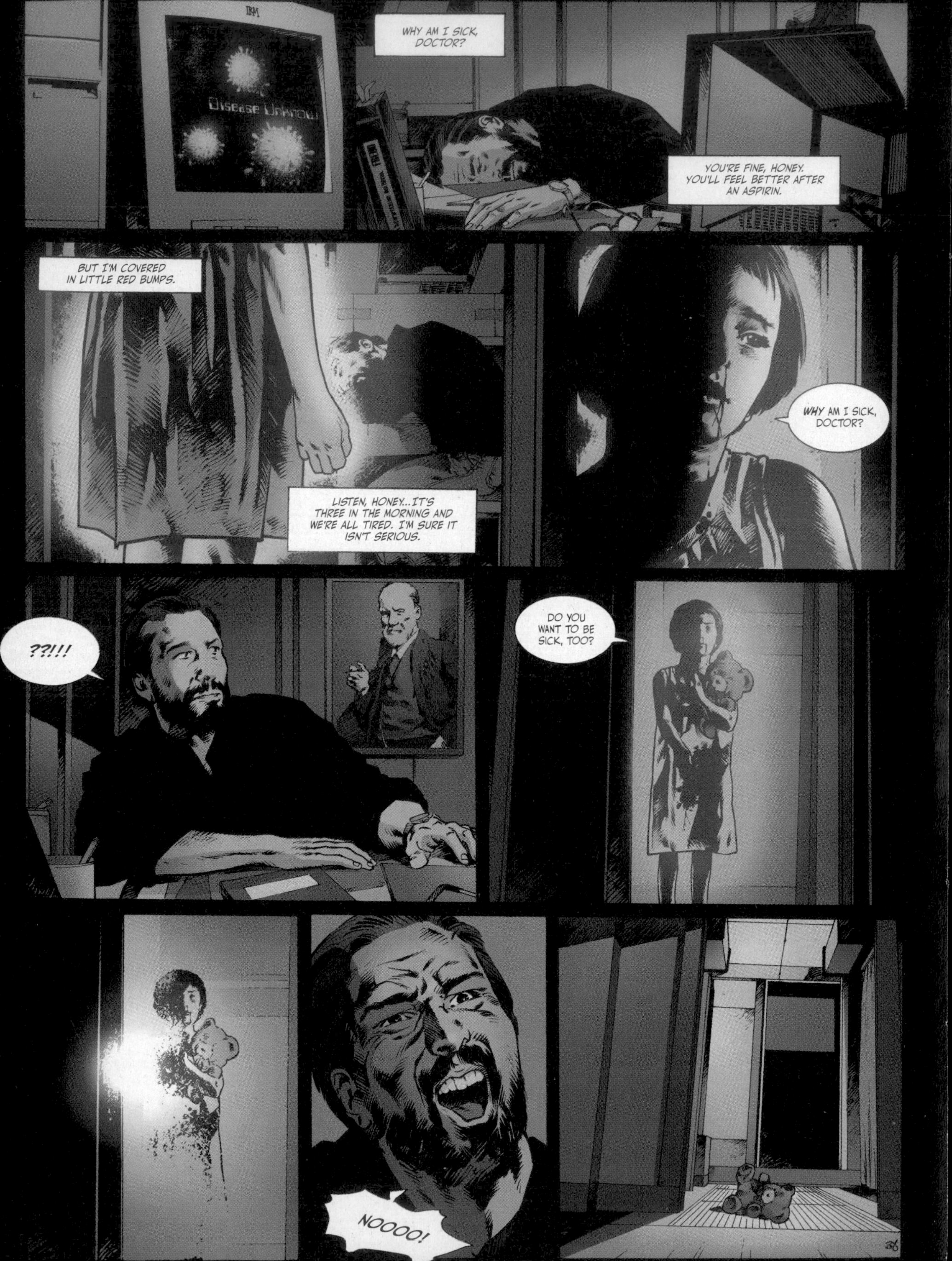
WHY AM I SICK, DOCTOR?
Disease Unknown
YOU'RE FINE, HONEY. YOU'LL FEEL BETTER AFTER AN ASPIRIN.
BUT I'M COVERED IN LITTLE RED BUMPS.
LISTEN, HONEY...IT'S THREE IN THE MORNING AND WE'RE ALL TIRED. I'M SURE IT ISN'T SERIOUS.
WHY AM I SICK, DOCTOR?
??!!!
DO YOU WANT TO BE SICK, TOO?
NOOOO!

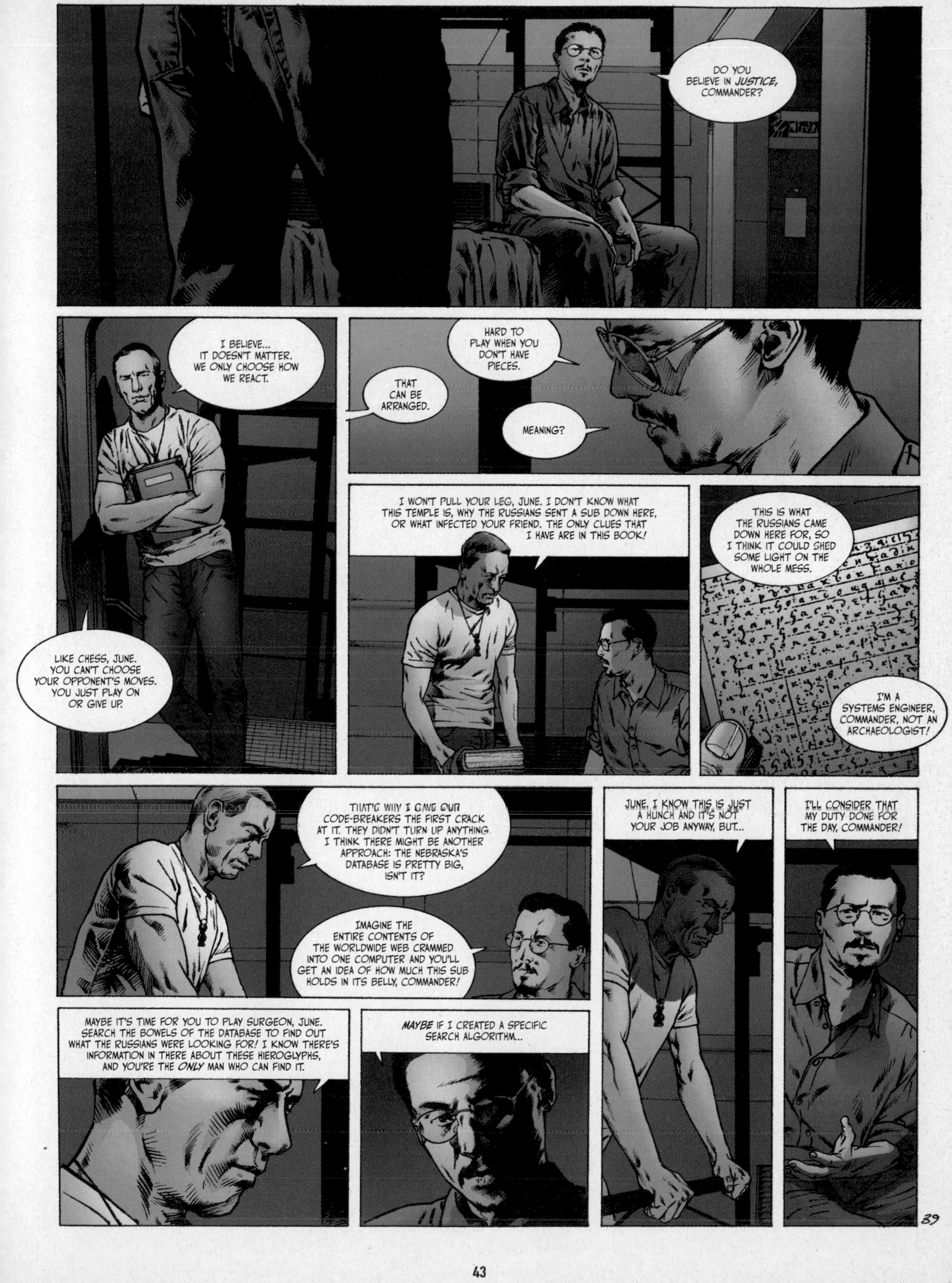
DO YOU BELIEVE IN *JUSTICE*, COMMANDER?
I BELIEVE... IT DOESN'T MATTER. WE ONLY CHOOSE HOW WE REACT.
LIKE CHESS, JUNE. YOU CAN'T CHOOSE YOUR OPPONENT'S MOVES. YOU JUST PLAY ON OR GIVE UP.
HARD TO PLAY WHEN YOU DON'T HAVE PIECES.
THAT CAN BE ARRANGED.
MEANING?
I WON'T PULL YOUR LEG, JUNE. I DON'T KNOW WHAT THIS TEMPLE IS, WHY THE RUSSIANS SENT A SUB DOWN HERE, OR WHAT INFECTED YOUR FRIEND. THE ONLY CLUES THAT I HAVE ARE IN THIS BOOK!
THIS IS WHAT THE RUSSIANS CAME DOWN HERE FOR, SO I THINK IT COULD SHED SOME LIGHT ON THE WHOLE MESS.
I'M A SYSTEMS ENGINEER, COMMANDER, NOT AN ARCHAEOLOGIST!
THAT'S WHY I GAVE OUR CODE-BREAKERS THE FIRST CRACK AT IT. THEY DIDN'T TURN UP ANYTHING. I THINK THERE MIGHT BE ANOTHER APPROACH: THE NEBRASKA'S DATABASE IS PRETTY BIG, ISN'T IT?
IMAGINE THE ENTIRE CONTENTS OF THE WORLDWIDE WEB CRAMMED INTO ONE COMPUTER AND YOU'LL GET AN IDEA OF HOW MUCH THIS SUB HOLDS IN ITS BELLY, COMMANDER!
MAYBE IT'S TIME FOR YOU TO PLAY SURGEON, JUNE. SEARCH THE BOWELS OF THE DATABASE TO FIND OUT WHAT THE RUSSIANS WERE LOOKING FOR! I KNOW THERE'S INFORMATION IN THERE ABOUT THESE HIEROGLYPHS, AND YOU'RE THE *ONLY* MAN WHO CAN FIND IT.
MAYBE IF I CREATED A SPECIFIC SEARCH ALGORITHM...
JUNE, I KNOW THIS IS JUST A HUNCH AND IT'S NOT YOUR JOB ANYWAY, BUT...
I'LL CONSIDER THAT MY DUTY DONE FOR THE DAY, COMMANDER!

39

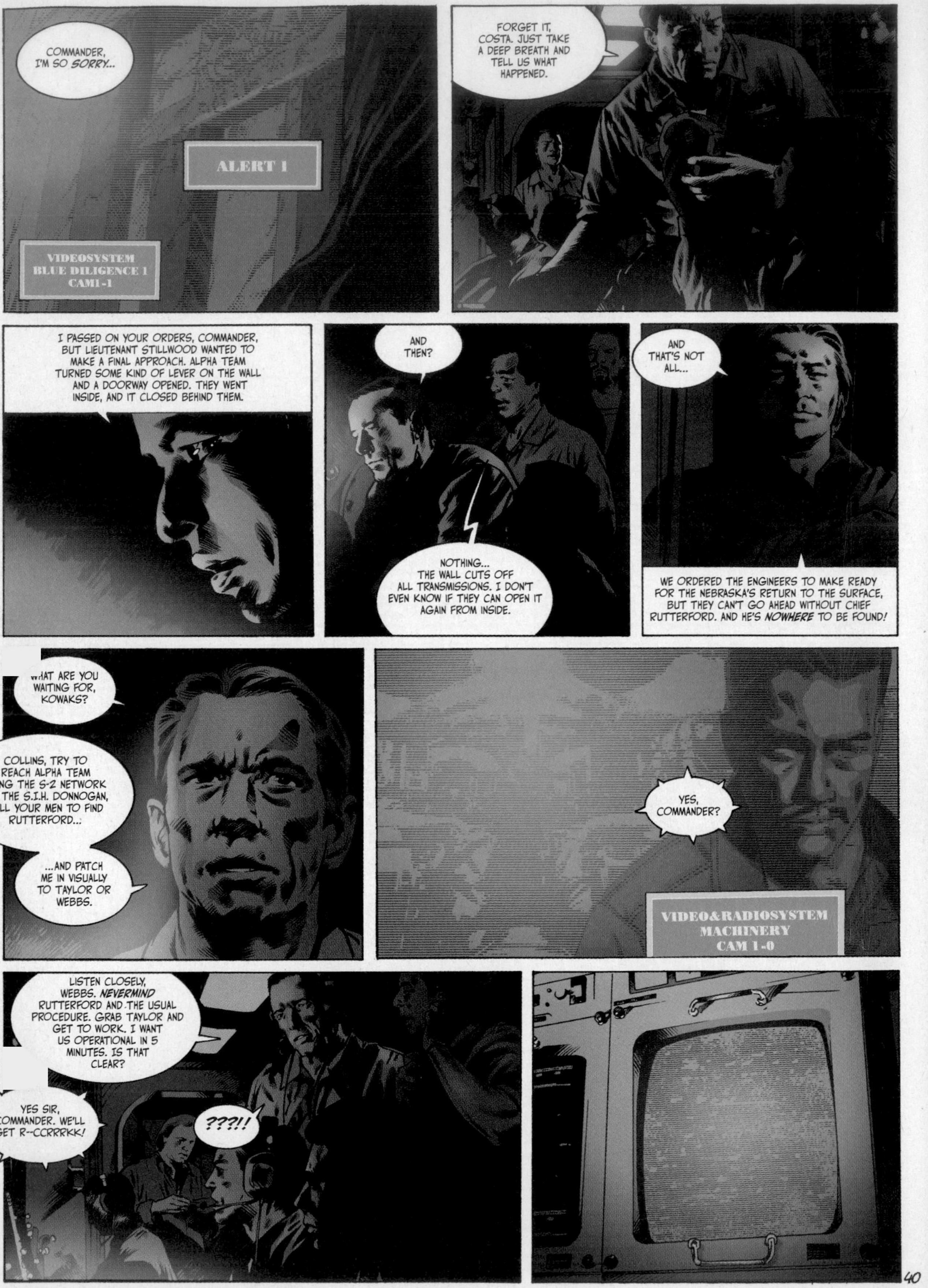
COMMANDER, I'M SO SORRY...
ALERT 1
VIDEOSYSTEM BLUE DILIGENCE 1 CAM1-1
FORGET IT, COSTA. JUST TAKE A DEEP BREATH AND TELL US WHAT HAPPENED.
I PASSED ON YOUR ORDERS, COMMANDER, BUT LIEUTENANT STILLWOOD WANTED TO MAKE A FINAL APPROACH. ALPHA TEAM TURNED SOME KIND OF LEVER ON THE WALL AND A DOORWAY OPENED. THEY WENT INSIDE, AND IT CLOSED BEHIND THEM.
AND THEN?
NOTHING... THE WALL CUTS OFF ALL TRANSMISSIONS. I DON'T EVEN KNOW IF THEY CAN OPEN IT AGAIN FROM INSIDE.
AND THAT'S NOT ALL...
WE ORDERED THE ENGINEERS TO MAKE READY FOR THE NEBRASKA'S RETURN TO THE SURFACE, BUT THEY CAN'T GO AHEAD WITHOUT CHIEF RUTTERFORD. AND HE'S NOWHERE TO BE FOUND!
WHAT ARE YOU WAITING FOR, KOWAKS?
COLLINS, TRY TO REACH ALPHA TEAM USING THE S-2 NETWORK OR THE S.I.H. DONNOGAN, TELL YOUR MEN TO FIND RUTTERFORD...
...AND PATCH ME IN VISUALLY TO TAYLOR OR WEBBS.
YES, COMMANDER?
VIDEO&RADIOSYSTEM MACHINERY CAM 1-0
LISTEN CLOSELY, WEBBS. NEVERMIND RUTTERFORD AND THE USUAL PROCEDURE. GRAB TAYLOR AND GET TO WORK. I WANT US OPERATIONAL IN 5 MINUTES. IS THAT CLEAR?
YES SIR, COMMANDER. WE'LL GET R--CCRRRKK!
???!!
40

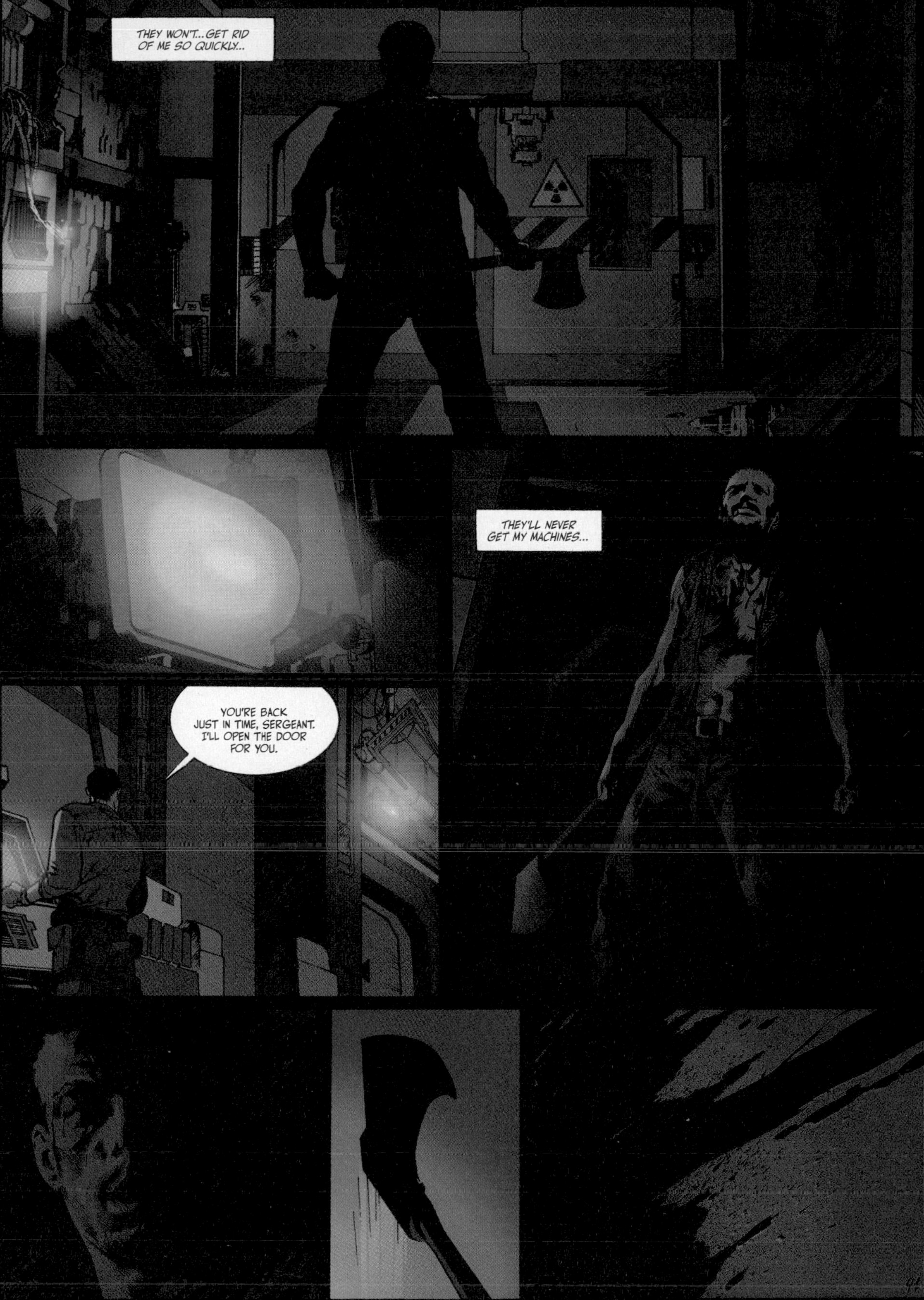
THEY WON'T...GET RID OF ME SO QUICKLY...
THEY'LL NEVER GET MY MACHINES...
YOU'RE BACK JUST IN TIME, SERGEANT. I'LL OPEN THE DOOR FOR YOU.

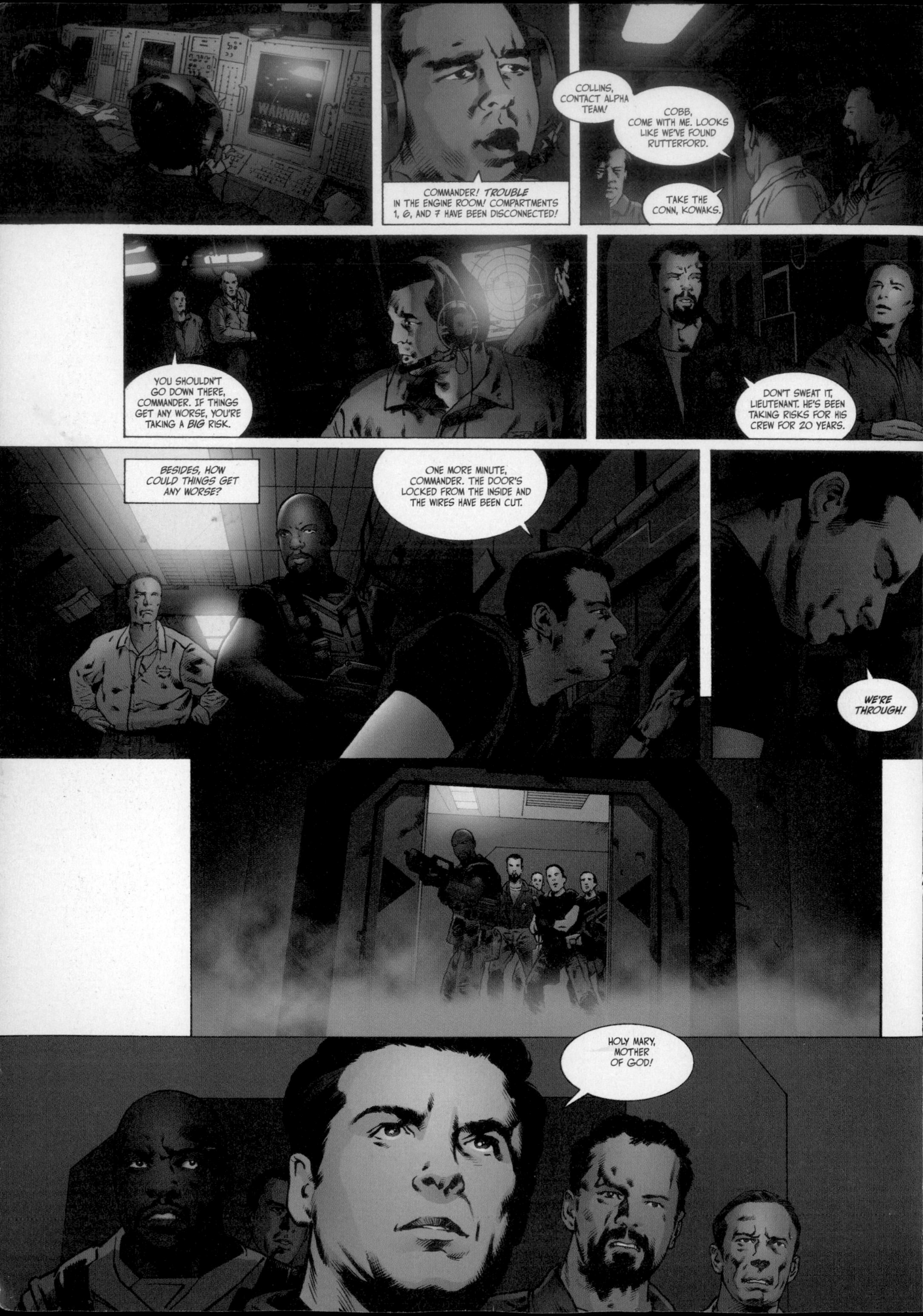
WARNING
COMMANDER! *TROUBLE* IN THE ENGINE ROOM! COMPARTMENTS 1, 6, AND 7 HAVE BEEN DISCONNECTED!
COLLINS, CONTACT ALPHA TEAM!
COBB, COME WITH ME. LOOKS LIKE WE'VE FOUND RUTTERFORD.
TAKE THE CONN, KOWAKS.
YOU SHOULDN'T GO DOWN THERE, COMMANDER. IF THINGS GET ANY WORSE, YOU'RE TAKING A *BIG* RISK.
DON'T SWEAT IT, LIEUTENANT. HE'S BEEN TAKING RISKS FOR HIS CREW FOR 20 YEARS.
BESIDES, HOW COULD THINGS GET ANY WORSE?
ONE MORE MINUTE, COMMANDER. THE DOOR'S LOCKED FROM THE INSIDE AND THE WIRES HAVE BEEN CUT.
WE'RE THROUGH!
HOLY MARY, MOTHER OF GOD!

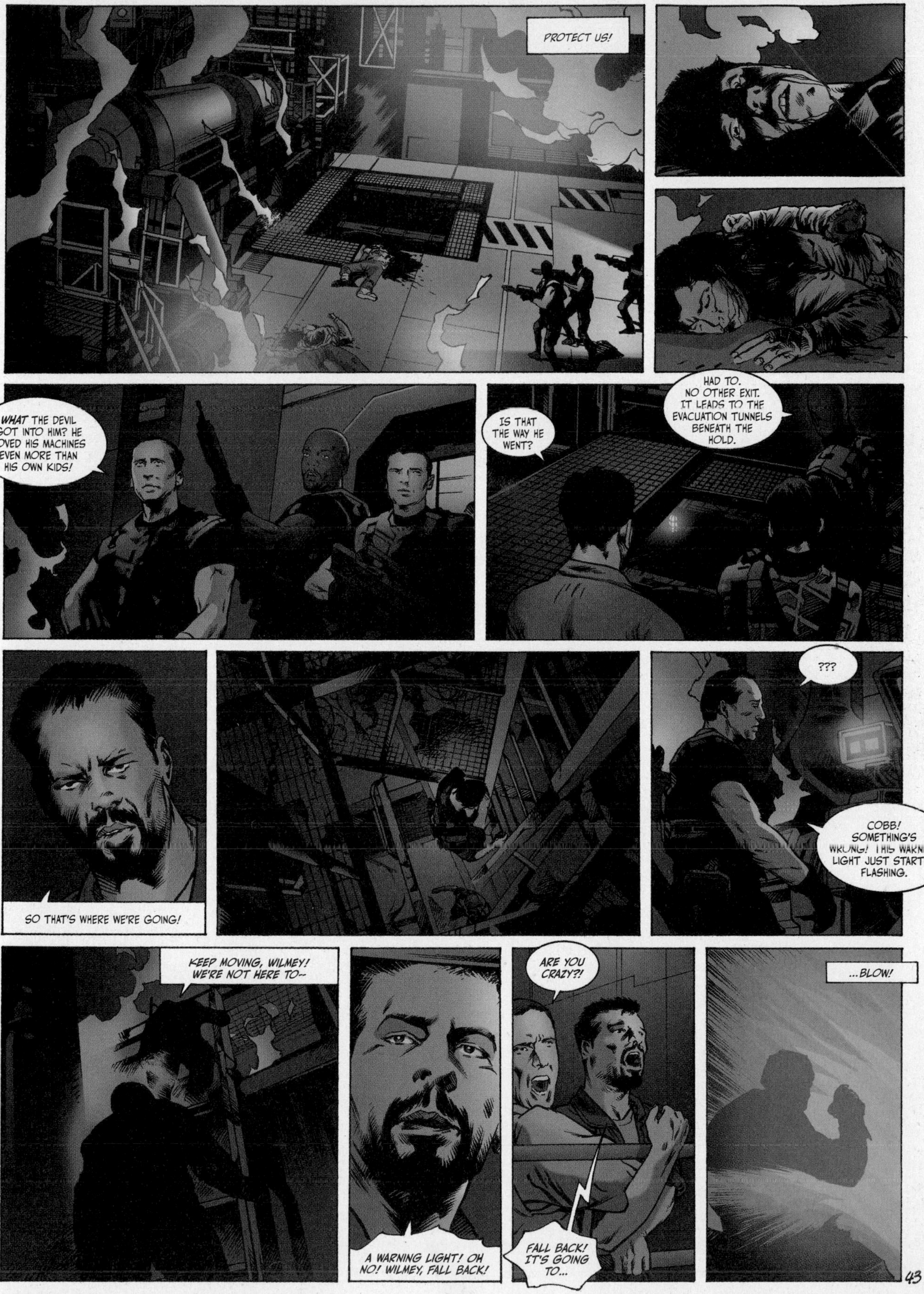
PROTECT US!
WHAT THE DEVIL GOT INTO HIM? HE LOVED HIS MACHINES EVEN MORE THAN HIS OWN KIDS!
IS THAT THE WAY HE WENT?
HAD TO. NO OTHER EXIT. IT LEADS TO THE EVACUATION TUNNELS BENEATH THE HOLD.
SO THAT'S WHERE WE'RE GOING!
???
COBB! SOMETHING'S WRONG! THIS WARNING LIGHT JUST STARTED FLASHING.
KEEP MOVING, WILMEY! WE'RE NOT HERE TO--
A WARNING LIGHT! OH NO! WILMEY, FALL BACK!
ARE YOU CRAZY?!
FALL BACK! IT'S GOING TO...
...BLOW!
43

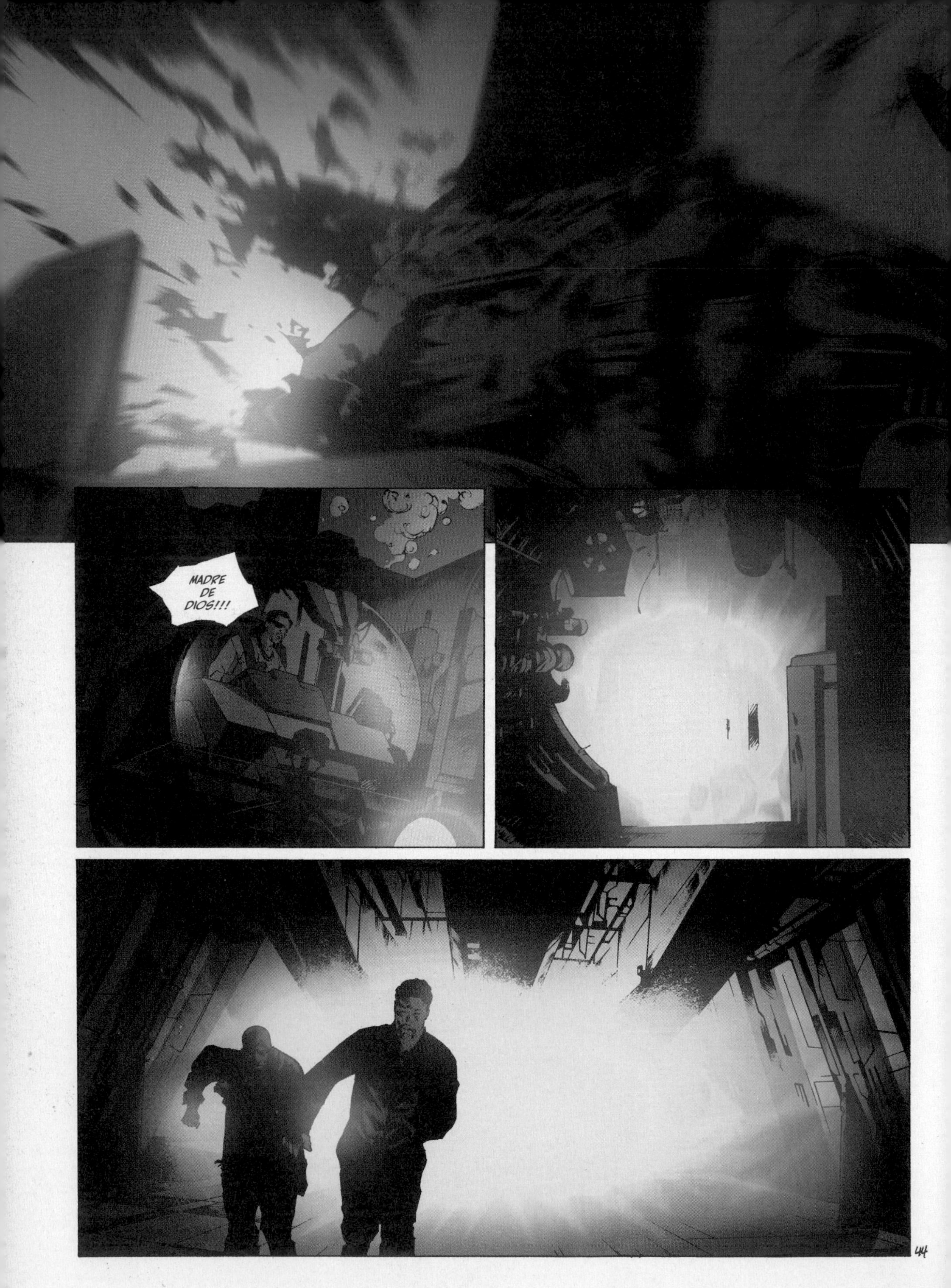
MADRE DE DIOS!!!
44

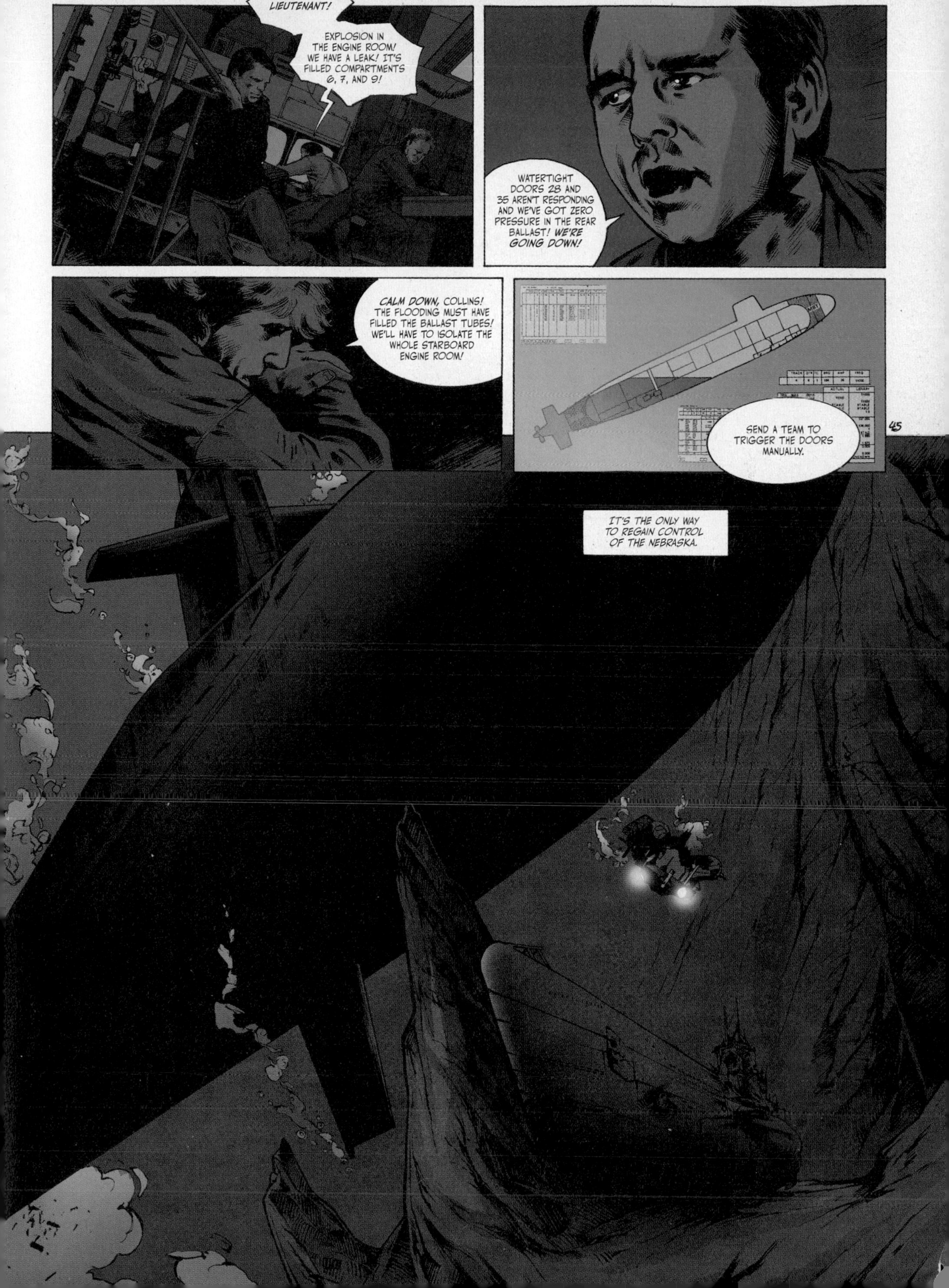
LIEUTENANT!
EXPLOSION IN THE ENGINE ROOM! WE HAVE A LEAK! IT'S FILLED COMPARTMENTS 6, 7, AND 9!
WATERTIGHT DOORS 28 AND 35 AREN'T RESPONDING AND WE'VE GOT ZERO PRESSURE IN THE REAR BALLAST! WE'RE GOING DOWN!
CALM DOWN, COLLINS! THE FLOODING MUST HAVE FILLED THE BALLAST TUBES! WE'LL HAVE TO ISOLATE THE WHOLE STARBOARD ENGINE ROOM!
SEND A TEAM TO TRIGGER THE DOORS MANUALLY.
IT'S THE ONLY WAY TO REGAIN CONTROL OF THE NEBRASKA.

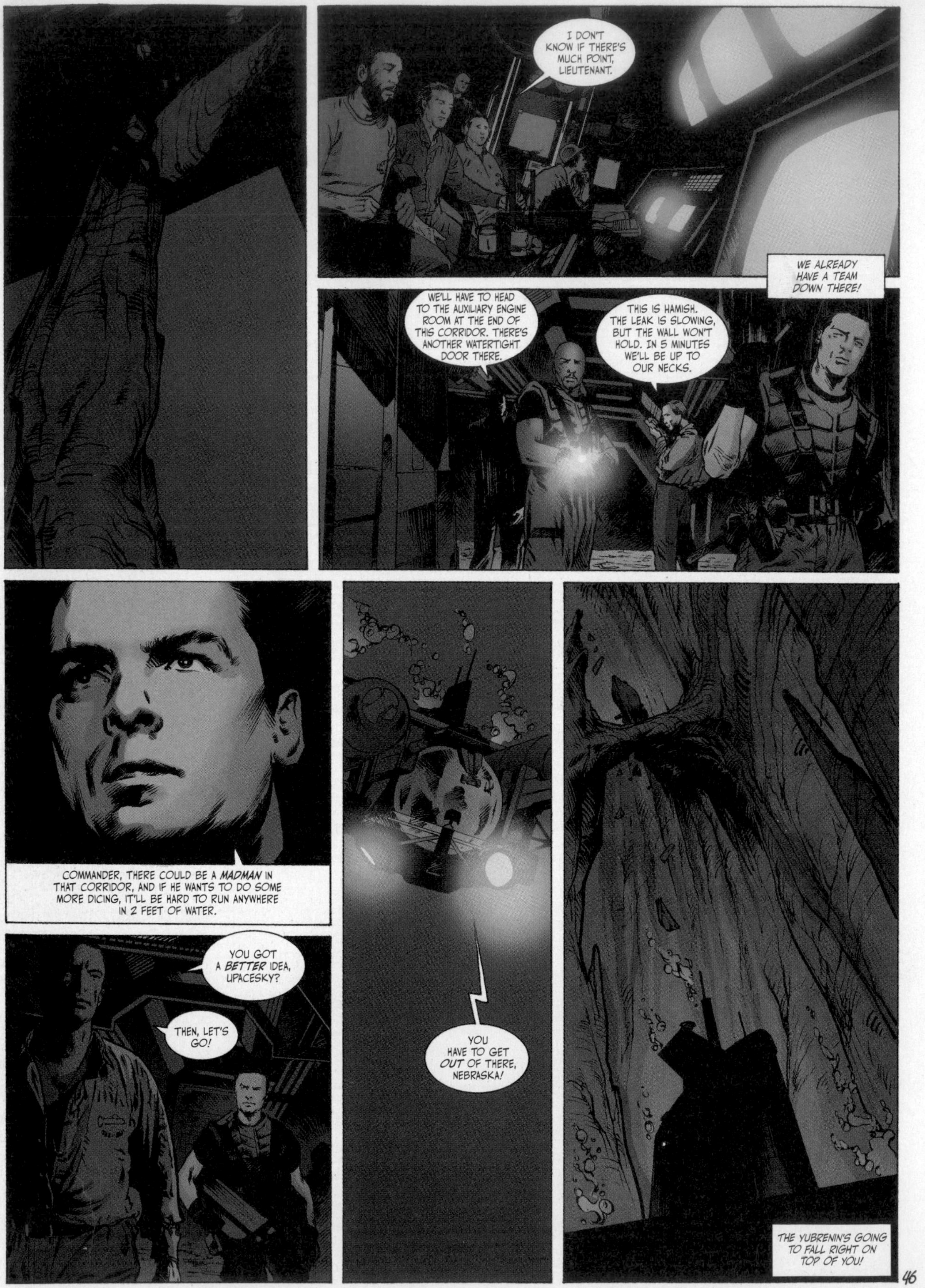
I DON'T KNOW IF THERE'S MUCH POINT, LIEUTENANT.
WE ALREADY HAVE A TEAM DOWN THERE!
WE'LL HAVE TO HEAD TO THE AUXILIARY ENGINE ROOM AT THE END OF THIS CORRIDOR. THERE'S ANOTHER WATERTIGHT DOOR THERE.
THIS IS HAMISH. THE LEAK IS SLOWING, BUT THE WALL WON'T HOLD. IN 5 MINUTES WE'LL BE UP TO OUR NECKS.
COMMANDER, THERE COULD BE A MADMAN IN THAT CORRIDOR, AND IF HE WANTS TO DO SOME MORE DICING, IT'LL BE HARD TO RUN ANYWHERE IN 2 FEET OF WATER.
YOU GOT A BETTER IDEA, UPACESKY?
THEN, LET'S GO!
YOU HAVE TO GET OUT OF THERE, NEBRASKA!
THE YUBRENIN'S GOING TO FALL RIGHT ON TOP OF YOU!
46

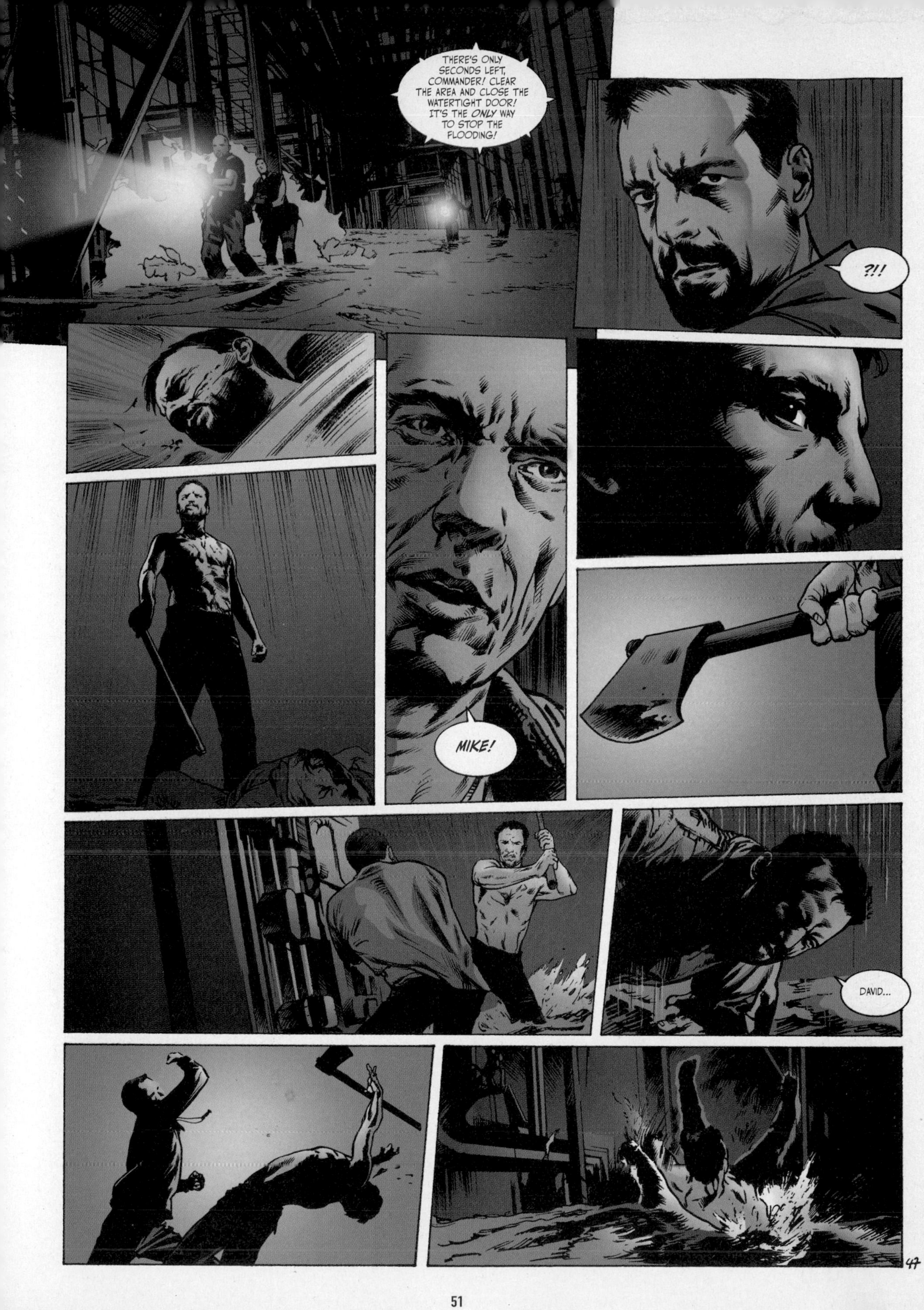
THERE'S ONLY SECONDS LEFT, COMMANDER! CLEAR THE AREA AND CLOSE THE WATERTIGHT DOOR! IT'S THE *ONLY* WAY TO STOP THE FLOODING!
?!!
MIKE!
DAVID...
47

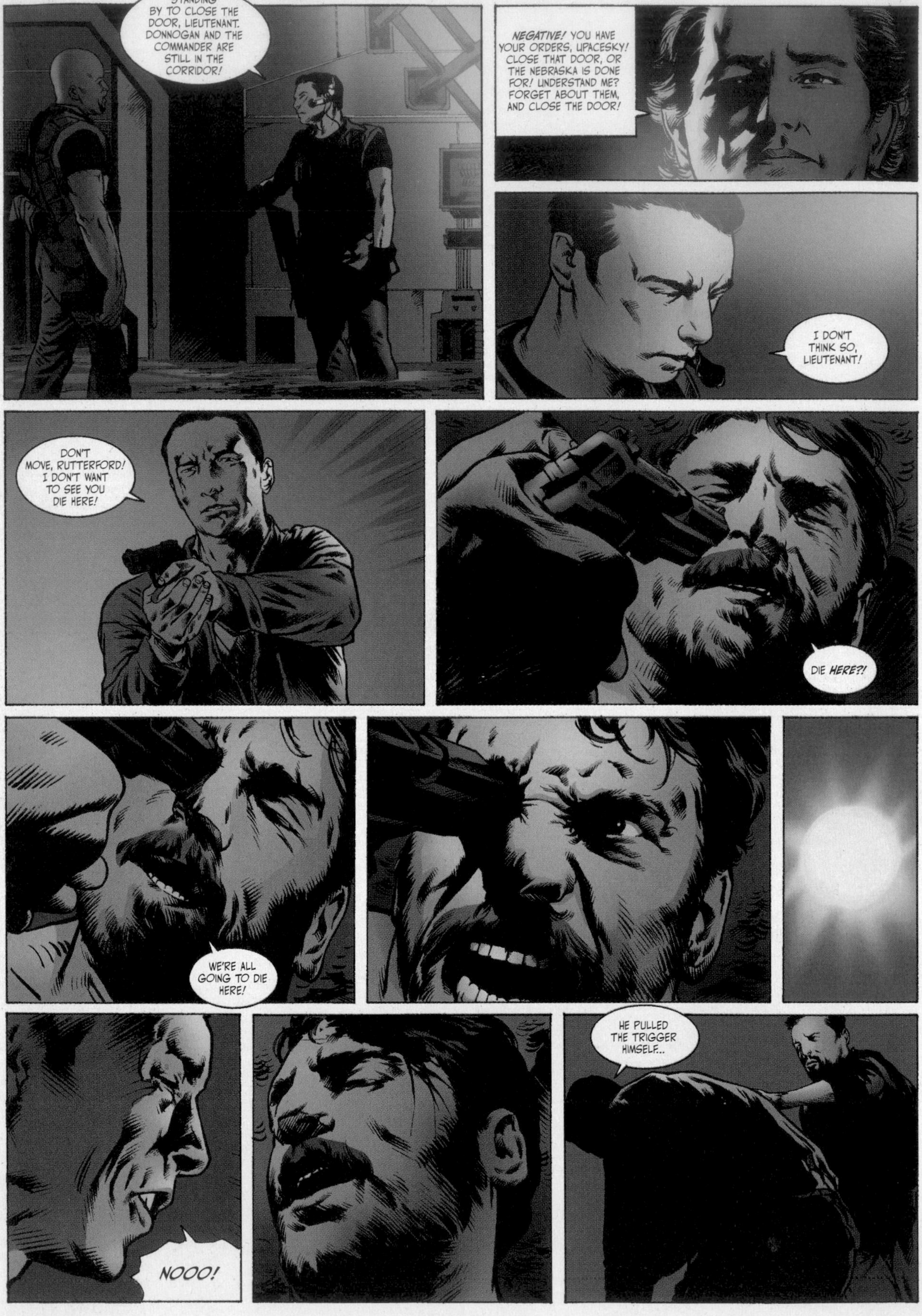
STANDING BY TO CLOSE THE DOOR, LIEUTENANT. DONNOGAN AND THE COMMANDER ARE STILL IN THE CORRIDOR!
NEGATIVE! YOU HAVE YOUR ORDERS, UPACESKY! CLOSE THAT DOOR, OR THE NEBRASKA IS DONE FOR! UNDERSTAND ME? FORGET ABOUT THEM, AND CLOSE THE DOOR!
I DON'T THINK SO, LIEUTENANT!
DON'T MOVE, RUTTERFORD! I DON'T WANT TO SEE YOU DIE HERE!
DIE HERE?!
WE'RE ALL GOING TO DIE HERE!
NOOO!
HE PULLED THE TRIGGER HIMSELF...

48

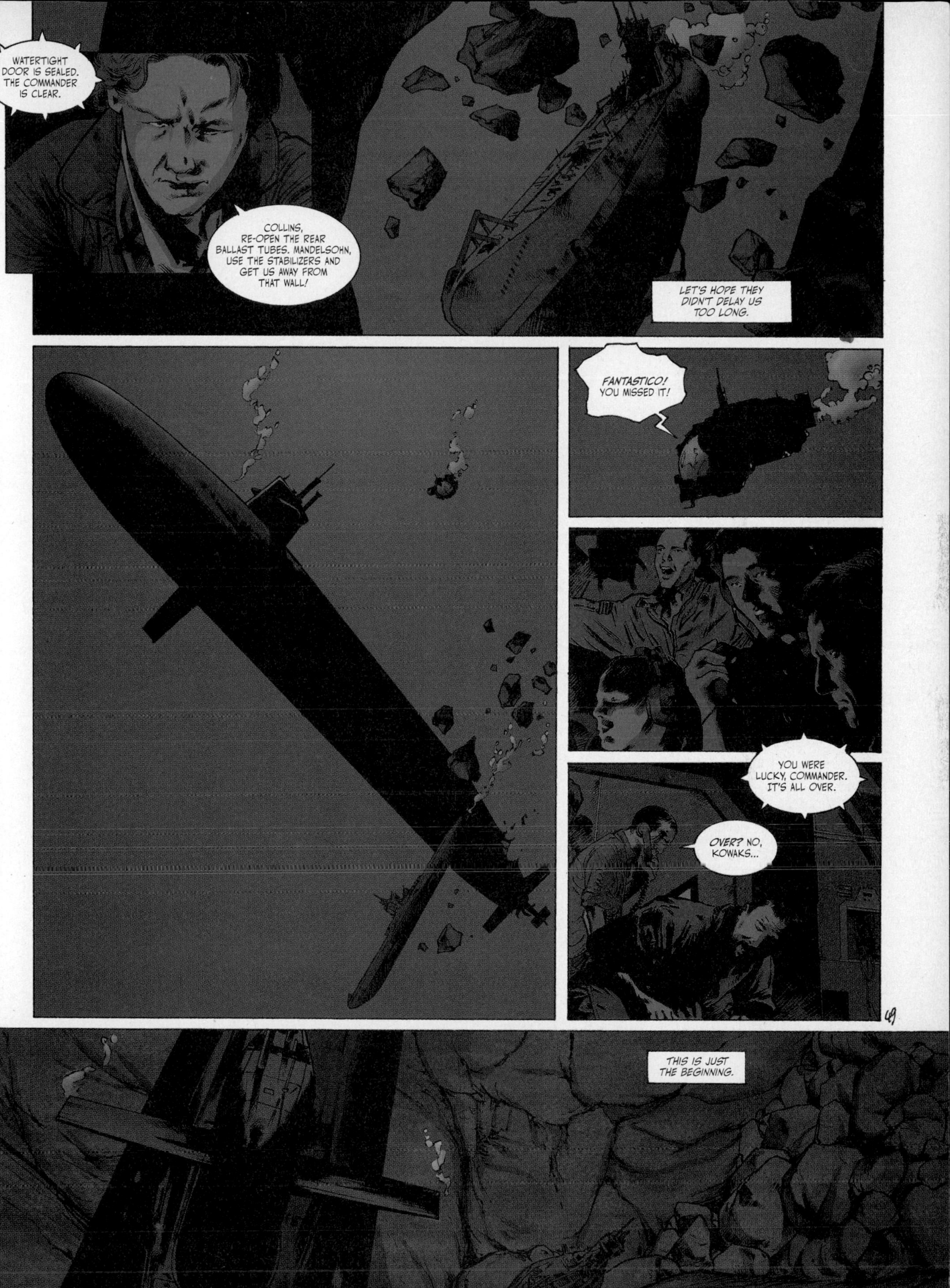
WATERTIGHT DOOR IS SEALED. THE COMMANDER IS CLEAR.
COLLINS, RE-OPEN THE REAR BALLAST TUBES. MANDELSOHN, USE THE STABILIZERS AND GET US AWAY FROM THAT WALL!
LET'S HOPE THEY DIDN'T DELAY US TOO LONG.
FANTASTICO! YOU MISSED IT!
YOU WERE LUCKY, COMMANDER. IT'S ALL OVER.
OVER? NO, KOWAKS...
49
THIS IS JUST THE BEGINNING.

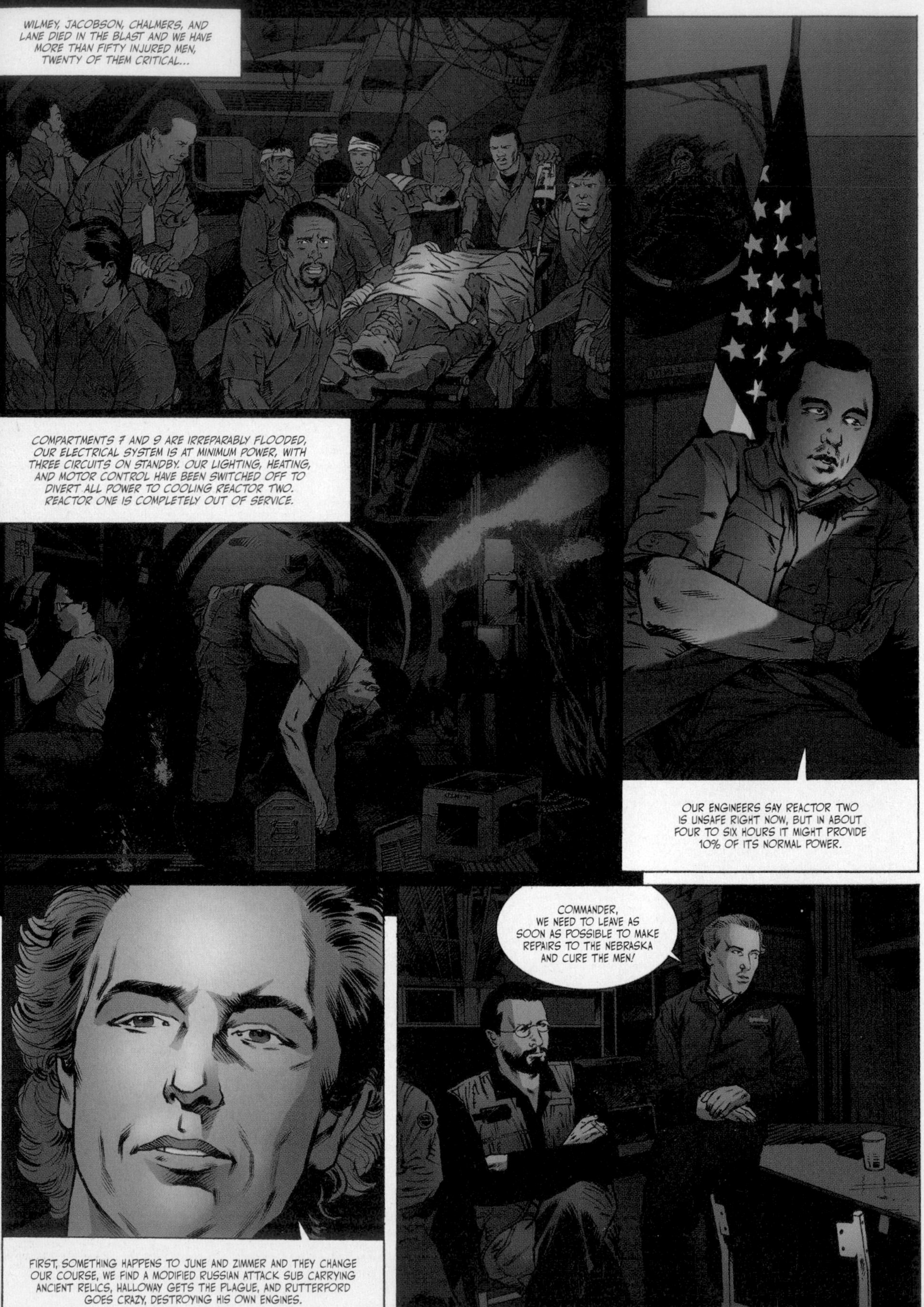
WILMEY, JACOBSON, CHALMERS, AND LANE DIED IN THE BLAST AND WE HAVE MORE THAN FIFTY INJURED MEN, TWENTY OF THEM CRITICAL...
COMPARTMENTS 7 AND 9 ARE IRREPARABLY FLOODED, OUR ELECTRICAL SYSTEM IS AT MINIMUM POWER, WITH THREE CIRCUITS ON STANDBY. OUR LIGHTING, HEATING, AND MOTOR CONTROL HAVE BEEN SWITCHED OFF TO DIVERT ALL POWER TO COOLING REACTOR TWO. REACTOR ONE IS COMPLETELY OUT OF SERVICE.
OUR ENGINEERS SAY REACTOR TWO IS UNSAFE RIGHT NOW, BUT IN ABOUT FOUR TO SIX HOURS IT MIGHT PROVIDE 10% OF ITS NORMAL POWER.
FIRST, SOMETHING HAPPENS TO JUNE AND ZIMMER AND THEY CHANGE OUR COURSE, WE FIND A MODIFIED RUSSIAN ATTACK SUB CARRYING ANCIENT RELICS, HALLOWAY GETS THE PLAGUE, AND RUTTERFORD GOES CRAZY, DESTROYING HIS OWN ENGINES.
COMMANDER, WE NEED TO LEAVE AS SOON AS POSSIBLE TO MAKE REPAIRS TO THE NEBRASKA AND CURE THE MEN!

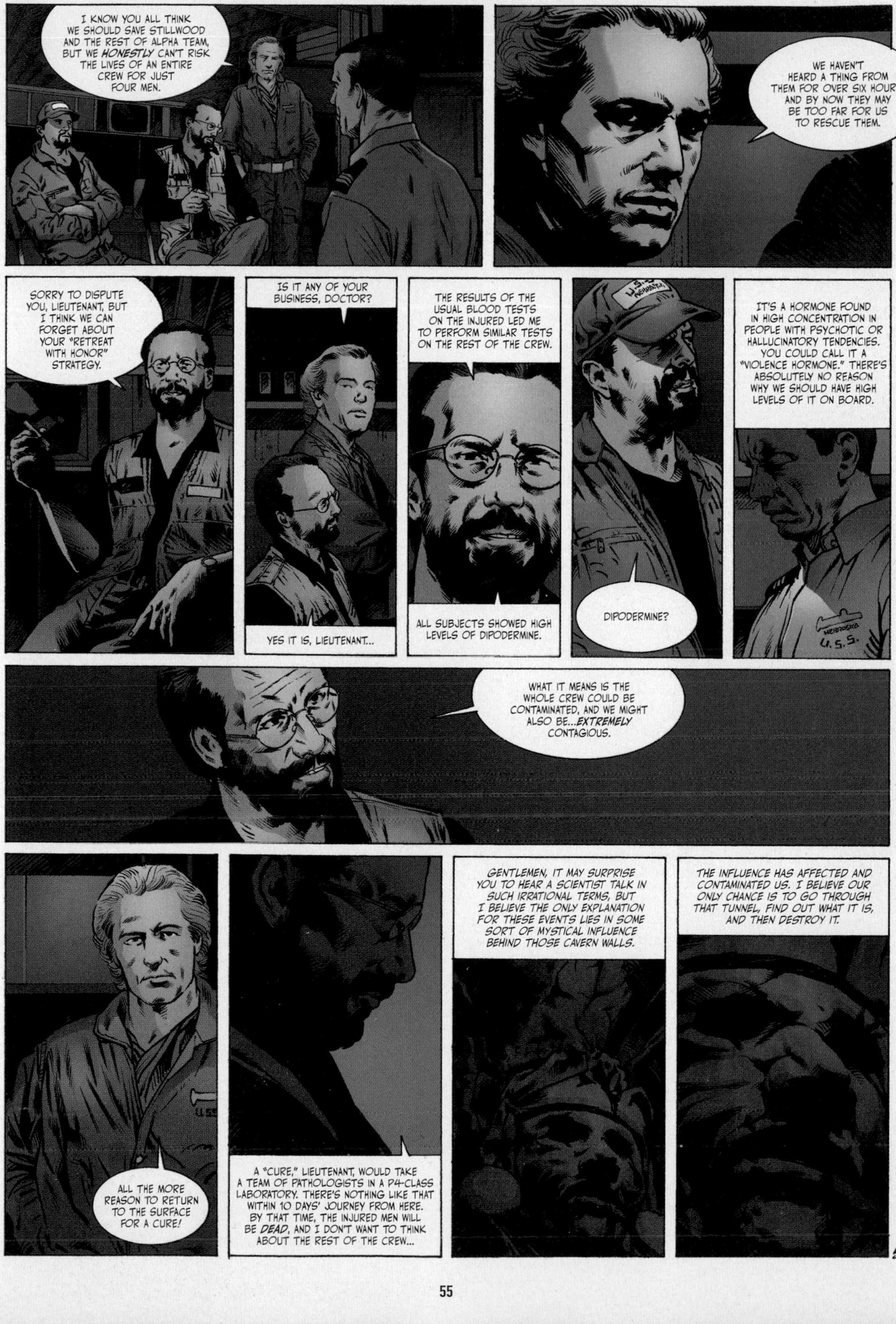
I KNOW YOU ALL THINK WE SHOULD SAVE STILLWOOD AND THE REST OF ALPHA TEAM, BUT WE *HONESTLY* CAN'T RISK THE LIVES OF AN ENTIRE CREW FOR JUST FOUR MEN.
WE HAVEN'T HEARD A THING FROM THEM FOR OVER SIX HOURS, AND BY NOW THEY MAY BE TOO FAR FOR US TO RESCUE THEM.
SORRY TO DISPUTE YOU, LIEUTENANT, BUT I THINK WE CAN FORGET ABOUT YOUR "RETREAT WITH HONOR" STRATEGY.
IS IT ANY OF YOUR BUSINESS, DOCTOR?
YES IT IS, LIEUTENANT...
THE RESULTS OF THE USUAL BLOOD TESTS ON THE INJURED LED ME TO PERFORM SIMILAR TESTS ON THE REST OF THE CREW.
ALL SUBJECTS SHOWED HIGH LEVELS OF DIPODERMINE.
DIPODERMINE?
IT'S A HORMONE FOUND IN HIGH CONCENTRATION IN PEOPLE WITH PSYCHOTIC OR HALLUCINATORY TENDENCIES. YOU COULD CALL IT A "VIOLENCE HORMONE." THERE'S ABSOLUTELY NO REASON WHY WE SHOULD HAVE HIGH LEVELS OF IT ON BOARD.
U.S.S.
WHAT IT MEANS IS THE WHOLE CREW COULD BE CONTAMINATED, AND WE MIGHT ALSO BE...*EXTREMELY* CONTAGIOUS.
ALL THE MORE REASON TO RETURN TO THE SURFACE FOR A CURE!
A "CURE," LIEUTENANT, WOULD TAKE A TEAM OF PATHOLOGISTS IN A P4-CLASS LABORATORY. THERE'S NOTHING LIKE THAT WITHIN 10 DAYS' JOURNEY FROM HERE. BY THAT TIME, THE INJURED MEN WILL BE *DEAD*, AND I DON'T WANT TO THINK ABOUT THE REST OF THE CREW...
GENTLEMEN, IT MAY SURPRISE YOU TO HEAR A SCIENTIST TALK IN SUCH IRRATIONAL TERMS, BUT I BELIEVE THE ONLY EXPLANATION FOR THESE EVENTS LIES IN SOME SORT OF MYSTICAL INFLUENCE BEHIND THOSE CAVERN WALLS.
THE INFLUENCE HAS AFFECTED AND CONTAMINATED US. I BELIEVE OUR ONLY CHANCE IS TO GO THROUGH THAT TUNNEL, FIND OUT WHAT IT IS, AND THEN DESTROY IT.
51

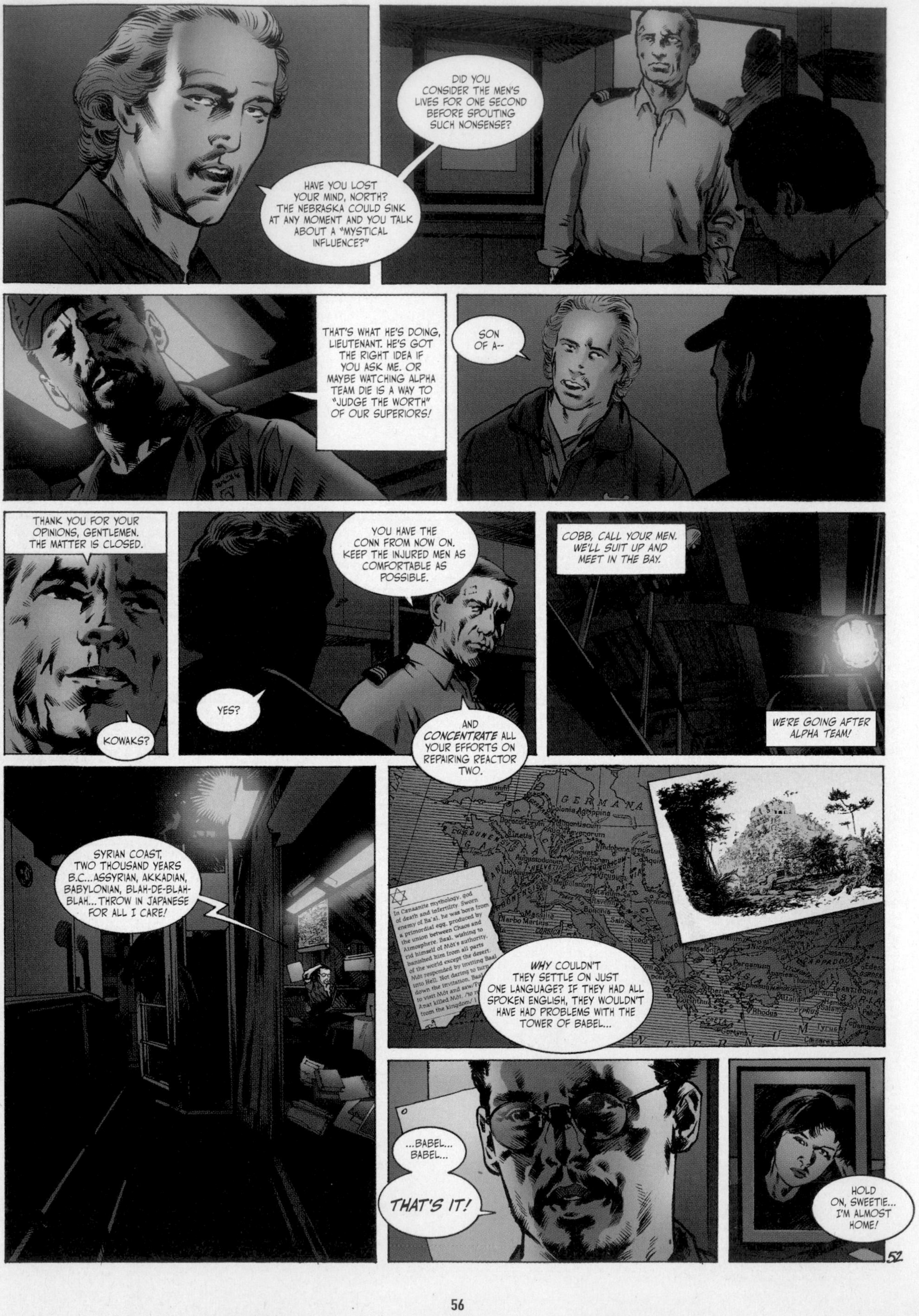
HAVE YOU LOST YOUR MIND, NORTH? THE NEBRASKA COULD SINK AT ANY MOMENT AND YOU TALK ABOUT A "MYSTICAL INFLUENCE?"
DID YOU CONSIDER THE MEN'S LIVES FOR ONE SECOND BEFORE SPOUTING SUCH NONSENSE?
THAT'S WHAT HE'S DOING, LIEUTENANT. HE'S GOT THE RIGHT IDEA IF YOU ASK ME. OR MAYBE WATCHING ALPHA TEAM DIE IS A WAY TO "JUDGE THE WORTH" OF OUR SUPERIORS!
SON OF A--
THANK YOU FOR YOUR OPINIONS, GENTLEMEN. THE MATTER IS CLOSED.
KOWAKS?
YES?
YOU HAVE THE CONN FROM NOW ON. KEEP THE INJURED MEN AS COMFORTABLE AS POSSIBLE.
AND CONCENTRATE ALL YOUR EFFORTS ON REPAIRING REACTOR TWO.
COBB, CALL YOUR MEN. WE'LL SUIT UP AND MEET IN THE BAY.
WE'RE GOING AFTER ALPHA TEAM!
SYRIAN COAST, TWO THOUSAND YEARS B.C...ASSYRIAN, AKKADIAN, BABYLONIAN, BLAH-DE-BLAH-BLAH...THROW IN JAPANESE FOR ALL I CARE!
WHY COULDN'T THEY SETTLE ON JUST ONE LANGUAGE? IF THEY HAD ALL SPOKEN ENGLISH, THEY WOULDN'T HAVE HAD PROBLEMS WITH THE TOWER OF BABEL...
...BABEL... BABEL...
THAT'S IT!
HOLD ON, SWEETIE... I'M ALMOST HOME!
52

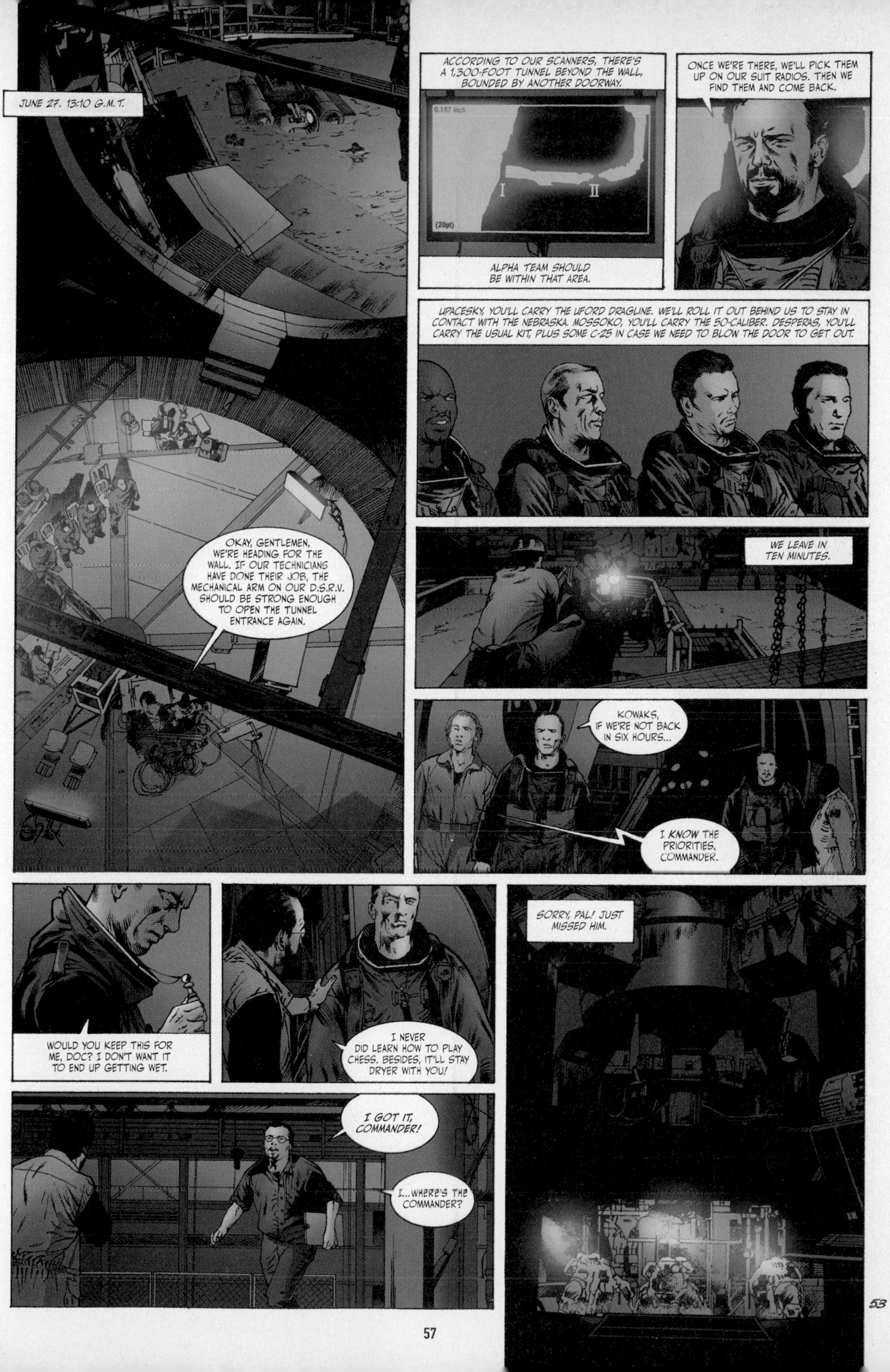
JUNE 27. 13:10 G.M.T.
OKAY, GENTLEMEN, WE'RE HEADING FOR THE WALL. IF OUR TECHNICIANS HAVE DONE THEIR JOB, THE MECHANICAL ARM ON OUR D.S.R.V. SHOULD BE STRONG ENOUGH TO OPEN THE TUNNEL ENTRANCE AGAIN.
ACCORDING TO OUR SCANNERS, THERE'S A 1,300-FOOT TUNNEL BEYOND THE WALL, BOUNDED BY ANOTHER DOORWAY.
I
II
ALPHA TEAM SHOULD BE WITHIN THAT AREA.
ONCE WE'RE THERE, WE'LL PICK THEM UP ON OUR SUIT RADIOS. THEN WE FIND THEM AND COME BACK.
UPACESKY, YOU'LL CARRY THE UFORD DRAGLINE. WE'LL ROLL IT OUT BEHIND US TO STAY IN CONTACT WITH THE NEBRASKA. MOSSOKO, YOU'LL CARRY THE 50-CALIBER. DESPERAS, YOU'LL CARRY THE USUAL KIT, PLUS SOME C-25 IN CASE WE NEED TO BLOW THE DOOR TO GET OUT.
WE LEAVE IN TEN MINUTES.
KOWAKS, IF WE'RE NOT BACK IN SIX HOURS...
I KNOW THE PRIORITIES, COMMANDER.
WOULD YOU KEEP THIS FOR ME, DOC? I DON'T WANT IT TO END UP GETTING WET.
I NEVER DID LEARN HOW TO PLAY CHESS. BESIDES, IT'LL STAY DRYER WITH YOU!
I GOT IT, COMMANDER!
I...WHERE'S THE COMMANDER?
SORRY, PAL! JUST MISSED HIM.
53

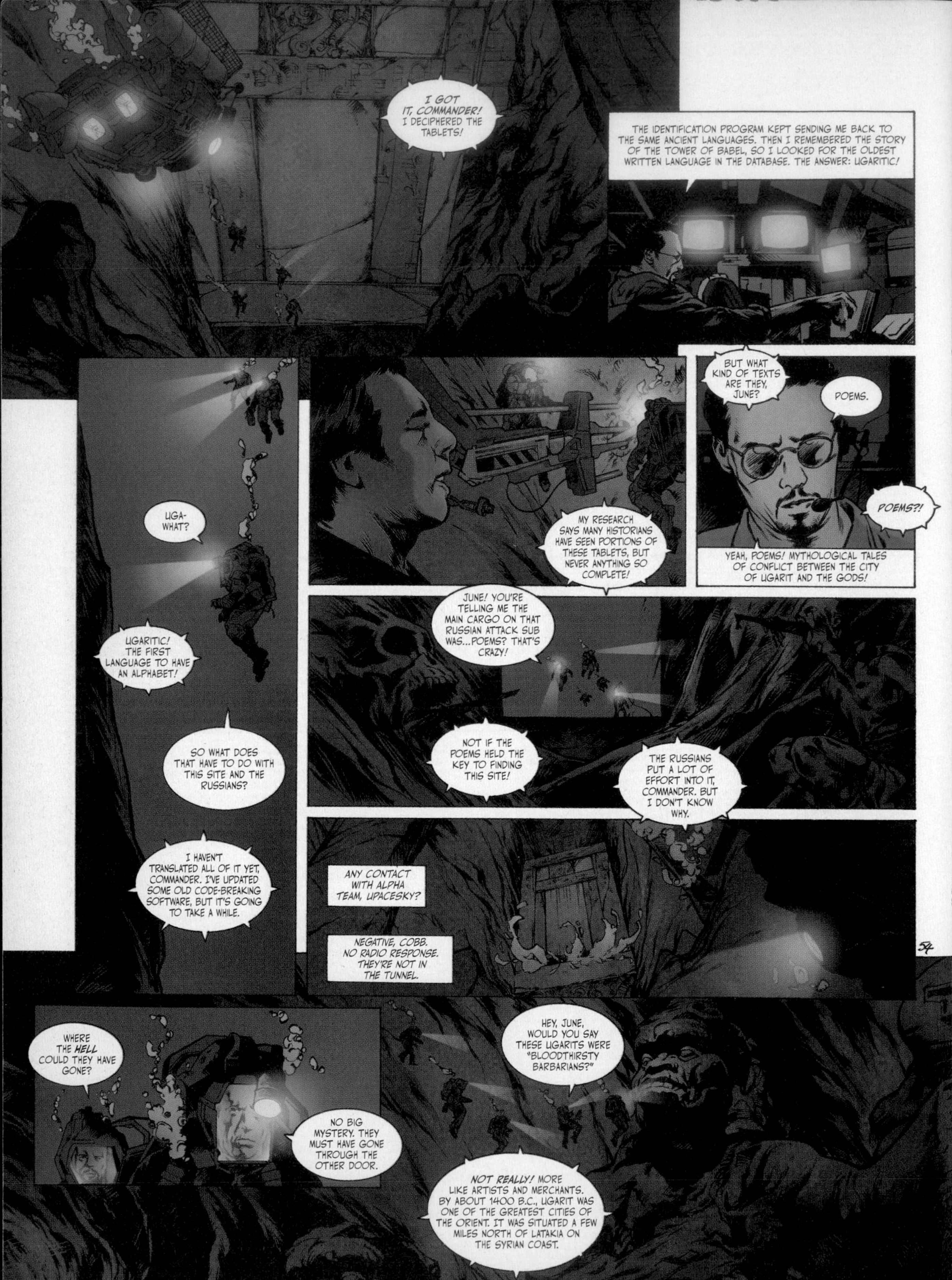
I GOT IT, COMMANDER! I DECIPHERED THE TABLETS!
THE IDENTIFICATION PROGRAM KEPT SENDING ME BACK TO THE SAME ANCIENT LANGUAGES. THEN I REMEMBERED THE STORY OF THE TOWER OF BABEL, SO I LOOKED FOR THE OLDEST WRITTEN LANGUAGE IN THE DATABASE. THE ANSWER: UGARITIC!
UGA-WHAT?
UGARITIC! THE FIRST LANGUAGE TO HAVE AN ALPHABET!
SO WHAT DOES THAT HAVE TO DO WITH THIS SITE AND THE RUSSIANS?
I HAVEN'T TRANSLATED ALL OF IT YET, COMMANDER. I'VE UPDATED SOME OLD CODE-BREAKING SOFTWARE, BUT IT'S GOING TO TAKE A WHILE.
MY RESEARCH SAYS MANY HISTORIANS HAVE SEEN PORTIONS OF THESE TABLETS, BUT NEVER ANYTHING SO COMPLETE!
BUT WHAT KIND OF TEXTS ARE THEY, JUNE?
POEMS.
POEMS?!
YEAH, POEMS! MYTHOLOGICAL TALES OF CONFLICT BETWEEN THE CITY OF UGARIT AND THE GODS!
JUNE! YOU'RE TELLING ME THE MAIN CARGO ON THAT RUSSIAN ATTACK SUB WAS...POEMS? THAT'S CRAZY!
NOT IF THE POEMS HELD THE KEY TO FINDING THIS SITE!
THE RUSSIANS PUT A LOT OF EFFORT INTO IT, COMMANDER. BUT I DON'T KNOW WHY.
ANY CONTACT WITH ALPHA TEAM, UPACESKY?
NEGATIVE, COBB. NO RADIO RESPONSE. THEY'RE NOT IN THE TUNNEL.
54
WHERE THE HELL COULD THEY HAVE GONE?
NO BIG MYSTERY. THEY MUST HAVE GONE THROUGH THE OTHER DOOR.
HEY, JUNE, WOULD YOU SAY THESE UGARITS WERE "BLOODTHIRSTY BARBARIANS?"
NOT REALLY! MORE LIKE ARTISTS AND MERCHANTS. BY ABOUT 1400 B.C., UGARIT WAS ONE OF THE GREATEST CITIES OF THE ORIENT. IT WAS SITUATED A FEW MILES NORTH OF LATAKIA ON THE SYRIAN COAST.

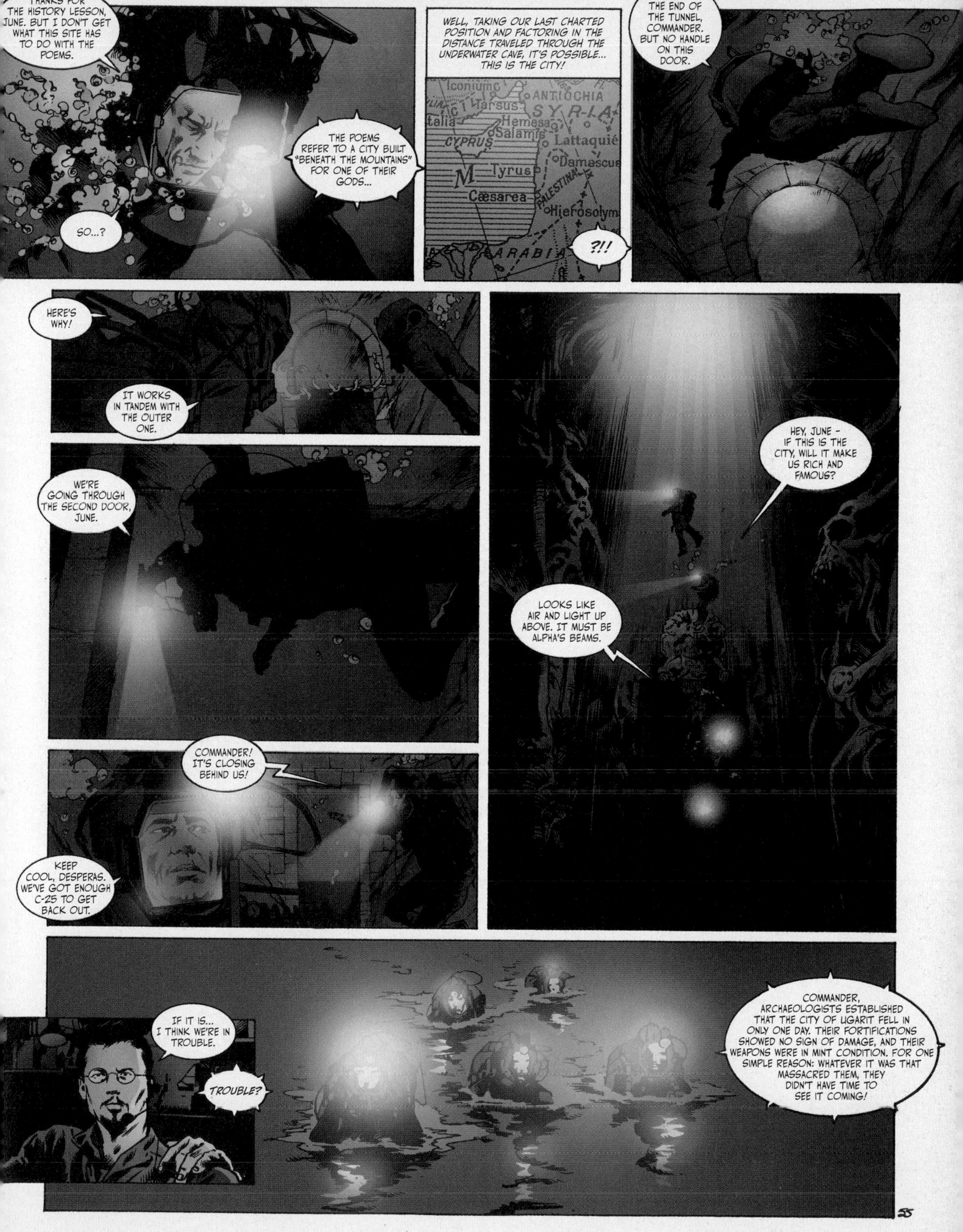
THANKS FOR THE HISTORY LESSON, JUNE. BUT I DON'T GET WHAT THIS SITE HAS TO DO WITH THE POEMS.
THE POEMS REFER TO A CITY BUILT "BENEATH THE MOUNTAINS" FOR ONE OF THEIR GODS...
SO...?
WELL, TAKING OUR LAST CHARTED POSITION AND FACTORING IN THE DISTANCE TRAVELED THROUGH THE UNDERWATER CAVE, IT'S POSSIBLE... THIS IS THE CITY!
Iconium
ANTIOCHIA
Tarsus
SYRIA
Hemesa
Salamis
CYPRUS
Lattaquié
Damescus
Tyrus
Cæsarea
PALESTINA
Hierosolyma
ARABIA
?!!
IT'S THE END OF THE TUNNEL, COMMANDER. BUT NO HANDLE ON THIS DOOR.
HERE'S WHY!
IT WORKS IN TANDEM WITH THE OUTER ONE.
WE'RE GOING THROUGH THE SECOND DOOR, JUNE.
COMMANDER! IT'S CLOSING BEHIND US!
KEEP COOL, DESPERAS. WE'VE GOT ENOUGH C-25 TO GET BACK OUT.
HEY, JUNE - IF THIS IS THE CITY, WILL IT MAKE US RICH AND FAMOUS?
LOOKS LIKE AIR AND LIGHT UP ABOVE. IT MUST BE ALPHA'S BEAMS.
IF IT IS... I THINK WE'RE IN TROUBLE.
TROUBLE?
COMMANDER, ARCHAEOLOGISTS ESTABLISHED THAT THE CITY OF UGARIT FELL IN ONLY ONE DAY. THEIR FORTIFICATIONS SHOWED NO SIGN OF DAMAGE, AND THEIR WEAPONS WERE IN MINT CONDITION. FOR ONE SIMPLE REASON: WHATEVER IT WAS THAT MASSACRED THEM, THEY DIDN'T HAVE TIME TO SEE IT COMING!

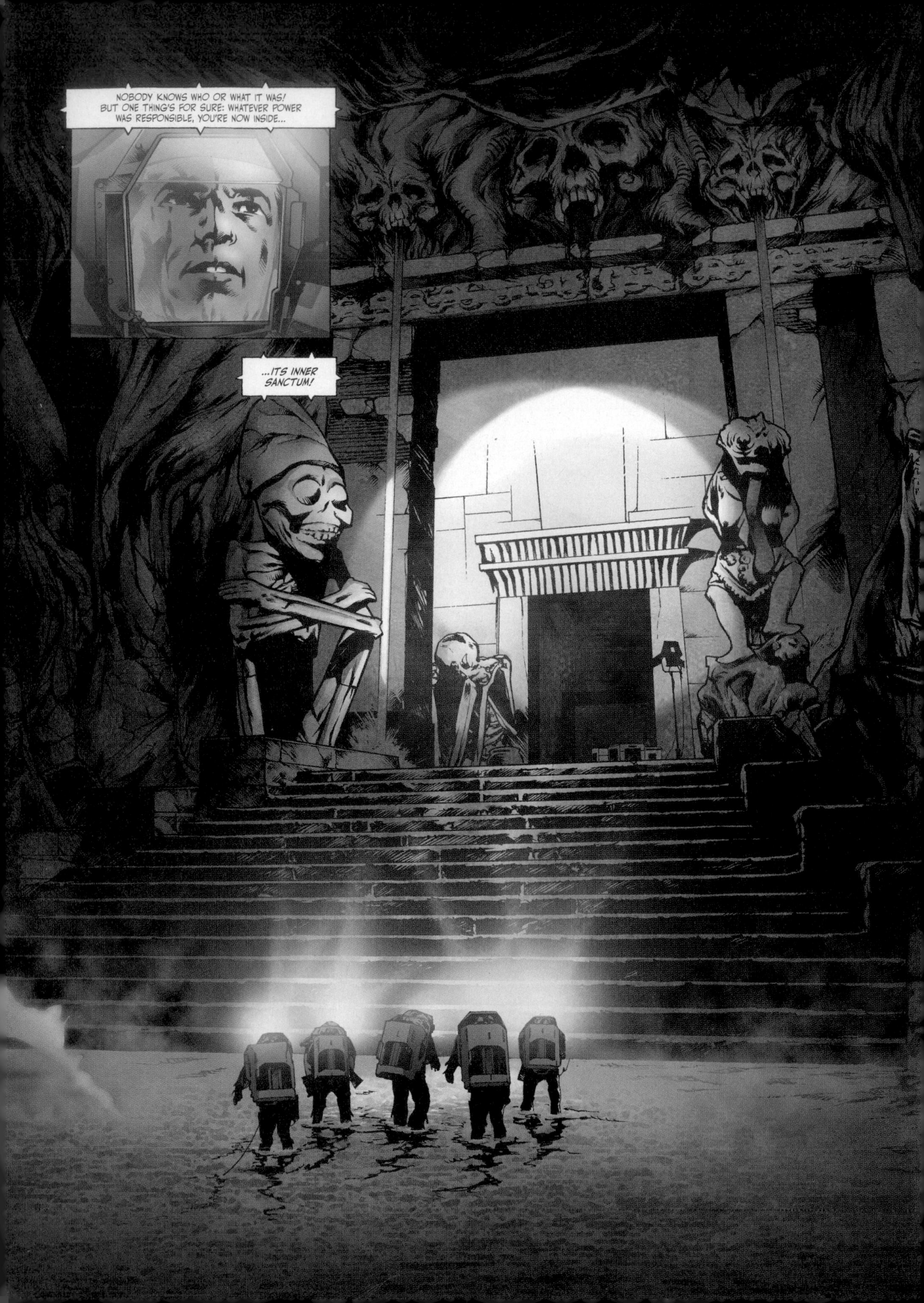
NOBODY KNOWS WHO OR WHAT IT WAS! BUT ONE THING'S FOR SURE: WHATEVER POWER WAS RESPONSIBLE, YOU'RE NOW INSIDE...
...ITS INNER SANCTUM!

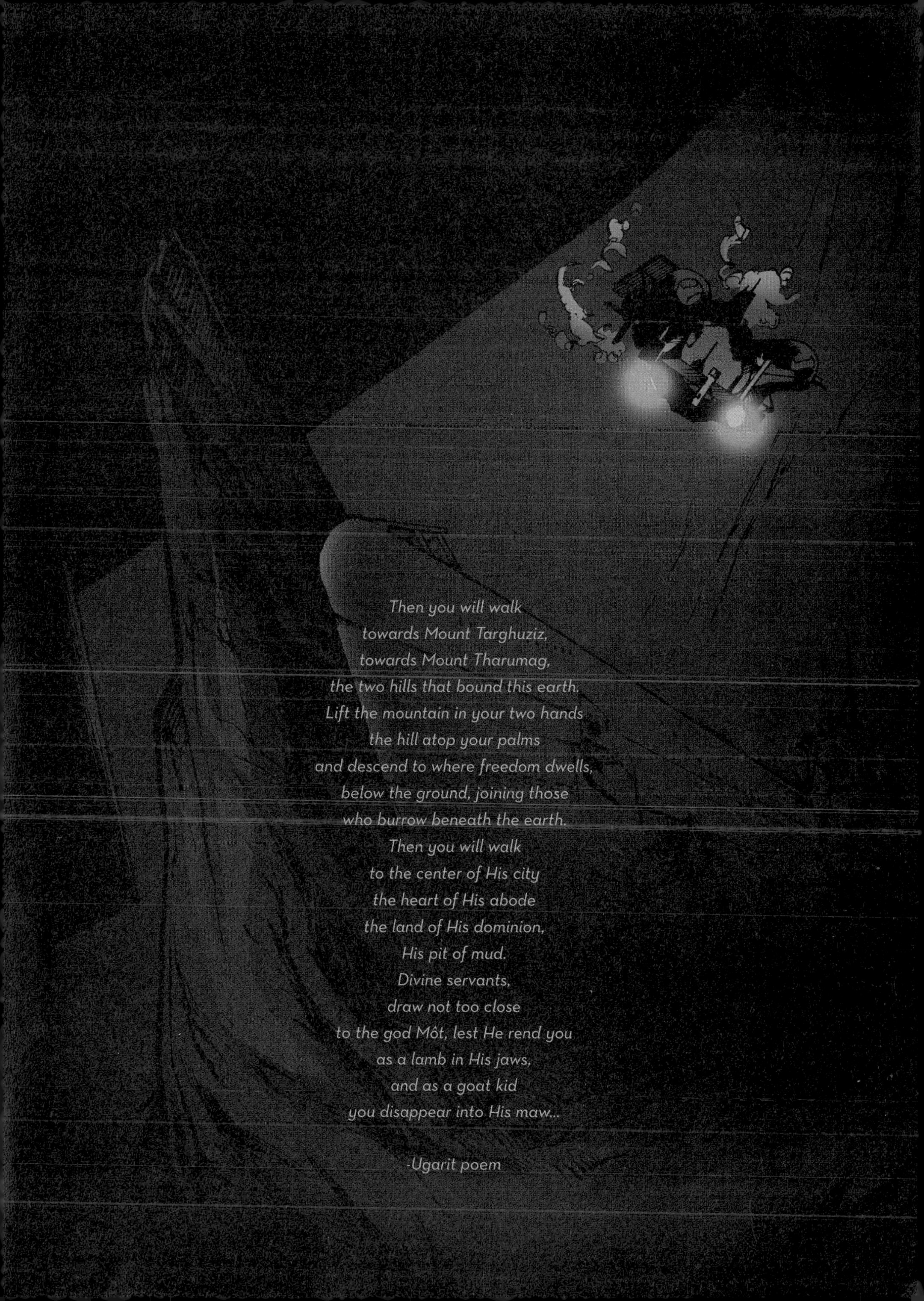

Then you will walk
towards Mount Targhuziz,
towards Mount Tharumag,
the two hills that bound this earth.
Lift the mountain in your two hands
the hill atop your palms
and descend to where freedom dwells,
below the ground, joining those
who burrow beneath the earth.
Then you will walk
to the center of His city
the heart of His abode
the land of His dominion,
His pit of mud.
Divine servants,
draw not too close
to the god Môt, lest He rend you
as a lamb in His jaws,
and as a goat kid
you disappear into His maw...

-Ugarit poem

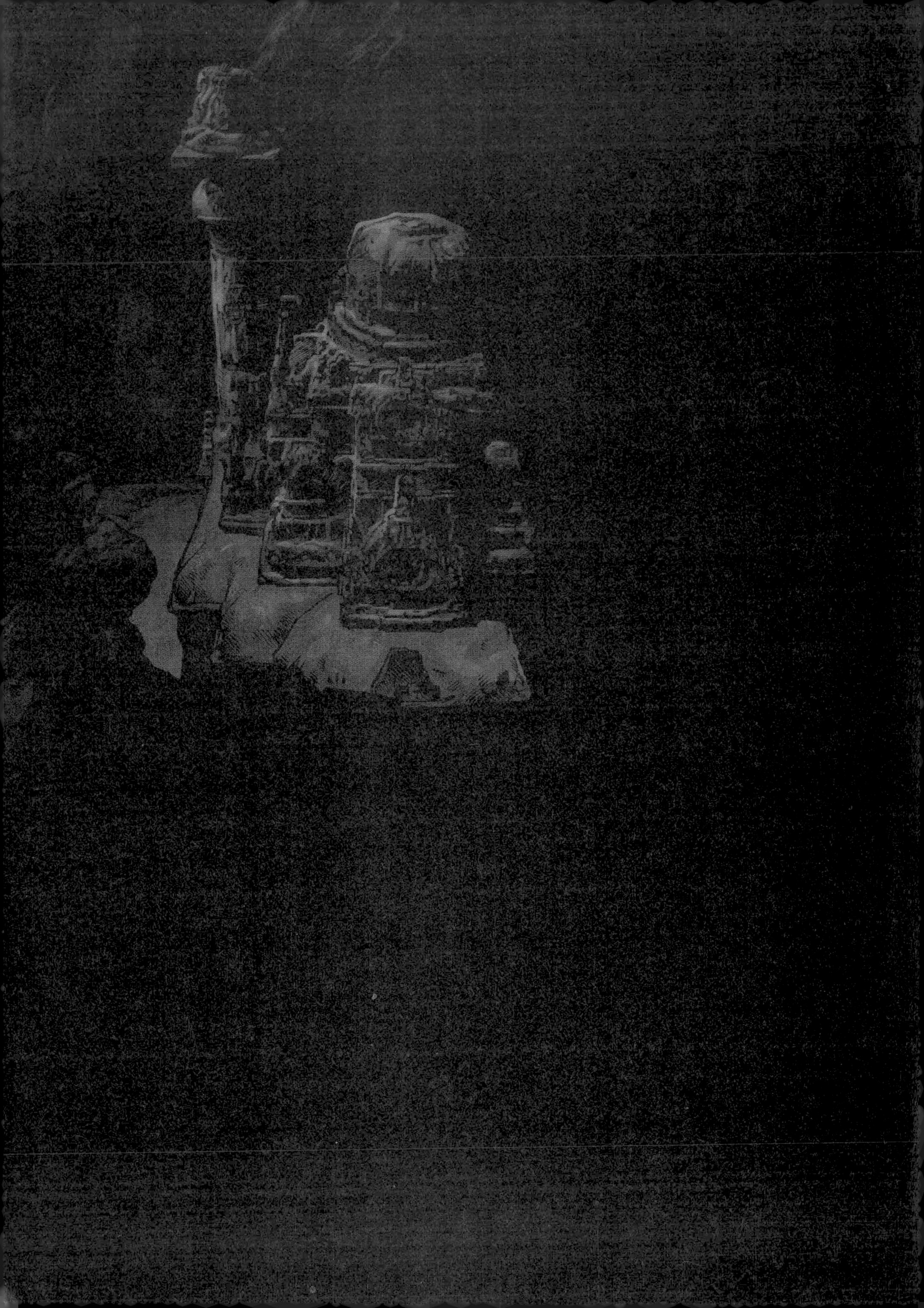

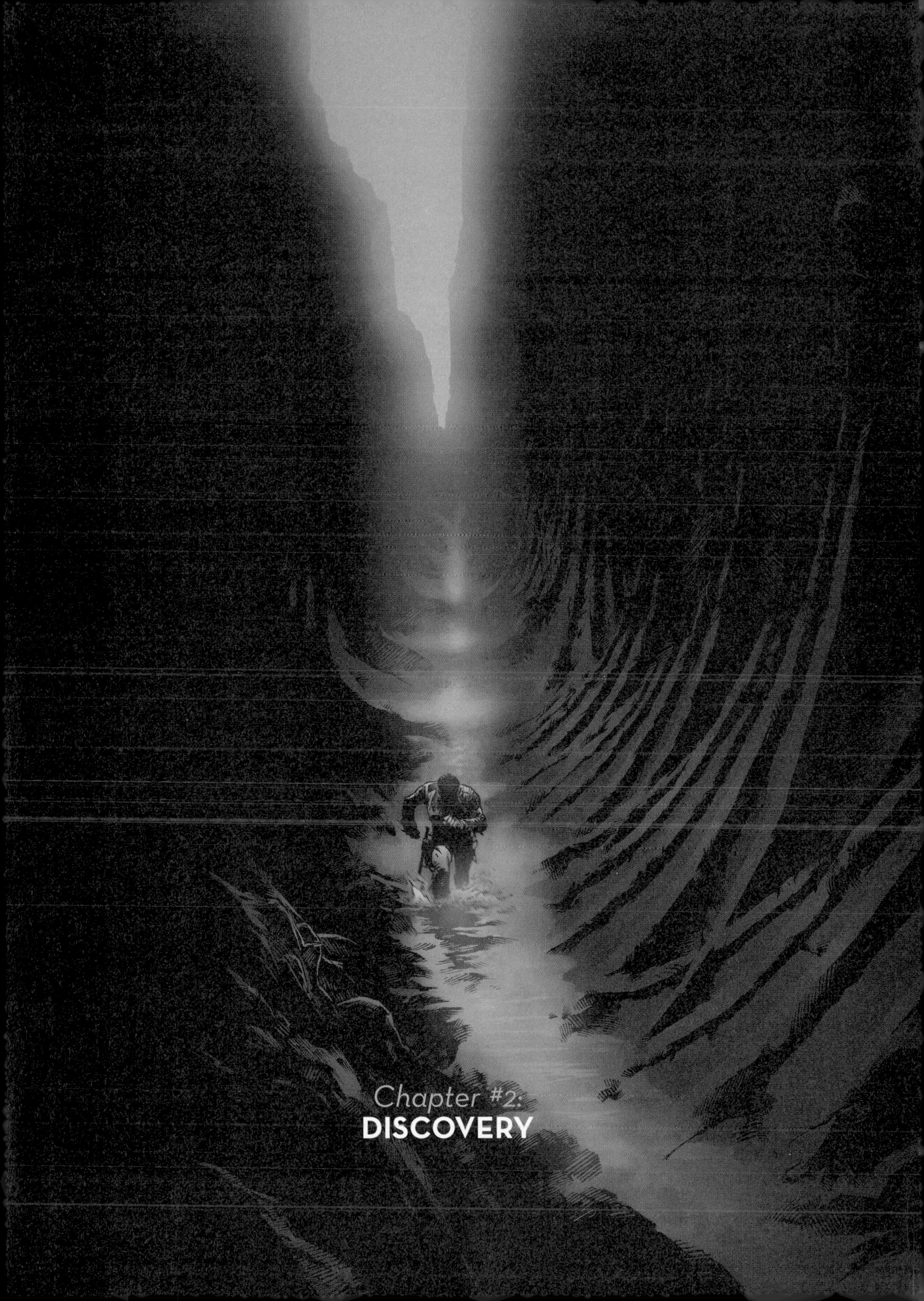

Chapter #2:
DISCOVERY

As you struck Lotan, the running snake,
As you finished the twisting serpent, the seven-headed tyrant,
As you burned and weakened the skies,
I will crush you, I will eat your splattered parts,
I will break your strength;
You will dive into the throat of the divine Môt,

Word, favorite words of El,
His appetite is the appetite of lions in the savanna,
Or the appetite of a shark in the sea, or the cistern
Who attracts the savage bulls, or the source of the doe.
If my desire is truly to consume soil,
With my two hands, I will devour...

- Ugarit poem

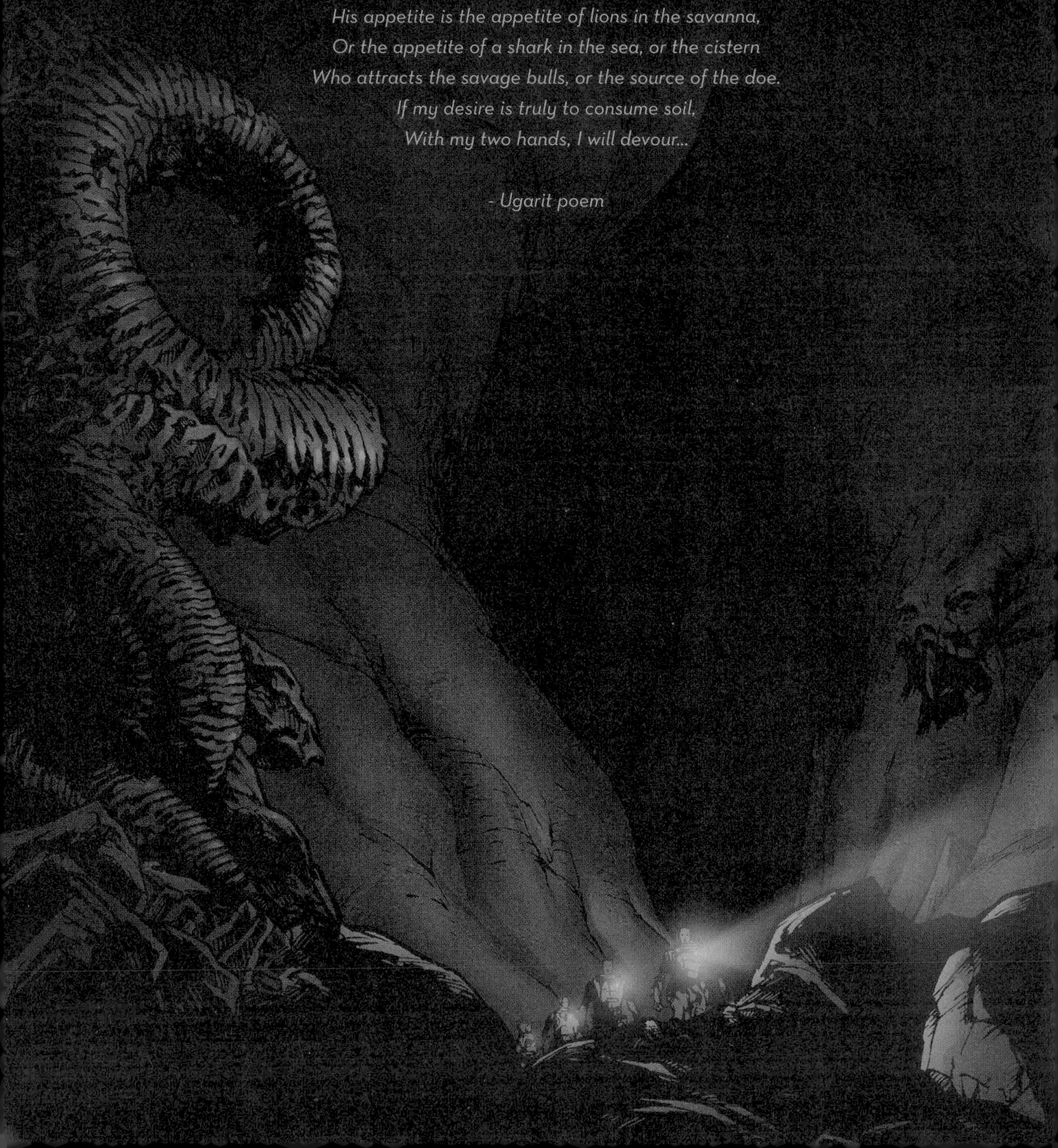

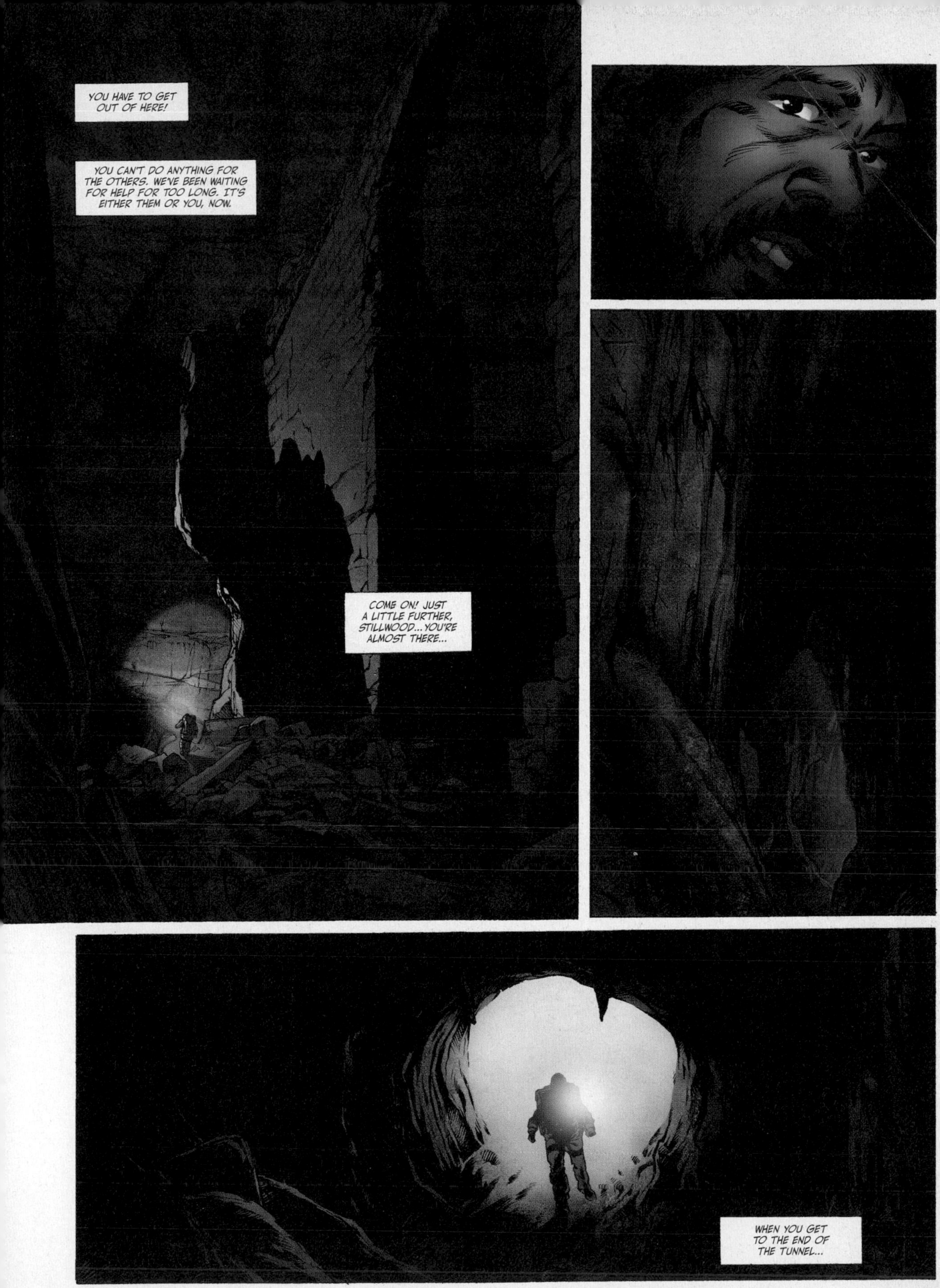
YOU HAVE TO GET OUT OF HERE!
YOU CAN'T DO ANYTHING FOR THE OTHERS. WE'VE BEEN WAITING FOR HELP FOR TOO LONG. IT'S EITHER THEM OR YOU, NOW.
COME ON! JUST A LITTLE FURTHER, STILLWOOD... YOU'RE ALMOST THERE...
WHEN YOU GET TO THE END OF THE TUNNEL...

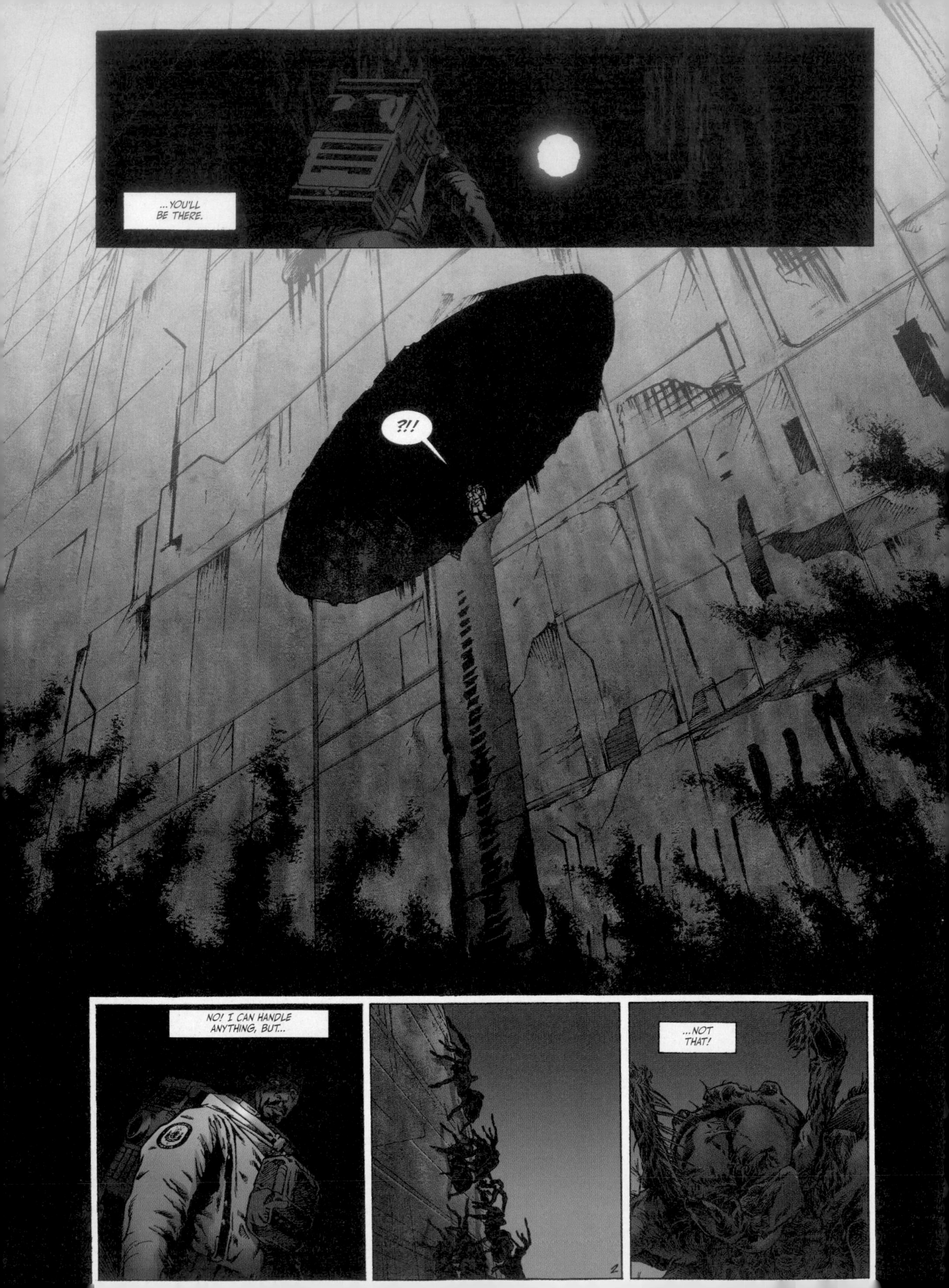
...YOU'LL BE THERE.
?!!
NO! I CAN HANDLE ANYTHING, BUT...
...NOT THAT!

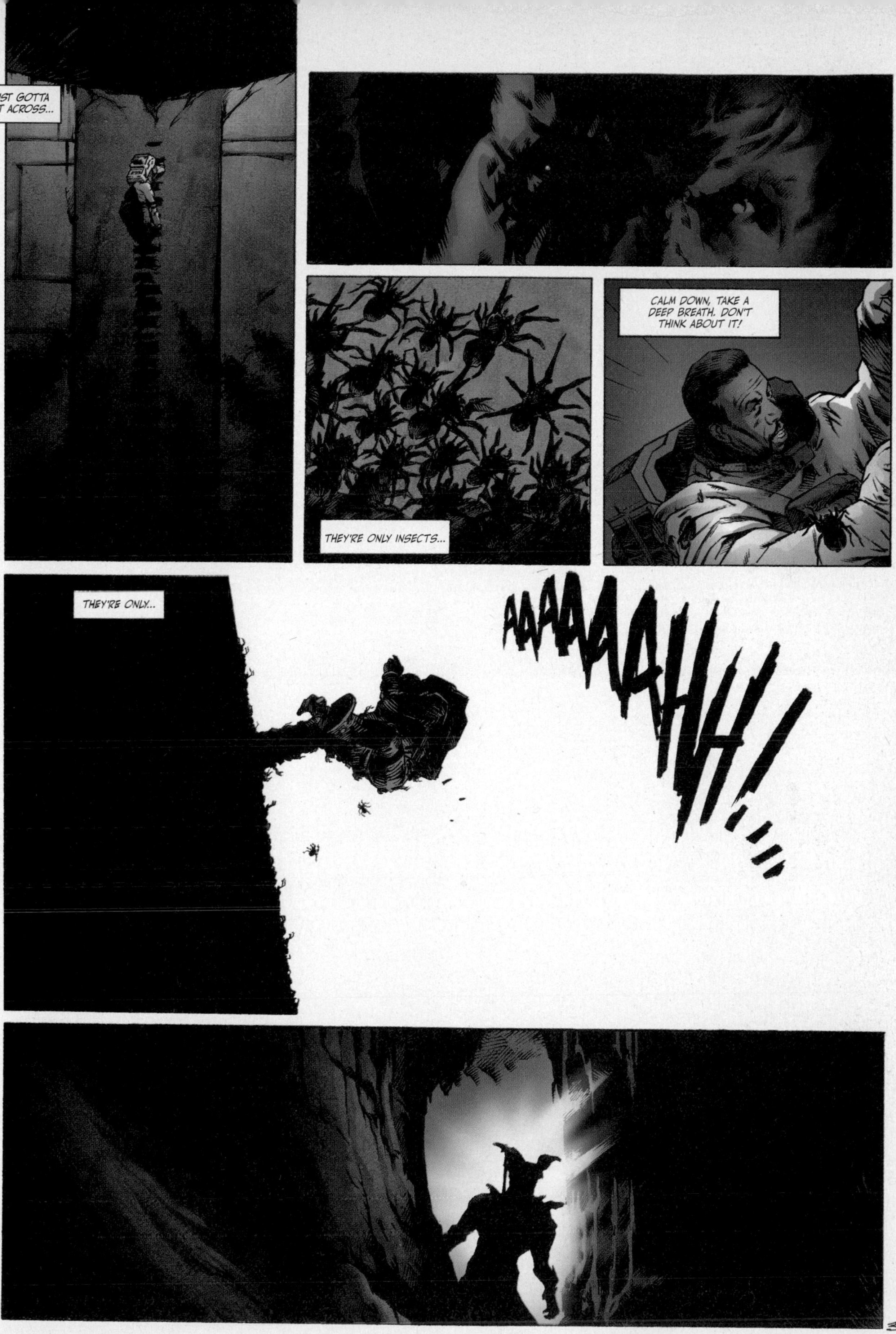
JUST GOTTA GET ACROSS...
THEY'RE ONLY INSECTS...
CALM DOWN, TAKE A DEEP BREATH. DON'T THINK ABOUT IT!
THEY'RE ONLY...
AAAAAAAHH!
3

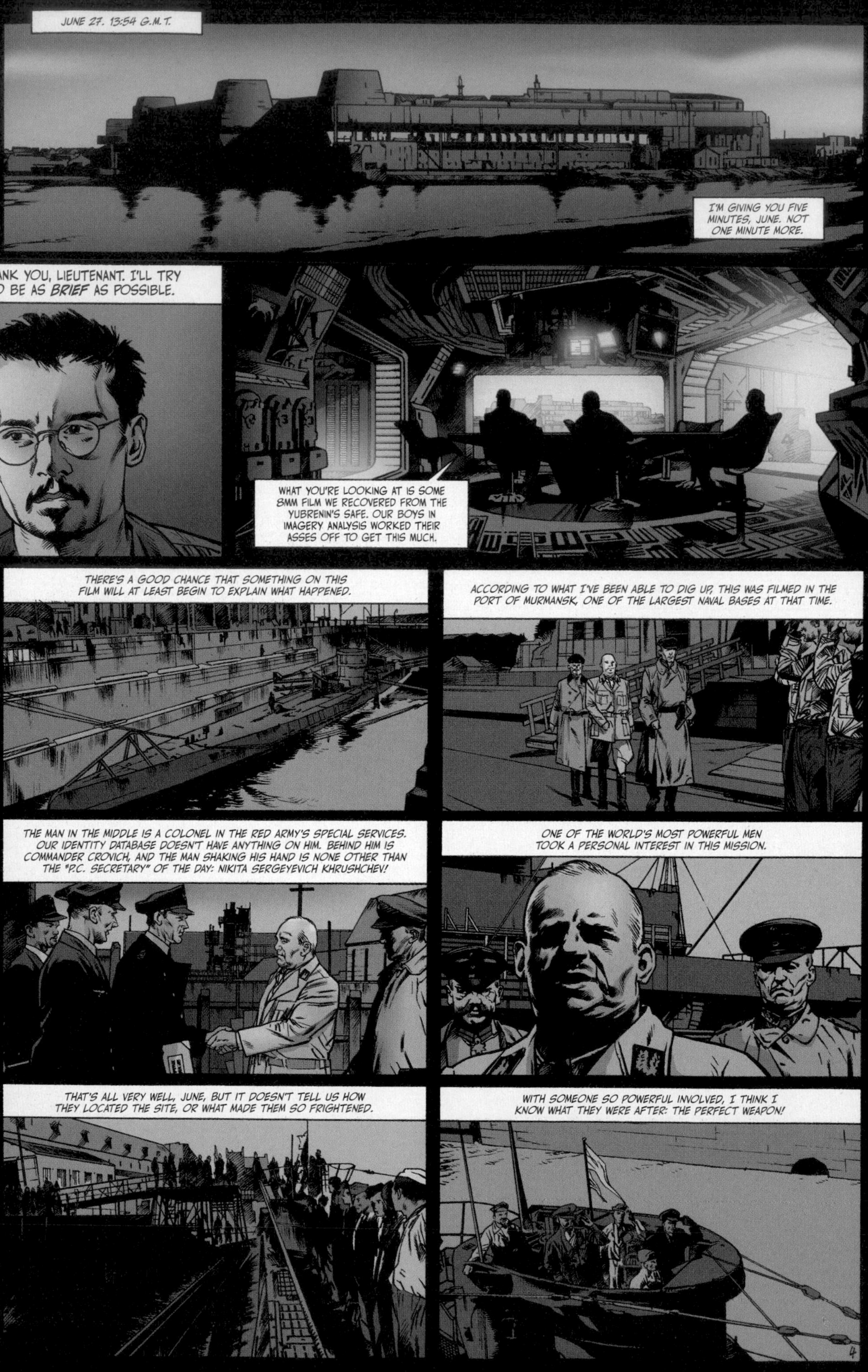
JUNE 27. 13:54 G.M.T.
I'M GIVING YOU FIVE MINUTES, JUNE. NOT ONE MINUTE MORE.
THANK YOU, LIEUTENANT. I'LL TRY TO BE AS BRIEF AS POSSIBLE.
WHAT YOU'RE LOOKING AT IS SOME 8MM FILM WE RECOVERED FROM THE YUBRENIN'S SAFE. OUR BOYS IN IMAGERY ANALYSIS WORKED THEIR ASSES OFF TO GET THIS MUCH.
THERE'S A GOOD CHANCE THAT SOMETHING ON THIS FILM WILL AT LEAST BEGIN TO EXPLAIN WHAT HAPPENED.
ACCORDING TO WHAT I'VE BEEN ABLE TO DIG UP, THIS WAS FILMED IN THE PORT OF MURMANSK, ONE OF THE LARGEST NAVAL BASES AT THAT TIME.
THE MAN IN THE MIDDLE IS A COLONEL IN THE RED ARMY'S SPECIAL SERVICES. OUR IDENTITY DATABASE DOESN'T HAVE ANYTHING ON HIM. BEHIND HIM IS COMMANDER CROVICH, AND THE MAN SHAKING HIS HAND IS NONE OTHER THAN THE "P.C. SECRETARY" OF THE DAY: NIKITA SERGEYEVICH KHRUSHCHEV!
ONE OF THE WORLD'S MOST POWERFUL MEN TOOK A PERSONAL INTEREST IN THIS MISSION.
THAT'S ALL VERY WELL, JUNE, BUT IT DOESN'T TELL US HOW THEY LOCATED THE SITE, OR WHAT MADE THEM SO FRIGHTENED.
WITH SOMEONE SO POWERFUL INVOLVED, I THINK I KNOW WHAT THEY WERE AFTER: THE PERFECT WEAPON!

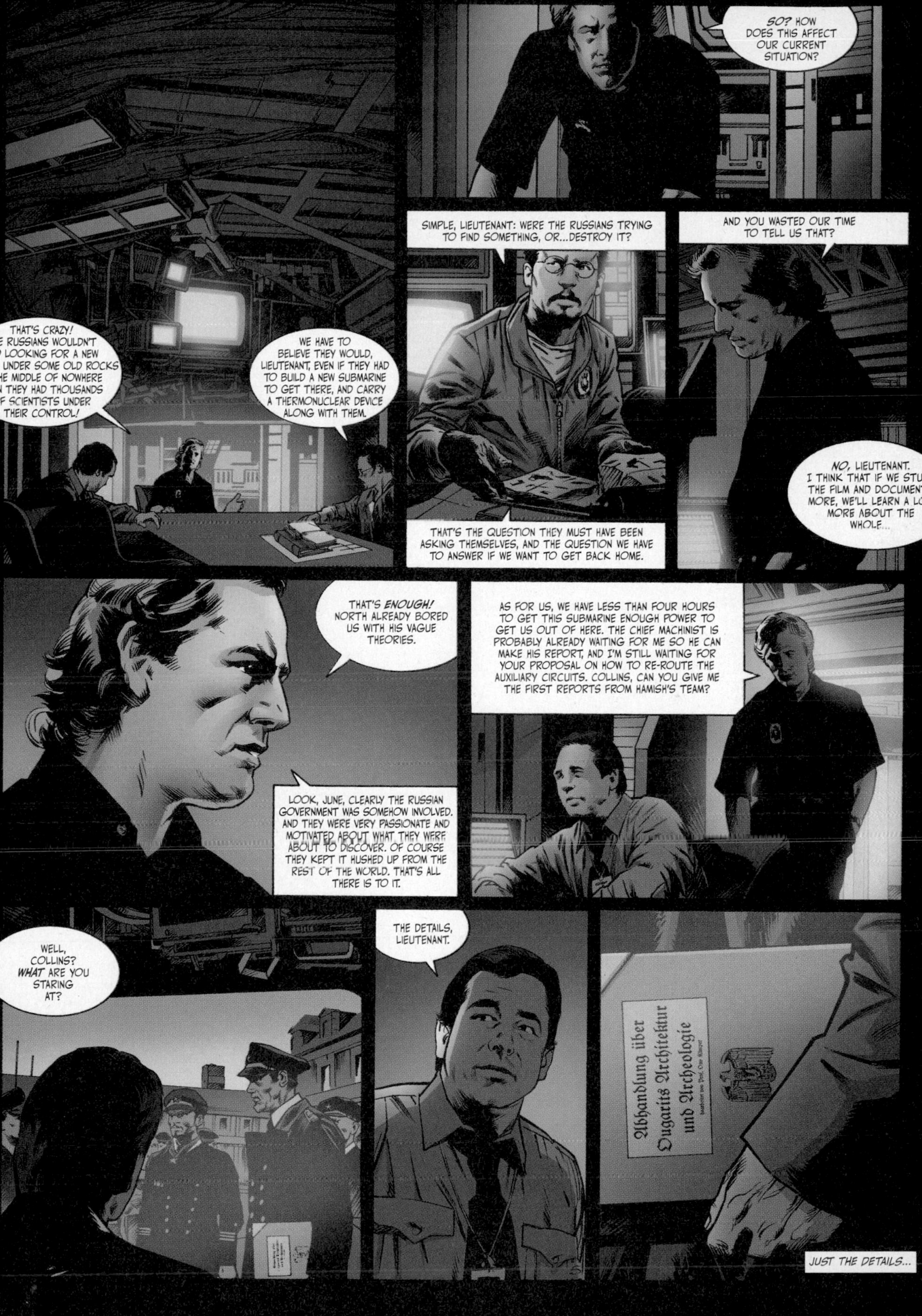
SO? HOW DOES THIS AFFECT OUR CURRENT SITUATION?
THAT'S CRAZY! THE RUSSIANS WOULDN'T GO LOOKING FOR A NEW WEAPON UNDER SOME OLD ROCKS IN THE MIDDLE OF NOWHERE WHEN THEY HAD THOUSANDS OF SCIENTISTS UNDER THEIR CONTROL!
WE HAVE TO BELIEVE THEY WOULD, LIEUTENANT, EVEN IF THEY HAD TO BUILD A NEW SUBMARINE TO GET THERE, AND CARRY A THERMONUCLEAR DEVICE ALONG WITH THEM.
SIMPLE, LIEUTENANT: WERE THE RUSSIANS TRYING TO FIND SOMETHING, OR...DESTROY IT?
THAT'S THE QUESTION THEY MUST HAVE BEEN ASKING THEMSELVES, AND THE QUESTION WE HAVE TO ANSWER IF WE WANT TO GET BACK HOME.
AND YOU WASTED OUR TIME TO TELL US THAT?
NO, LIEUTENANT. I THINK THAT IF WE STUDY THE FILM AND DOCUMENTS MORE, WE'LL LEARN A LOT MORE ABOUT THE WHOLE...
THAT'S ENOUGH! NORTH ALREADY BORED US WITH HIS VAGUE THEORIES.
LOOK, JUNE, CLEARLY THE RUSSIAN GOVERNMENT WAS SOMEHOW INVOLVED. AND THEY WERE VERY PASSIONATE AND MOTIVATED ABOUT WHAT THEY WERE ABOUT TO DISCOVER. OF COURSE THEY KEPT IT HUSHED UP FROM THE REST OF THE WORLD. THAT'S ALL THERE IS TO IT.
AS FOR US, WE HAVE LESS THAN FOUR HOURS TO GET THIS SUBMARINE ENOUGH POWER TO GET US OUT OF HERE. THE CHIEF MACHINIST IS PROBABLY ALREADY WAITING FOR ME SO HE CAN MAKE HIS REPORT, AND I'M STILL WAITING FOR YOUR PROPOSAL ON HOW TO RE-ROUTE THE AUXILIARY CIRCUITS. COLLINS, CAN YOU GIVE ME THE FIRST REPORTS FROM HAMISH'S TEAM?
WELL, COLLINS? WHAT ARE YOU STARING AT?
THE DETAILS, LIEUTENANT.
Abhandlung über Ougarits Architektur und Archeologie
JUST THE DETAILS...

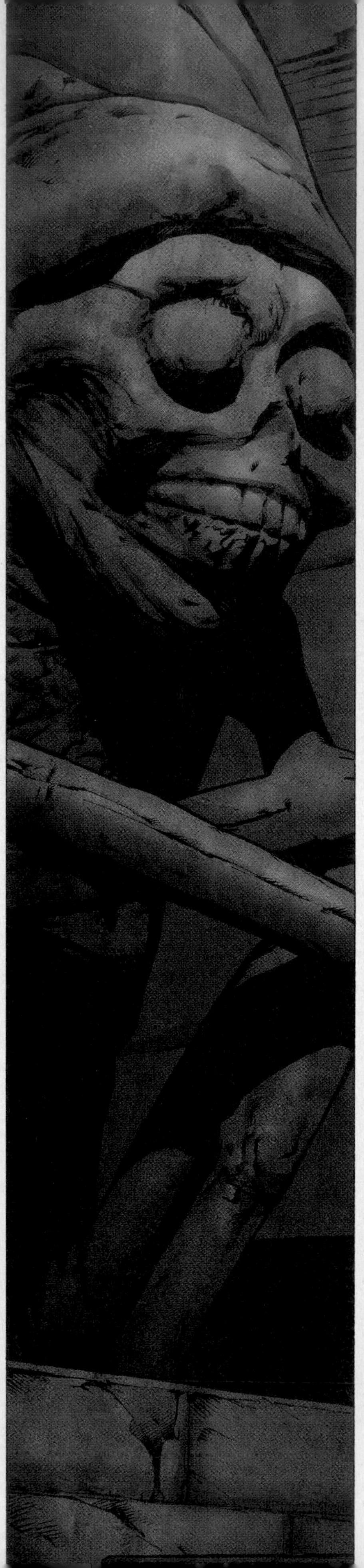

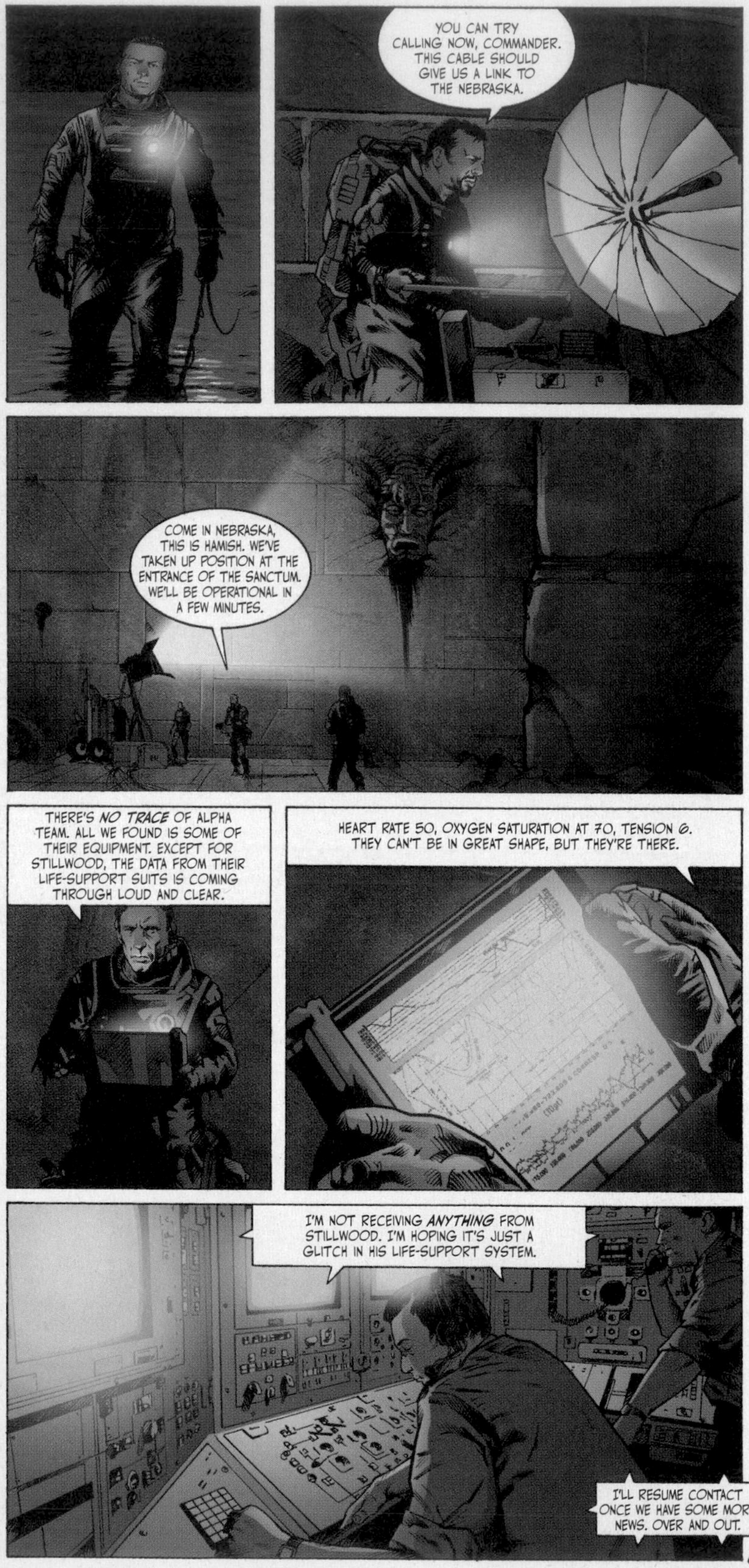
YOU CAN TRY CALLING NOW, COMMANDER. THIS CABLE SHOULD GIVE US A LINK TO THE NEBRASKA.
COME IN NEBRASKA, THIS IS HAMISH. WE'VE TAKEN UP POSITION AT THE ENTRANCE OF THE SANCTUM. WE'LL BE OPERATIONAL IN A FEW MINUTES.
THERE'S *NO TRACE* OF ALPHA TEAM. ALL WE FOUND IS SOME OF THEIR EQUIPMENT. EXCEPT FOR STILLWOOD, THE DATA FROM THEIR LIFE-SUPPORT SUITS IS COMING THROUGH LOUD AND CLEAR.
HEART RATE 50, OXYGEN SATURATION AT 70, TENSION 6. THEY CAN'T BE IN GREAT SHAPE, BUT THEY'RE THERE.
I'M NOT RECEIVING ***ANYTHING*** FROM STILLWOOD. I'M HOPING IT'S JUST A GLITCH IN HIS LIFE-SUPPORT SYSTEM.
I'LL RESUME CONTACT ONCE WE HAVE SOME MORE NEWS. OVER AND OUT.
6

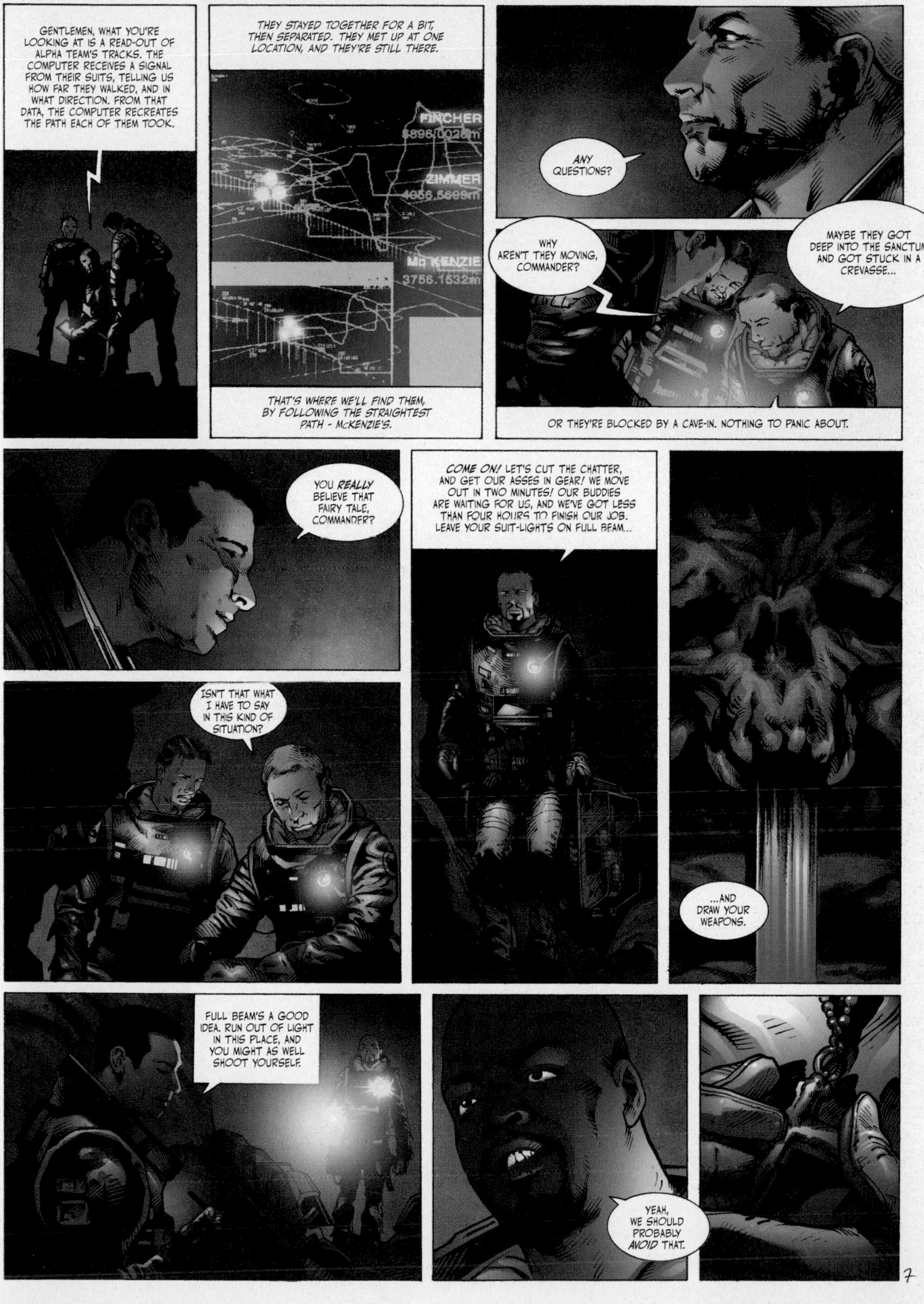
GENTLEMEN, WHAT YOU'RE LOOKING AT IS A READ-OUT OF ALPHA TEAM'S TRACKS. THE COMPUTER RECEIVES A SIGNAL FROM THEIR SUITS, TELLING US HOW FAR THEY WALKED, AND IN WHAT DIRECTION. FROM THAT DATA, THE COMPUTER RECREATES THE PATH EACH OF THEM TOOK.
THEY STAYED TOGETHER FOR A BIT, THEN SEPARATED. THEY MET UP AT ONE LOCATION, AND THEY'RE STILL THERE.
FINCHER
ZIMMER
McKENZIE
3756.1532m
THAT'S WHERE WE'LL FIND THEM, BY FOLLOWING THE STRAIGHTEST PATH - McKENZIE'S.
ANY QUESTIONS?
WHY AREN'T THEY MOVING, COMMANDER?
MAYBE THEY GOT DEEP INTO THE SANCTUM AND GOT STUCK IN A CREVASSE...
OR THEY'RE BLOCKED BY A CAVE-IN. NOTHING TO PANIC ABOUT.
YOU REALLY BELIEVE THAT FAIRY TALE, COMMANDER?
ISN'T THAT WHAT I HAVE TO SAY IN THIS KIND OF SITUATION?
COME ON! LET'S CUT THE CHATTER, AND GET OUR ASSES IN GEAR! WE MOVE OUT IN TWO MINUTES! OUR BUDDIES ARE WAITING FOR US, AND WE'VE GOT LESS THAN FOUR HOURS TO FINISH OUR JOB. LEAVE YOUR SUIT-LIGHTS ON FULL BEAM...
...AND DRAW YOUR WEAPONS.
FULL BEAM'S A GOOD IDEA. RUN OUT OF LIGHT IN THIS PLACE, AND YOU MIGHT AS WELL SHOOT YOURSELF.
YEAH, WE SHOULD PROBABLY AVOID THAT.
7

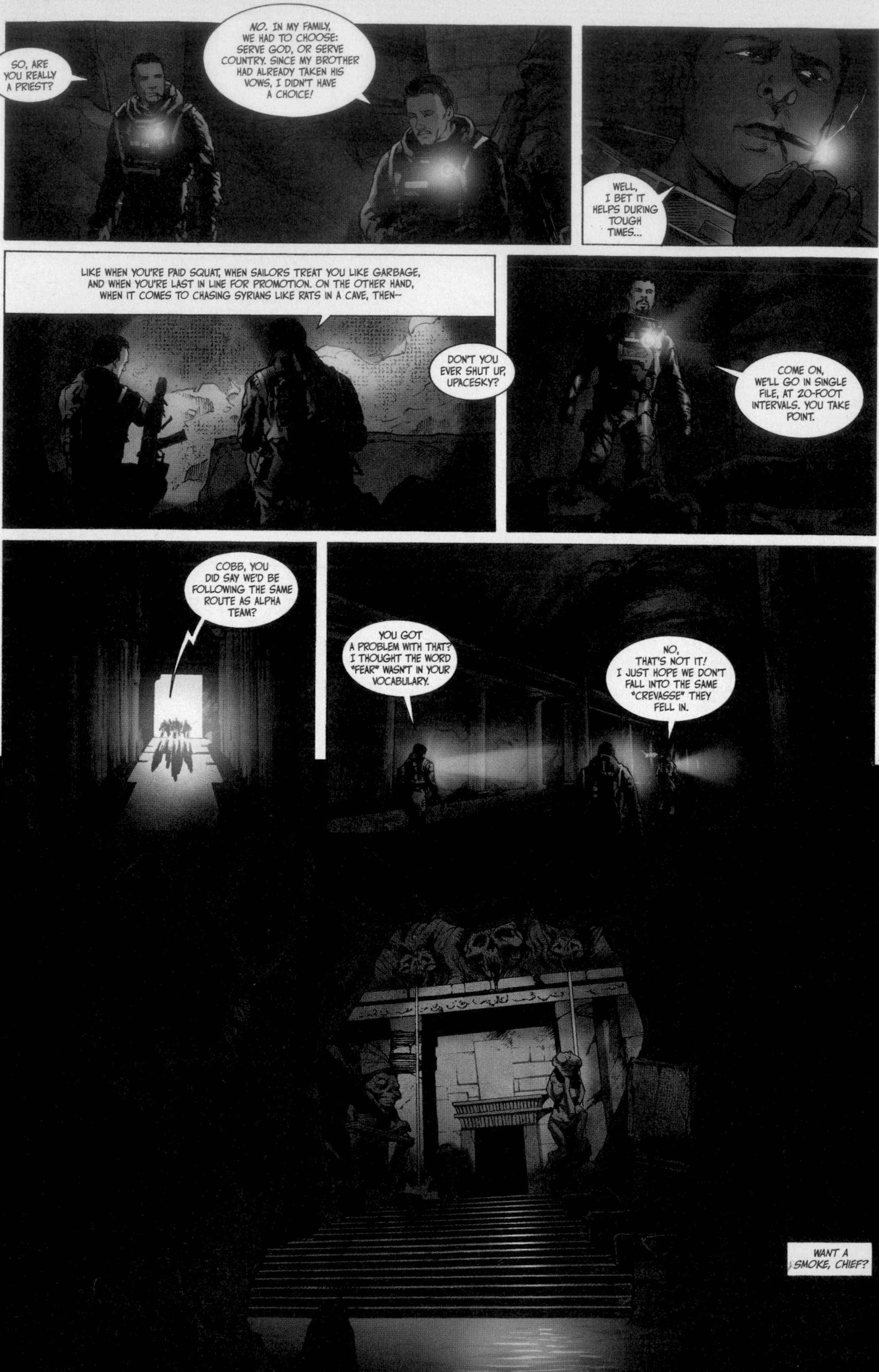

SO, ARE YOU REALLY A PRIEST?
NO. IN MY FAMILY, WE HAD TO CHOOSE: SERVE GOD, OR SERVE COUNTRY. SINCE MY BROTHER HAD ALREADY TAKEN HIS VOWS, I DIDN'T HAVE A CHOICE!
WELL, I BET IT HELPS DURING TOUGH TIMES...
LIKE WHEN YOU'RE PAID SQUAT, WHEN SAILORS TREAT YOU LIKE GARBAGE, AND WHEN YOU'RE LAST IN LINE FOR PROMOTION. ON THE OTHER HAND, WHEN IT COMES TO CHASING SYRIANS LIKE RATS IN A CAVE, THEN--
DON'T YOU EVER SHUT UP, UPACESKY?
COME ON, WE'LL GO IN SINGLE FILE, AT 20-FOOT INTERVALS. YOU TAKE POINT.
COBB, YOU DID SAY WE'D BE FOLLOWING THE SAME ROUTE AS ALPHA TEAM?
YOU GOT A PROBLEM WITH THAT? I THOUGHT THE WORD "FEAR" WASN'T IN YOUR VOCABULARY.
NO, THAT'S NOT IT! I JUST HOPE WE DON'T FALL INTO THE SAME "CREVASSE" THEY FELL IN.
WANT A SMOKE, CHIEF?

8

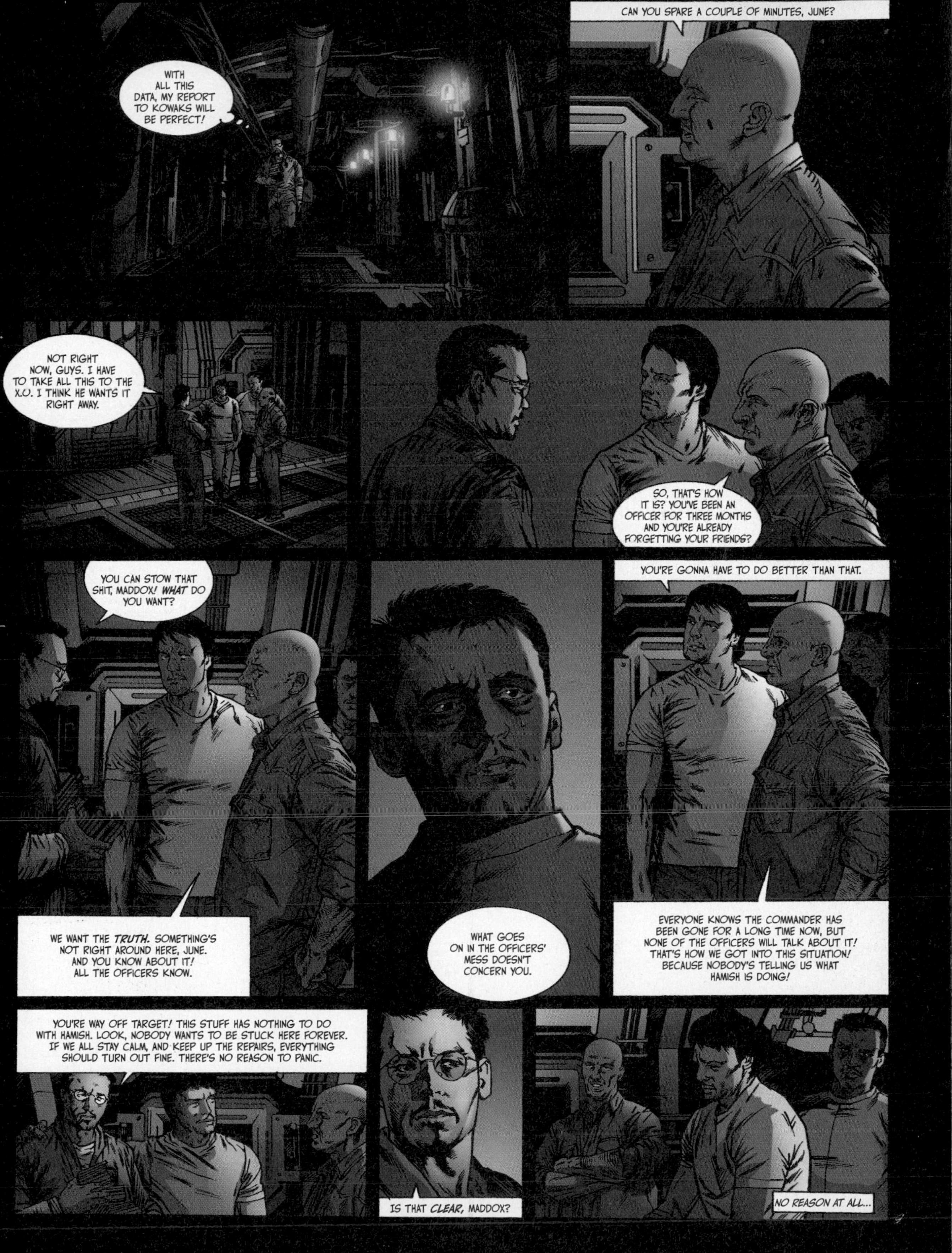
WITH ALL THIS DATA, MY REPORT TO KOWAKS WILL BE PERFECT!
CAN YOU SPARE A COUPLE OF MINUTES, JUNE?
NOT RIGHT NOW, GUYS. I HAVE TO TAKE ALL THIS TO THE X.O. I THINK HE WANTS IT RIGHT AWAY.
SO, THAT'S HOW IT IS? YOU'VE BEEN AN OFFICER FOR THREE MONTHS AND YOU'RE ALREADY FORGETTING YOUR FRIENDS?
YOU CAN STOW THAT SHIT, MADDOX! WHAT DO YOU WANT?
WE WANT THE TRUTH. SOMETHING'S NOT RIGHT AROUND HERE, JUNE. AND YOU KNOW ABOUT IT! ALL THE OFFICERS KNOW.
WHAT GOES ON IN THE OFFICERS' MESS DOESN'T CONCERN YOU.
YOU'RE GONNA HAVE TO DO BETTER THAN THAT.
EVERYONE KNOWS THE COMMANDER HAS BEEN GONE FOR A LONG TIME NOW, BUT NONE OF THE OFFICERS WILL TALK ABOUT IT! THAT'S HOW WE GOT INTO THIS SITUATION! BECAUSE NOBODY'S TELLING US WHAT HAMISH IS DOING!
YOU'RE WAY OFF TARGET! THIS STUFF HAS NOTHING TO DO WITH HAMISH. LOOK, NOBODY WANTS TO BE STUCK HERE FOREVER. IF WE ALL STAY CALM, AND KEEP UP THE REPAIRS, EVERYTHING SHOULD TURN OUT FINE. THERE'S NO REASON TO PANIC.
IS THAT CLEAR, MADDOX?
NO REASON AT ALL...

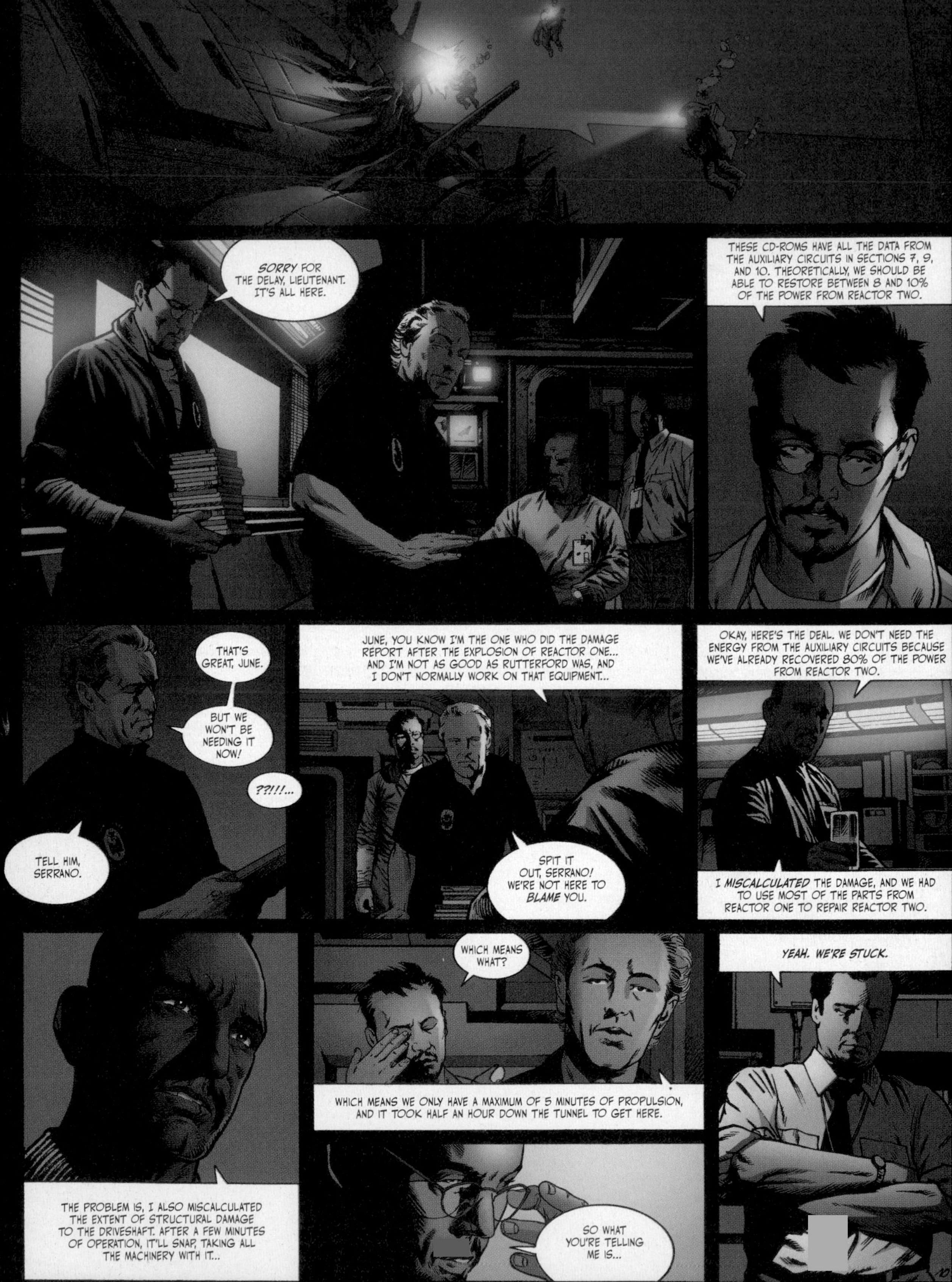
SORRY FOR THE DELAY, LIEUTENANT. IT'S ALL HERE.
THESE CD-ROMS HAVE ALL THE DATA FROM THE AUXILIARY CIRCUITS IN SECTIONS 7, 9, AND 10. THEORETICALLY, WE SHOULD BE ABLE TO RESTORE BETWEEN 8 AND 10% OF THE POWER FROM REACTOR TWO.
THAT'S GREAT, JUNE.
BUT WE WON'T BE NEEDING IT NOW!
??!!!...
TELL HIM, SERRANO.
JUNE, YOU KNOW I'M THE ONE WHO DID THE DAMAGE REPORT AFTER THE EXPLOSION OF REACTOR ONE... AND I'M NOT AS GOOD AS RUTTERFORD WAS, AND I DON'T NORMALLY WORK ON THAT EQUIPMENT...
SPIT IT OUT, SERRANO! WE'RE NOT HERE TO BLAME YOU.
OKAY, HERE'S THE DEAL. WE DON'T NEED THE ENERGY FROM THE AUXILIARY CIRCUITS BECAUSE WE'VE ALREADY RECOVERED 80% OF THE POWER FROM REACTOR TWO.
I MISCALCULATED THE DAMAGE, AND WE HAD TO USE MOST OF THE PARTS FROM REACTOR ONE TO REPAIR REACTOR TWO.
THE PROBLEM IS, I ALSO MISCALCULATED THE EXTENT OF STRUCTURAL DAMAGE TO THE DRIVESHAFT. AFTER A FEW MINUTES OF OPERATION, IT'LL SNAP, TAKING ALL THE MACHINERY WITH IT...
WHICH MEANS WHAT?
WHICH MEANS WE ONLY HAVE A MAXIMUM OF 5 MINUTES OF PROPULSION, AND IT TOOK HALF AN HOUR DOWN THE TUNNEL TO GET HERE.
SO WHAT YOU'RE TELLING ME IS...
YEAH. WE'RE STUCK.

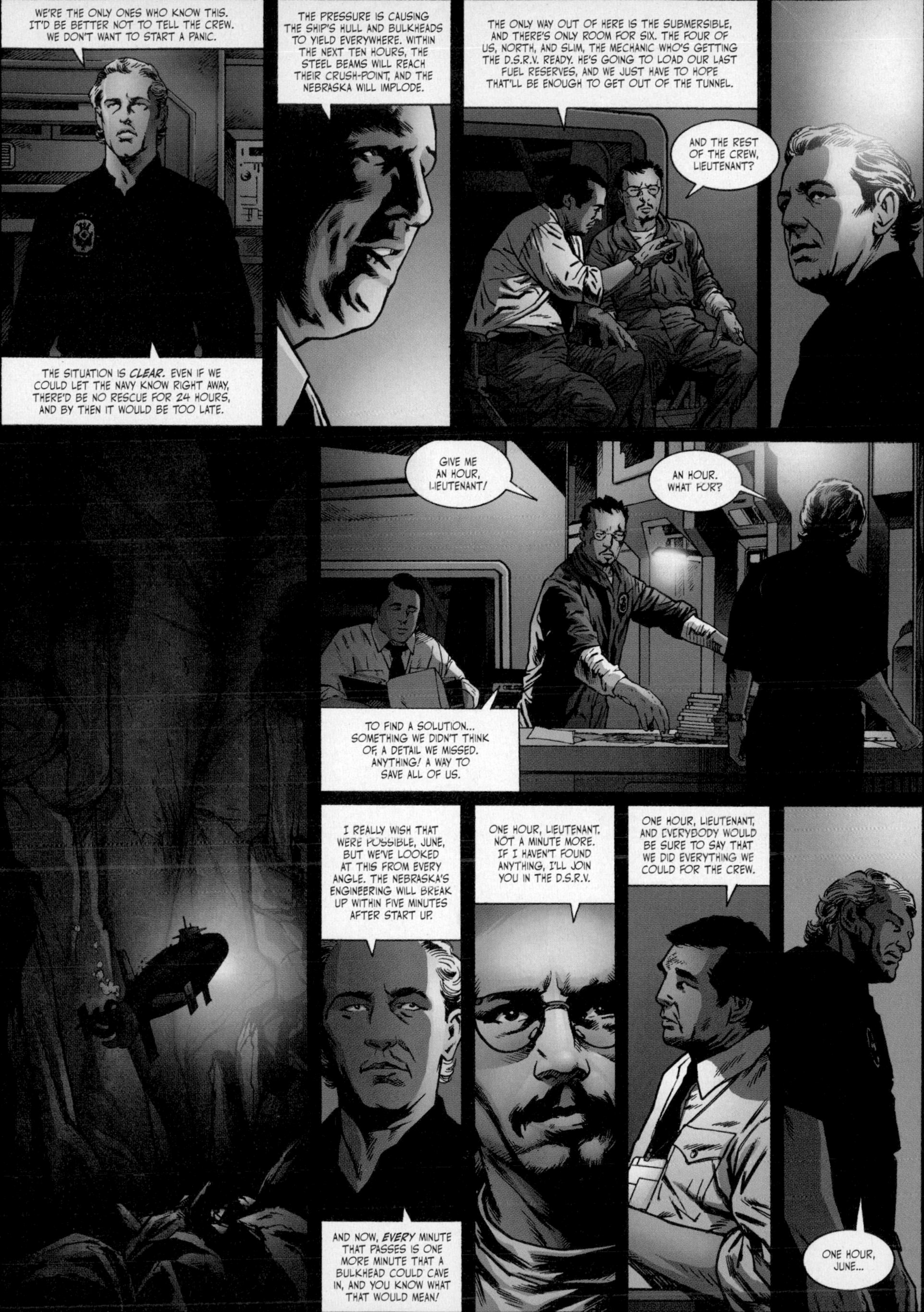
WE'RE THE ONLY ONES WHO KNOW THIS. IT'D BE BETTER NOT TO TELL THE CREW. WE DON'T WANT TO START A PANIC.
THE SITUATION IS CLEAR. EVEN IF WE COULD LET THE NAVY KNOW RIGHT AWAY, THERE'D BE NO RESCUE FOR 24 HOURS, AND BY THEN IT WOULD BE TOO LATE.
THE PRESSURE IS CAUSING THE SHIP'S HULL AND BULKHEADS TO YIELD EVERYWHERE. WITHIN THE NEXT TEN HOURS, THE STEEL BEAMS WILL REACH THEIR CRUSH-POINT, AND THE NEBRASKA WILL IMPLODE.
THE ONLY WAY OUT OF HERE IS THE SUBMERSIBLE, AND THERE'S ONLY ROOM FOR SIX. THE FOUR OF US, NORTH, AND SLIM, THE MECHANIC WHO'S GETTING THE D.S.R.V. READY. HE'S GOING TO LOAD OUR LAST FUEL RESERVES, AND WE JUST HAVE TO HOPE THAT'LL BE ENOUGH TO GET OUT OF THE TUNNEL.
AND THE REST OF THE CREW, LIEUTENANT?
GIVE ME AN HOUR, LIEUTENANT!
AN HOUR. WHAT FOR?
TO FIND A SOLUTION... SOMETHING WE DIDN'T THINK OF, A DETAIL WE MISSED. ANYTHING! A WAY TO SAVE ALL OF US.
I REALLY WISH THAT WERE POSSIBLE, JUNE, BUT WE'VE LOOKED AT THIS FROM EVERY ANGLE. THE NEBRASKA'S ENGINEERING WILL BREAK UP WITHIN FIVE MINUTES AFTER START UP.
AND NOW, EVERY MINUTE THAT PASSES IS ONE MORE MINUTE THAT A BULKHEAD COULD CAVE IN, AND YOU KNOW WHAT THAT WOULD MEAN!
ONE HOUR, LIEUTENANT. NOT A MINUTE MORE. IF I HAVEN'T FOUND ANYTHING, I'LL JOIN YOU IN THE D.S.R.V.
ONE HOUR, LIEUTENANT, AND EVERYBODY WOULD BE SURE TO SAY THAT WE DID EVERYTHING WE COULD FOR THE CREW.
ONE HOUR, JUNE...

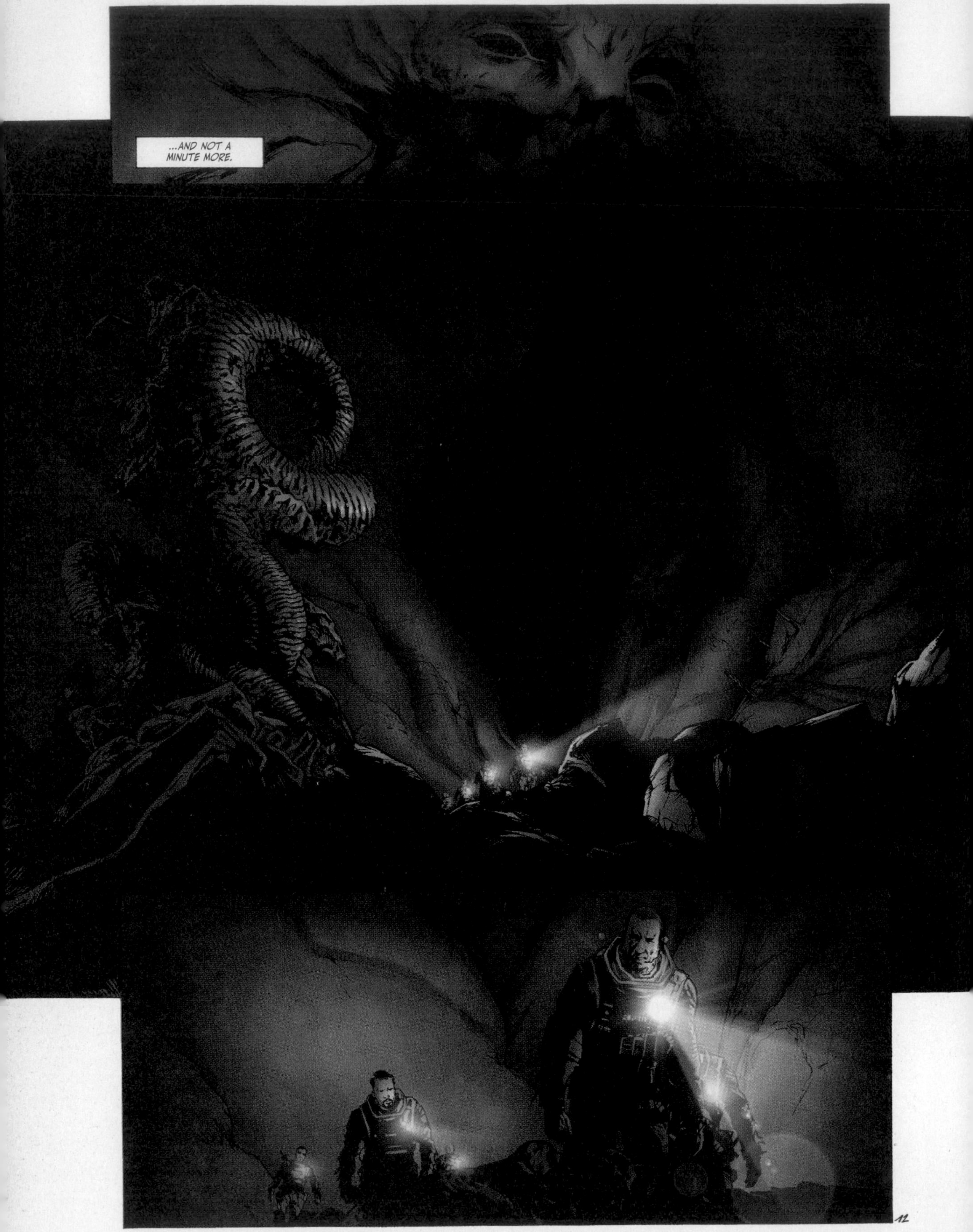
...AND NOT A MINUTE MORE.
12

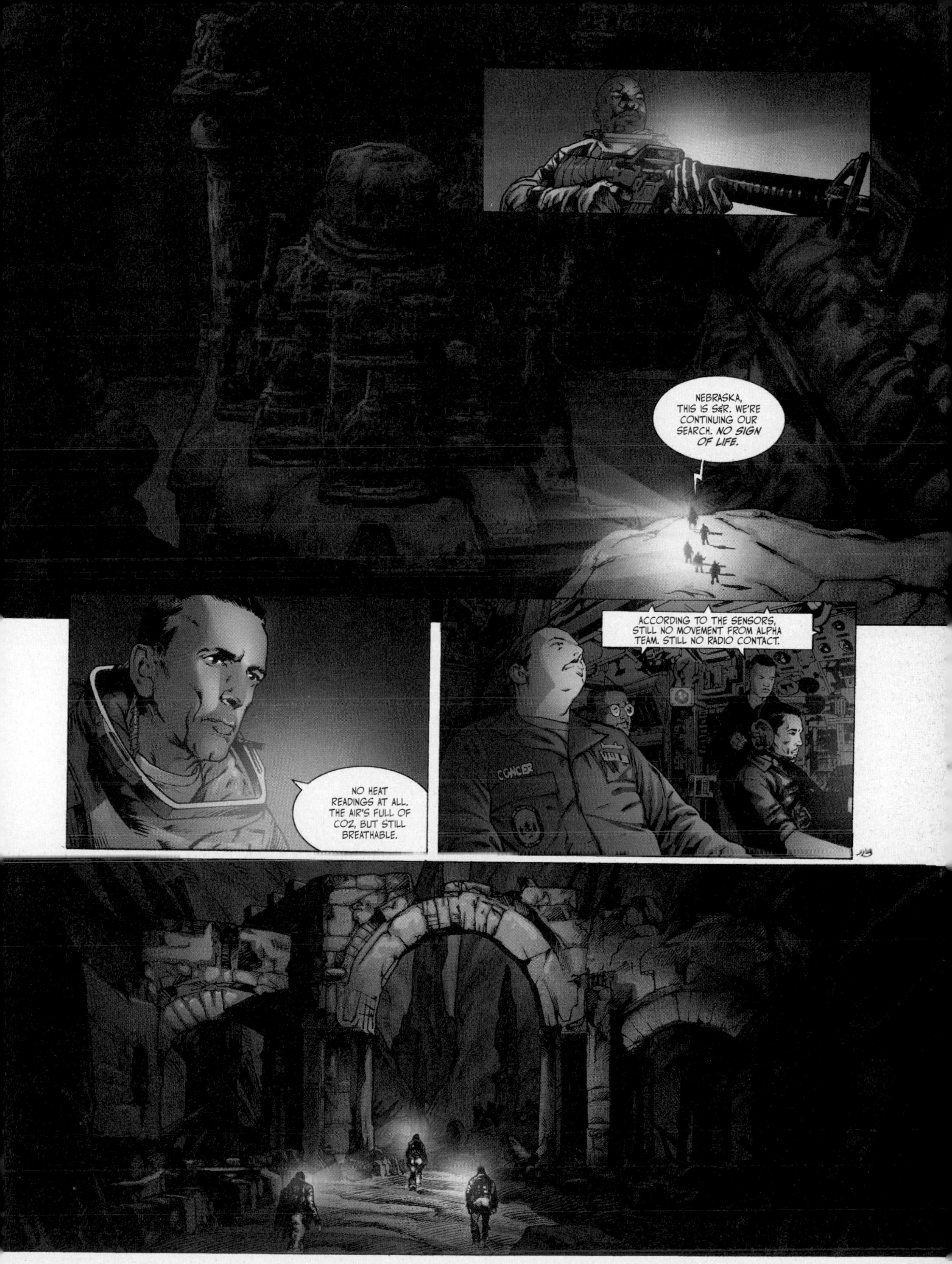

NEBRASKA, THIS IS S&R. WE'RE CONTINUING OUR SEARCH. *NO SIGN OF LIFE.*
NO HEAT READINGS AT ALL. THE AIR'S FULL OF CO2, BUT STILL BREATHABLE.
ACCORDING TO THE SENSORS, STILL NO MOVEMENT FROM ALPHA TEAM. STILL NO RADIO CONTACT.

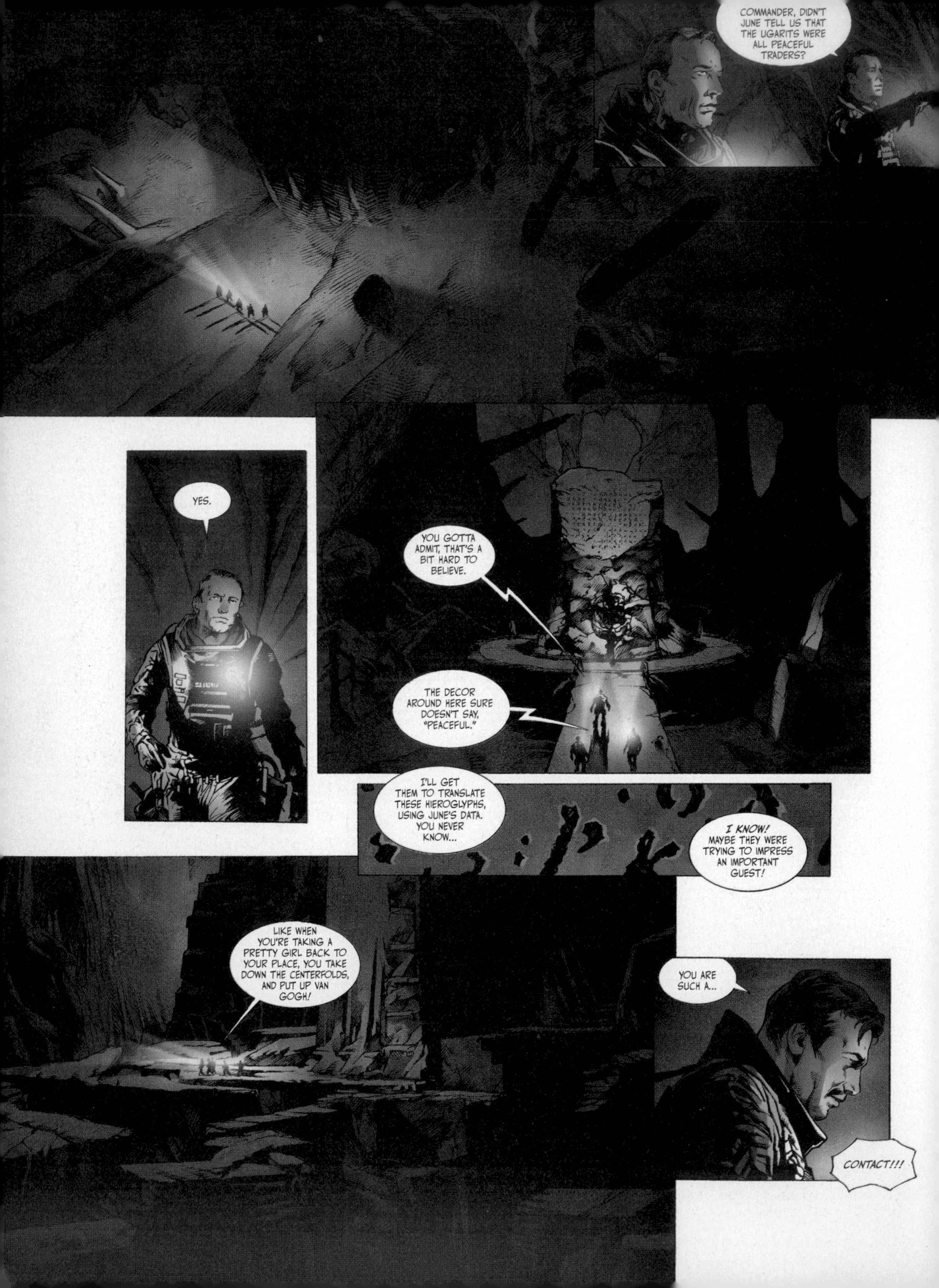
COMMANDER, DIDN'T JUNE TELL US THAT THE UGARITS WERE ALL PEACEFUL TRADERS?
YES.
YOU GOTTA ADMIT, THAT'S A BIT HARD TO BELIEVE.
THE DECOR AROUND HERE SURE DOESN'T SAY, "PEACEFUL."
I'LL GET THEM TO TRANSLATE THESE HIEROGLYPHS, USING JUNE'S DATA. YOU NEVER KNOW...
I KNOW! MAYBE THEY WERE TRYING TO IMPRESS AN IMPORTANT GUEST!
LIKE WHEN YOU'RE TAKING A PRETTY GIRL BACK TO YOUR PLACE, YOU TAKE DOWN THE CENTERFOLDS, AND PUT UP VAN GOGH!
YOU ARE SUCH A...
CONTACT!!!

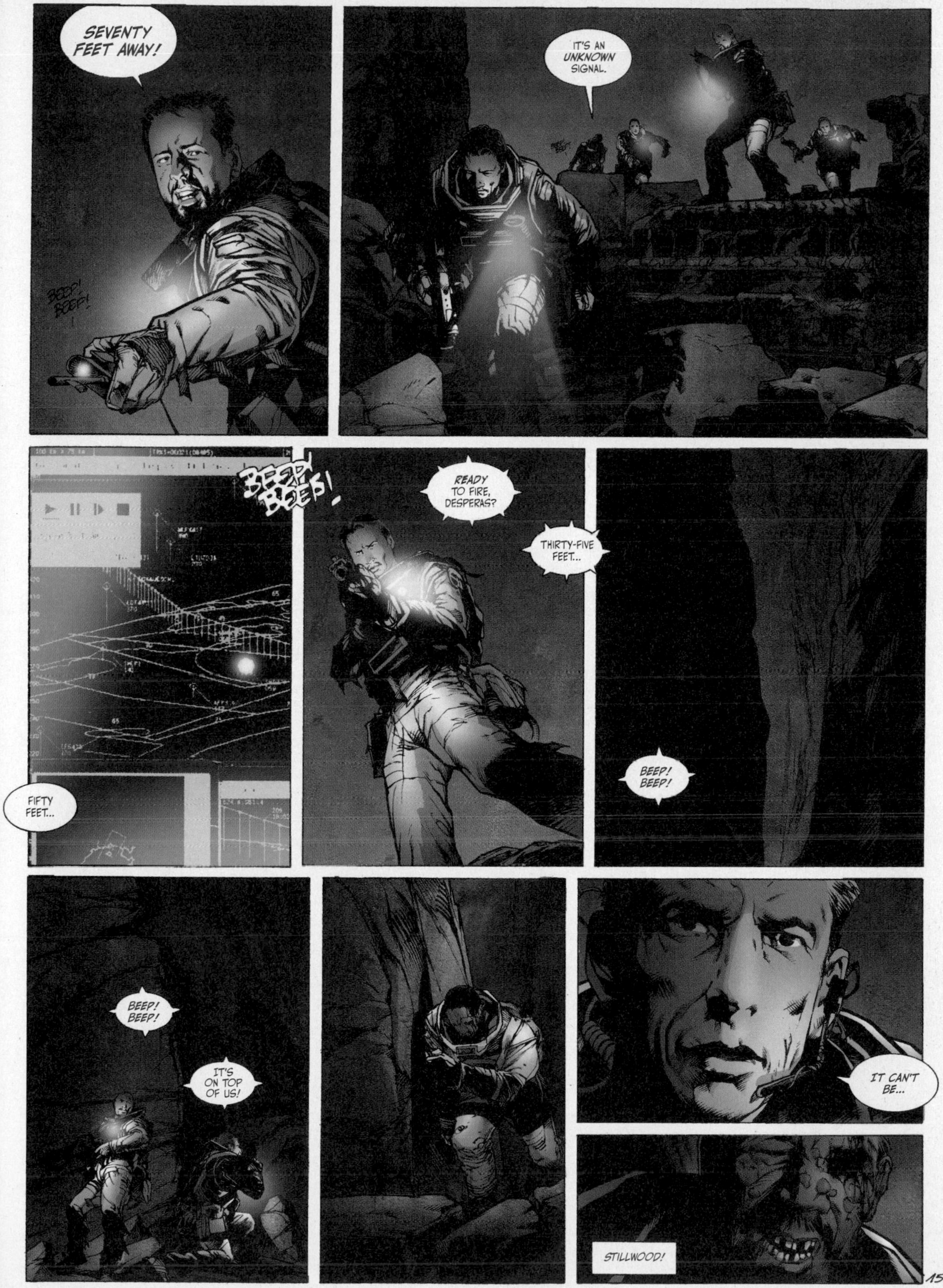
SEVENTY FEET AWAY!
BEEP! BEEP!
IT'S AN UNKNOWN SIGNAL.
BEEP! BEEP!
FIFTY FEET...
READY TO FIRE, DESPERAS?
THIRTY-FIVE FEET...
BEEP! BEEP!
BEEP! BEEP!
IT'S ON TOP OF US!
IT CAN'T BE...
STILLWOOD!
15

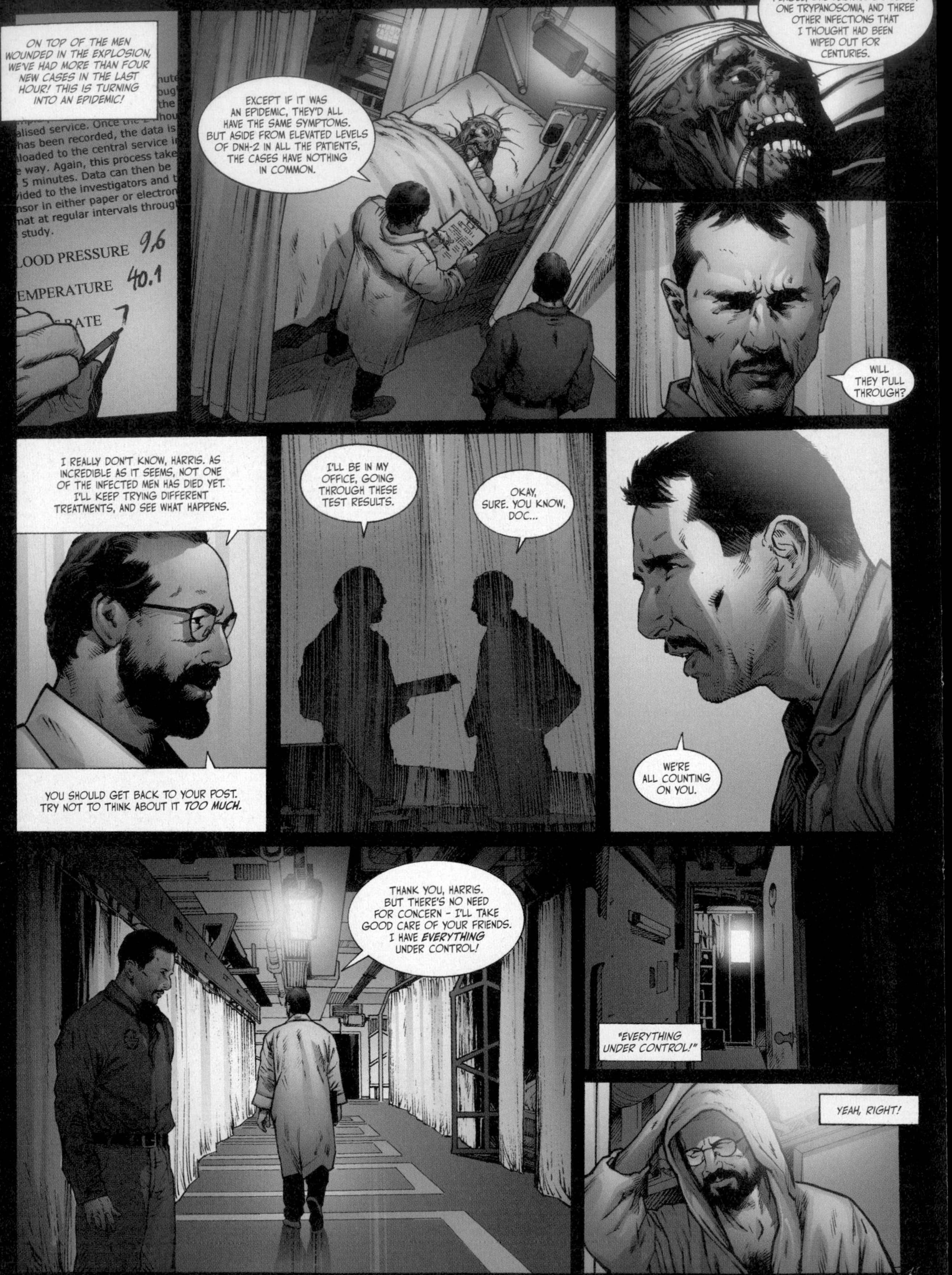

ON TOP OF THE MEN WOUNDED IN THE EXPLOSION, WE'VE HAD MORE THAN FOUR NEW CASES IN THE LAST HOUR! THIS IS TURNING INTO AN EPIDEMIC!
alised service. Once the ... has been recorded, the data is ...loaded to the central service in ... way. Again, this process take... 5 minutes. Data can then be ...vided to the investigators and t... ...nsor in either paper or electron... ...mat at regular intervals throug... study.
LOOD PRESSURE 9,6
EMPERATURE 40.1
RATE 7
EXCEPT IF IT WAS AN EPIDEMIC, THEY'D ALL HAVE THE SAME SYMPTOMS. BUT ASIDE FROM ELEVATED LEVELS OF DNH-2 IN ALL THE PATIENTS, THE CASES HAVE NOTHING IN COMMON.
IN THE LAST HOUR, I'VE SEEN ONE CASE OF BUBONIC PLAGUE, ONE LEISHMAN'S DISEASE, ONE TRYPANOSOMIA, AND THREE OTHER INFECTIONS THAT I THOUGHT HAD BEEN WIPED OUT FOR CENTURIES.
WILL THEY PULL THROUGH?
I REALLY DON'T KNOW, HARRIS. AS INCREDIBLE AS IT SEEMS, NOT ONE OF THE INFECTED MEN HAS DIED YET. I'LL KEEP TRYING DIFFERENT TREATMENTS, AND SEE WHAT HAPPENS.
YOU SHOULD GET BACK TO YOUR POST. TRY NOT TO THINK ABOUT IT TOO MUCH.
I'LL BE IN MY OFFICE, GOING THROUGH THESE TEST RESULTS.
OKAY, SURE. YOU KNOW, DOC...
WE'RE ALL COUNTING ON YOU.
THANK YOU, HARRIS. BUT THERE'S NO NEED FOR CONCERN - I'LL TAKE GOOD CARE OF YOUR FRIENDS. I HAVE EVERYTHING UNDER CONTROL!
"EVERYTHING UNDER CONTROL!"
YEAH, RIGHT!

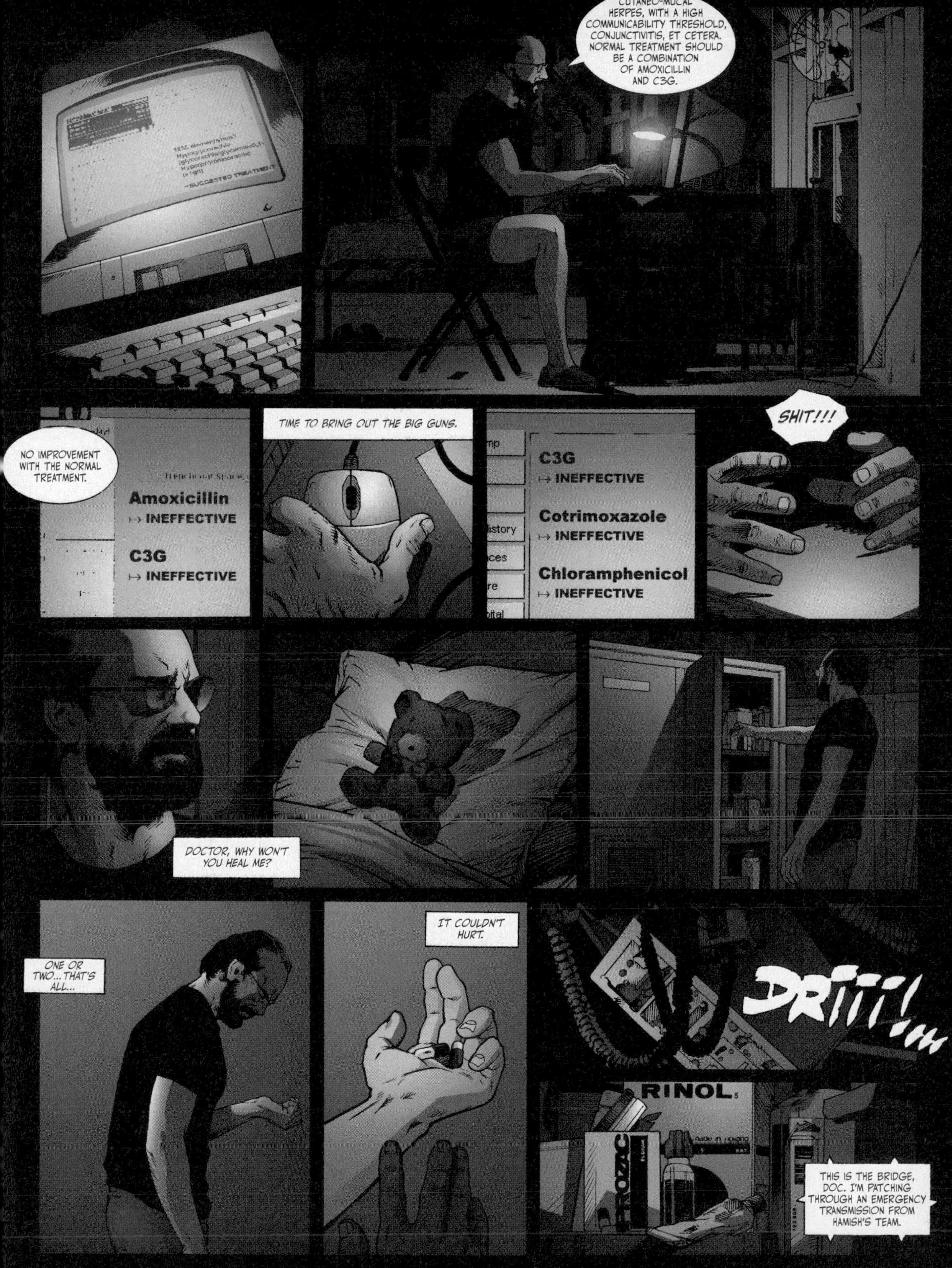
CUTANEO-MUCAL HERPES, WITH A HIGH COMMUNICABILITY THRESHOLD, CONJUNCTIVITIS, ET CETERA. NORMAL TREATMENT SHOULD BE A COMBINATION OF AMOXICILLIN AND C3G.
NO IMPROVEMENT WITH THE NORMAL TREATMENT.
Amoxicillin
↦ INEFFECTIVE
C3G
↦ INEFFECTIVE
TIME TO BRING OUT THE BIG GUNS.
C3G
↦ INEFFECTIVE
Cotrimoxazole
↦ INEFFECTIVE
Chloramphenicol
↦ INEFFECTIVE
SHIT!!!
DOCTOR, WHY WON'T YOU HEAL ME?
ONE OR TWO... THAT'S ALL...
IT COULDN'T HURT.
DRIII!...
RINOL
FROZAC
THIS IS THE BRIDGE, DOC. I'M PATCHING THROUGH AN EMERGENCY TRANSMISSION FROM HAMISH'S TEAM.

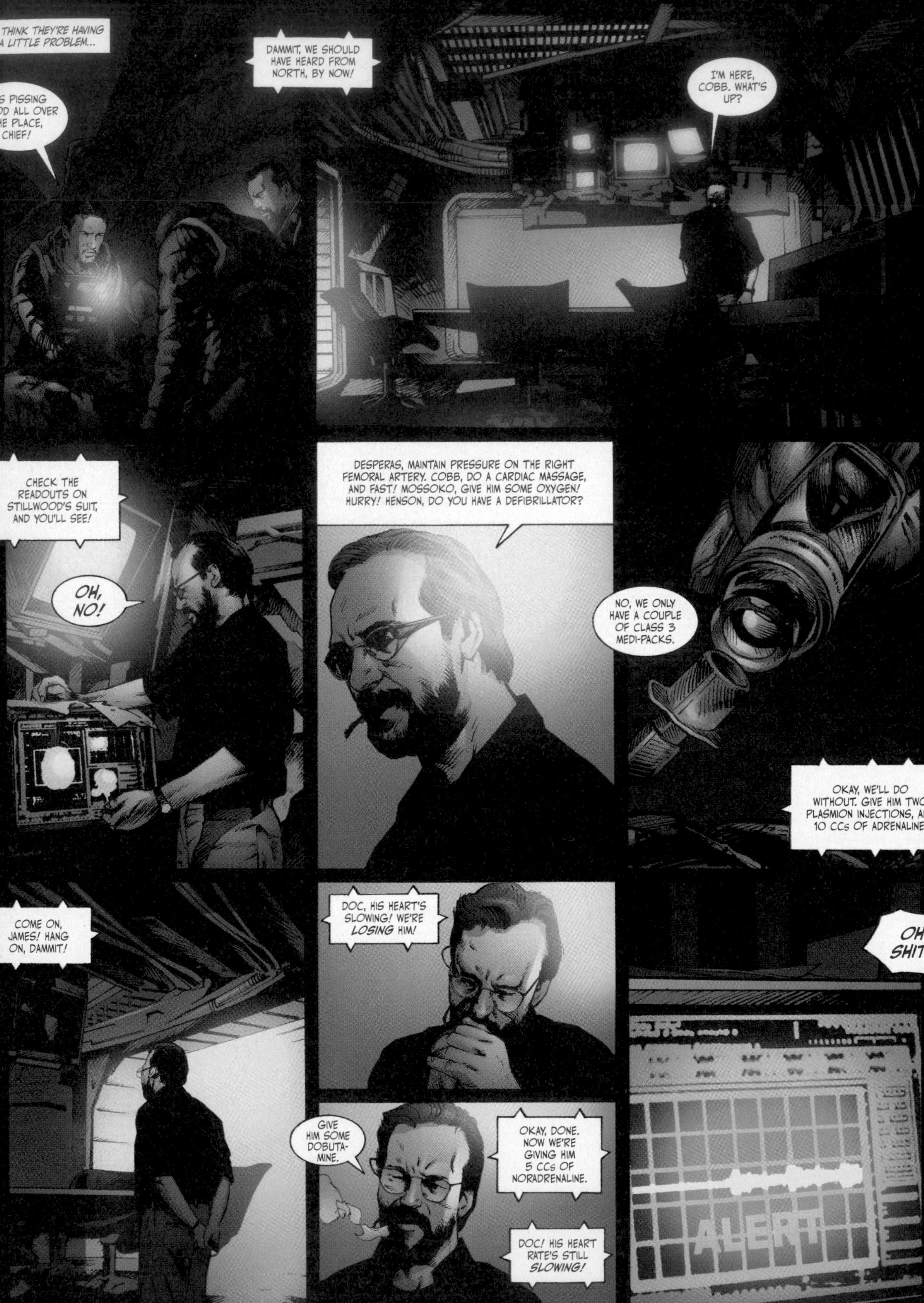
I THINK THEY'RE HAVING A LITTLE PROBLEM...
HE'S PISSING BLOOD ALL OVER THE PLACE, CHIEF!
DAMMIT, WE SHOULD HAVE HEARD FROM NORTH, BY NOW!
I'M HERE, COBB. WHAT'S UP?
CHECK THE READOUTS ON STILLWOOD'S SUIT, AND YOU'LL SEE!
OH, NO!
DESPERAS, MAINTAIN PRESSURE ON THE RIGHT FEMORAL ARTERY. COBB, DO A CARDIAC MASSAGE, AND FAST! MOSSOKO, GIVE HIM SOME OXYGEN! HURRY! HENSON, DO YOU HAVE A DEFIBRILLATOR?
NO, WE ONLY HAVE A COUPLE OF CLASS 3 MEDI-PACKS.
OKAY, WE'LL DO WITHOUT. GIVE HIM TWO PLASMION INJECTIONS, AND 10 CCs OF ADRENALINE.
COME ON, JAMES! HANG ON, DAMMIT!
DOC, HIS HEART'S SLOWING! WE'RE LOSING HIM!
GIVE HIM SOME DOBUTA-MINE.
OKAY, DONE. NOW WE'RE GIVING HIM 5 CCs OF NORADRENALINE.
DOC! HIS HEART RATE'S STILL SLOWING!
OH SHIT!
ALERT

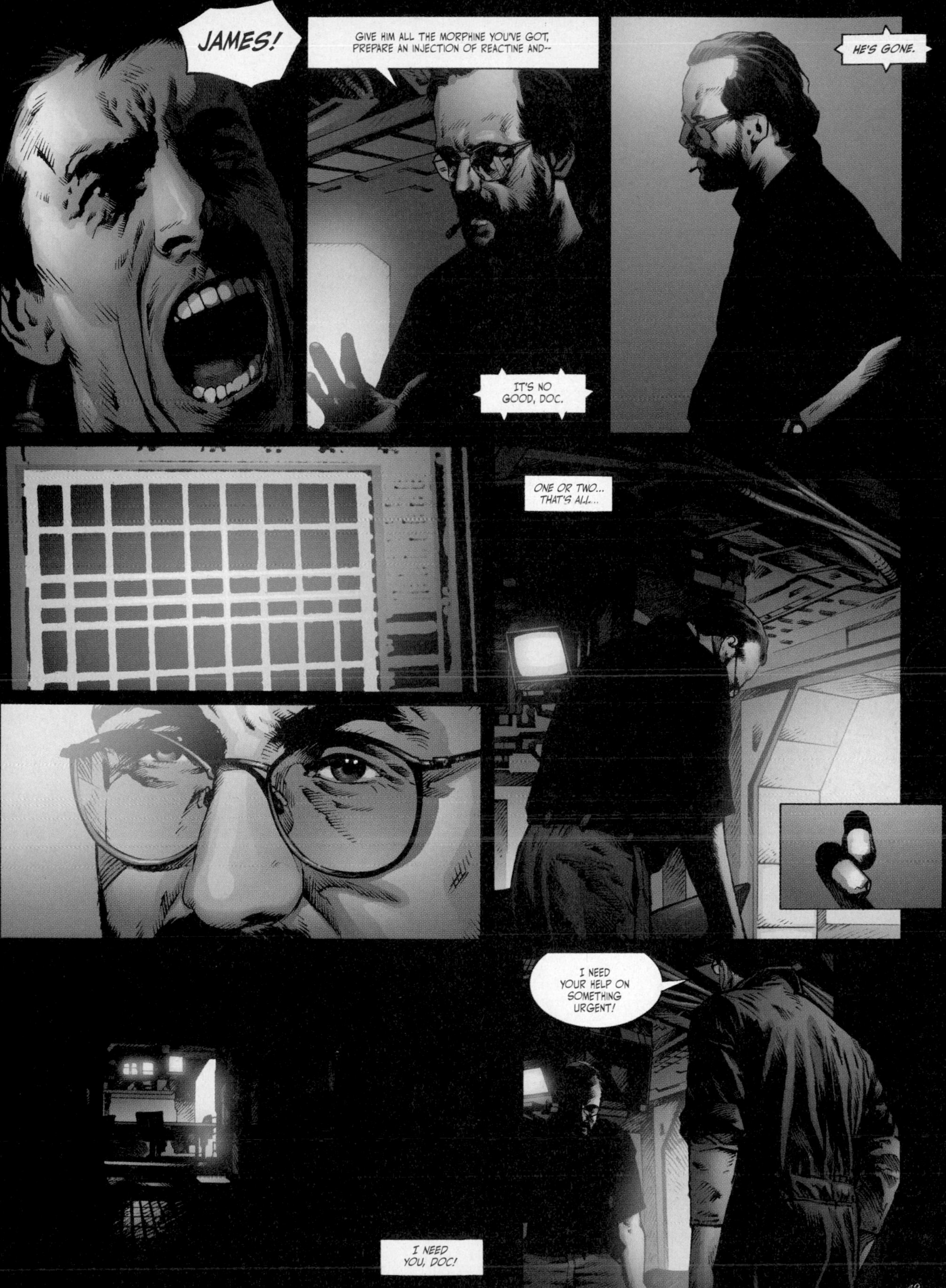
JAMES!
GIVE HIM ALL THE MORPHINE YOU'VE GOT, PREPARE AN INJECTION OF REACTINE AND--
IT'S NO GOOD, DOC.
HE'S GONE.
ONE OR TWO... THAT'S ALL...
I NEED YOUR HELP ON SOMETHING URGENT!
I NEED YOU, DOC!

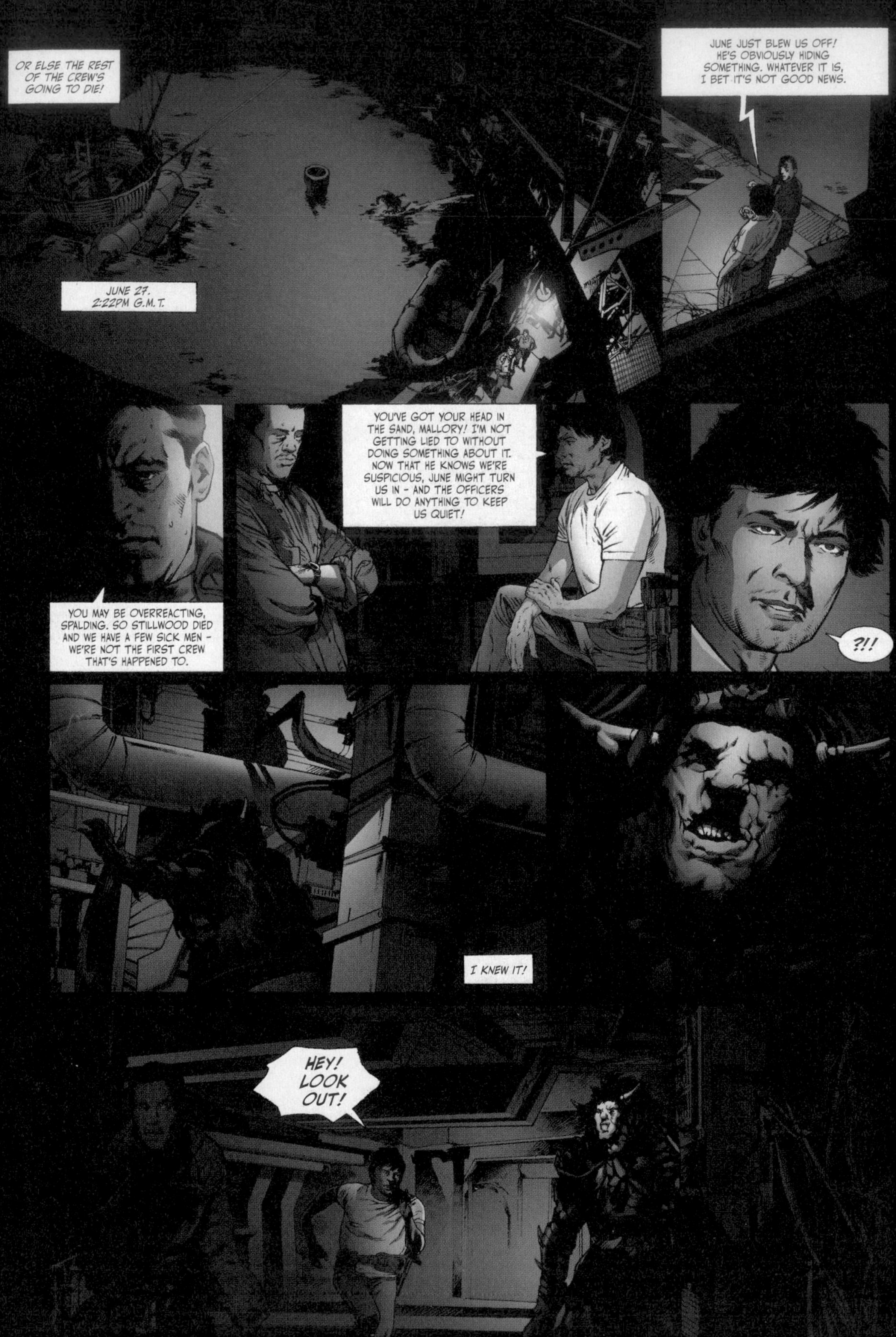
OR ELSE THE REST OF THE CREW'S GOING TO DIE!
JUNE 27. 2:22PM G.M.T.
JUNE JUST BLEW US OFF! HE'S OBVIOUSLY HIDING SOMETHING. WHATEVER IT IS, I BET IT'S NOT GOOD NEWS.
YOU MAY BE OVERREACTING, SPALDING. SO STILLWOOD DIED AND WE HAVE A FEW SICK MEN - WE'RE NOT THE FIRST CREW THAT'S HAPPENED TO.
YOU'VE GOT YOUR HEAD IN THE SAND, MALLORY! I'M NOT GETTING LIED TO WITHOUT DOING SOMETHING ABOUT IT. NOW THAT HE KNOWS WE'RE SUSPICIOUS, JUNE MIGHT TURN US IN - AND THE OFFICERS WILL DO ANYTHING TO KEEP US QUIET!
?!!
I KNEW IT!
HEY! LOOK OUT!

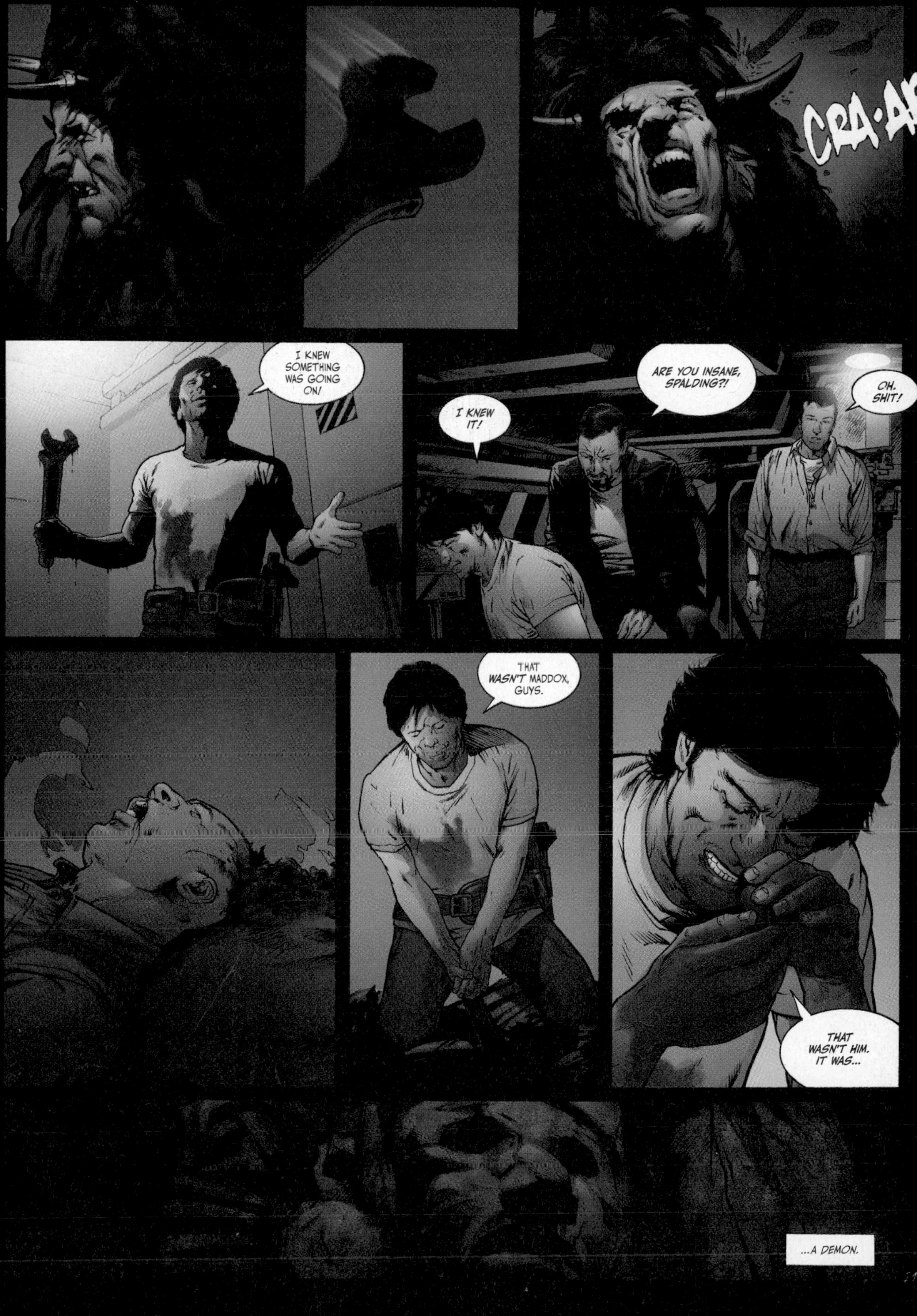
CRA-AK!
I KNEW SOMETHING WAS GOING ON!
I KNEW IT!
ARE YOU INSANE, SPALDING?!
OH. SHIT!
THAT WASN'T MADDOX, GUYS.
THAT WASN'T HIM. IT WAS...
...A DEMON.

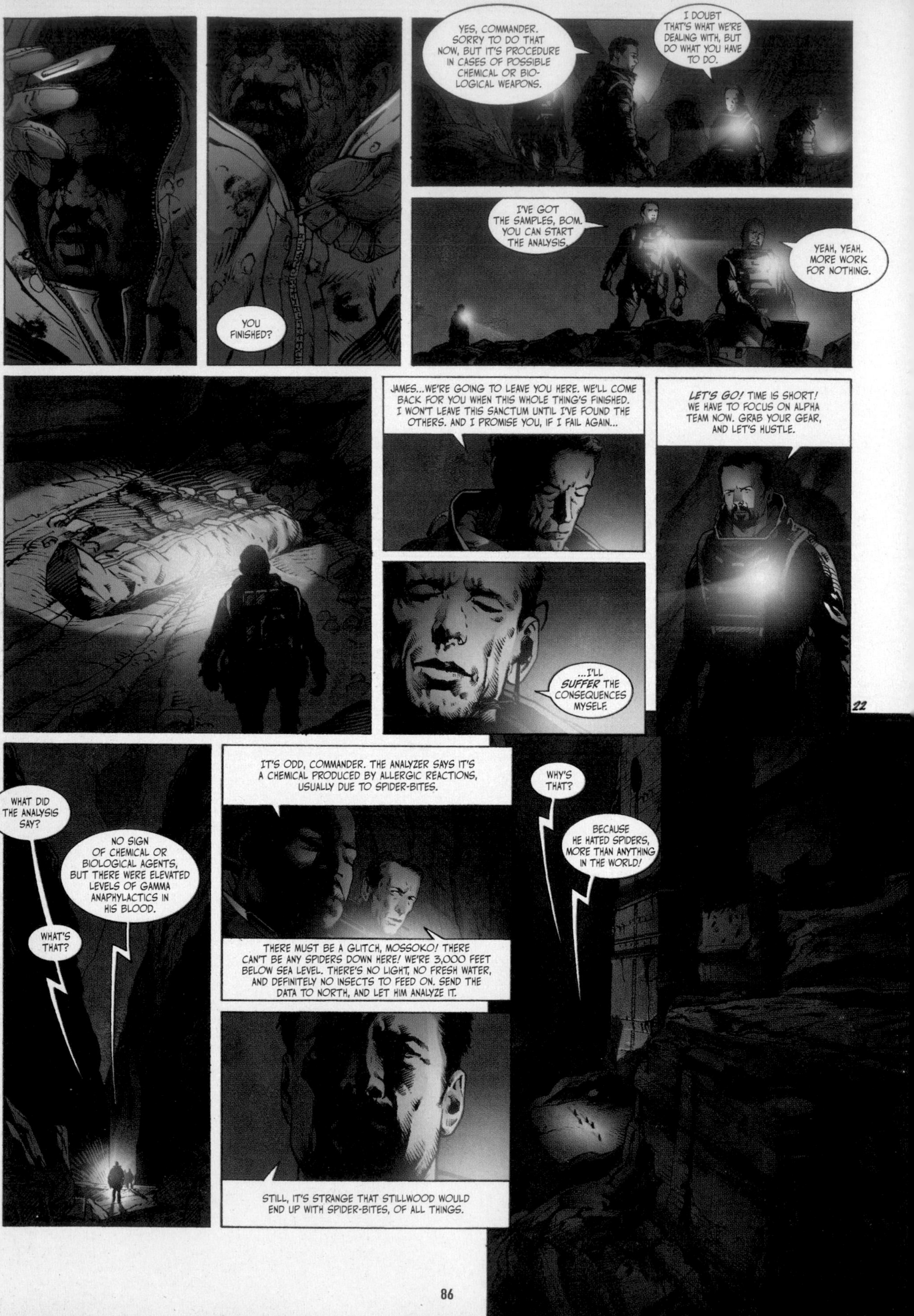
YES, COMMANDER. SORRY TO DO THAT NOW, BUT IT'S PROCEDURE IN CASES OF POSSIBLE CHEMICAL OR BIO-LOGICAL WEAPONS.
I DOUBT THAT'S WHAT WE'RE DEALING WITH, BUT DO WHAT YOU HAVE TO DO.
YOU FINISHED?
I'VE GOT THE SAMPLES, BOM. YOU CAN START THE ANALYSIS.
YEAH, YEAH. MORE WORK FOR NOTHING.
JAMES...WE'RE GOING TO LEAVE YOU HERE. WE'LL COME BACK FOR YOU WHEN THIS WHOLE THING'S FINISHED. I WON'T LEAVE THIS SANCTUM UNTIL I'VE FOUND THE OTHERS. AND I PROMISE YOU, IF I FAIL AGAIN...
...I'LL *SUFFER* THE CONSEQUENCES MYSELF.
LET'S GO! TIME IS SHORT! WE HAVE TO FOCUS ON ALPHA TEAM NOW. GRAB YOUR GEAR, AND LET'S HUSTLE.
22
WHAT DID THE ANALYSIS SAY?
NO SIGN OF CHEMICAL OR BIOLOGICAL AGENTS, BUT THERE WERE ELEVATED LEVELS OF GAMMA ANAPHYLACTICS IN HIS BLOOD.
WHAT'S THAT?
IT'S ODD, COMMANDER. THE ANALYZER SAYS IT'S A CHEMICAL PRODUCED BY ALLERGIC REACTIONS, USUALLY DUE TO SPIDER-BITES.
THERE MUST BE A GLITCH, MOSSOKO! THERE CAN'T BE ANY SPIDERS DOWN HERE! WE'RE 3,000 FEET BELOW SEA LEVEL. THERE'S NO LIGHT, NO FRESH WATER, AND DEFINITELY NO INSECTS TO FEED ON. SEND THE DATA TO NORTH, AND LET HIM ANALYZE IT.
STILL, IT'S STRANGE THAT STILLWOOD WOULD END UP WITH SPIDER-BITES, OF ALL THINGS.
WHY'S THAT?
BECAUSE HE HATED SPIDERS, MORE THAN ANYTHING IN THE WORLD!

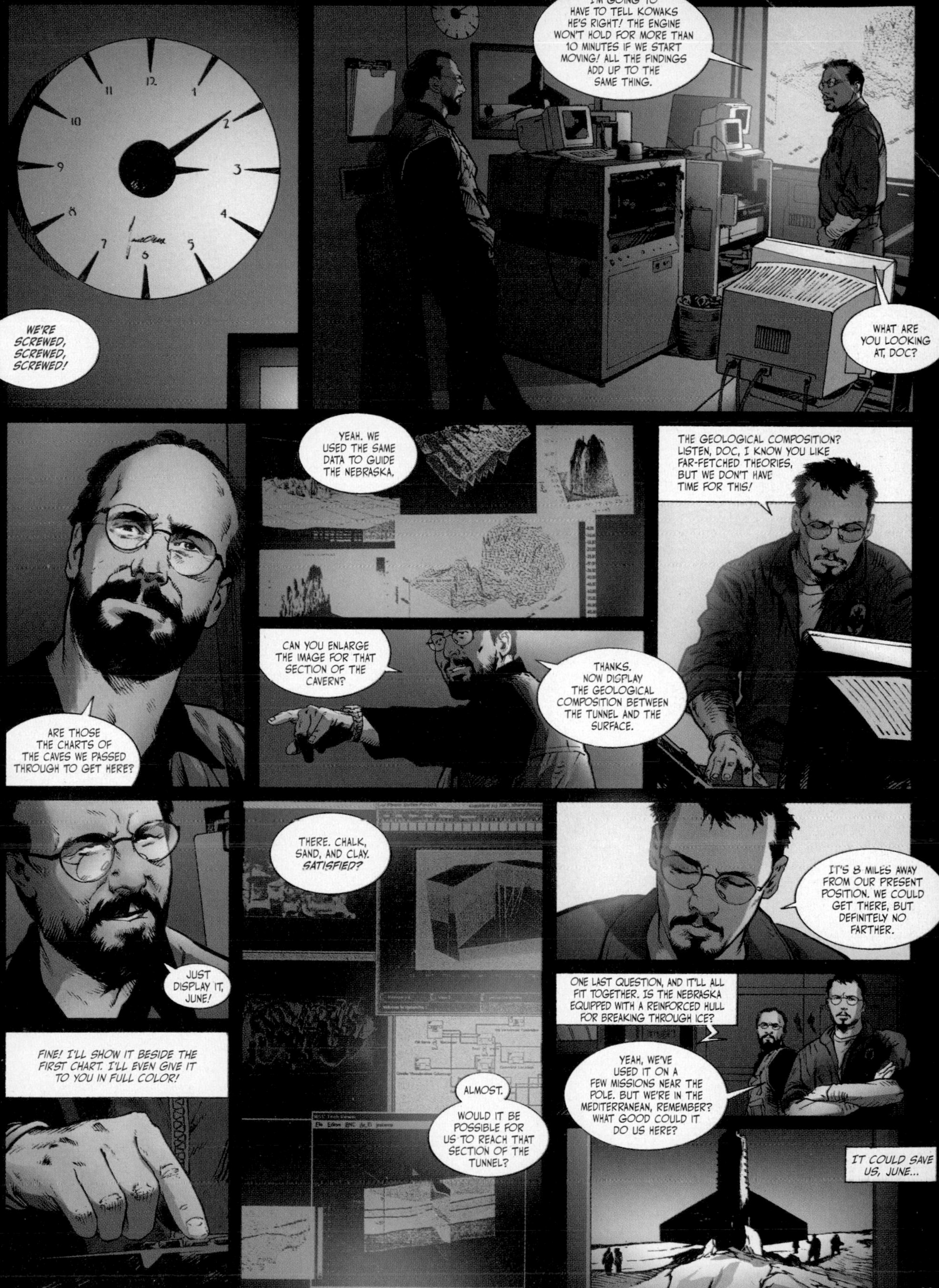
I'M GOING TO HAVE TO TELL KOWAKS HE'S RIGHT! THE ENGINE WON'T HOLD FOR MORE THAN 10 MINUTES IF WE START MOVING! ALL THE FINDINGS ADD UP TO THE SAME THING.
WE'RE SCREWED, SCREWED, SCREWED!
WHAT ARE YOU LOOKING AT, DOC?
YEAH. WE USED THE SAME DATA TO GUIDE THE NEBRASKA.
THE GEOLOGICAL COMPOSITION? LISTEN, DOC, I KNOW YOU LIKE FAR-FETCHED THEORIES, BUT WE DON'T HAVE TIME FOR THIS!
ARE THOSE THE CHARTS OF THE CAVES WE PASSED THROUGH TO GET HERE?
CAN YOU ENLARGE THE IMAGE FOR THAT SECTION OF THE CAVERN?
THANKS. NOW DISPLAY THE GEOLOGICAL COMPOSITION BETWEEN THE TUNNEL AND THE SURFACE.
JUST DISPLAY IT, JUNE!
THERE. CHALK, SAND, AND CLAY. SATISFIED?
IT'S 8 MILES AWAY FROM OUR PRESENT POSITION. WE COULD GET THERE, BUT DEFINITELY NO FARTHER.
FINE! I'LL SHOW IT BESIDE THE FIRST CHART. I'LL EVEN GIVE IT TO YOU IN FULL COLOR!
ALMOST.
WOULD IT BE POSSIBLE FOR US TO REACH THAT SECTION OF THE TUNNEL?
ONE LAST QUESTION, AND IT'LL ALL FIT TOGETHER. IS THE NEBRASKA EQUIPPED WITH A REINFORCED HULL FOR BREAKING THROUGH ICE?
YEAH, WE'VE USED IT ON A FEW MISSIONS NEAR THE POLE. BUT WE'RE IN THE MEDITERRANEAN, REMEMBER? WHAT GOOD COULD IT DO US HERE?
IT COULD SAVE US, JUNE...

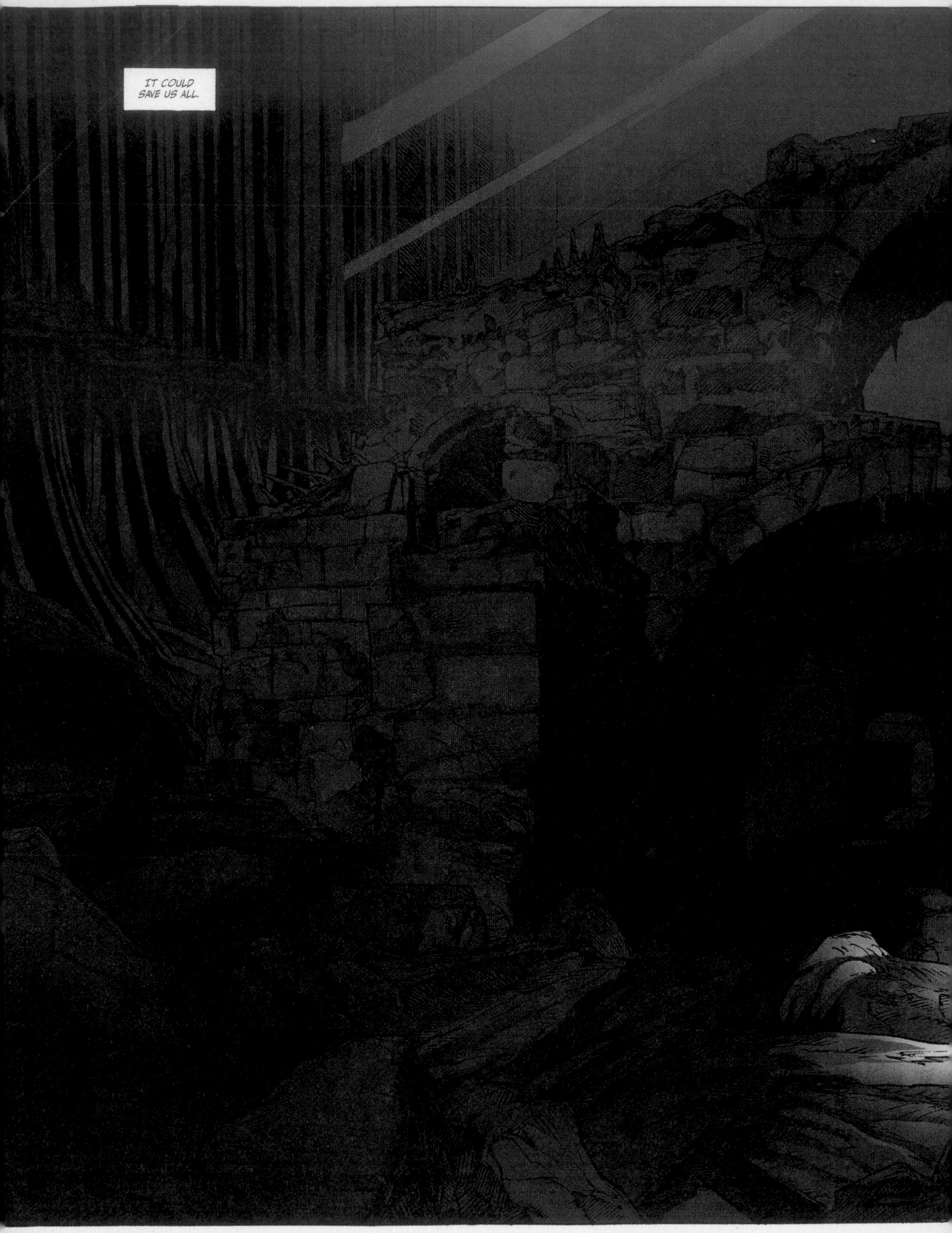
IT COULD SAVE US ALL.

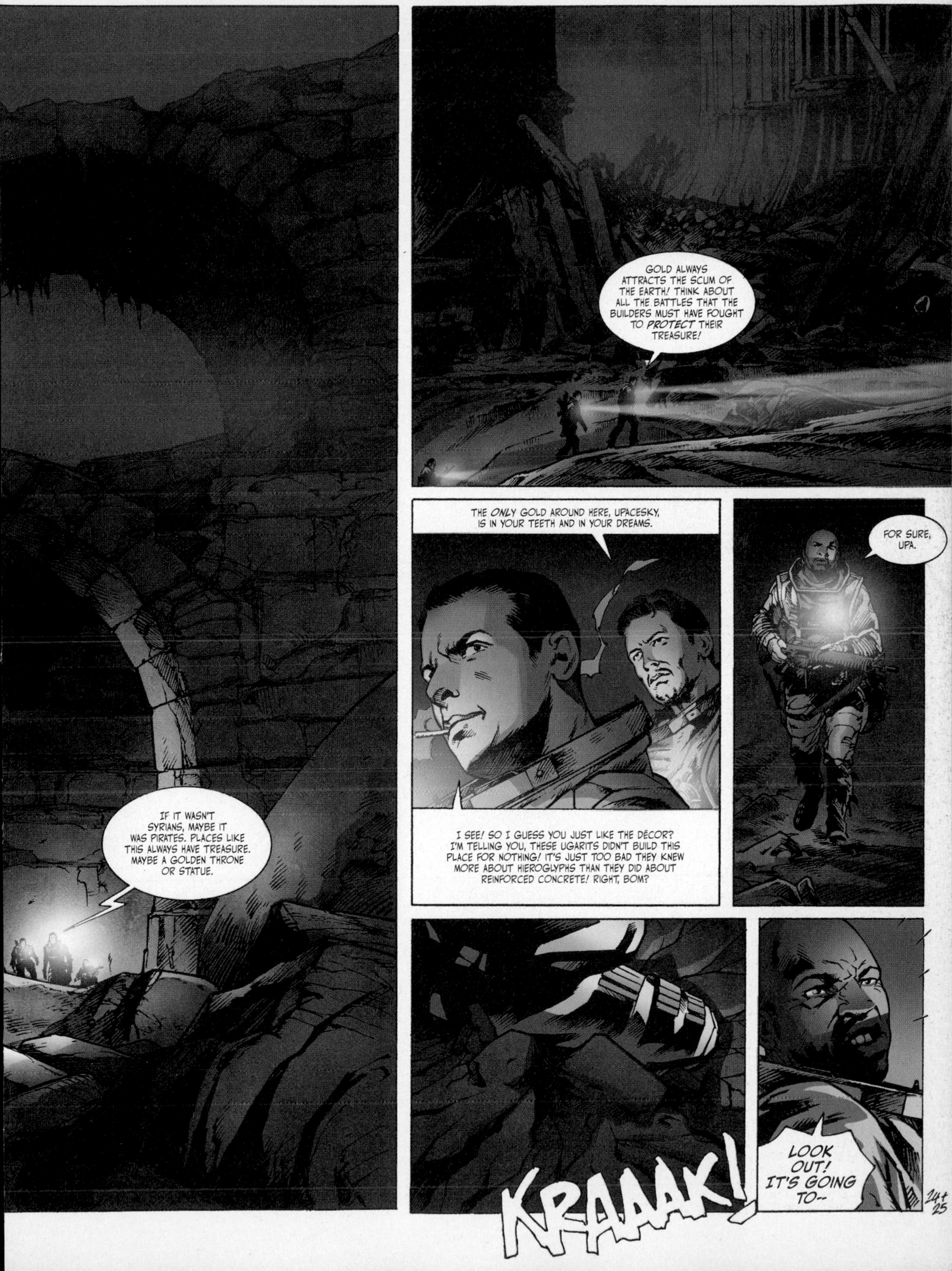
IF IT WASN'T SYRIANS, MAYBE IT WAS PIRATES. PLACES LIKE THIS ALWAYS HAVE TREASURE. MAYBE A GOLDEN THRONE OR STATUE.
GOLD ALWAYS ATTRACTS THE SCUM OF THE EARTH! THINK ABOUT ALL THE BATTLES THAT THE BUILDERS MUST HAVE FOUGHT TO PROTECT THEIR TREASURE!
THE ONLY GOLD AROUND HERE, UPACESKY, IS IN YOUR TEETH AND IN YOUR DREAMS.
I SEE! SO I GUESS YOU JUST LIKE THE DÉCOR? I'M TELLING YOU, THESE UGARITS DIDN'T BUILD THIS PLACE FOR NOTHING! IT'S JUST TOO BAD THEY KNEW MORE ABOUT HIEROGLYPHS THAN THEY DID ABOUT REINFORCED CONCRETE! RIGHT, BOM?
FOR SURE, UPA.
KRAAAK!
LOOK OUT! IT'S GOING TO--

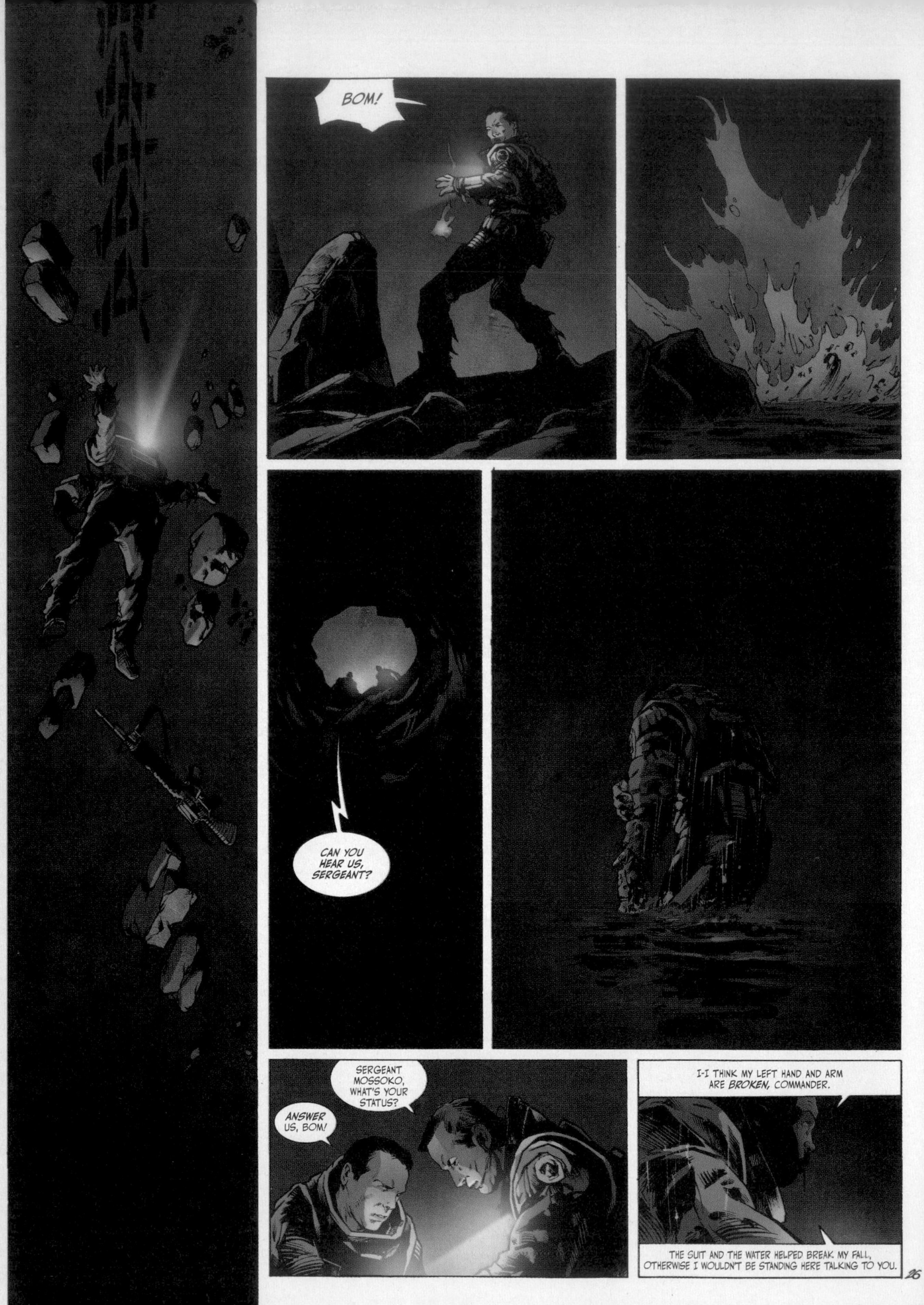
BOM!
CAN YOU HEAR US, SERGEANT?
SERGEANT MOSSOKO, WHAT'S YOUR STATUS?
ANSWER US, BOM!
I-I THINK MY LEFT HAND AND ARM ARE BROKEN, COMMANDER.
THE SUIT AND THE WATER HELPED BREAK MY FALL, OTHERWISE I WOULDN'T BE STANDING HERE TALKING TO YOU.
26

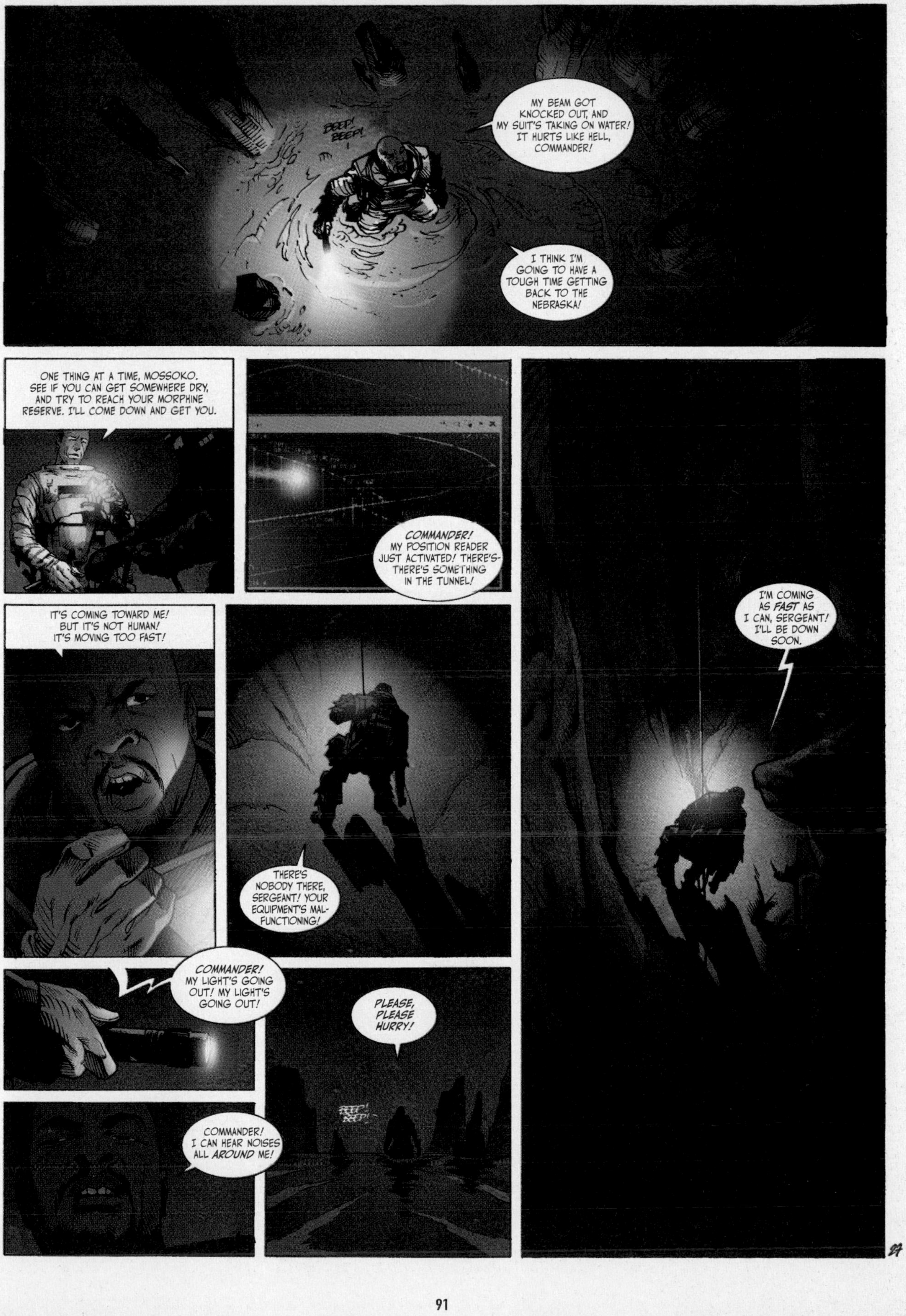
BEEP! BEEP!
MY BEAM GOT KNOCKED OUT, AND MY SUIT'S TAKING ON WATER! IT HURTS LIKE HELL, COMMANDER!
I THINK I'M GOING TO HAVE A TOUGH TIME GETTING BACK TO THE NEBRASKA!
ONE THING AT A TIME, MOSSOKO. SEE IF YOU CAN GET SOMEWHERE DRY, AND TRY TO REACH YOUR MORPHINE RESERVE. I'LL COME DOWN AND GET YOU.
COMMANDER! MY POSITION READER JUST ACTIVATED! THERE'S- THERE'S SOMETHING IN THE TUNNEL!
I'M COMING AS FAST AS I CAN, SERGEANT! I'LL BE DOWN SOON.
IT'S COMING TOWARD ME! BUT IT'S NOT HUMAN! IT'S MOVING TOO FAST!
THERE'S NOBODY THERE, SERGEANT! YOUR EQUIPMENT'S MAL- FUNCTIONING!
COMMANDER! MY LIGHT'S GOING OUT! MY LIGHT'S GOING OUT!
PLEASE, PLEASE HURRY!
COMMANDER! I CAN HEAR NOISES ALL AROUND ME!
BEEP! BEEP!
27

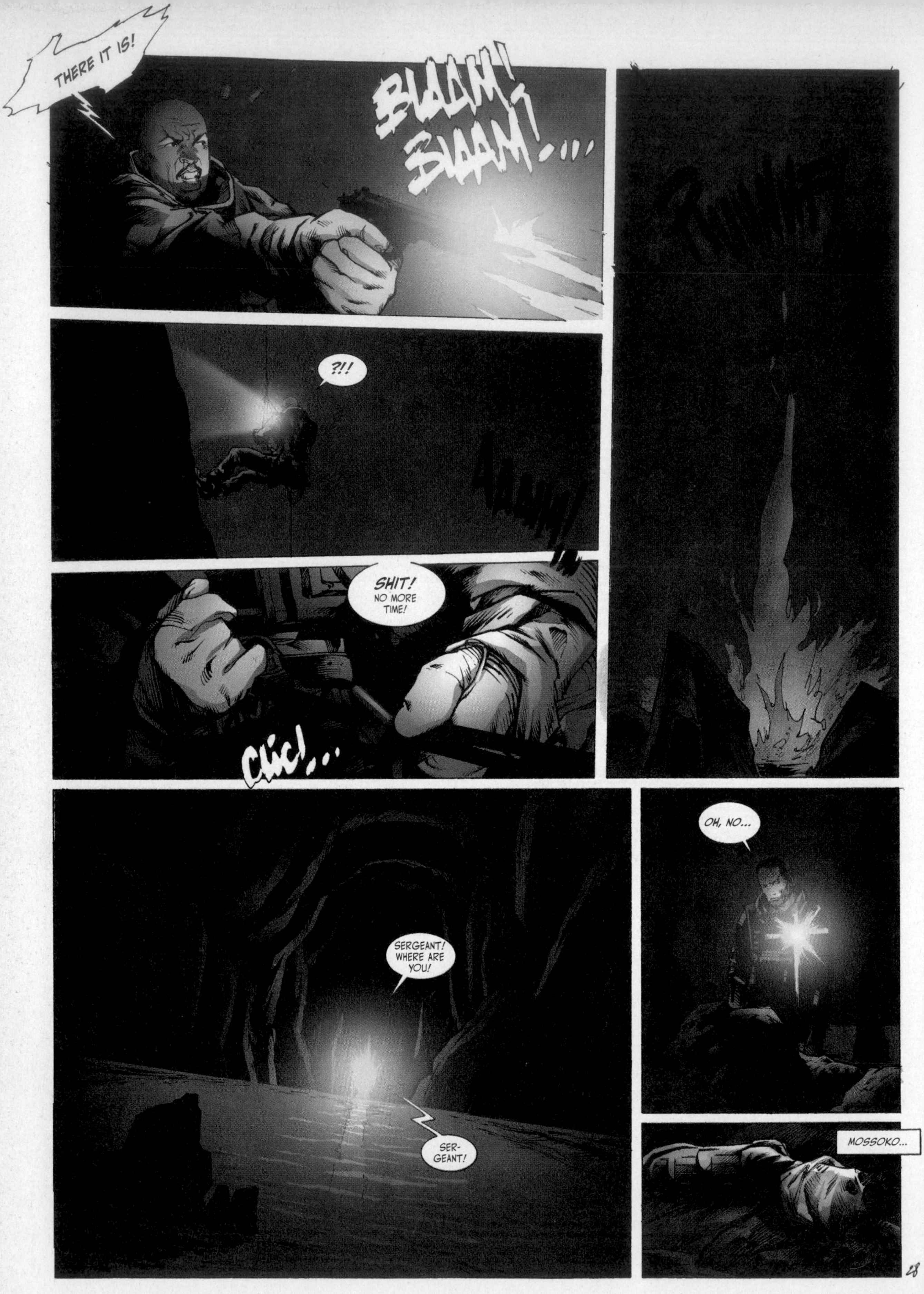
THERE IT IS!
BLAAM! BLAAM!...
?!!
SHIT! NO MORE TIME!
CLIC!...
SERGEANT! WHERE ARE YOU!
SER-GEANT!
OH, NO...
MOSSOKO...

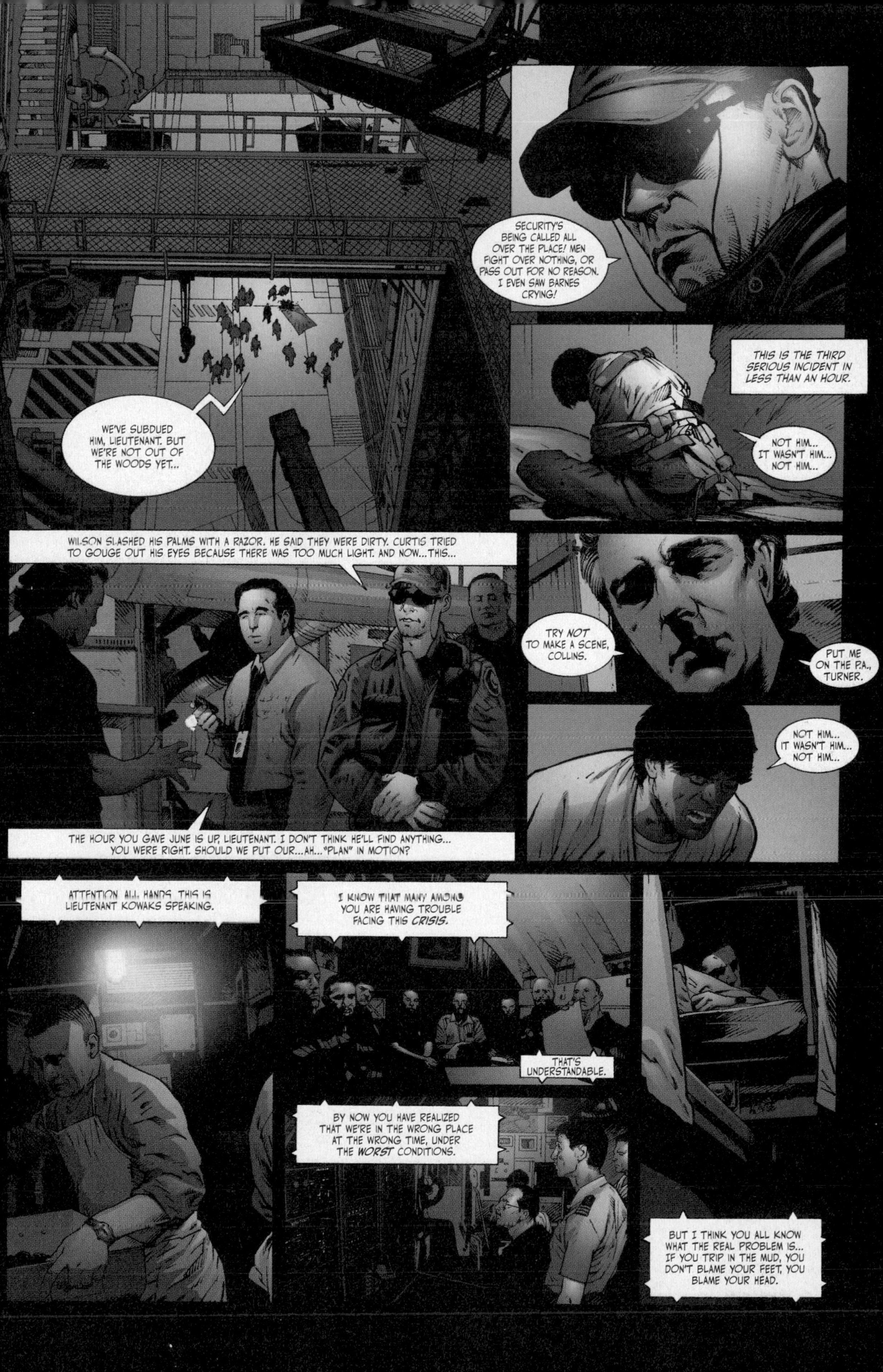
SECURITY'S BEING CALLED ALL OVER THE PLACE! MEN FIGHT OVER NOTHING, OR PASS OUT FOR NO REASON. I EVEN SAW BARNES CRYING!
WE'VE SUBDUED HIM, LIEUTENANT. BUT WE'RE NOT OUT OF THE WOODS YET...
THIS IS THE THIRD SERIOUS INCIDENT IN LESS THAN AN HOUR.
NOT HIM... IT WASN'T HIM... NOT HIM...
WILSON SLASHED HIS PALMS WITH A RAZOR. HE SAID THEY WERE DIRTY. CURTIS TRIED TO GOUGE OUT HIS EYES BECAUSE THERE WAS TOO MUCH LIGHT. AND NOW... THIS...
THE HOUR YOU GAVE JUNE IS UP, LIEUTENANT. I DON'T THINK HE'LL FIND ANYTHING... YOU WERE RIGHT. SHOULD WE PUT OUR... AH... "PLAN" IN MOTION?
TRY NOT TO MAKE A SCENE, COLLINS.
PUT ME ON THE P.A., TURNER.
NOT HIM... IT WASN'T HIM... NOT HIM...
ATTENTION ALL HANDS. THIS IS LIEUTENANT KOWAKS SPEAKING.
I KNOW THAT MANY AMONG YOU ARE HAVING TROUBLE FACING THIS CRISIS.
THAT'S UNDERSTANDABLE.
BY NOW YOU HAVE REALIZED THAT WE'RE IN THE WRONG PLACE AT THE WRONG TIME, UNDER THE WORST CONDITIONS.
BUT I THINK YOU ALL KNOW WHAT THE REAL PROBLEM IS... IF YOU TRIP IN THE MUD, YOU DON'T BLAME YOUR FEET, YOU BLAME YOUR HEAD.

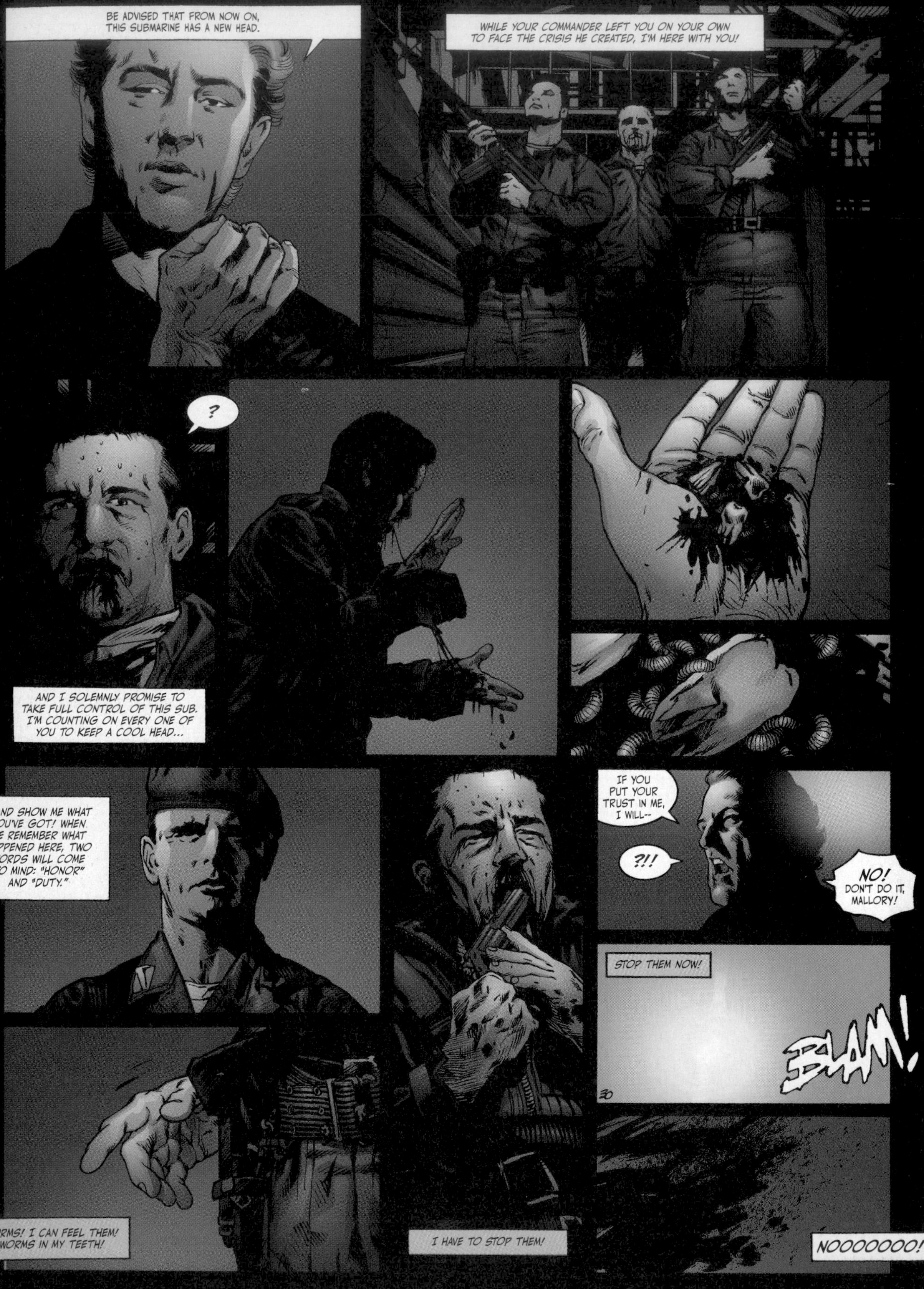
BE ADVISED THAT FROM NOW ON, THIS SUBMARINE HAS A NEW HEAD.
WHILE YOUR COMMANDER LEFT YOU ON YOUR OWN TO FACE THE CRISIS HE CREATED, I'M HERE WITH YOU!
?
AND I SOLEMNLY PROMISE TO TAKE FULL CONTROL OF THIS SUB. I'M COUNTING ON EVERY ONE OF YOU TO KEEP A COOL HEAD...
...AND SHOW ME WHAT YOU'VE GOT! WHEN WE REMEMBER WHAT HAPPENED HERE, TWO WORDS WILL COME TO MIND: "HONOR" AND "DUTY."
WORMS! I CAN FEEL THEM! WORMS IN MY TEETH!
I HAVE TO STOP THEM!
IF YOU PUT YOUR TRUST IN ME, I WILL--
?!!
NO! DON'T DO IT, MALLORY!
STOP THEM NOW!
BLAM!
30
NOOOOOOO!

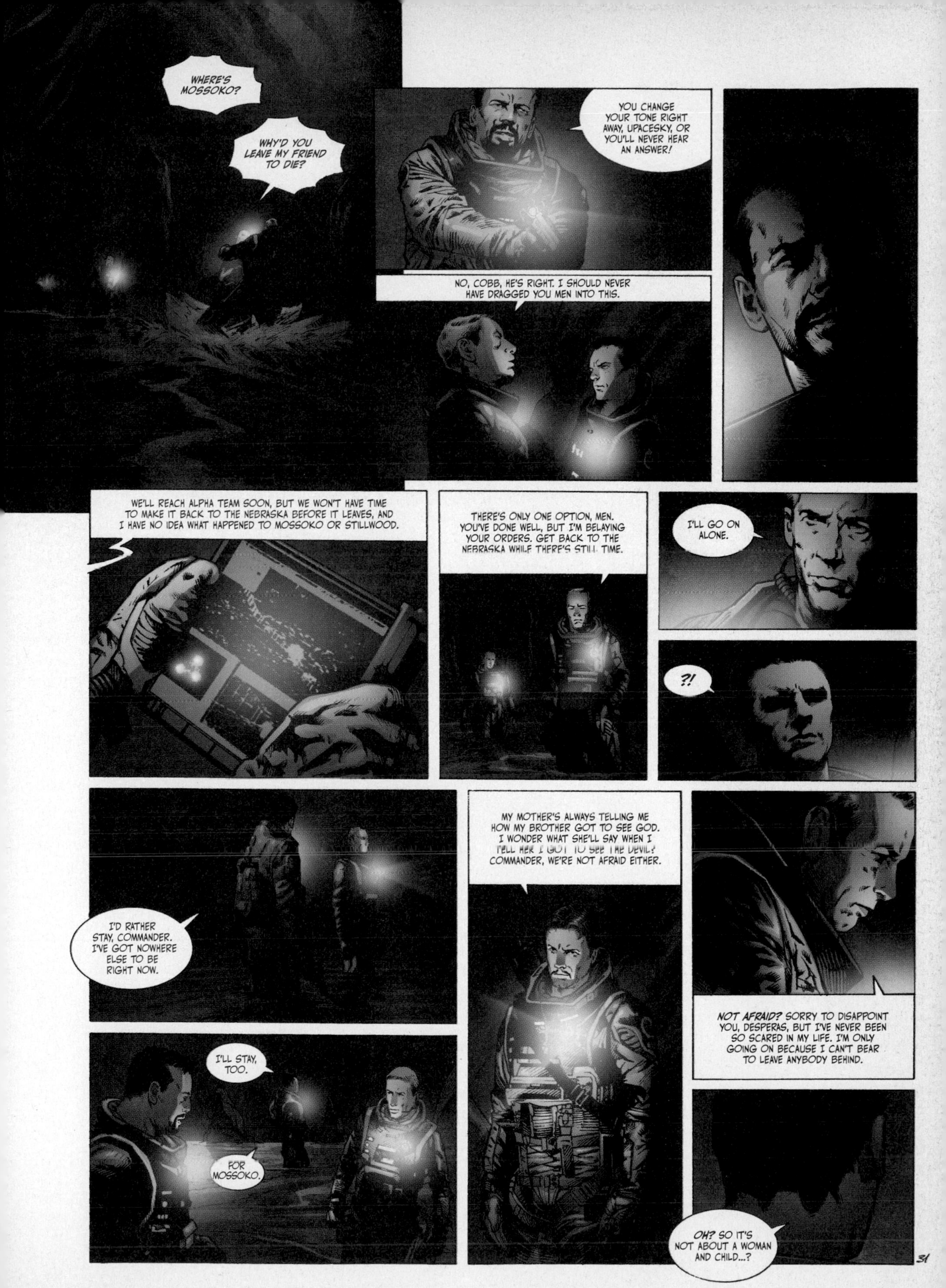
WHERE'S MOSSOKO?
WHY'D YOU LEAVE MY FRIEND TO DIE?
YOU CHANGE YOUR TONE RIGHT AWAY, UPACESKY, OR YOU'LL NEVER HEAR AN ANSWER!
NO, COBB, HE'S RIGHT. I SHOULD NEVER HAVE DRAGGED YOU MEN INTO THIS.
WE'LL REACH ALPHA TEAM SOON, BUT WE WON'T HAVE TIME TO MAKE IT BACK TO THE NEBRASKA BEFORE IT LEAVES, AND I HAVE NO IDEA WHAT HAPPENED TO MOSSOKO OR STILLWOOD.
THERE'S ONLY ONE OPTION, MEN. YOU'VE DONE WELL, BUT I'M BELAYING YOUR ORDERS. GET BACK TO THE NEBRASKA WHILE THERE'S STILL TIME.
I'LL GO ON ALONE.
?!
I'D RATHER STAY, COMMANDER. I'VE GOT NOWHERE ELSE TO BE RIGHT NOW.
I'LL STAY, TOO.
FOR MOSSOKO.
MY MOTHER'S ALWAYS TELLING ME HOW MY BROTHER GOT TO SEE GOD. I WONDER WHAT SHE'LL SAY WHEN I TELL HER I GOT TO SEE THE DEVIL? COMMANDER, WE'RE NOT AFRAID EITHER.
NOT AFRAID? SORRY TO DISAPPOINT YOU, DESPERAS, BUT I'VE NEVER BEEN SO SCARED IN MY LIFE. I'M ONLY GOING ON BECAUSE I CAN'T BEAR TO LEAVE ANYBODY BEHIND.
OH? SO IT'S NOT ABOUT A WOMAN AND CHILD...?
31

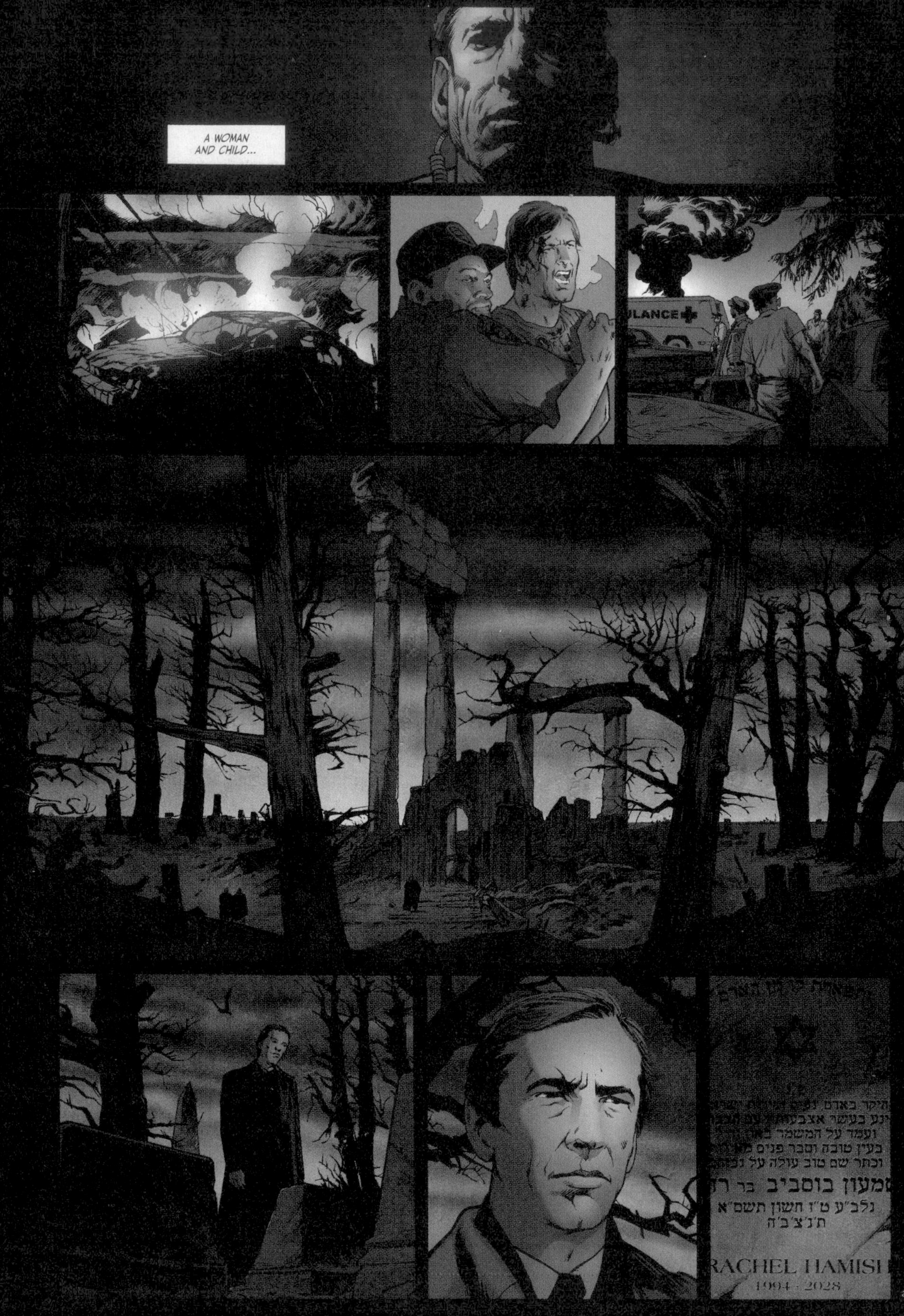
A WOMAN AND CHILD...
RACHEL HAMISI
1994 - 2028

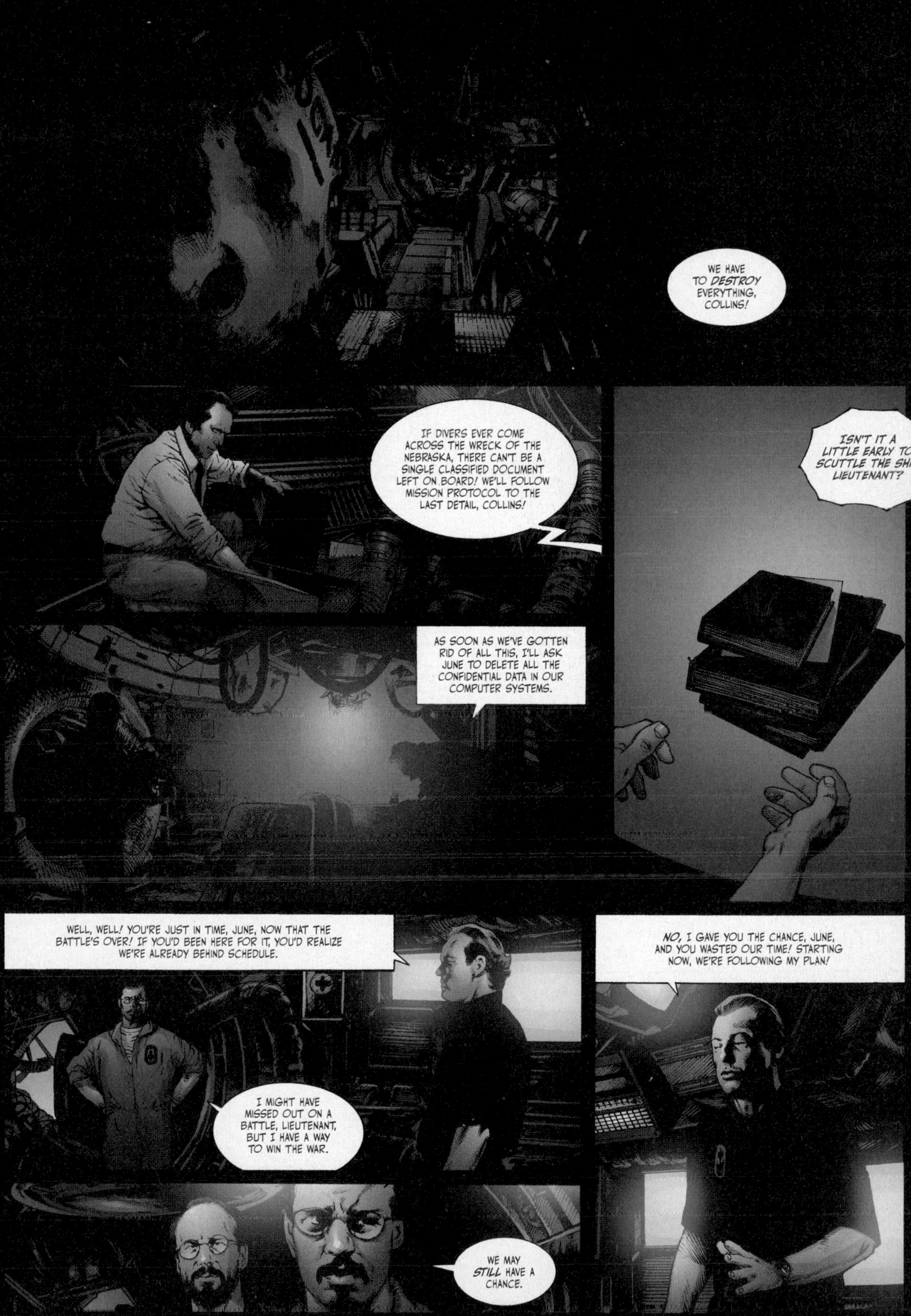
WE HAVE TO DESTROY EVERYTHING, COLLINS!
IF DIVERS EVER COME ACROSS THE WRECK OF THE NEBRASKA, THERE CAN'T BE A SINGLE CLASSIFIED DOCUMENT LEFT ON BOARD! WE'LL FOLLOW MISSION PROTOCOL TO THE LAST DETAIL, COLLINS!
ISN'T IT A LITTLE EARLY TO SCUTTLE THE SHIP, LIEUTENANT?
AS SOON AS WE'VE GOTTEN RID OF ALL THIS, I'LL ASK JUNE TO DELETE ALL THE CONFIDENTIAL DATA IN OUR COMPUTER SYSTEMS.
WELL, WELL! YOU'RE JUST IN TIME, JUNE, NOW THAT THE BATTLE'S OVER! IF YOU'D BEEN HERE FOR IT, YOU'D REALIZE WE'RE ALREADY BEHIND SCHEDULE.
I MIGHT HAVE MISSED OUT ON A BATTLE, LIEUTENANT, BUT I HAVE A WAY TO WIN THE WAR.
WE MAY STILL HAVE A CHANCE.
NO, I GAVE YOU THE CHANCE, JUNE, AND YOU WASTED OUR TIME! STARTING NOW, WE'RE FOLLOWING MY PLAN!

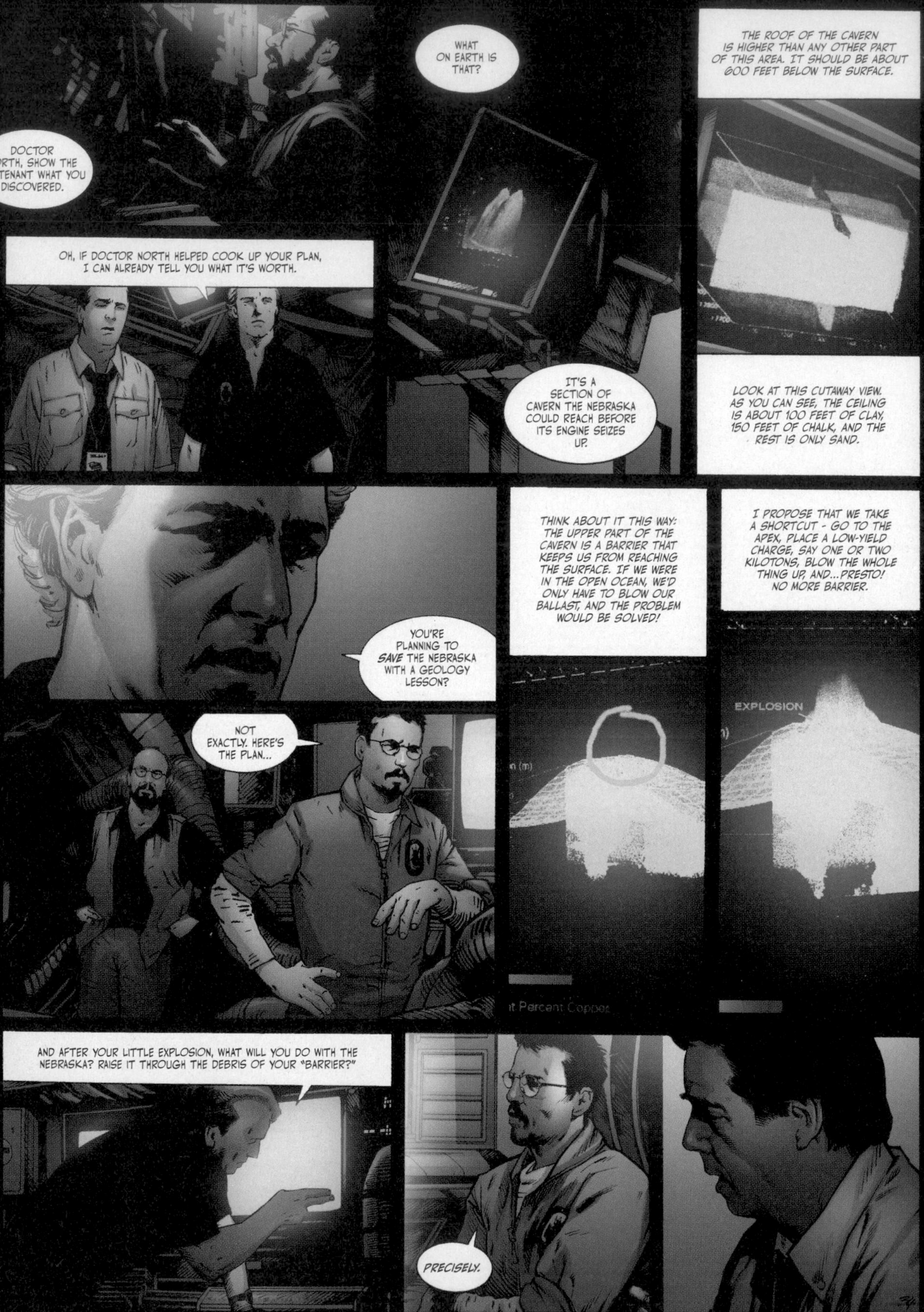
DOCTOR NORTH, SHOW THE LIEUTENANT WHAT YOU DISCOVERED.
OH, IF DOCTOR NORTH HELPED COOK UP YOUR PLAN, I CAN ALREADY TELL YOU WHAT IT'S WORTH.
WHAT ON EARTH IS THAT?
IT'S A SECTION OF CAVERN THE NEBRASKA COULD REACH BEFORE ITS ENGINE SEIZES UP.
THE ROOF OF THE CAVERN IS HIGHER THAN ANY OTHER PART OF THIS AREA. IT SHOULD BE ABOUT 600 FEET BELOW THE SURFACE.
LOOK AT THIS CUTAWAY VIEW. AS YOU CAN SEE, THE CEILING IS ABOUT 100 FEET OF CLAY, 150 FEET OF CHALK, AND THE REST IS ONLY SAND.
YOU'RE PLANNING TO *SAVE* THE NEBRASKA WITH A GEOLOGY LESSON?
NOT EXACTLY. HERE'S THE PLAN...
THINK ABOUT IT THIS WAY: THE UPPER PART OF THE CAVERN IS A BARRIER THAT KEEPS US FROM REACHING THE SURFACE. IF WE WERE IN THE OPEN OCEAN, WE'D ONLY HAVE TO BLOW OUR BALLAST, AND THE PROBLEM WOULD BE SOLVED!
I PROPOSE THAT WE TAKE A SHORTCUT - GO TO THE APEX, PLACE A LOW-YIELD CHARGE, SAY ONE OR TWO KILOTONS, BLOW THE WHOLE THING UP, AND...PRESTO! NO MORE BARRIER.
EXPLOSION
AND AFTER YOUR LITTLE EXPLOSION, WHAT WILL YOU DO WITH THE NEBRASKA? RAISE IT THROUGH THE DEBRIS OF YOUR "BARRIER?"
PRECISELY.

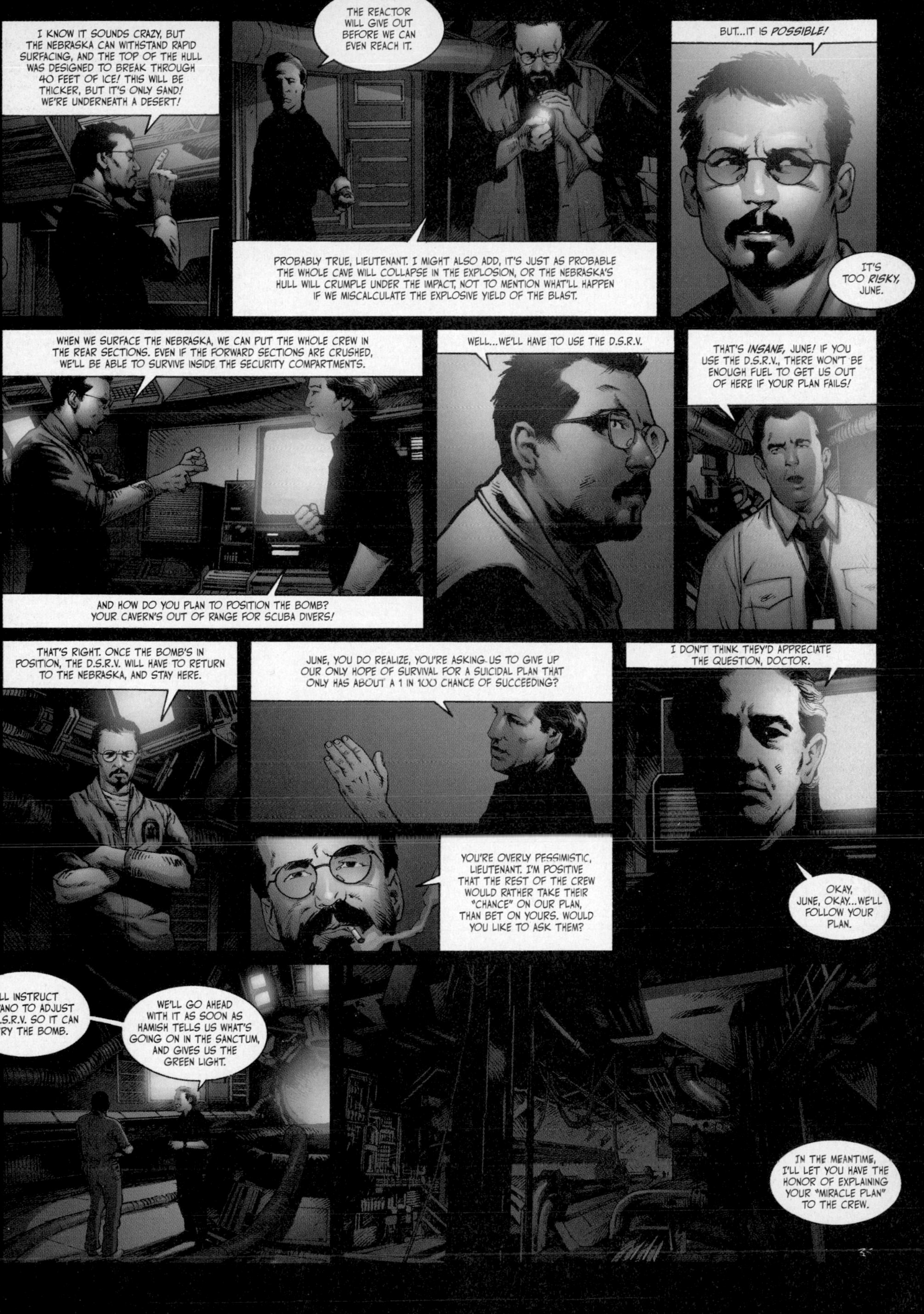
I KNOW IT SOUNDS CRAZY, BUT THE NEBRASKA CAN WITHSTAND RAPID SURFACING, AND THE TOP OF THE HULL WAS DESIGNED TO BREAK THROUGH 40 FEET OF ICE! THIS WILL BE THICKER, BUT IT'S ONLY SAND! WE'RE UNDERNEATH A DESERT!
THE REACTOR WILL GIVE OUT BEFORE WE CAN EVEN REACH IT.
PROBABLY TRUE, LIEUTENANT. I MIGHT ALSO ADD, IT'S JUST AS PROBABLE THE WHOLE CAVE WILL COLLAPSE IN THE EXPLOSION, OR THE NEBRASKA'S HULL WILL CRUMPLE UNDER THE IMPACT, NOT TO MENTION WHAT'LL HAPPEN IF WE MISCALCULATE THE EXPLOSIVE YIELD OF THE BLAST.
BUT...IT IS POSSIBLE!
IT'S TOO RISKY, JUNE.
WHEN WE SURFACE THE NEBRASKA, WE CAN PUT THE WHOLE CREW IN THE REAR SECTIONS. EVEN IF THE FORWARD SECTIONS ARE CRUSHED, WE'LL BE ABLE TO SURVIVE INSIDE THE SECURITY COMPARTMENTS.
AND HOW DO YOU PLAN TO POSITION THE BOMB? YOUR CAVERN'S OUT OF RANGE FOR SCUBA DIVERS!
WELL...WE'LL HAVE TO USE THE D.S.R.V.
THAT'S INSANE, JUNE! IF YOU USE THE D.S.R.V., THERE WON'T BE ENOUGH FUEL TO GET US OUT OF HERE IF YOUR PLAN FAILS!
THAT'S RIGHT. ONCE THE BOMB'S IN POSITION, THE D.S.R.V. WILL HAVE TO RETURN TO THE NEBRASKA, AND STAY HERE.
JUNE, YOU DO REALIZE, YOU'RE ASKING US TO GIVE UP OUR ONLY HOPE OF SURVIVAL FOR A SUICIDAL PLAN THAT ONLY HAS ABOUT A 1 IN 100 CHANCE OF SUCCEEDING?
YOU'RE OVERLY PESSIMISTIC, LIEUTENANT. I'M POSITIVE THAT THE REST OF THE CREW WOULD RATHER TAKE THEIR "CHANCE" ON OUR PLAN, THAN BET ON YOURS. WOULD YOU LIKE TO ASK THEM?
I DON'T THINK THEY'D APPRECIATE THE QUESTION, DOCTOR.
OKAY, JUNE, OKAY...WE'LL FOLLOW YOUR PLAN.
I'LL INSTRUCT SERRANO TO ADJUST THE D.S.R.V. SO IT CAN CARRY THE BOMB.
WE'LL GO AHEAD WITH IT AS SOON AS HAMISH TELLS US WHAT'S GOING ON IN THE SANCTUM, AND GIVES US THE GREEN LIGHT.
IN THE MEANTIME, I'LL LET YOU HAVE THE HONOR OF EXPLAINING YOUR "MIRACLE PLAN" TO THE CREW.

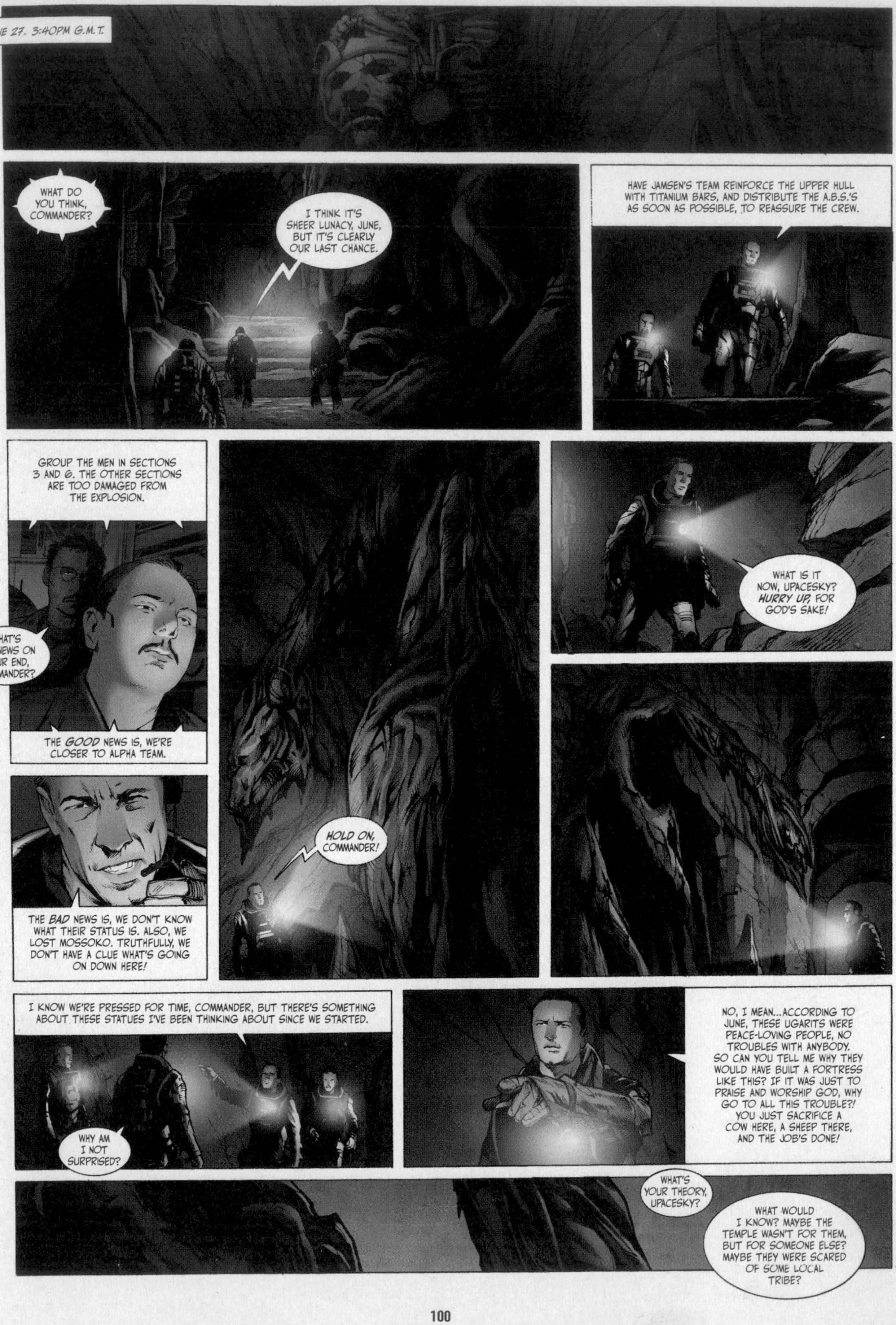

JUNE 27. 3:40PM G.M.T.
WHAT DO YOU THINK, COMMANDER?
I THINK IT'S SHEER LUNACY, JUNE, BUT IT'S CLEARLY OUR LAST CHANCE.
HAVE JAMSEN'S TEAM REINFORCE THE UPPER HULL WITH TITANIUM BARS, AND DISTRIBUTE THE A.B.S.'S AS SOON AS POSSIBLE, TO REASSURE THE CREW.
GROUP THE MEN IN SECTIONS 3 AND 6. THE OTHER SECTIONS ARE TOO DAMAGED FROM THE EXPLOSION.
WHAT'S THE NEWS ON YOUR END, COMMANDER?
THE GOOD NEWS IS, WE'RE CLOSER TO ALPHA TEAM.
THE BAD NEWS IS, WE DON'T KNOW WHAT THEIR STATUS IS. ALSO, WE LOST MOSSOKO. TRUTHFULLY, WE DON'T HAVE A CLUE WHAT'S GOING ON DOWN HERE!
HOLD ON, COMMANDER!
WHAT IS IT NOW, UPACESKY? HURRY UP, FOR GOD'S SAKE!
I KNOW WE'RE PRESSED FOR TIME, COMMANDER, BUT THERE'S SOMETHING ABOUT THESE STATUES I'VE BEEN THINKING ABOUT SINCE WE STARTED.
WHY AM I NOT SURPRISED?
NO, I MEAN...ACCORDING TO JUNE, THESE UGARITS WERE PEACE-LOVING PEOPLE, NO TROUBLES WITH ANYBODY. SO CAN YOU TELL ME WHY THEY WOULD HAVE BUILT A FORTRESS LIKE THIS? IF IT WAS JUST TO PRAISE AND WORSHIP GOD, WHY GO TO ALL THIS TROUBLE?! YOU JUST SACRIFICE A COW HERE, A SHEEP THERE, AND THE JOB'S DONE!
WHAT'S YOUR THEORY, UPACESKY?
WHAT WOULD I KNOW? MAYBE THE TEMPLE WASN'T FOR THEM, BUT FOR SOMEONE ELSE? MAYBE THEY WERE SCARED OF SOME LOCAL TRIBE?
36

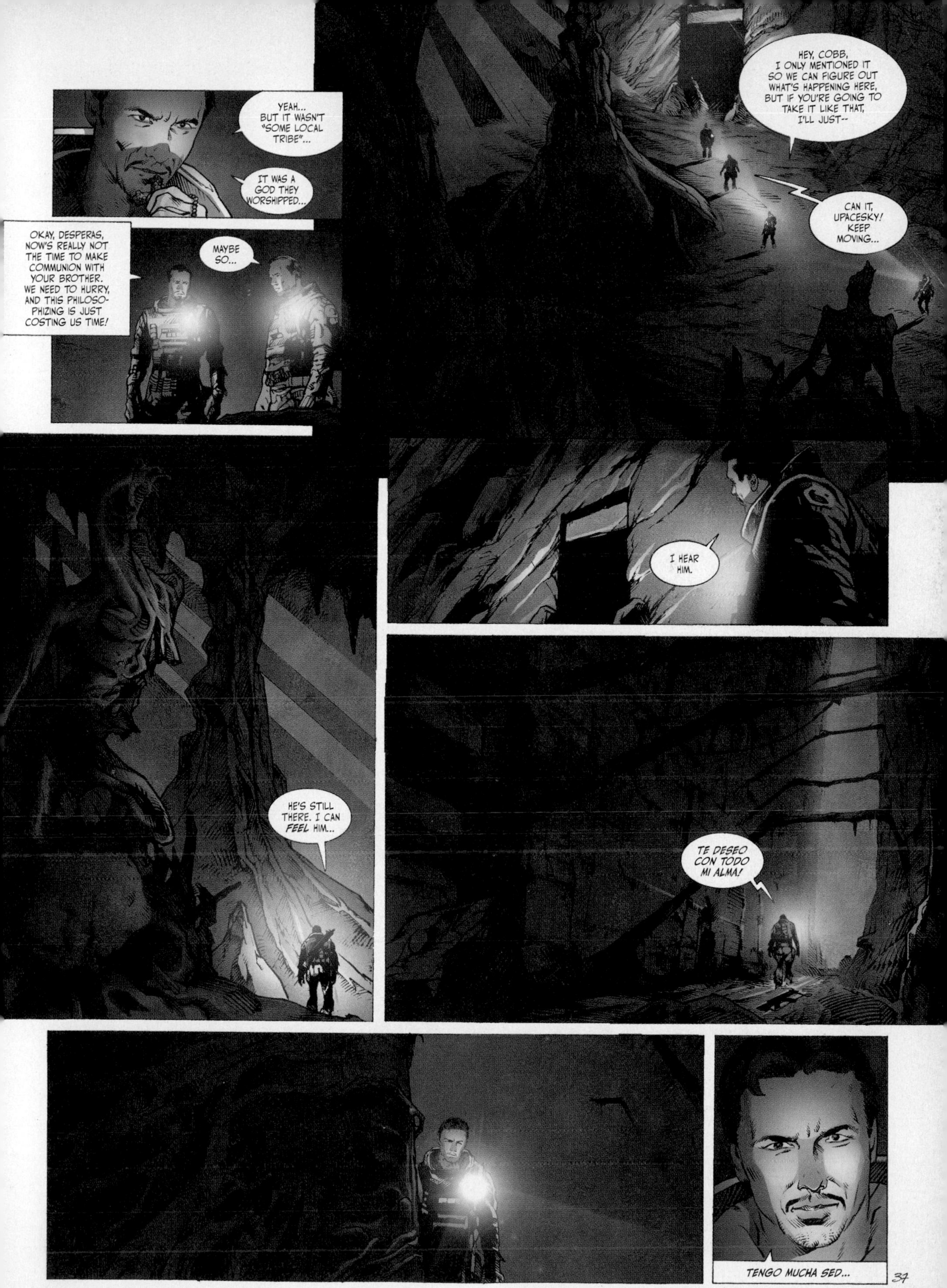
YEAH... BUT IT WASN'T "SOME LOCAL TRIBE"...
IT WAS A GOD THEY WORSHIPPED...
OKAY, DESPERAS, NOW'S REALLY NOT THE TIME TO MAKE COMMUNION WITH YOUR BROTHER. WE NEED TO HURRY, AND THIS PHILOSO-PHIZING IS JUST COSTING US TIME!
MAYBE SO...
HEY, COBB, I ONLY MENTIONED IT SO WE CAN FIGURE OUT WHAT'S HAPPENING HERE, BUT IF YOU'RE GOING TO TAKE IT LIKE THAT, I'LL JUST--
CAN IT, UPACESKY! KEEP MOVING...
HE'S STILL THERE. I CAN *FEEL* HIM...
I HEAR HIM.
TE DESEO CON TODO MI ALMA!
TENGO MUCHA SED...

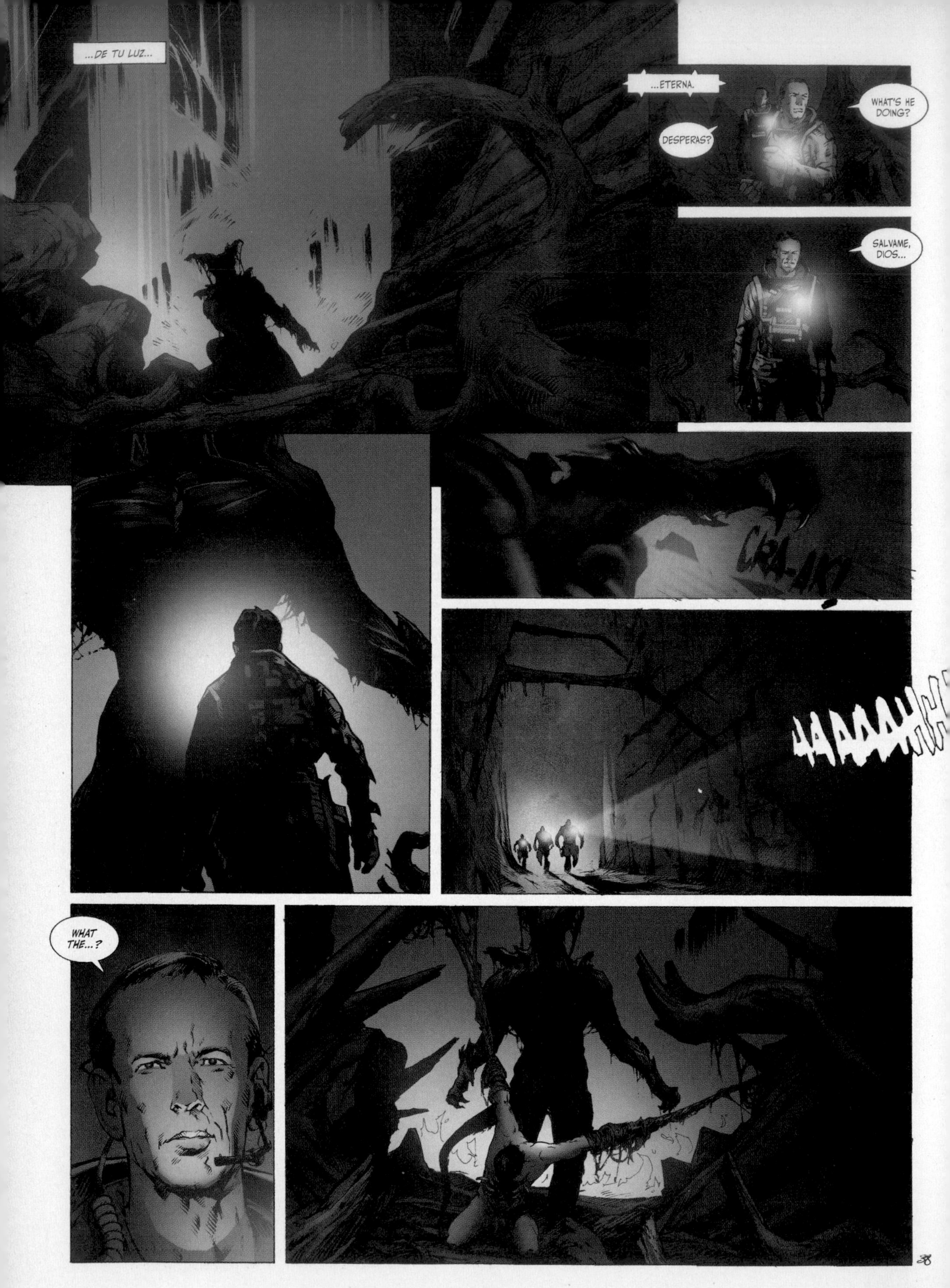
...DE TU LUZ...
...ETERNA.
DESPERAS?
WHAT'S HE DOING?
SALVAME, DIOS...
CRA-AK!
AAAAHH
WHAT THE...?

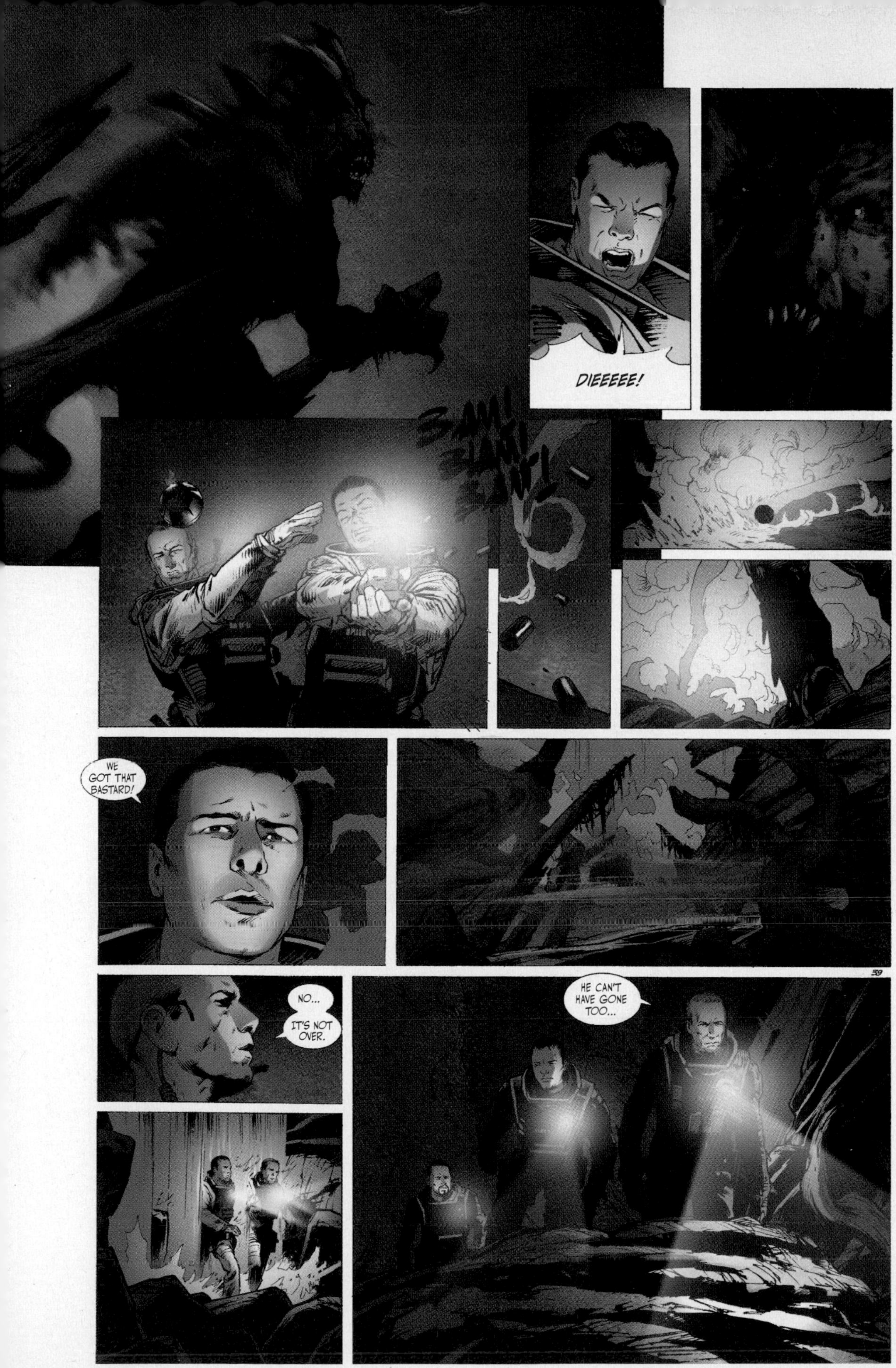
DIEEEEE!
BAM! BAM! BAM!
WE GOT THAT BASTARD!
NO... IT'S NOT OVER.
HE CAN'T HAVE GONE TOO...

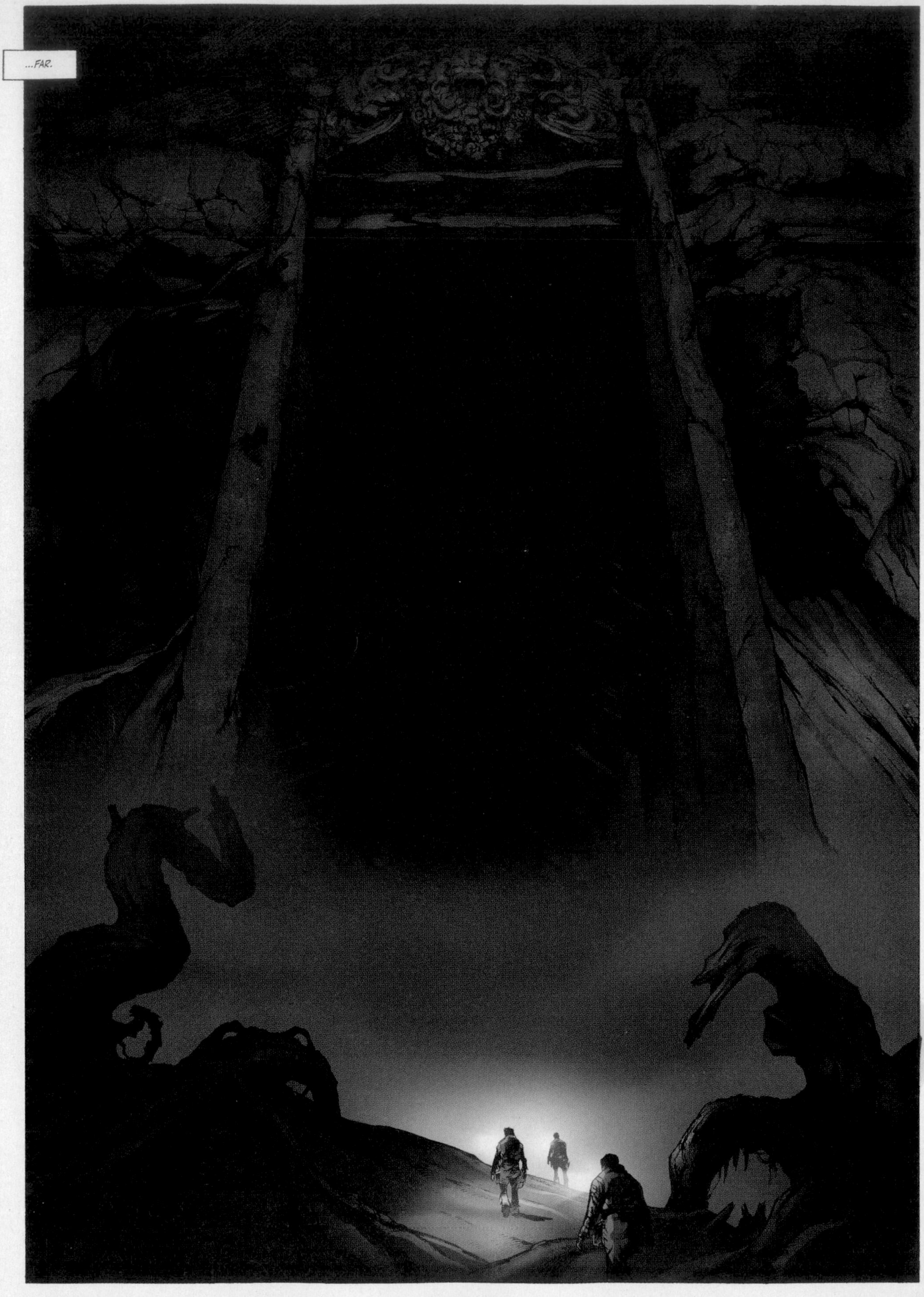
...FAR.

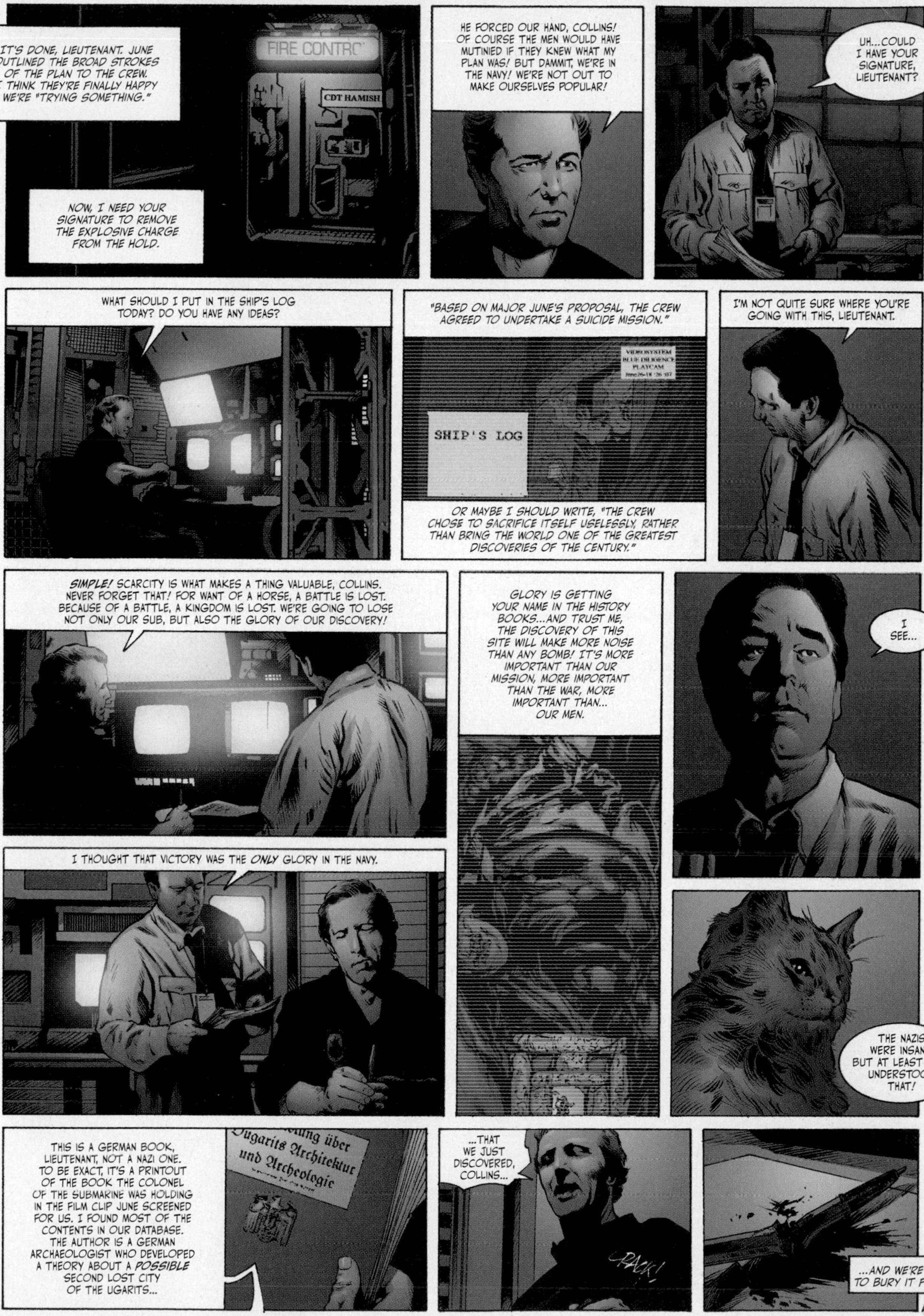
IT'S DONE, LIEUTENANT. JUNE OUTLINED THE BROAD STROKES OF THE PLAN TO THE CREW. I THINK THEY'RE FINALLY HAPPY WE'RE "TRYING SOMETHING."
FIRE CONTRO
CDT HAMISH
NOW, I NEED YOUR SIGNATURE TO REMOVE THE EXPLOSIVE CHARGE FROM THE HOLD.
HE FORCED OUR HAND, COLLINS! OF COURSE THE MEN WOULD HAVE MUTINIED IF THEY KNEW WHAT MY PLAN WAS! BUT DAMMIT, WE'RE IN THE NAVY! WE'RE NOT OUT TO MAKE OURSELVES POPULAR!
UH...COULD I HAVE YOUR SIGNATURE, LIEUTENANT?
WHAT SHOULD I PUT IN THE SHIP'S LOG TODAY? DO YOU HAVE ANY IDEAS?
"BASED ON MAJOR JUNE'S PROPOSAL, THE CREW AGREED TO UNDERTAKE A SUICIDE MISSION."
VIDEOSYSTEM
BLUE DILIGENCE
PLAYCAM
SHIP'S LOG
OR MAYBE I SHOULD WRITE, "THE CREW CHOSE TO SACRIFICE ITSELF USELESSLY, RATHER THAN BRING THE WORLD ONE OF THE GREATEST DISCOVERIES OF THE CENTURY."
I'M NOT QUITE SURE WHERE YOU'RE GOING WITH THIS, LIEUTENANT.
SIMPLE! SCARCITY IS WHAT MAKES A THING VALUABLE, COLLINS. NEVER FORGET THAT! FOR WANT OF A HORSE, A BATTLE IS LOST. BECAUSE OF A BATTLE, A KINGDOM IS LOST. WE'RE GOING TO LOSE NOT ONLY OUR SUB, BUT ALSO THE GLORY OF OUR DISCOVERY!
GLORY IS GETTING YOUR NAME IN THE HISTORY BOOKS...AND TRUST ME, THE DISCOVERY OF THIS SITE WILL MAKE MORE NOISE THAN ANY BOMB! IT'S MORE IMPORTANT THAN OUR MISSION, MORE IMPORTANT THAN THE WAR, MORE IMPORTANT THAN... OUR MEN.
I SEE...
I THOUGHT THAT VICTORY WAS THE ONLY GLORY IN THE NAVY.
THE NAZIS WERE INSANE, BUT AT LEAST THEY UNDERSTOOD THAT!
THIS IS A GERMAN BOOK, LIEUTENANT, NOT A NAZI ONE. TO BE EXACT, IT'S A PRINTOUT OF THE BOOK THE COLONEL OF THE SUBMARINE WAS HOLDING IN THE FILM CLIP JUNE SCREENED FOR US. I FOUND MOST OF THE CONTENTS IN OUR DATABASE. THE AUTHOR IS A GERMAN ARCHAEOLOGIST WHO DEVELOPED A THEORY ABOUT A POSSIBLE SECOND LOST CITY OF THE UGARITS...
Ugarits Architektur und Archeologie
...THAT WE JUST DISCOVERED, COLLINS...
CRACK!
...AND WE'RE GOING TO BURY IT FOREVER.
41

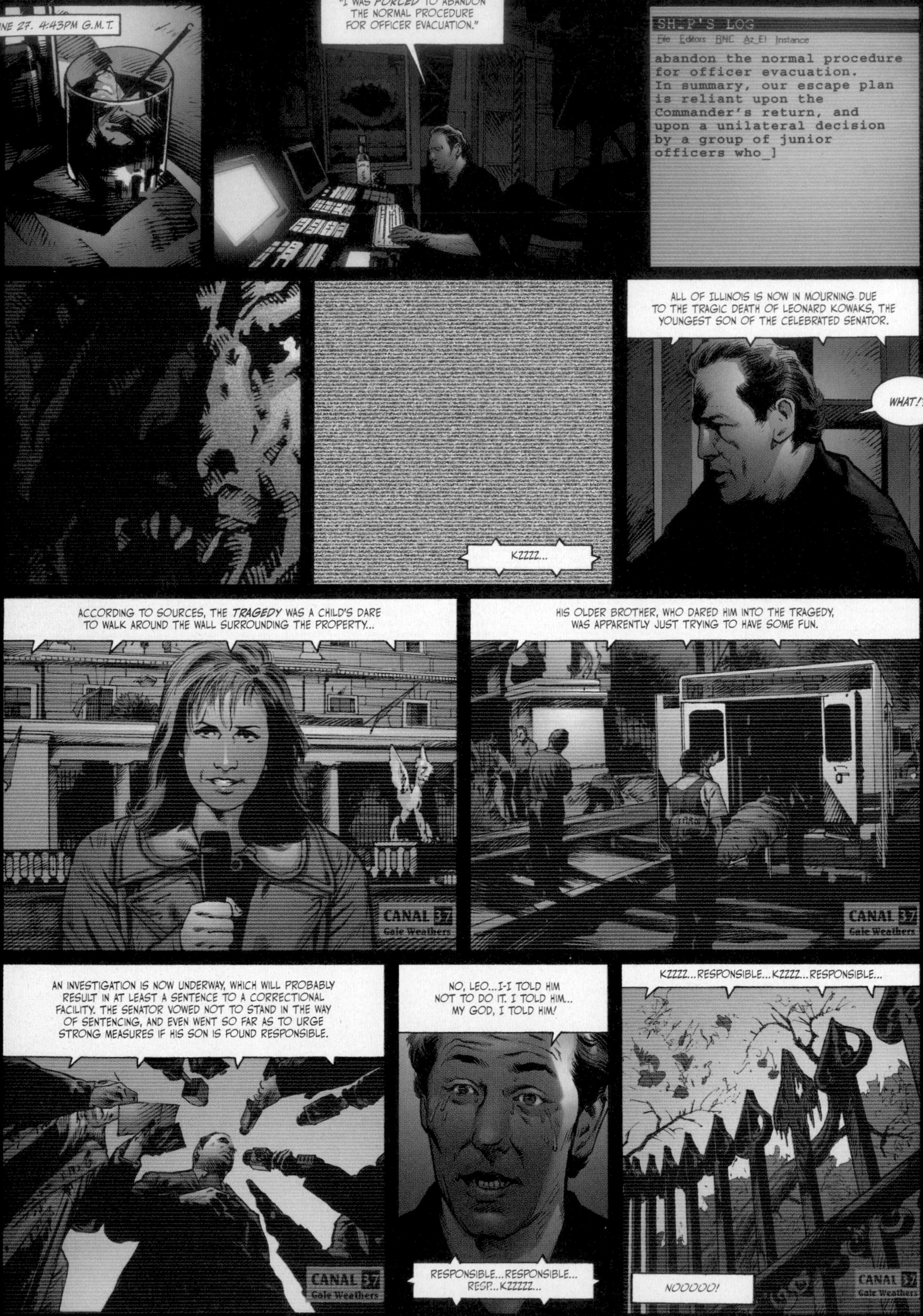
JUNE 27. 4:43PM G.M.T.
"I WAS FORCED TO ABANDON THE NORMAL PROCEDURE FOR OFFICER EVACUATION."
SHIP'S LOG
File Editors BNC Az El Instance
abandon the normal procedure for officer evacuation. In summary, our escape plan is reliant upon the Commander's return, and upon a unilateral decision by a group of junior officers who_]
KZZZZ...
ALL OF ILLINOIS IS NOW IN MOURNING DUE TO THE TRAGIC DEATH OF LEONARD KOWAKS, THE YOUNGEST SON OF THE CELEBRATED SENATOR.
WHAT!?
ACCORDING TO SOURCES, THE TRAGEDY WAS A CHILD'S DARE TO WALK AROUND THE WALL SURROUNDING THE PROPERTY...
CANAL 37
Gale Weathers
HIS OLDER BROTHER, WHO DARED HIM INTO THE TRAGEDY, WAS APPARENTLY JUST TRYING TO HAVE SOME FUN.
CANAL 37
Gale Weathers
AN INVESTIGATION IS NOW UNDERWAY, WHICH WILL PROBABLY RESULT IN AT LEAST A SENTENCE TO A CORRECTIONAL FACILITY. THE SENATOR VOWED NOT TO STAND IN THE WAY OF SENTENCING, AND EVEN WENT SO FAR AS TO URGE STRONG MEASURES IF HIS SON IS FOUND RESPONSIBLE.
CANAL 37
Gale Weathers
NO, LEO...I-I TOLD HIM NOT TO DO IT. I TOLD HIM... MY GOD, I TOLD HIM!
RESPONSIBLE...RESPONSIBLE... RESP...KZZZZZ...
KZZZZ...RESPONSIBLE...KZZZZ...RESPONSIBLE...
NOOOOO!
CANAL 37
Gale Weathers

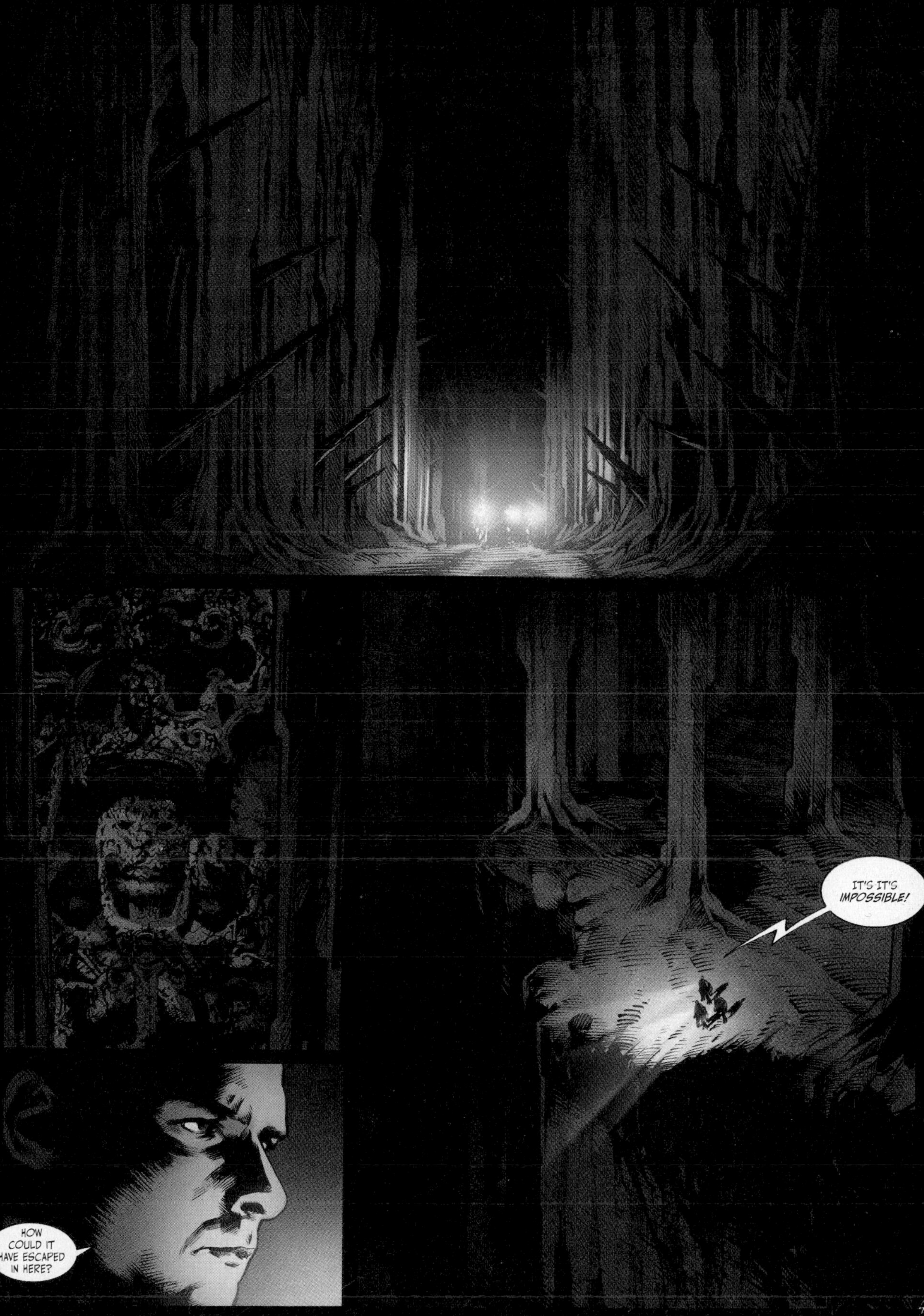
IT'S IT'S IMPOSSIBLE!
HOW COULD IT HAVE ESCAPED IN HERE?

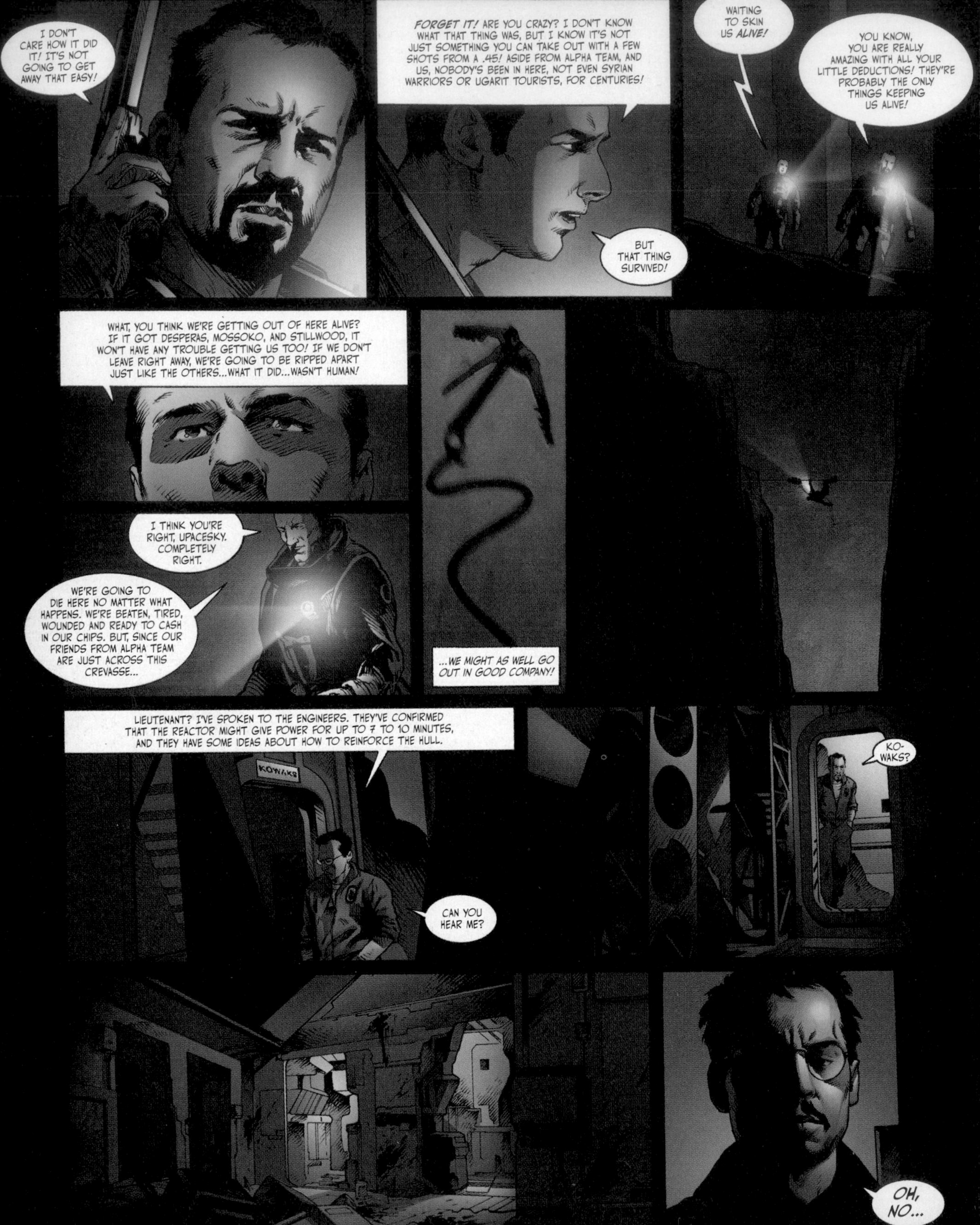

I DON'T CARE HOW IT DID IT! IT'S NOT GOING TO GET AWAY THAT EASY!
FORGET IT! ARE YOU CRAZY? I DON'T KNOW WHAT THAT THING WAS, BUT I KNOW IT'S NOT JUST SOMETHING YOU CAN TAKE OUT WITH A FEW SHOTS FROM A .45! ASIDE FROM ALPHA TEAM, AND US, NOBODY'S BEEN IN HERE, NOT EVEN SYRIAN WARRIORS OR UGARIT TOURISTS, FOR CENTURIES!
BUT THAT THING SURVIVED!
WAITING TO SKIN US ALIVE!
YOU KNOW, YOU ARE REALLY AMAZING WITH ALL YOUR LITTLE DEDUCTIONS! THEY'RE PROBABLY THE ONLY THINGS KEEPING US ALIVE!
WHAT, YOU THINK WE'RE GETTING OUT OF HERE ALIVE? IF IT GOT DESPERAS, MOSSOKO, AND STILLWOOD, IT WON'T HAVE ANY TROUBLE GETTING US TOO! IF WE DON'T LEAVE RIGHT AWAY, WE'RE GOING TO BE RIPPED APART JUST LIKE THE OTHERS...WHAT IT DID...WASN'T HUMAN!
I THINK YOU'RE RIGHT, UPACESKY. COMPLETELY RIGHT.
WE'RE GOING TO DIE HERE NO MATTER WHAT HAPPENS. WE'RE BEATEN, TIRED, WOUNDED AND READY TO CASH IN OUR CHIPS. BUT, SINCE OUR FRIENDS FROM ALPHA TEAM ARE JUST ACROSS THIS CREVASSE...
...WE MIGHT AS WELL GO OUT IN GOOD COMPANY!
LIEUTENANT? I'VE SPOKEN TO THE ENGINEERS. THEY'VE CONFIRMED THAT THE REACTOR MIGHT GIVE POWER FOR UP TO 7 TO 10 MINUTES, AND THEY HAVE SOME IDEAS ABOUT HOW TO REINFORCE THE HULL.
KOWAKS
CAN YOU HEAR ME?
KO-WAKS?
OH, NO...

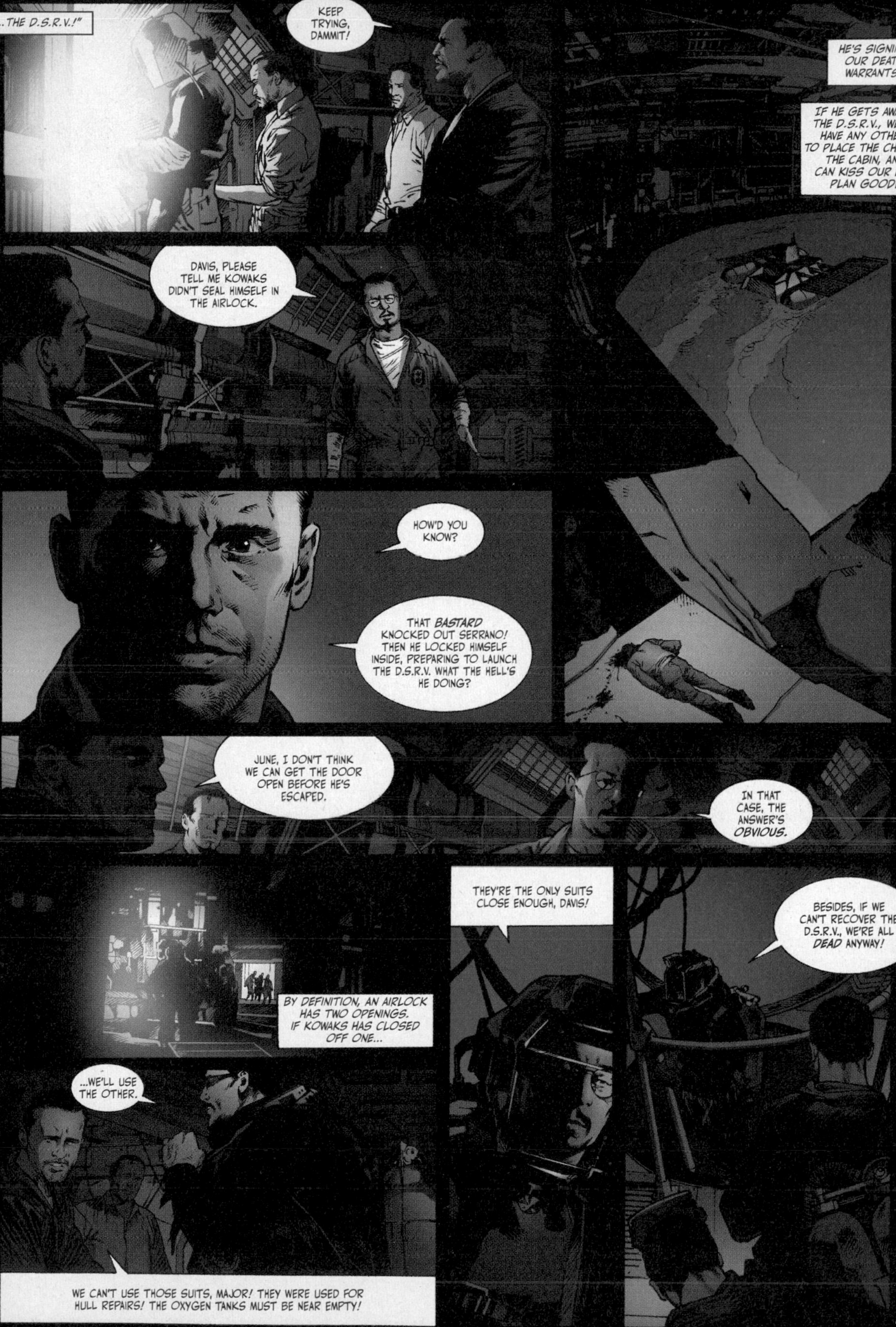
"...THE D.S.R.V.!"
KEEP TRYING, DAMMIT!
HE'S SIGNING OUR DEATH WARRANTS!
IF HE GETS AWAY WITH THE D.S.R.V., WE WON'T HAVE ANY OTHER WAY TO PLACE THE CHARGES IN THE CABIN, AND WE CAN KISS OUR ESCAPE PLAN GOODBYE!
DAVIS, PLEASE TELL ME KOWAKS DIDN'T SEAL HIMSELF IN THE AIRLOCK.
HOW'D YOU KNOW?
THAT BASTARD KNOCKED OUT SERRANO! THEN HE LOCKED HIMSELF INSIDE, PREPARING TO LAUNCH THE D.S.R.V. WHAT THE HELL'S HE DOING?
JUNE, I DON'T THINK WE CAN GET THE DOOR OPEN BEFORE HE'S ESCAPED.
IN THAT CASE, THE ANSWER'S OBVIOUS.
BY DEFINITION, AN AIRLOCK HAS TWO OPENINGS. IF KOWAKS HAS CLOSED OFF ONE...
...WE'LL USE THE OTHER.
WE CAN'T USE THOSE SUITS, MAJOR! THEY WERE USED FOR HULL REPAIRS! THE OXYGEN TANKS MUST BE NEAR EMPTY!
THEY'RE THE ONLY SUITS CLOSE ENOUGH, DAVIS!
BESIDES, IF WE CAN'T RECOVER THE D.S.R.V., WE'RE ALL DEAD ANYWAY!

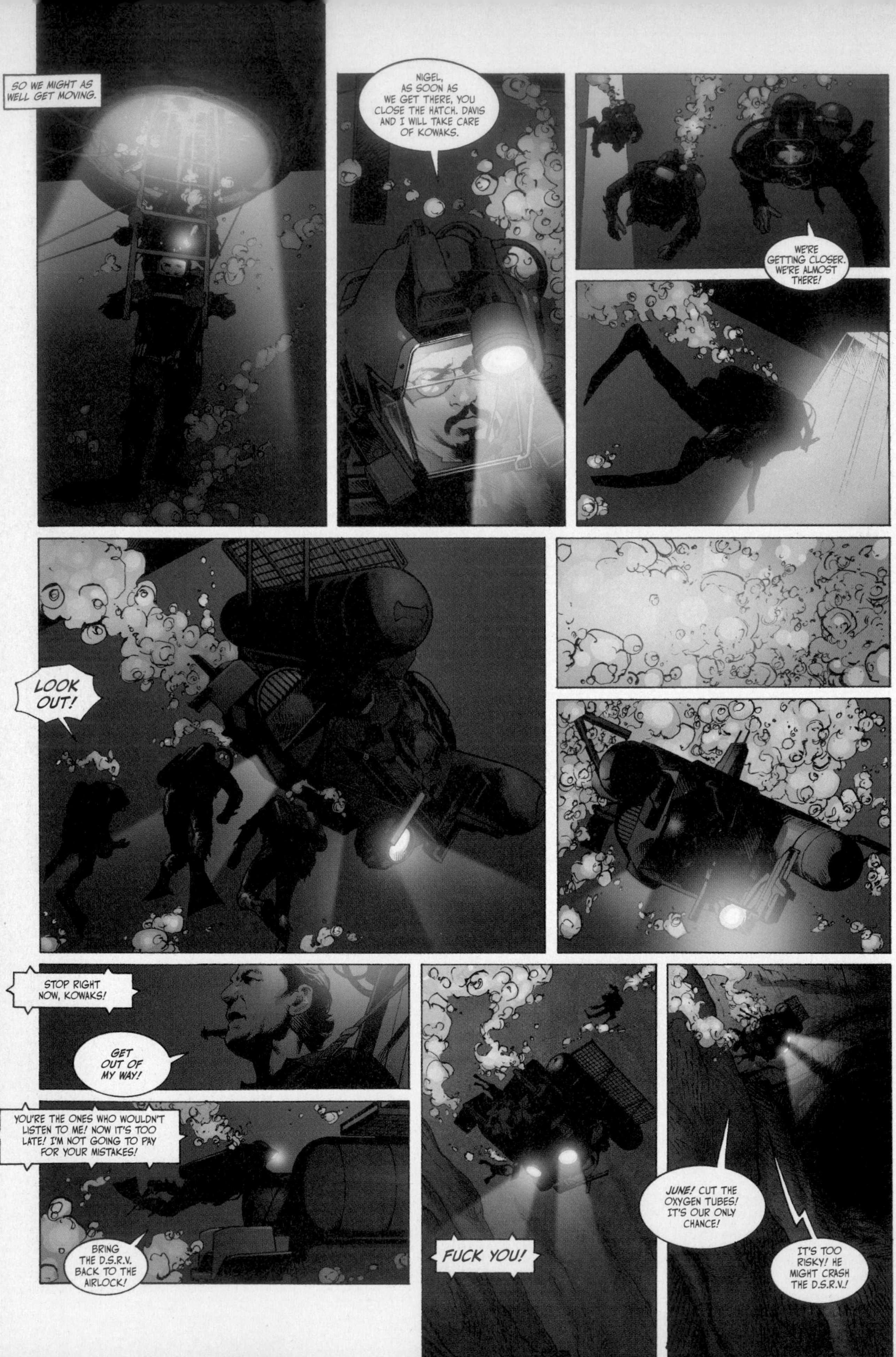
SO WE MIGHT AS WELL GET MOVING.
NIGEL, AS SOON AS WE GET THERE, YOU CLOSE THE HATCH. DAVIS AND I WILL TAKE CARE OF KOWAKS.
WE'RE GETTING CLOSER. WE'RE ALMOST THERE!
LOOK OUT!
STOP RIGHT NOW, KOWAKS!
GET OUT OF MY WAY!
YOU'RE THE ONES WHO WOULDN'T LISTEN TO ME! NOW IT'S TOO LATE! I'M NOT GOING TO PAY FOR YOUR MISTAKES!
BRING THE D.S.R.V. BACK TO THE AIRLOCK!
FUCK YOU!
JUNE! CUT THE OXYGEN TUBES! IT'S OUR ONLY CHANCE!
IT'S TOO RISKY! HE MIGHT CRASH THE D.S.R.V.!

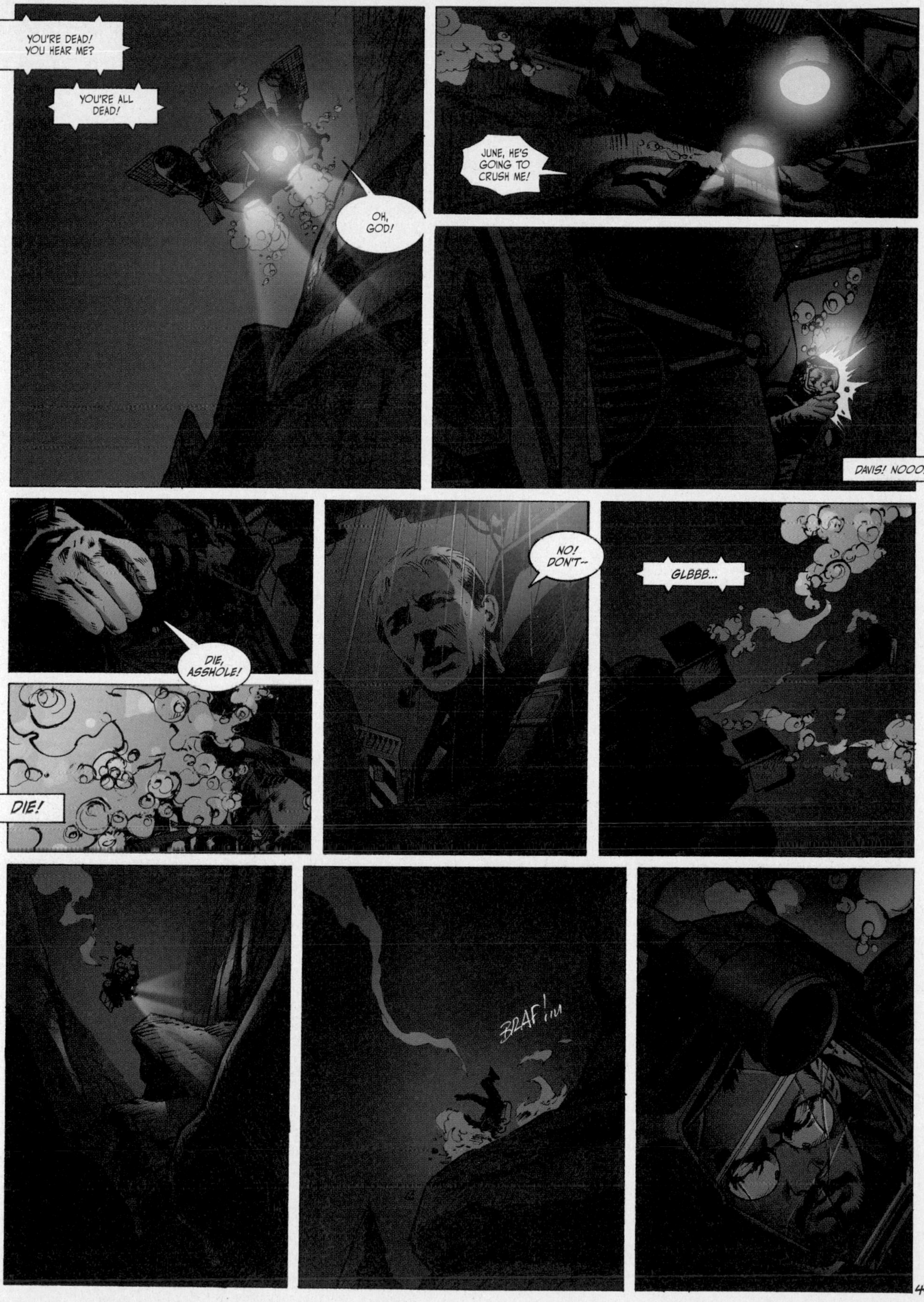
YOU'RE DEAD! YOU HEAR ME?
YOU'RE ALL DEAD!
OH, GOD!
JUNE, HE'S GOING TO CRUSH ME!
DAVIS! NOOO!
DIE, ASSHOLE!
DIE!
NO! DON'T--
GLBBB...
BRAF!
47

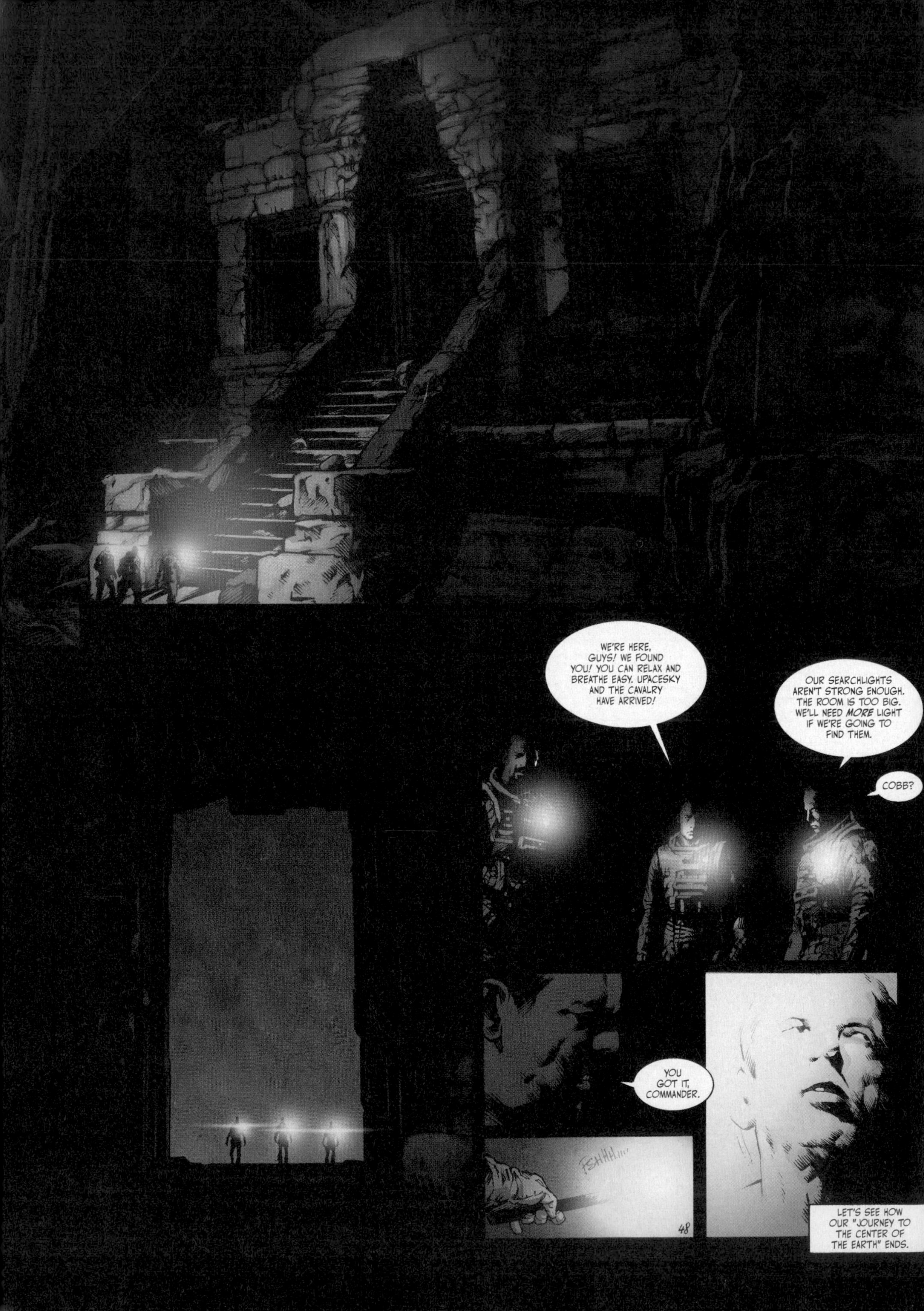
WE'RE HERE, GUYS! WE FOUND YOU! YOU CAN RELAX AND BREATHE EASY. UPACESKY AND THE CAVALRY HAVE ARRIVED!
OUR SEARCHLIGHTS AREN'T STRONG ENOUGH. THE ROOM IS TOO BIG. WE'LL NEED *MORE* LIGHT IF WE'RE GOING TO FIND THEM.
COBB?
YOU GOT IT, COMMANDER.
FSHHH...
LET'S SEE HOW OUR "JOURNEY TO THE CENTER OF THE EARTH" ENDS.

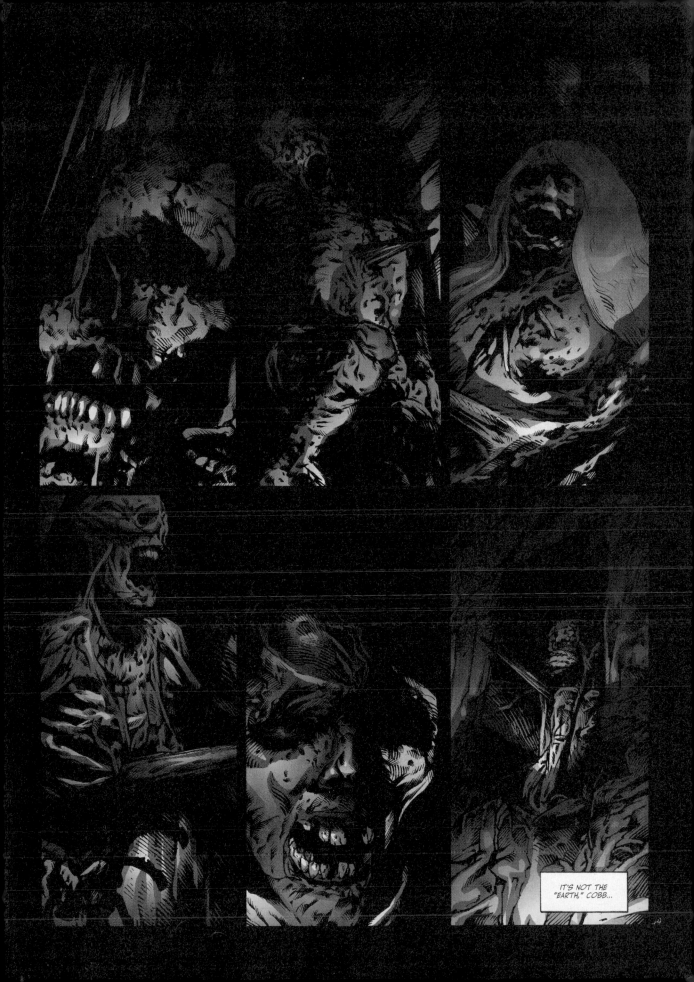

IT'S NOT THE "EARTH," COBB...

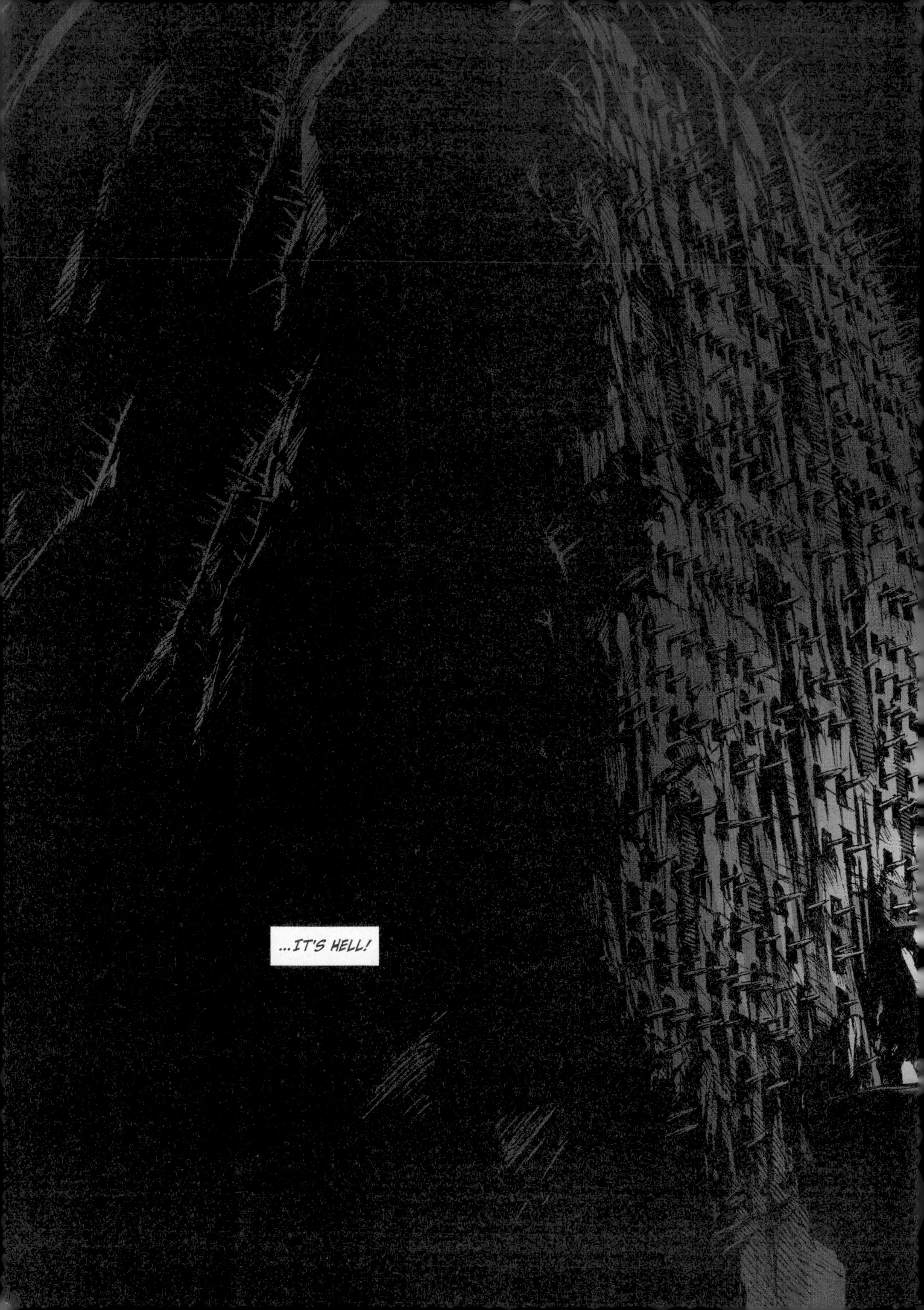
...IT'S HELL!

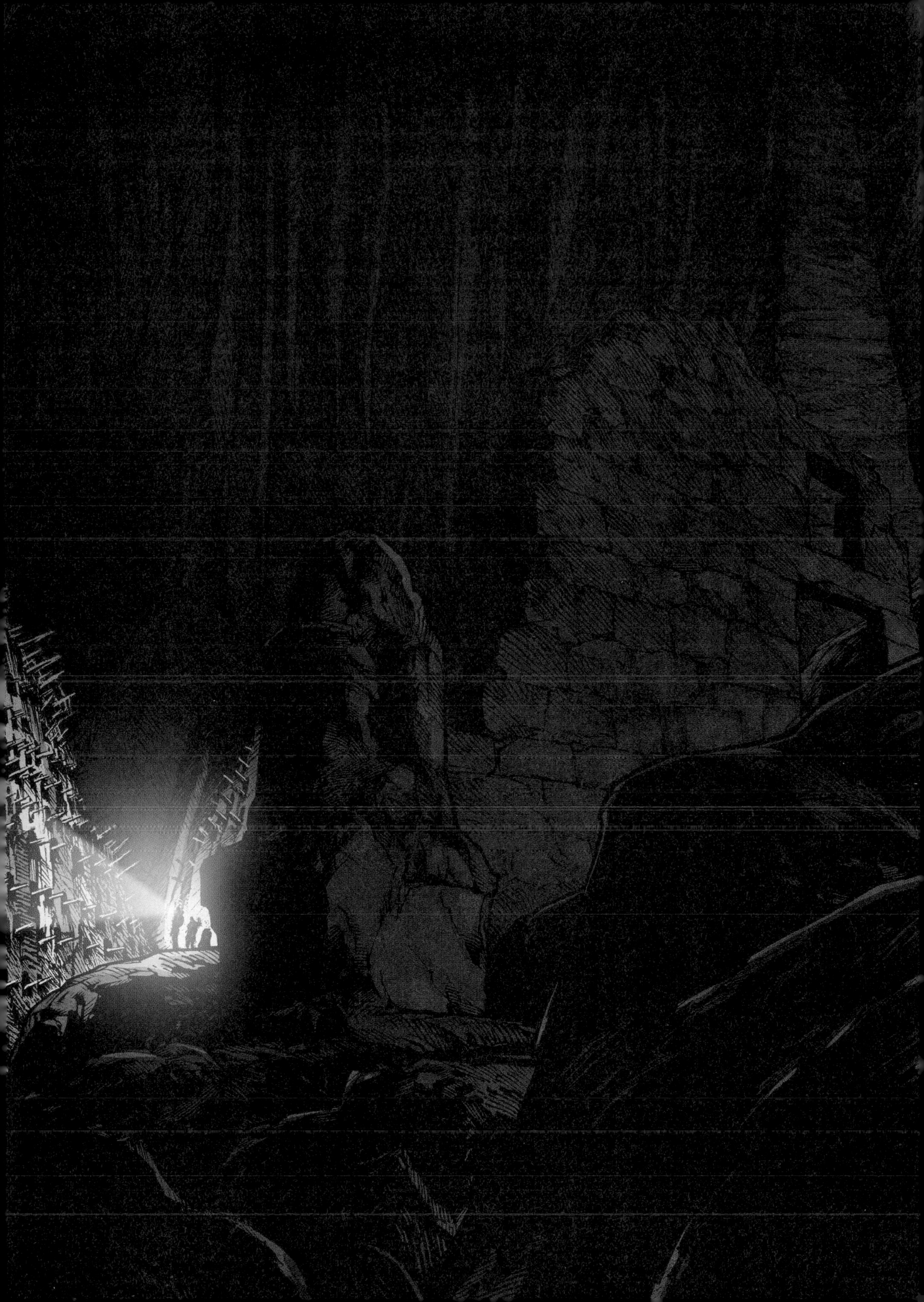

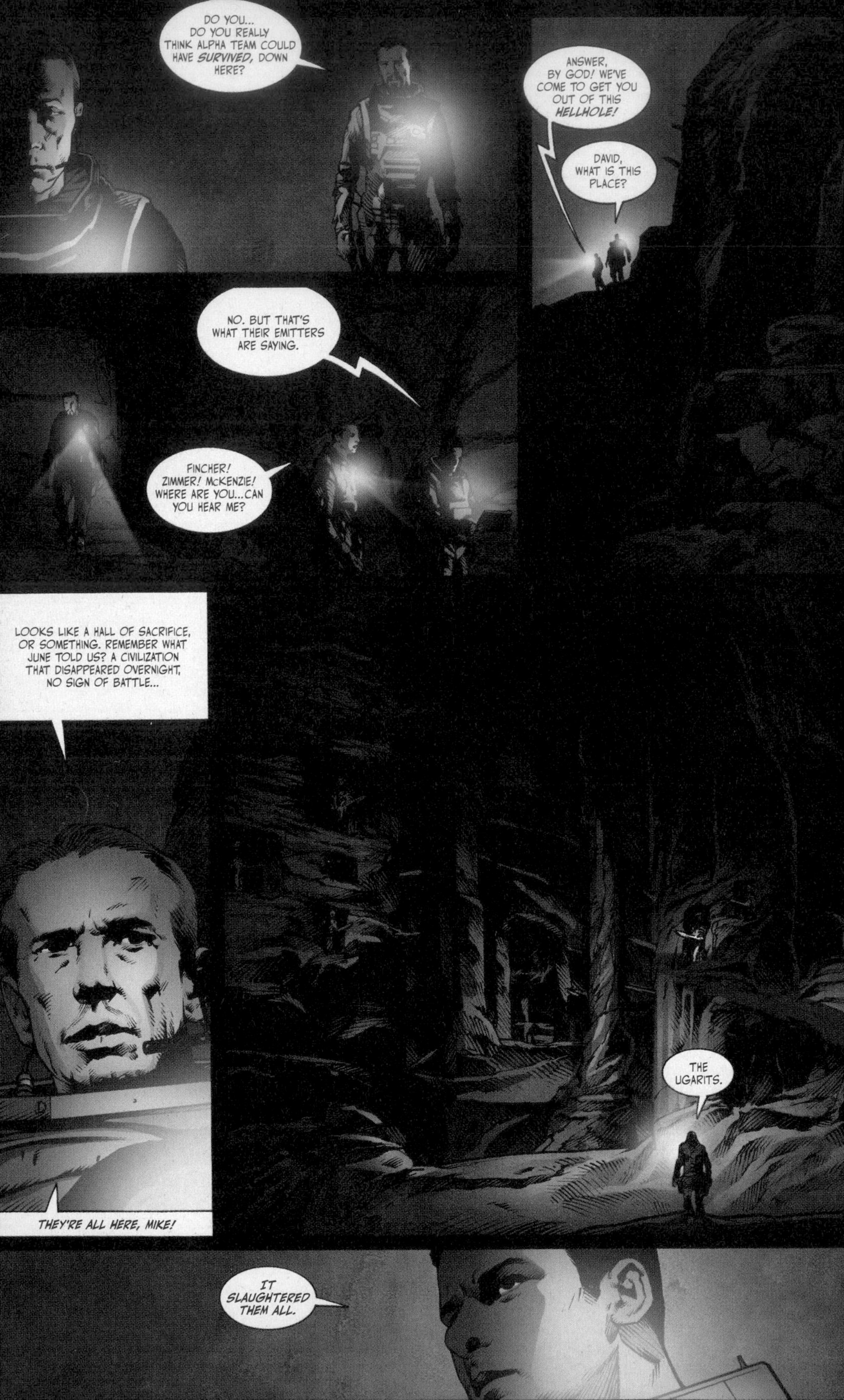
DO YOU... DO YOU REALLY THINK ALPHA TEAM COULD HAVE *SURVIVED,* DOWN HERE?
NO. BUT THAT'S WHAT THEIR EMITTERS ARE SAYING.
ANSWER, BY GOD! WE'VE COME TO GET YOU OUT OF THIS *HELLHOLE!*
FINCHER! ZIMMER! McKENZIE! WHERE ARE YOU...CAN YOU HEAR ME?
DAVID, WHAT IS THIS PLACE?
LOOKS LIKE A HALL OF SACRIFICE, OR SOMETHING. REMEMBER WHAT JUNE TOLD US? A CIVILIZATION THAT DISAPPEARED OVERNIGHT, NO SIGN OF BATTLE...
THE UGARITS.
THEY'RE ALL HERE, MIKE!
IT SLAUGHTERED THEM ALL.

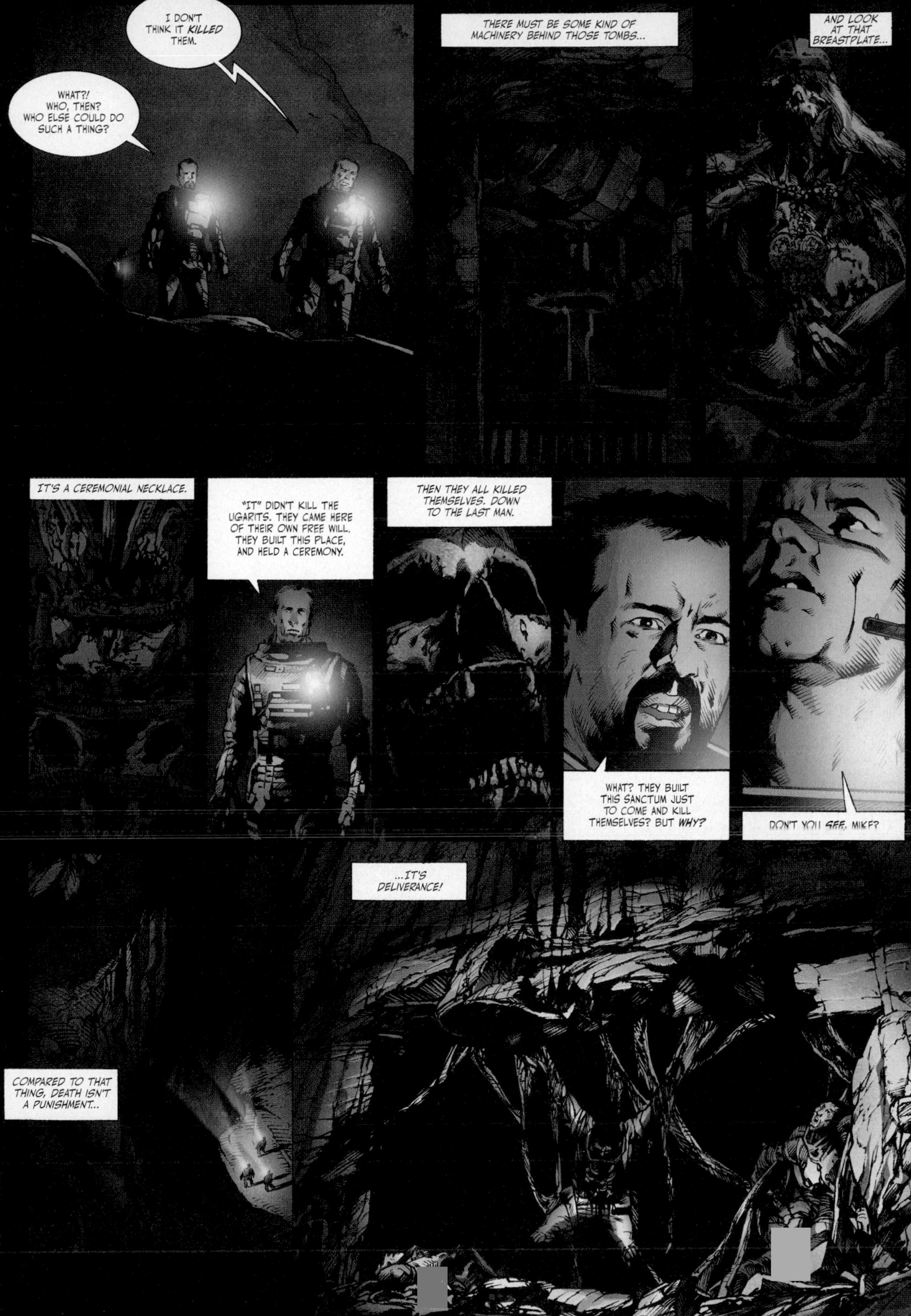

WHAT?! WHO, THEN? WHO ELSE COULD DO SUCH A THING?
I DON'T THINK IT KILLED THEM.
THERE MUST BE SOME KIND OF MACHINERY BEHIND THOSE TOMBS...
AND LOOK AT THAT BREASTPLATE...
IT'S A CEREMONIAL NECKLACE.
"IT" DIDN'T KILL THE UGARITS. THEY CAME HERE OF THEIR OWN FREE WILL. THEY BUILT THIS PLACE, AND HELD A CEREMONY.
THEN THEY ALL KILLED THEMSELVES. DOWN TO THE LAST MAN.
WHAT? THEY BUILT THIS SANCTUM JUST TO COME AND KILL THEMSELVES? BUT WHY?
DON'T YOU SEE, MIKE?
...IT'S DELIVERANCE!
COMPARED TO THAT THING, DEATH ISN'T A PUNISHMENT...

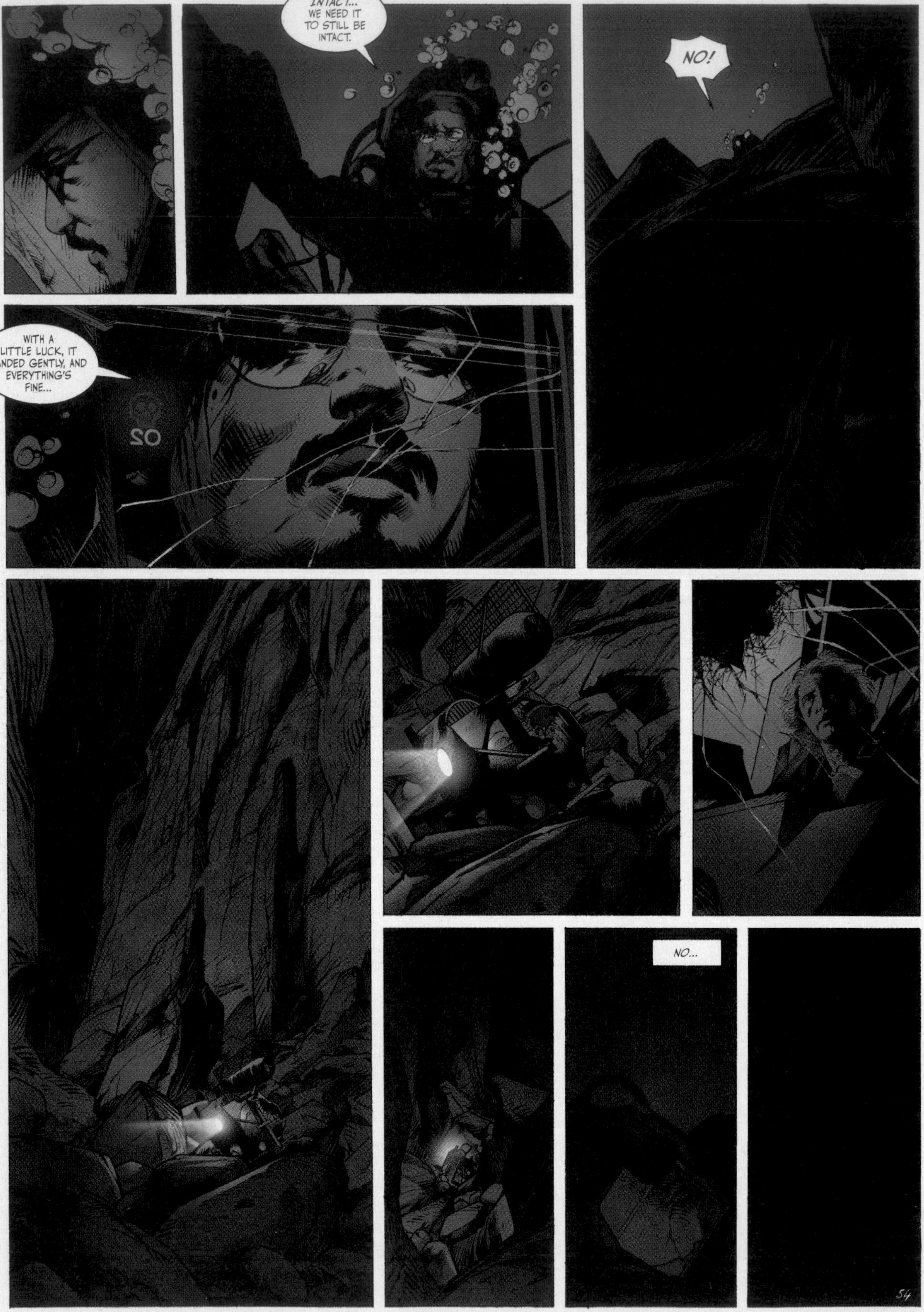

INTACT... WE NEED IT TO STILL BE INTACT.
NO!
WITH A LITTLE LUCK, IT LANDED GENTLY, AND EVERYTHING'S FINE...
O2
NO...
54

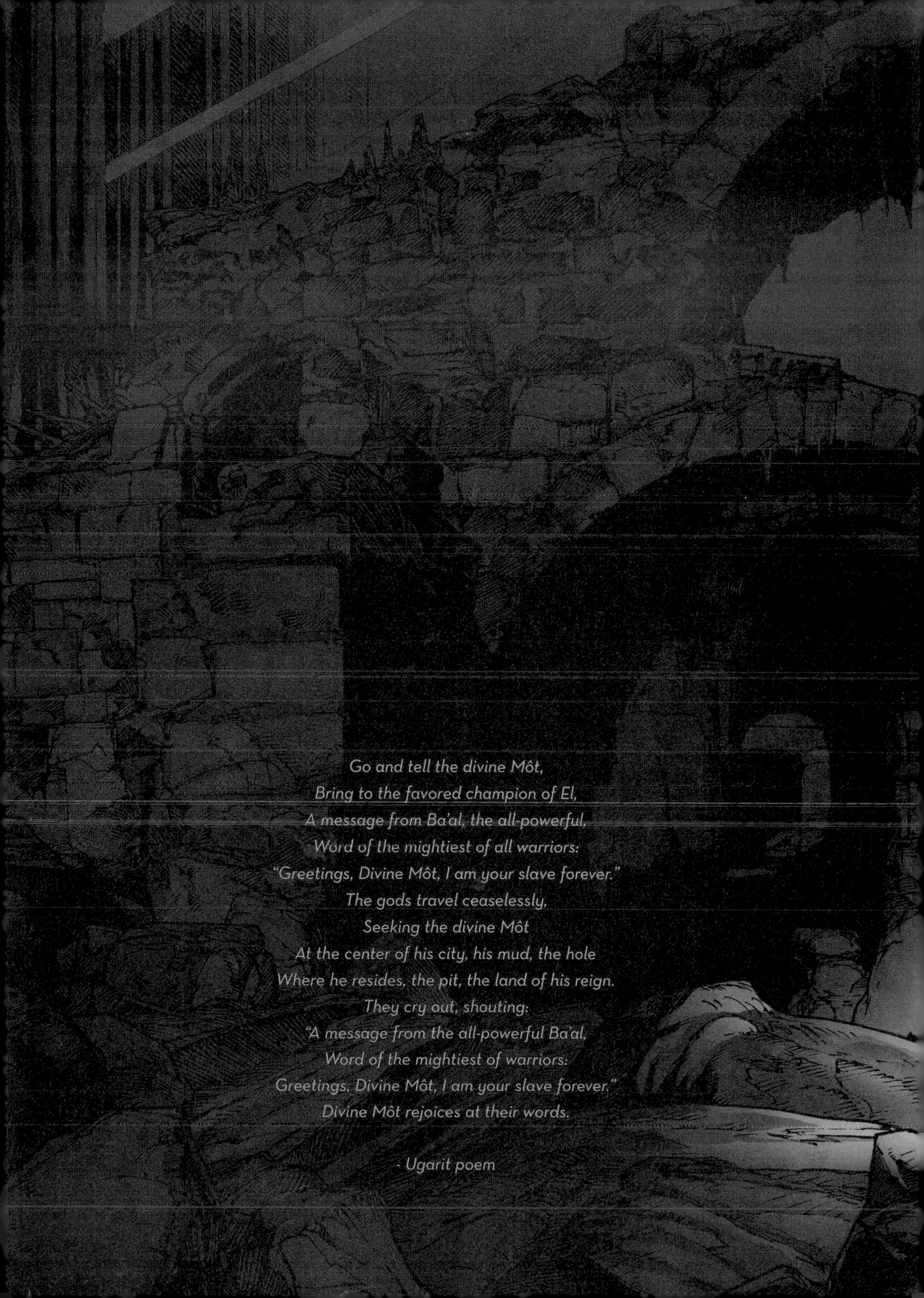

Go and tell the divine Môt,
Bring to the favored champion of El,
A message from Ba'al, the all-powerful,
Word of the mightiest of all warriors:
"Greetings, Divine Môt, I am your slave forever."
The gods travel ceaselessly,
Seeking the divine Môt
At the center of his city, his mud, the hole
Where he resides, the pit, the land of his reign.
They cry out, shouting:
"A message from the all-powerful Ba'al,
Word of the mightiest of warriors:
Greetings, Divine Môt, I am your slave forever."
Divine Môt rejoices at their words.

- Ugarit poem

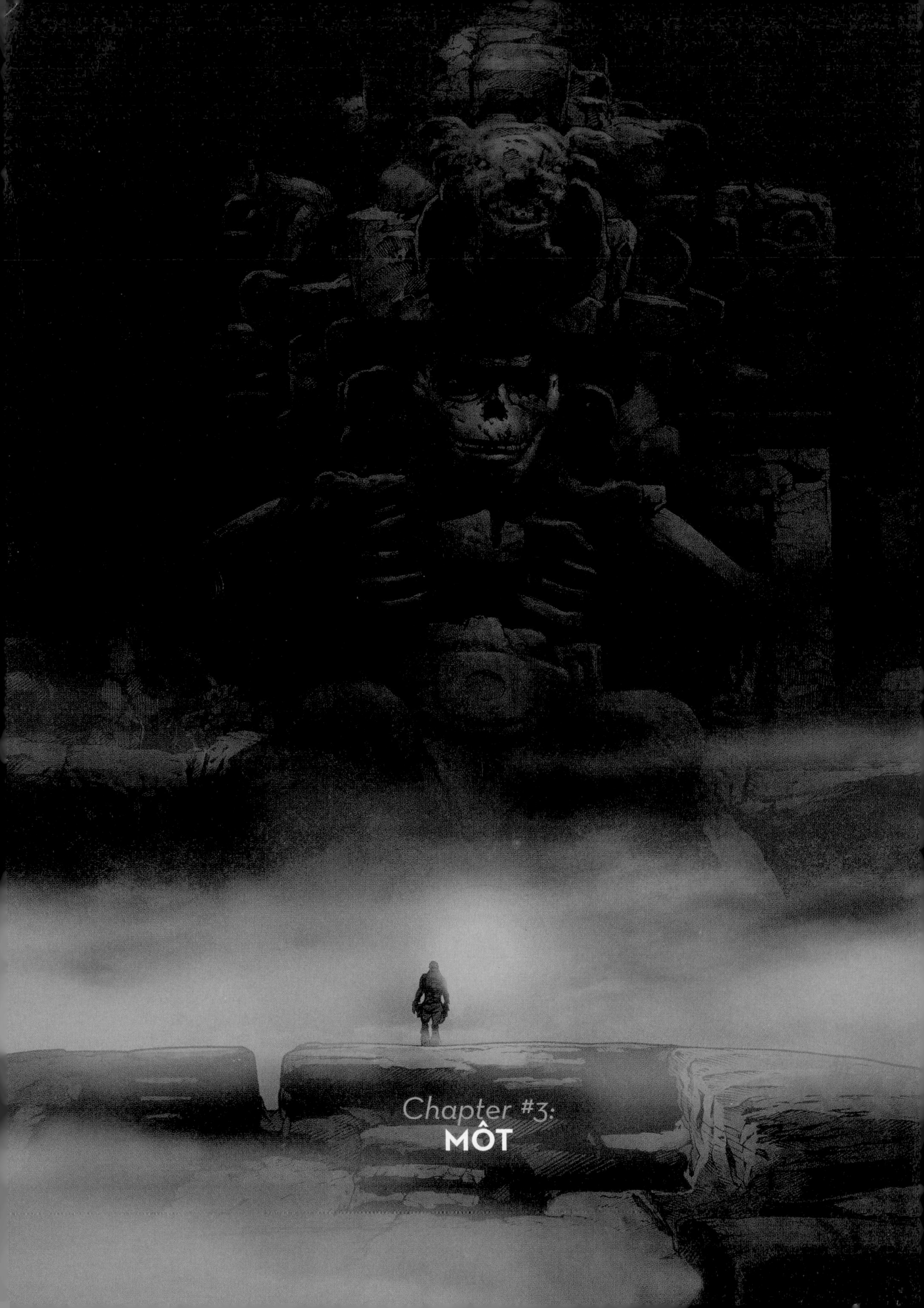
Chapter #3:
MÔT

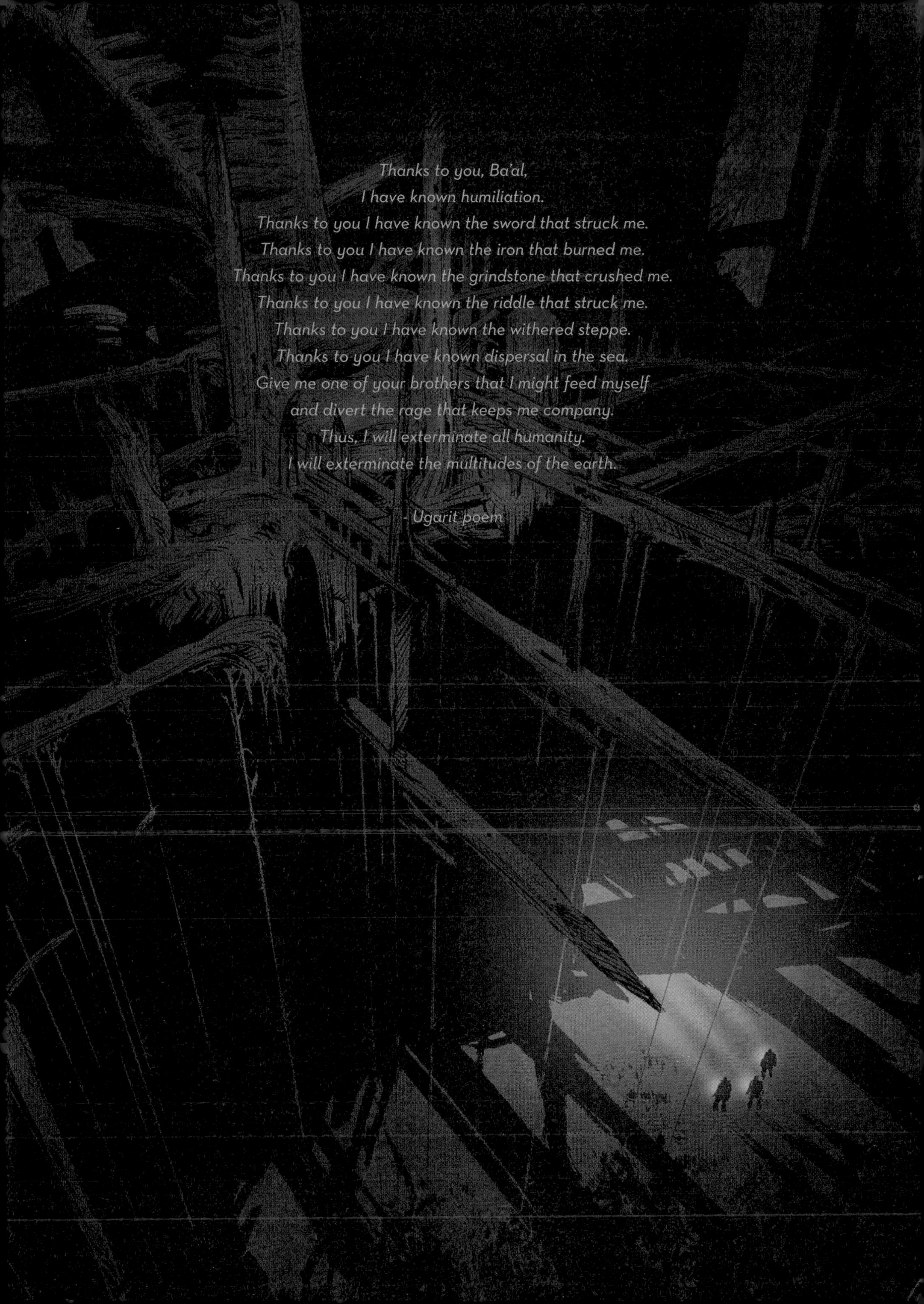

Thanks to you, Ba'al,
I have known humiliation.
Thanks to you I have known the sword that struck me.
Thanks to you I have known the iron that burned me.
Thanks to you I have known the grindstone that crushed me.
Thanks to you I have known the riddle that struck me.
Thanks to you I have known the withered steppe.
Thanks to you I have known dispersal in the sea.
Give me one of your brothers that I might feed myself
and divert the rage that keeps me company.
Thus, I will exterminate all humanity.
I will exterminate the multitudes of the earth.

- Ugarit poem

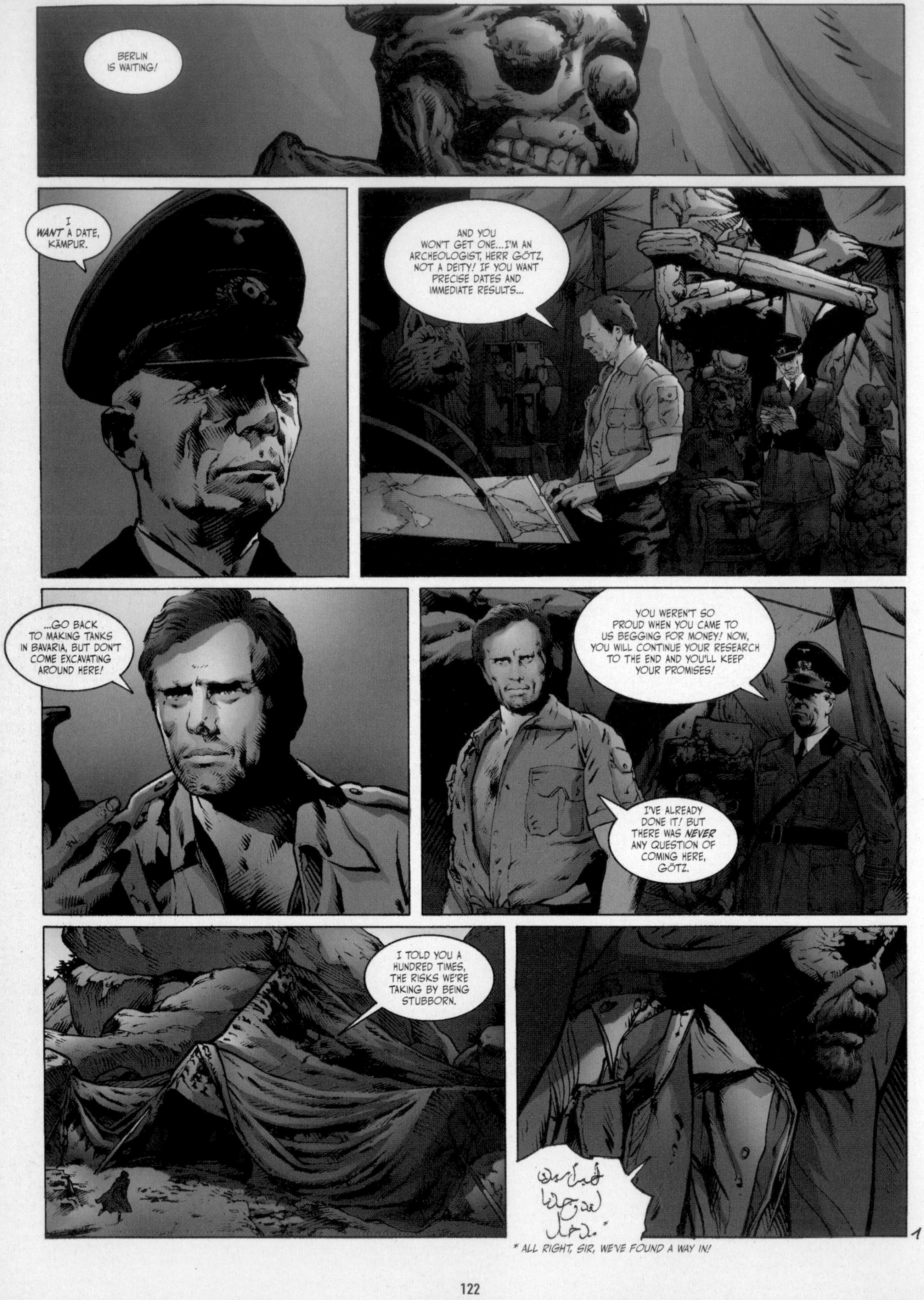
BERLIN IS WAITING!
I *WANT* A DATE, KÄMPUR.
AND YOU WON'T GET ONE...I'M AN ARCHEOLOGIST, HERR GÖTZ, NOT A DEITY! IF YOU WANT PRECISE DATES AND IMMEDIATE RESULTS...
...GO BACK TO MAKING TANKS IN BAVARIA, BUT DON'T COME EXCAVATING AROUND HERE!
YOU WEREN'T SO PROUD WHEN YOU CAME TO US BEGGING FOR MONEY! NOW, YOU WILL CONTINUE YOUR RESEARCH TO THE END AND YOU'LL KEEP YOUR PROMISES!
I'VE ALREADY DONE IT! BUT THERE WAS *NEVER* ANY QUESTION OF COMING HERE, GÖTZ.
I TOLD YOU A HUNDRED TIMES, THE RISKS WE'RE TAKING BY BEING STUBBORN.

* *ALL RIGHT, SIR, WE'VE FOUND A WAY IN!*

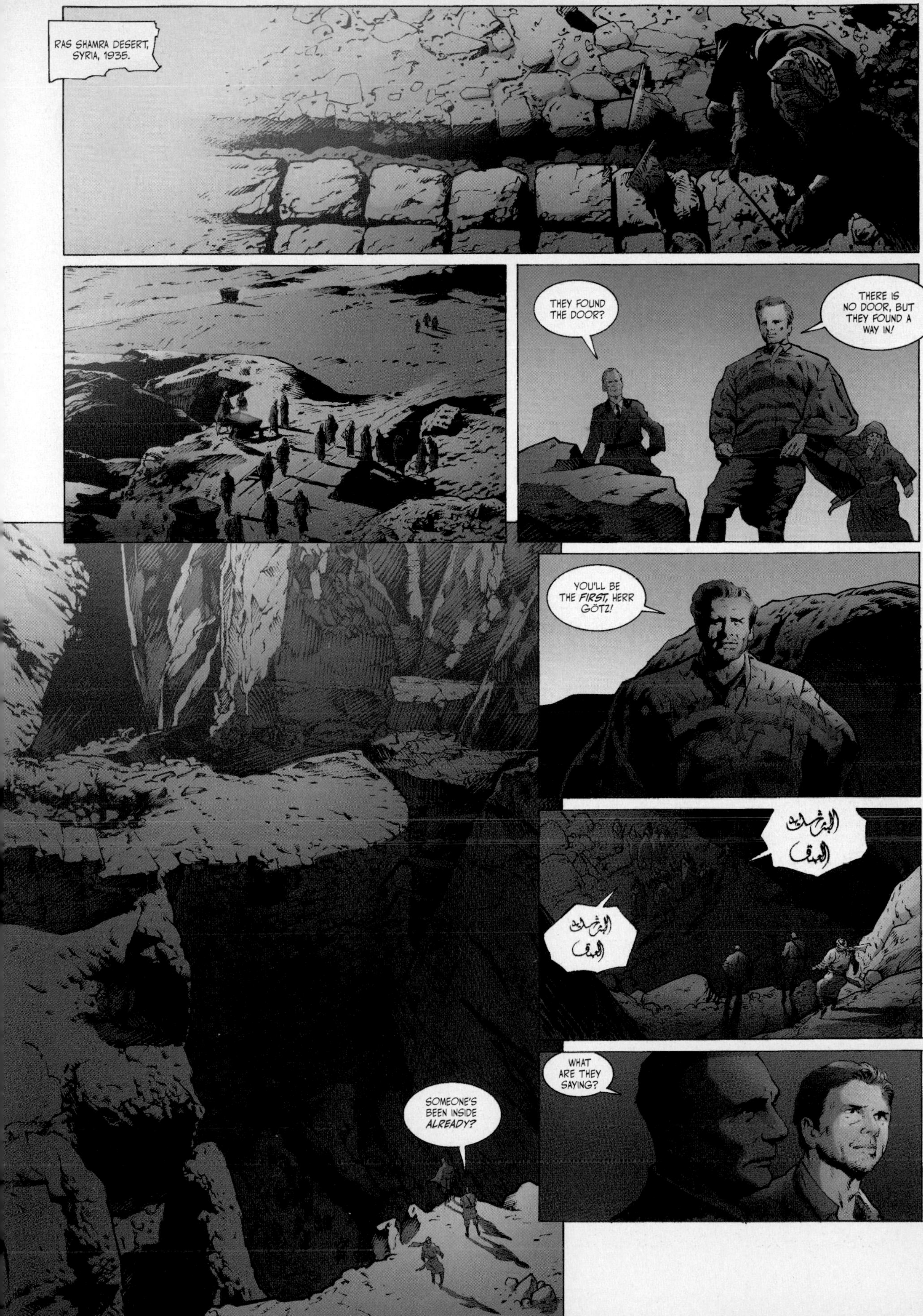
RAS SHAMRA DESERT, SYRIA, 1935.
THEY FOUND THE DOOR?
THERE IS NO DOOR, BUT THEY FOUND A WAY IN!
YOU'LL BE THE *FIRST,* HERR GÖTZ!
WHAT ARE THEY SAYING?
SOMEONE'S BEEN INSIDE *ALREADY?*

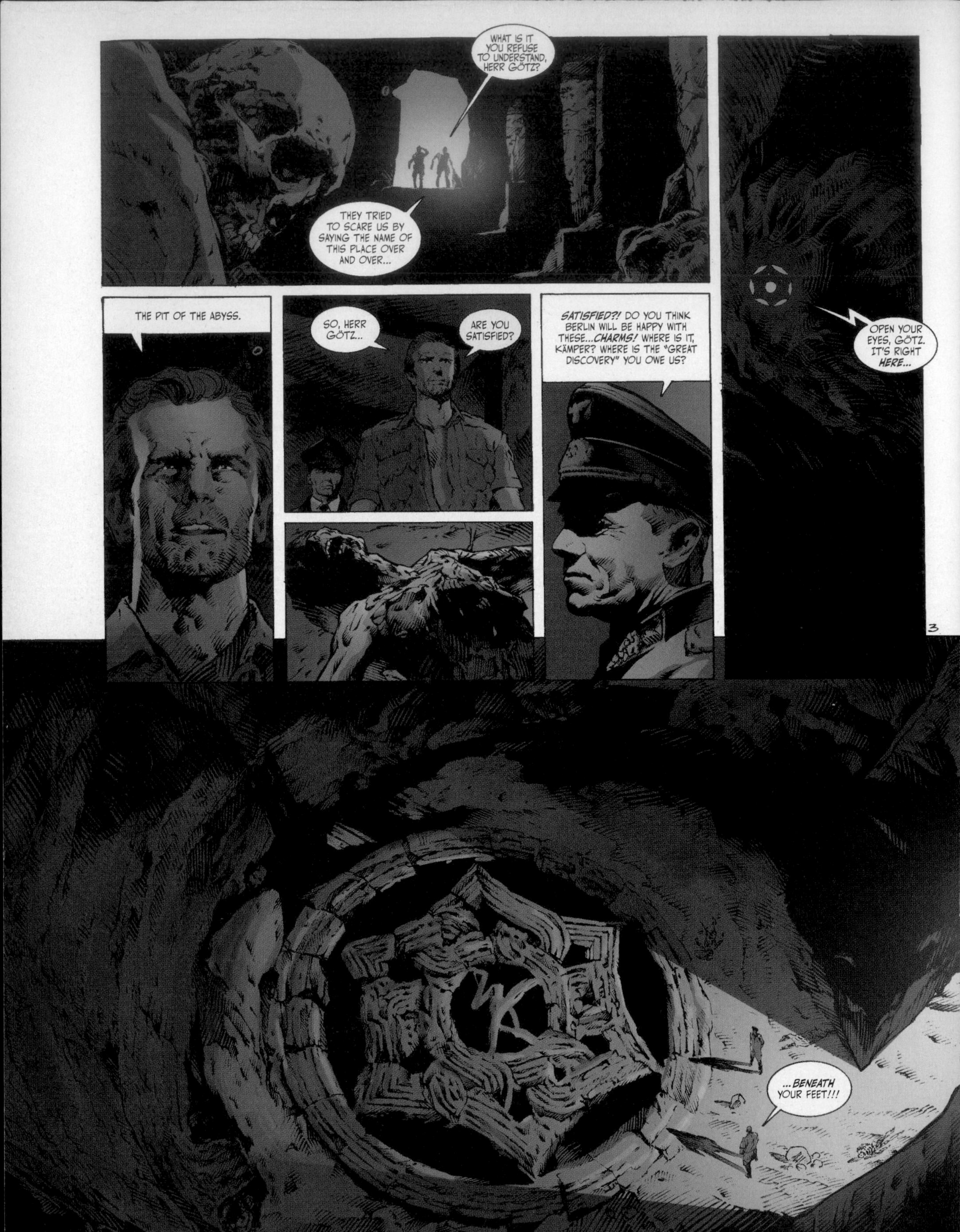
WHAT IS IT YOU REFUSE TO UNDERSTAND, HERR GÖTZ?
THEY TRIED TO SCARE US BY SAYING THE NAME OF THIS PLACE OVER AND OVER...
THE PIT OF THE ABYSS.
SO, HERR GÖTZ...
ARE YOU SATISFIED?
SATISFIED?! DO YOU THINK BERLIN WILL BE HAPPY WITH THESE...CHARMS! WHERE IS IT, KÄMPER? WHERE IS THE "GREAT DISCOVERY" YOU OWE US?
OPEN YOUR EYES, GÖTZ. IT'S RIGHT HERE...
...BENEATH YOUR FEET!!!

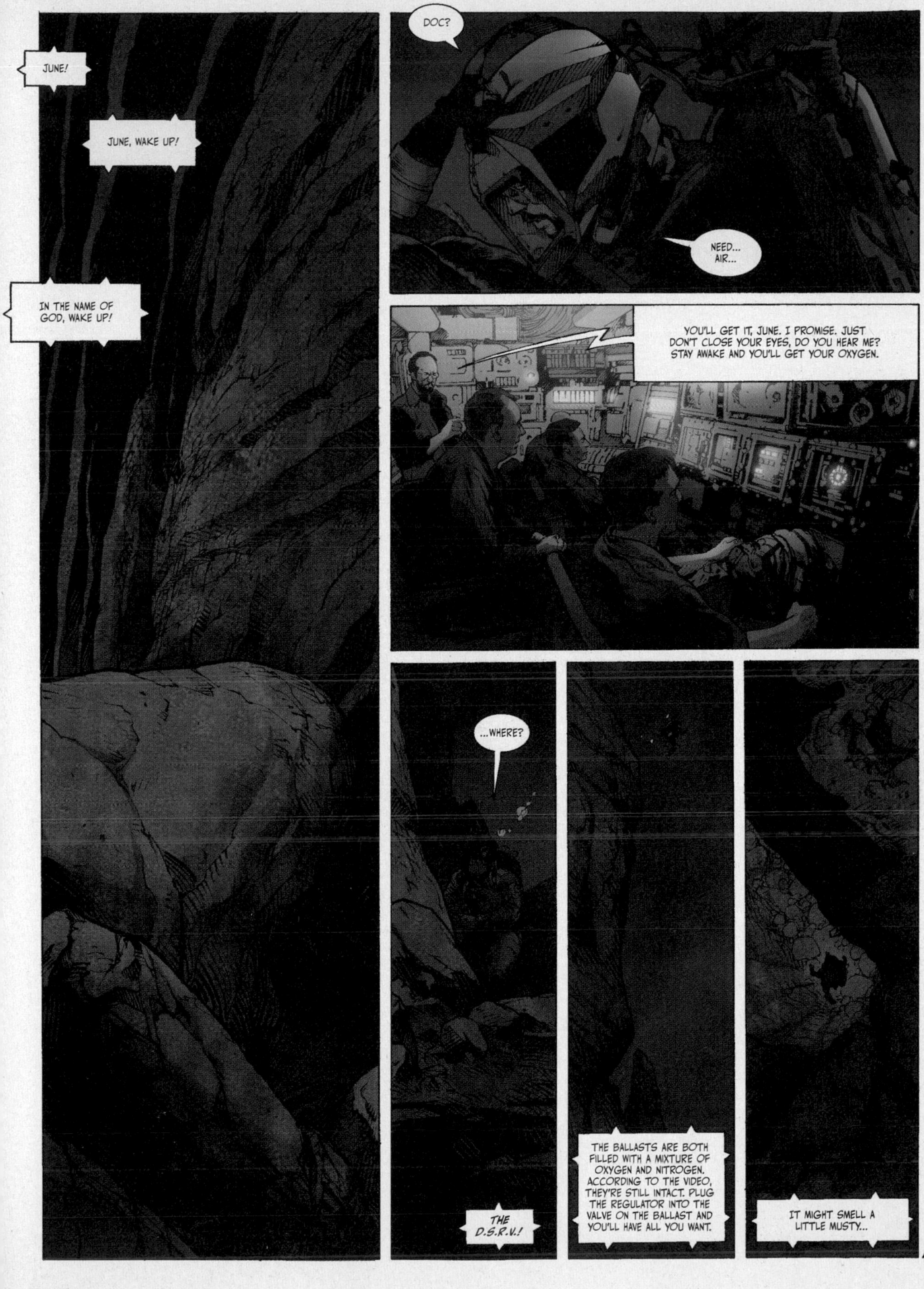

JUNE!
JUNE, WAKE UP!
IN THE NAME OF GOD, WAKE UP!
DOC?
NEED... AIR...
YOU'LL GET IT, JUNE. I PROMISE. JUST DON'T CLOSE YOUR EYES, DO YOU HEAR ME? STAY AWAKE AND YOU'LL GET YOUR OXYGEN.
...WHERE?
THE D.S.R.V.!
THE BALLASTS ARE BOTH FILLED WITH A MIXTURE OF OXYGEN AND NITROGEN. ACCORDING TO THE VIDEO, THEY'RE STILL INTACT. PLUG THE REGULATOR INTO THE VALVE ON THE BALLAST AND YOU'LL HAVE ALL YOU WANT.
IT MIGHT SMELL A LITTLE MUSTY...
4

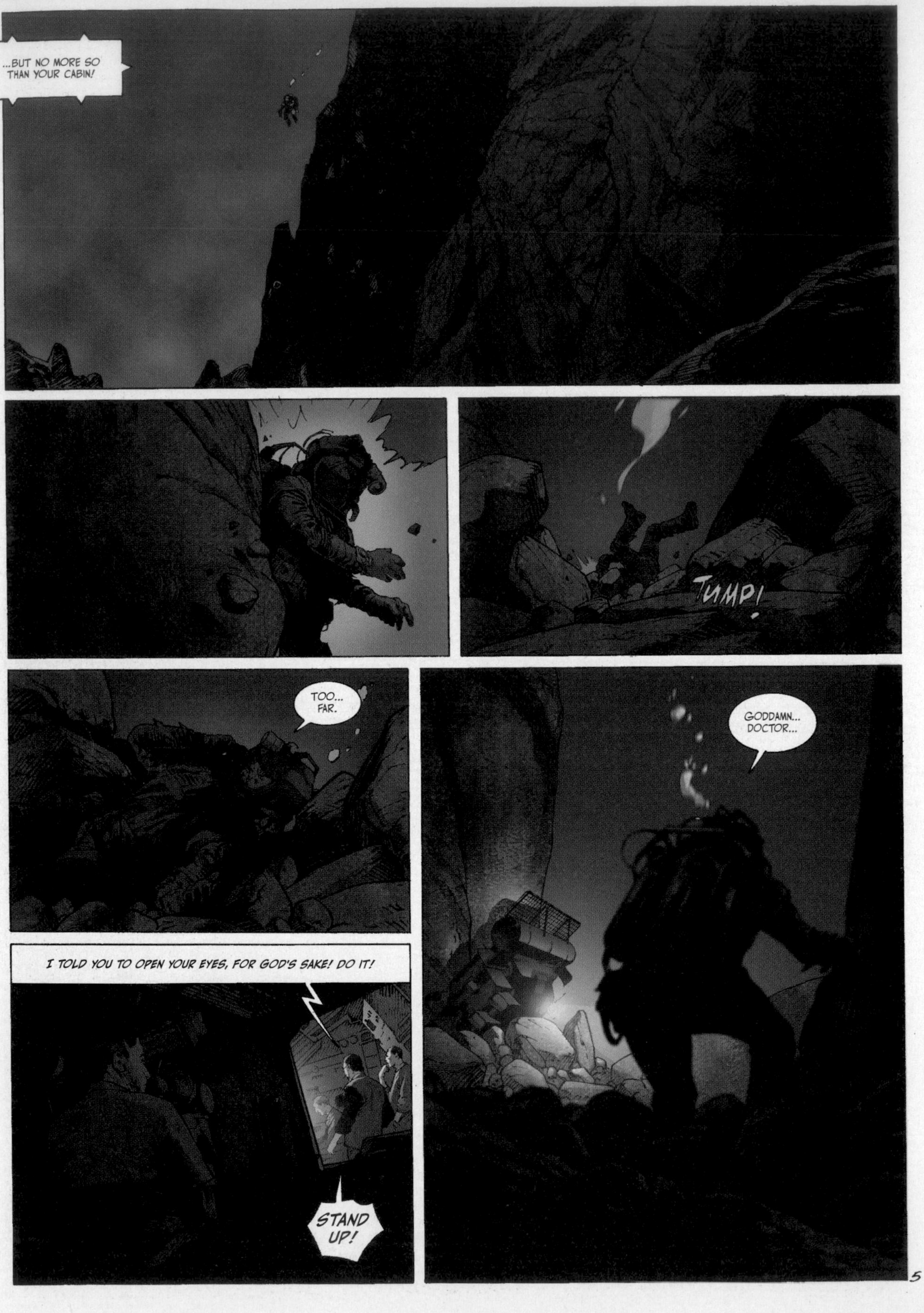
...BUT NO MORE SO THAN YOUR CABIN!
TUMP!
TOO... FAR.
GODDAMN... DOCTOR...
I TOLD YOU TO OPEN YOUR EYES, FOR GOD'S SAKE! DO IT!
STAND UP!
5

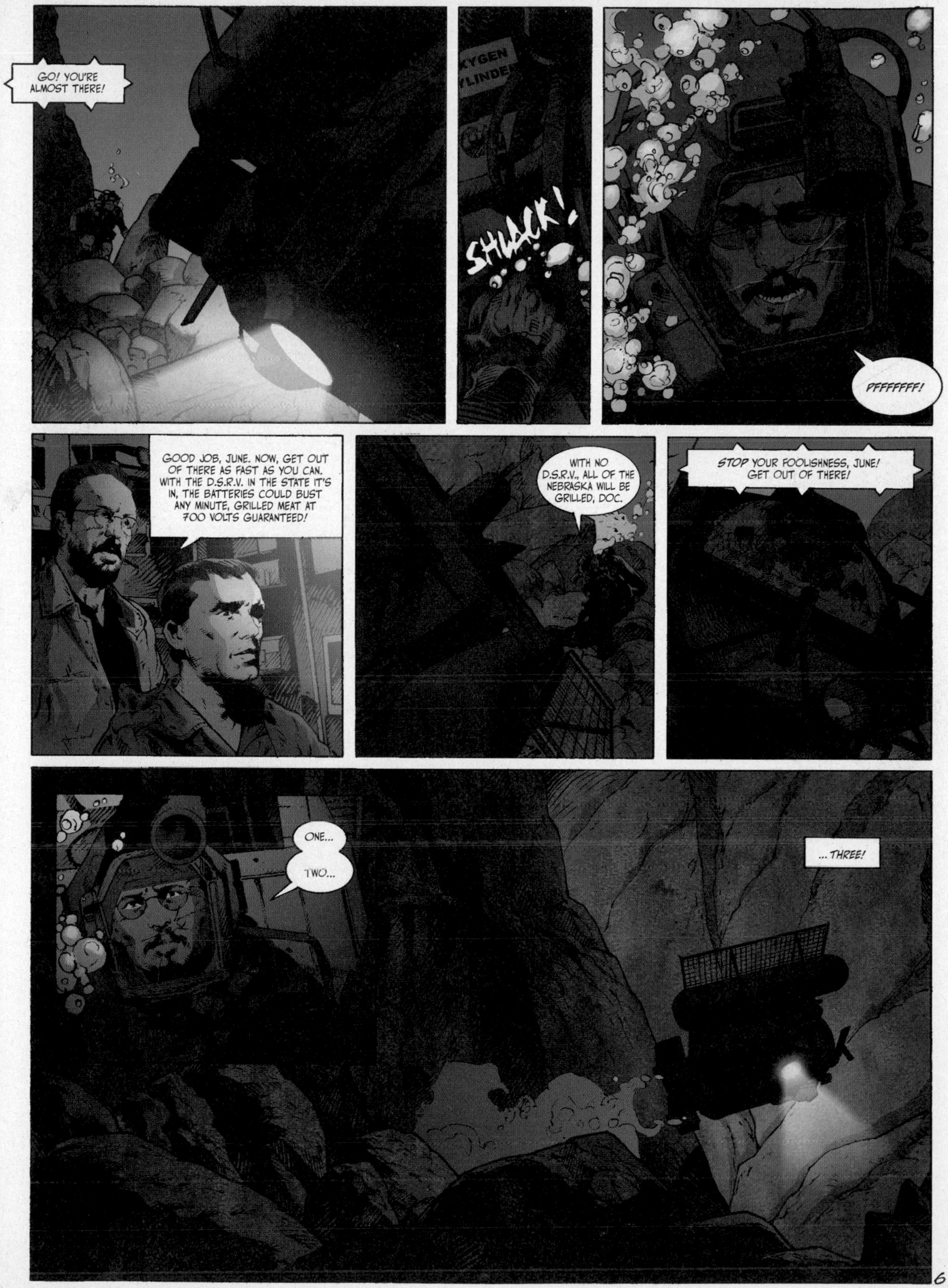
GO! YOU'RE ALMOST THERE!
SHLACK!
PFFFFFFF!
GOOD JOB, JUNE. NOW, GET OUT OF THERE AS FAST AS YOU CAN. WITH THE D.S.R.V. IN THE STATE IT'S IN, THE BATTERIES COULD BUST ANY MINUTE, GRILLED MEAT AT 700 VOLTS GUARANTEED!
WITH NO D.S.R.V., ALL OF THE NEBRASKA WILL BE GRILLED, DOC.
STOP YOUR FOOLISHNESS, JUNE! GET OUT OF THERE!
ONE...
TWO...
...THREE!
6

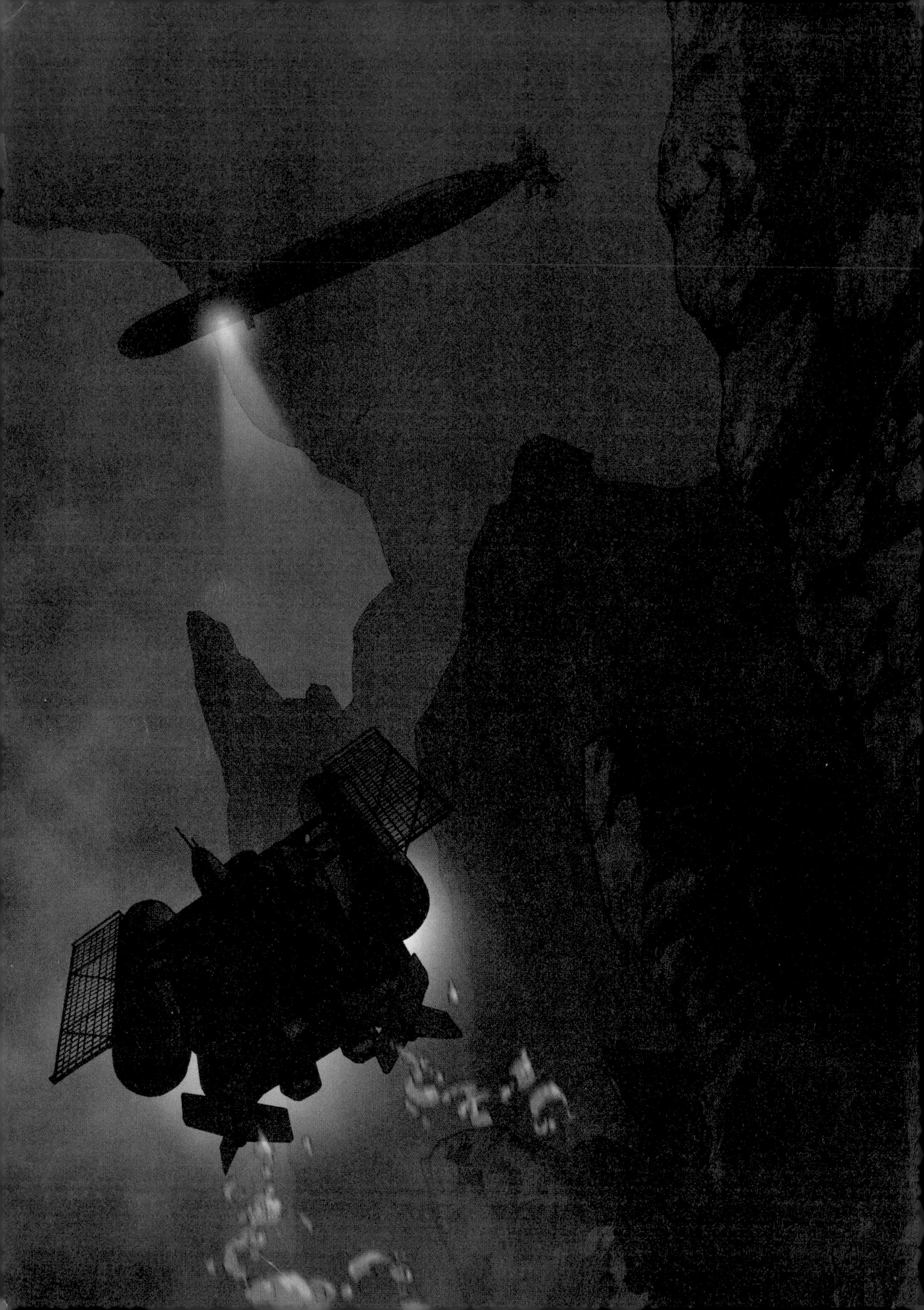

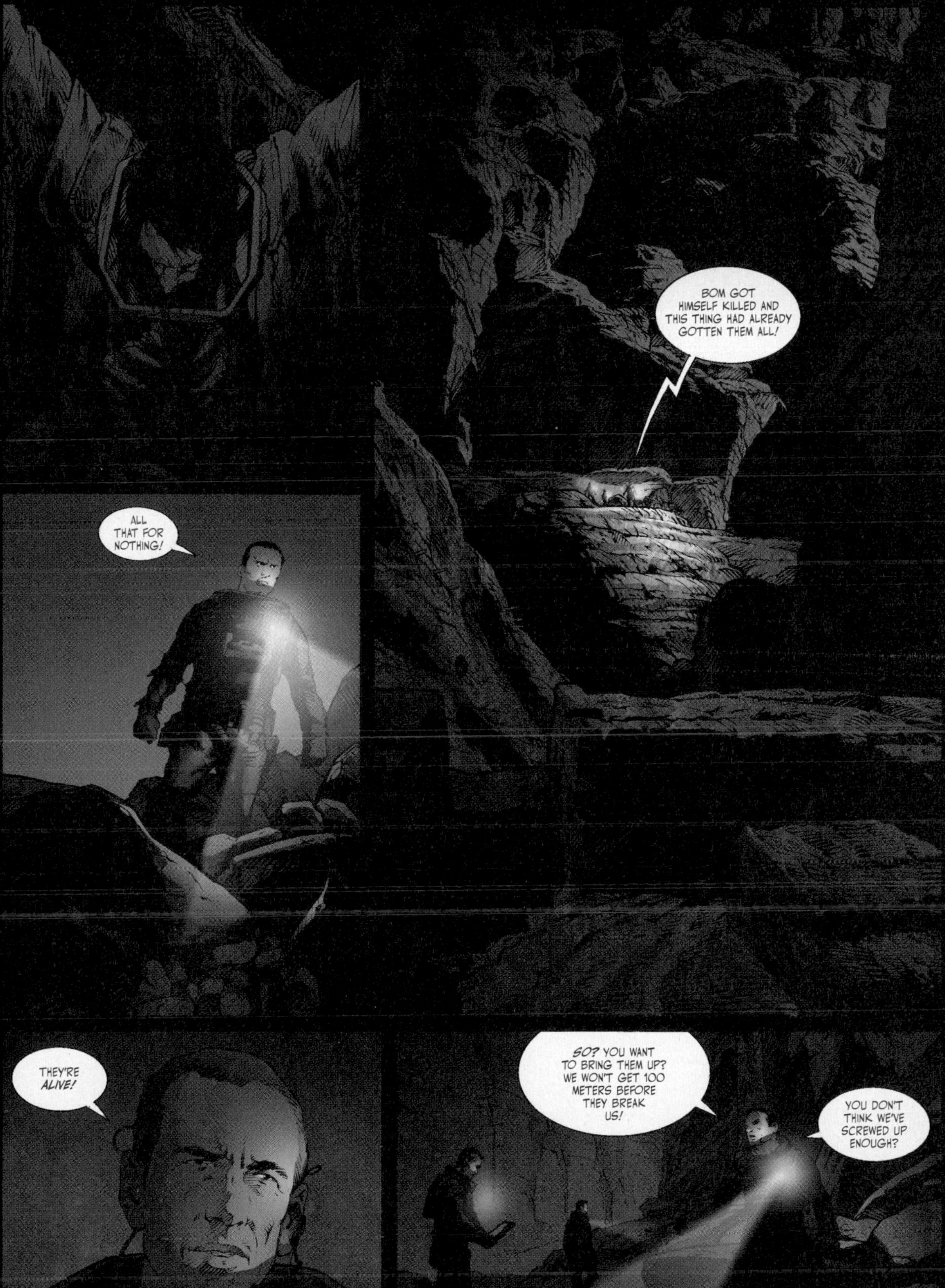
BOM GOT HIMSELF KILLED AND THIS THING HAD ALREADY GOTTEN THEM ALL!
ALL THAT FOR NOTHING!
THEY'RE *ALIVE!*
SO? YOU WANT TO BRING THEM UP? WE WON'T GET 100 METERS BEFORE THEY BREAK US!
YOU DON'T THINK WE'VE SCREWED UP ENOUGH?

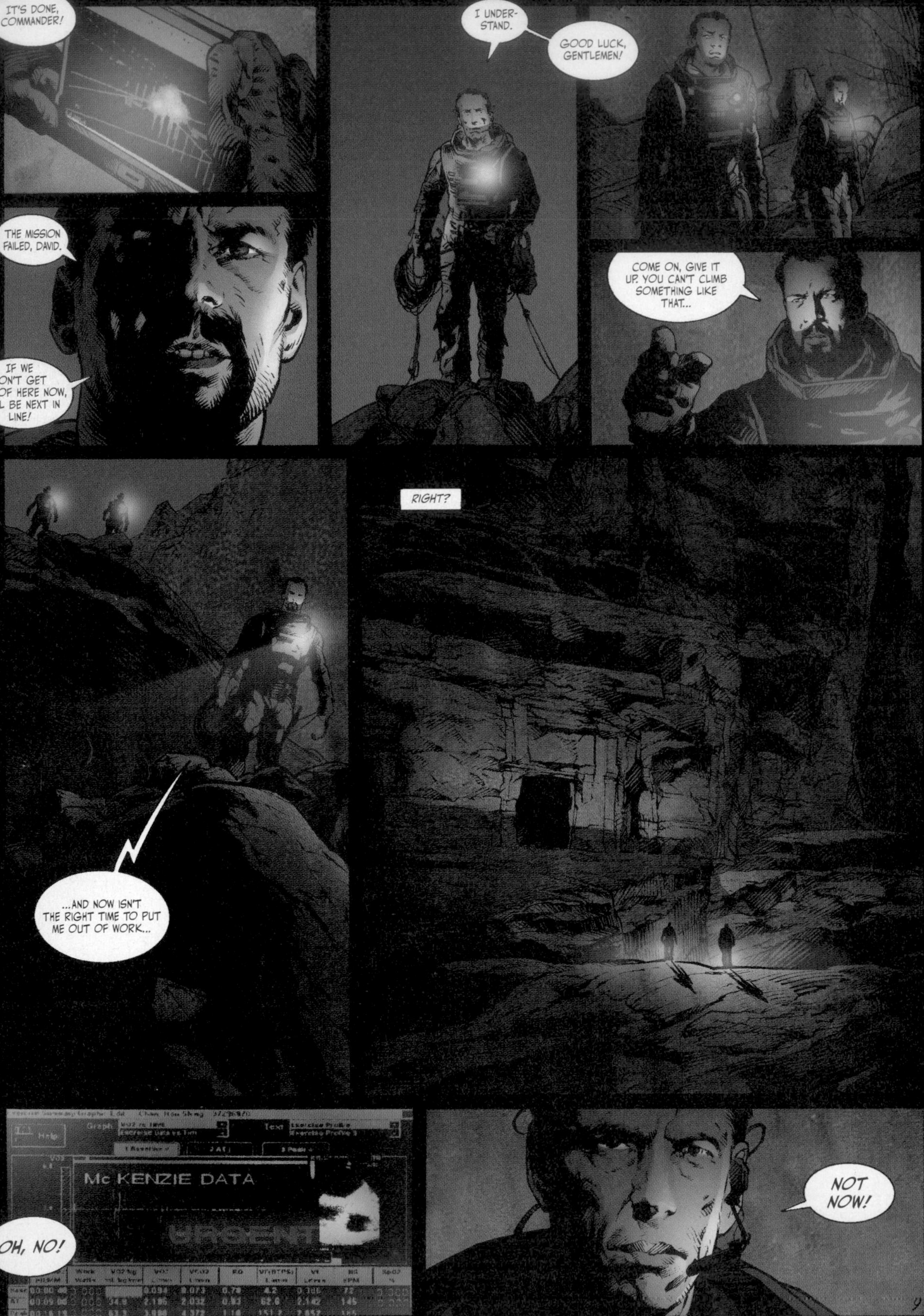
IT'S DONE, COMMANDER!
I UNDER-STAND.
GOOD LUCK, GENTLEMEN!
THE MISSION FAILED, DAVID.
IF WE DON'T GET OUT OF HERE NOW, WE'LL BE NEXT IN LINE!
COME ON, GIVE IT UP. YOU CAN'T CLIMB SOMETHING LIKE THAT...
RIGHT?
...AND NOW ISN'T THE RIGHT TIME TO PUT ME OUT OF WORK...
Mc KENZIE DATA
OH, NO!
NOT NOW!

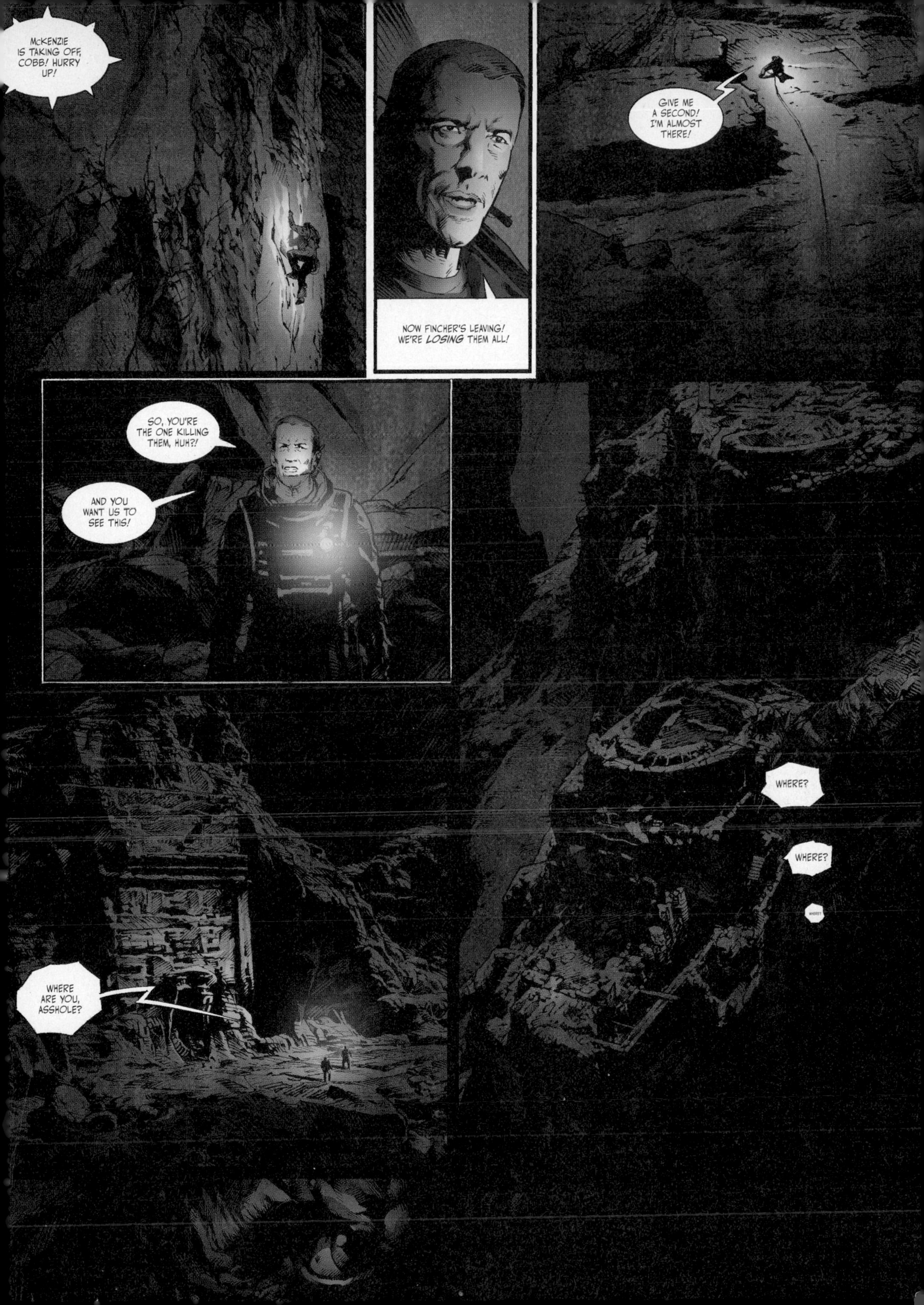
McKENZIE IS TAKING OFF, COBB! HURRY UP!
NOW FINCHER'S LEAVING! WE'RE *LOSING* THEM ALL!
GIVE ME A SECOND! I'M ALMOST THERE!
SO, YOU'RE THE ONE KILLING THEM, HUH?!
AND YOU WANT US TO SEE THIS!
WHERE ARE YOU, ASSHOLE?
WHERE?
WHERE?
WHERE?

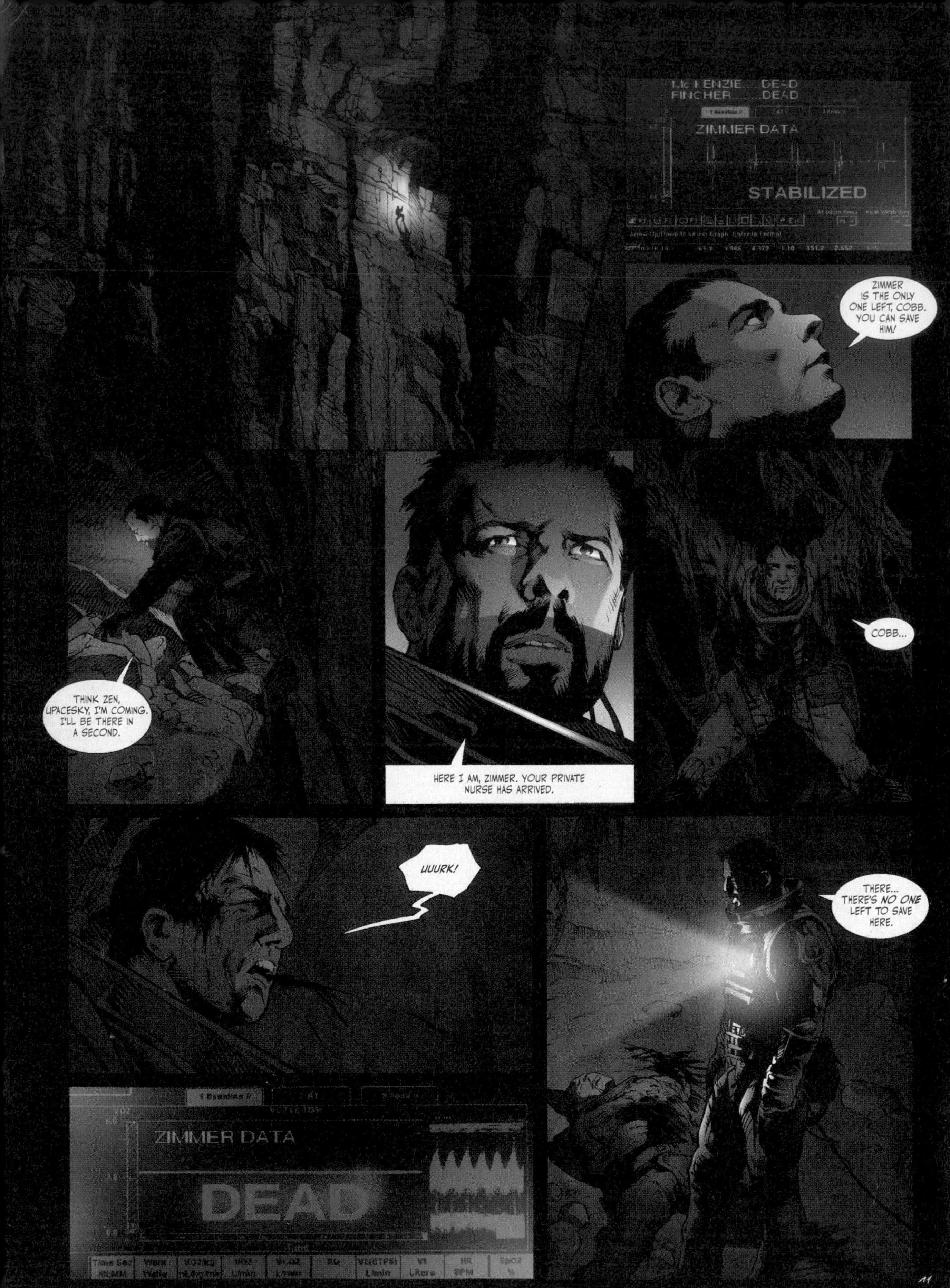
McKENZIE.....DEAD
FINCHER.......DEAD
ZIMMER DATA
STABILIZED
ZIMMER IS THE ONLY ONE LEFT, COBB. YOU CAN SAVE HIM!
THINK ZEN, UPACESKY, I'M COMING. I'LL BE THERE IN A SECOND.
HERE I AM, ZIMMER. YOUR PRIVATE NURSE HAS ARRIVED.
COBB...
UUURK!
ZIMMER DATA
DEAD
THERE... THERE'S *NO ONE* LEFT TO SAVE HERE.

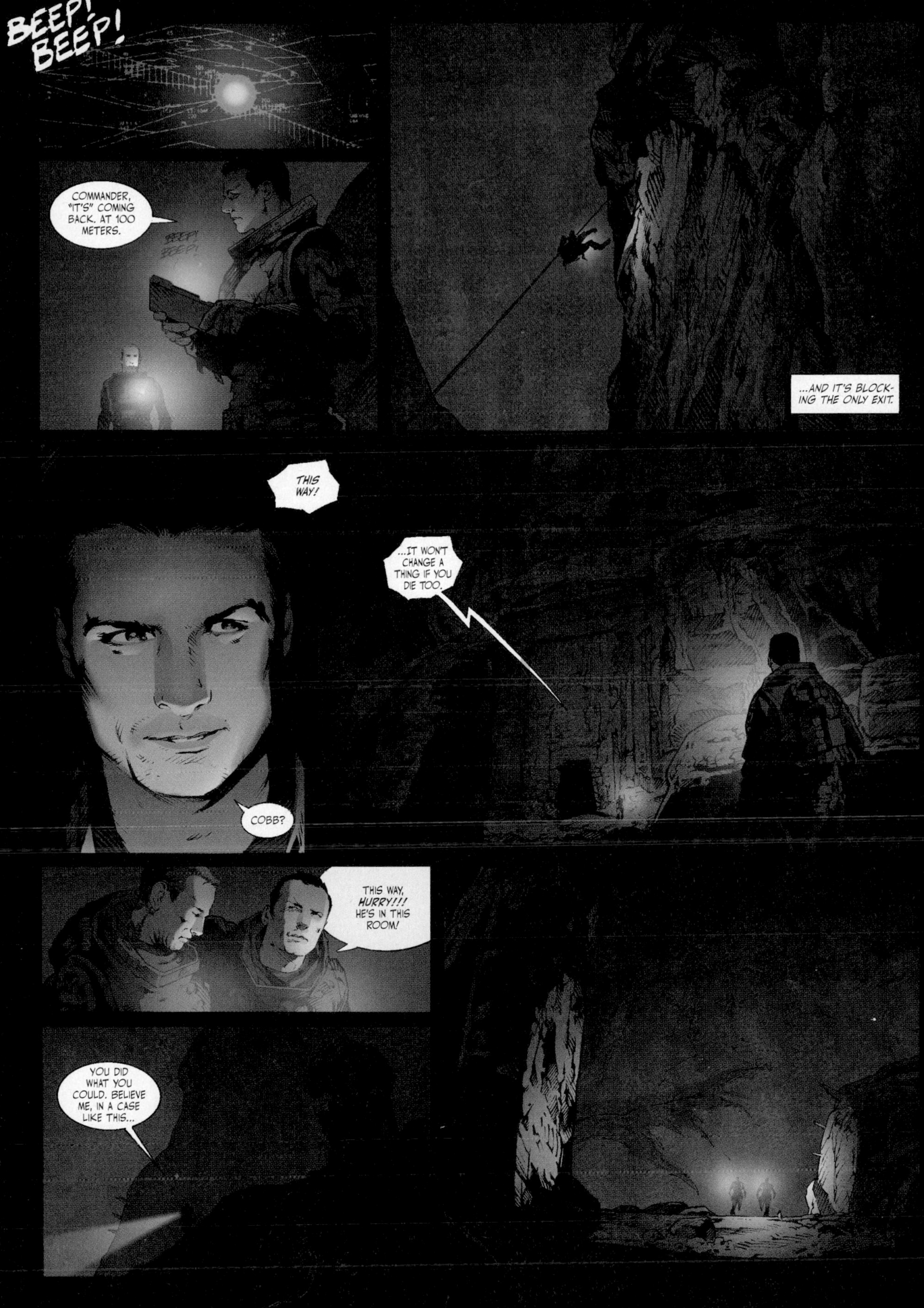
BEEP! BEEP!
COMMANDER, "IT'S" COMING BACK. AT 100 METERS.
BEEP! BEEP!
...AND IT'S BLOCKING THE ONLY EXIT.
THIS WAY!
...IT WON'T CHANGE A THING IF YOU DIE TOO.
COBB?
THIS WAY, HURRY!!! HE'S IN THIS ROOM!
YOU DID WHAT YOU COULD. BELIEVE ME, IN A CASE LIKE THIS...

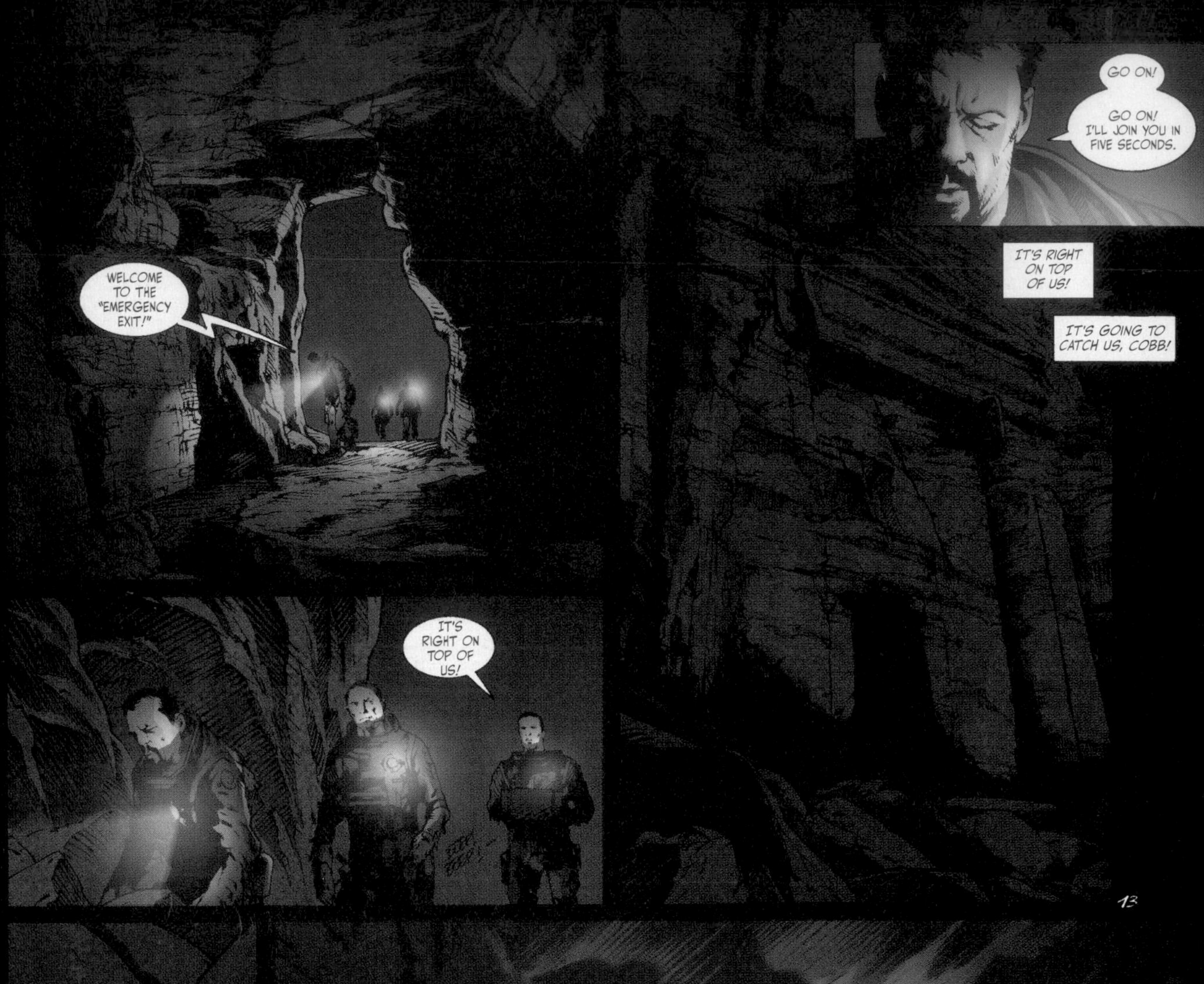

WELCOME TO THE "EMERGENCY EXIT!"
IT'S RIGHT ON TOP OF US!
GO ON!
GO ON! I'LL JOIN YOU IN FIVE SECONDS.
IT'S RIGHT ON TOP OF US!
IT'S GOING TO CATCH US, COBB!
NO, UPACESKY, NOT WITH THE PRESENT I LEFT FOR IT.
A PRESENT FROM ALPHA!

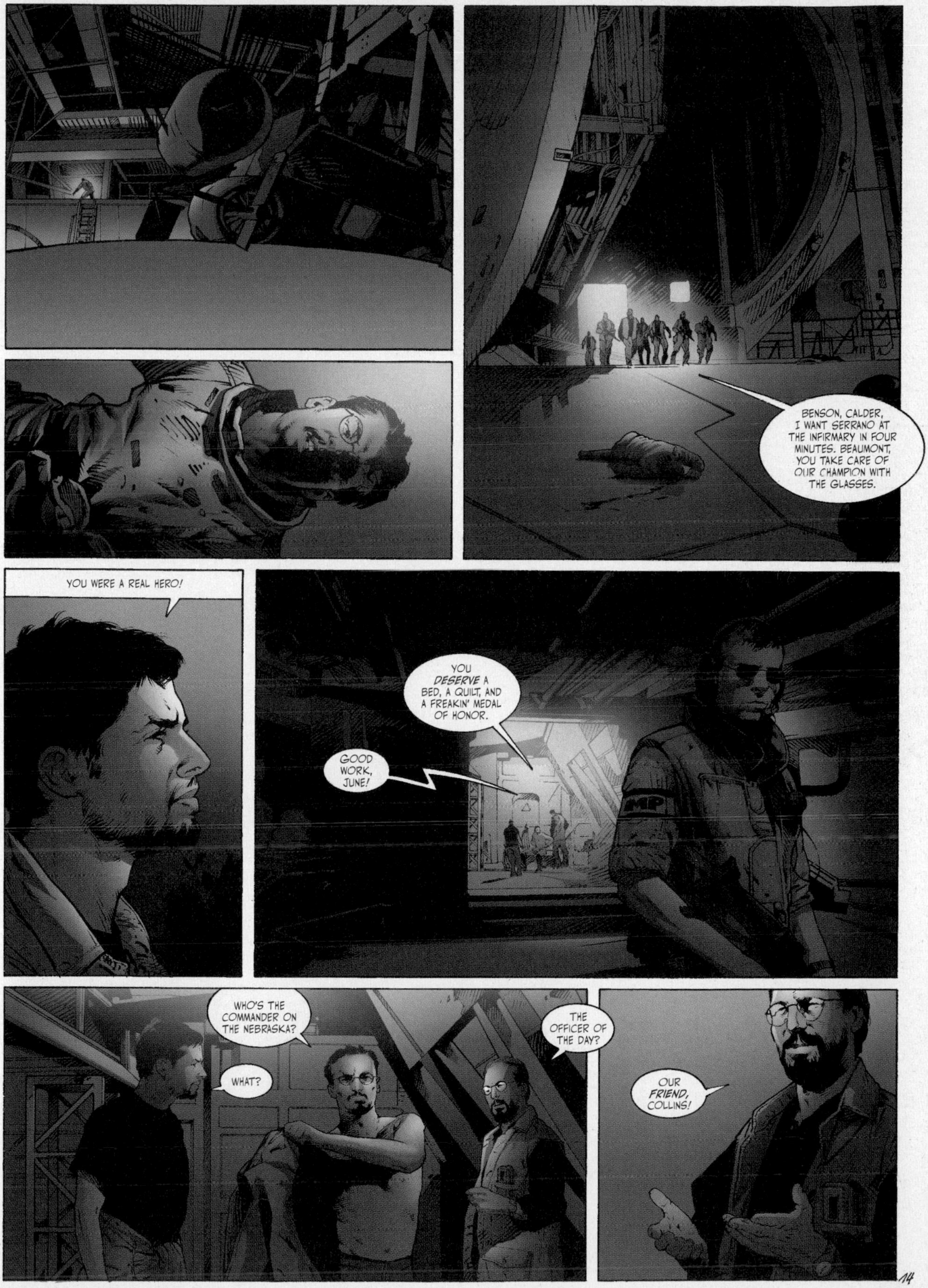
BENSON, CALDER, I WANT SERRANO AT THE INFIRMARY IN FOUR MINUTES. BEAUMONT, YOU TAKE CARE OF OUR CHAMPION WITH THE GLASSES.
YOU WERE A REAL HERO!
YOU DESERVE A BED, A QUILT, AND A FREAKIN' MEDAL OF HONOR.
GOOD WORK, JUNE!
WHO'S THE COMMANDER ON THE NEBRASKA?
WHAT?
THE OFFICER OF THE DAY?
OUR FRIEND, COLLINS!
14

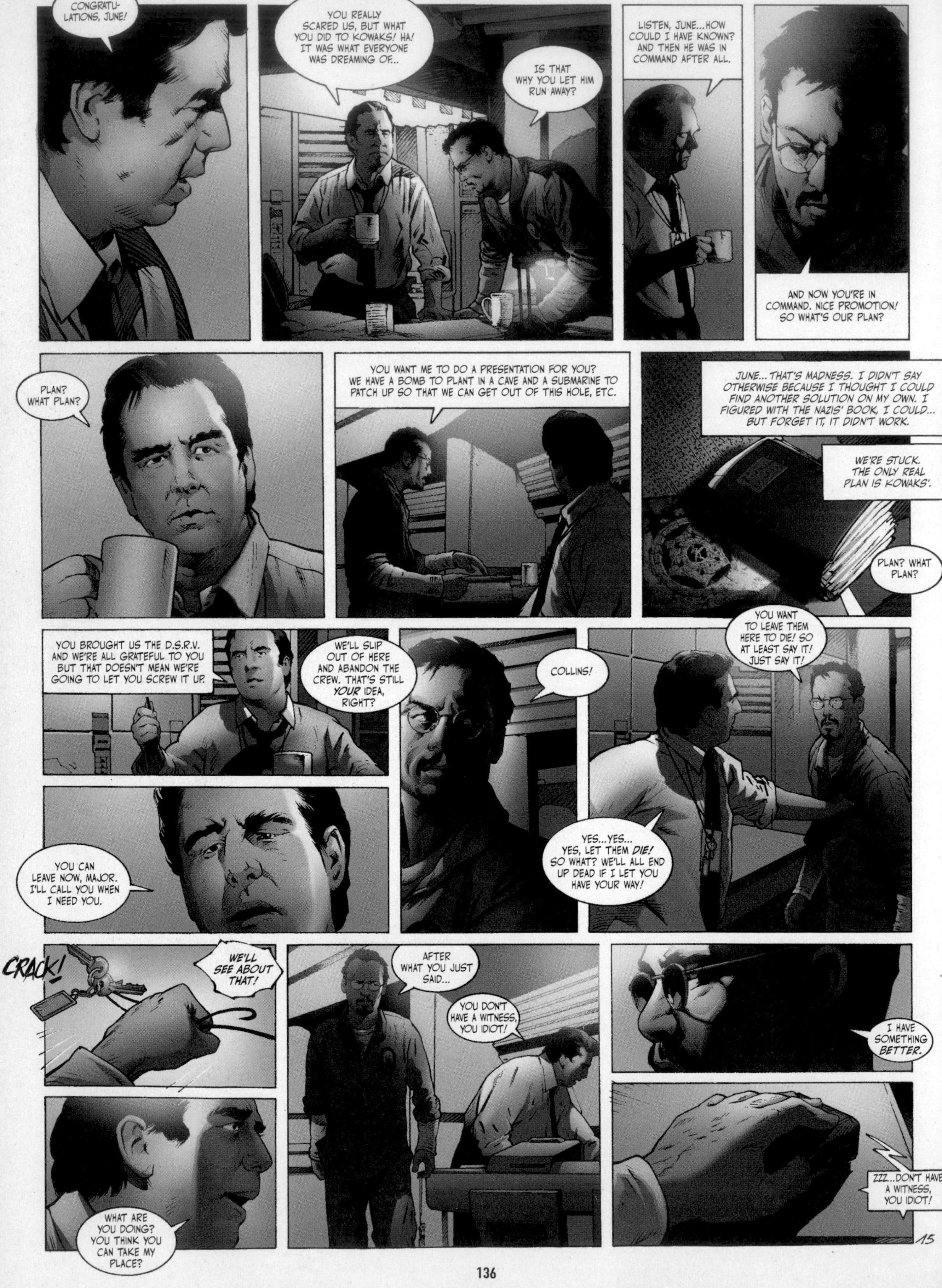
CONGRATU-LATIONS, JUNE!
YOU REALLY SCARED US, BUT WHAT YOU DID TO KOWAKS! HA! IT WAS WHAT EVERYONE WAS DREAMING OF...
IS THAT WHY YOU LET HIM RUN AWAY?
LISTEN, JUNE...HOW COULD I HAVE KNOWN? AND THEN HE WAS IN COMMAND AFTER ALL.
AND NOW YOU'RE IN COMMAND. NICE PROMOTION! SO WHAT'S OUR PLAN?
PLAN? WHAT PLAN?
YOU WANT ME TO DO A PRESENTATION FOR YOU? WE HAVE A BOMB TO PLANT IN A CAVE AND A SUBMARINE TO PATCH UP SO THAT WE CAN GET OUT OF THIS HOLE, ETC.
JUNE... THAT'S MADNESS. I DIDN'T SAY OTHERWISE BECAUSE I THOUGHT I COULD FIND ANOTHER SOLUTION ON MY OWN. I FIGURED WITH THE NAZIS' BOOK, I COULD... BUT FORGET IT, IT DIDN'T WORK.
WE'RE STUCK. THE ONLY REAL PLAN IS KOWAKS'.
PLAN? WHAT PLAN?
YOU BROUGHT US THE D.S.R.V. AND WE'RE ALL GRATEFUL TO YOU BUT THAT DOESN'T MEAN WE'RE GOING TO LET YOU SCREW IT UP.
WE'LL SLIP OUT OF HERE AND ABANDON THE CREW. THAT'S STILL YOUR IDEA, RIGHT?
COLLINS!
YOU WANT TO LEAVE THEM HERE TO DIE! SO AT LEAST SAY IT! JUST SAY IT!
YOU CAN LEAVE NOW, MAJOR. I'LL CALL YOU WHEN I NEED YOU.
YES...YES... YES, LET THEM DIE! SO WHAT? WE'LL ALL END UP DEAD IF I LET YOU HAVE YOUR WAY!
CRACK!
WE'LL SEE ABOUT THAT!
WHAT ARE YOU DOING? YOU THINK YOU CAN TAKE MY PLACE?
AFTER WHAT YOU JUST SAID...
YOU DON'T HAVE A WITNESS, YOU IDIOT!
I HAVE SOMETHING BETTER.
ZZZ...DON'T HAVE A WITNESS, YOU IDIOT!
15

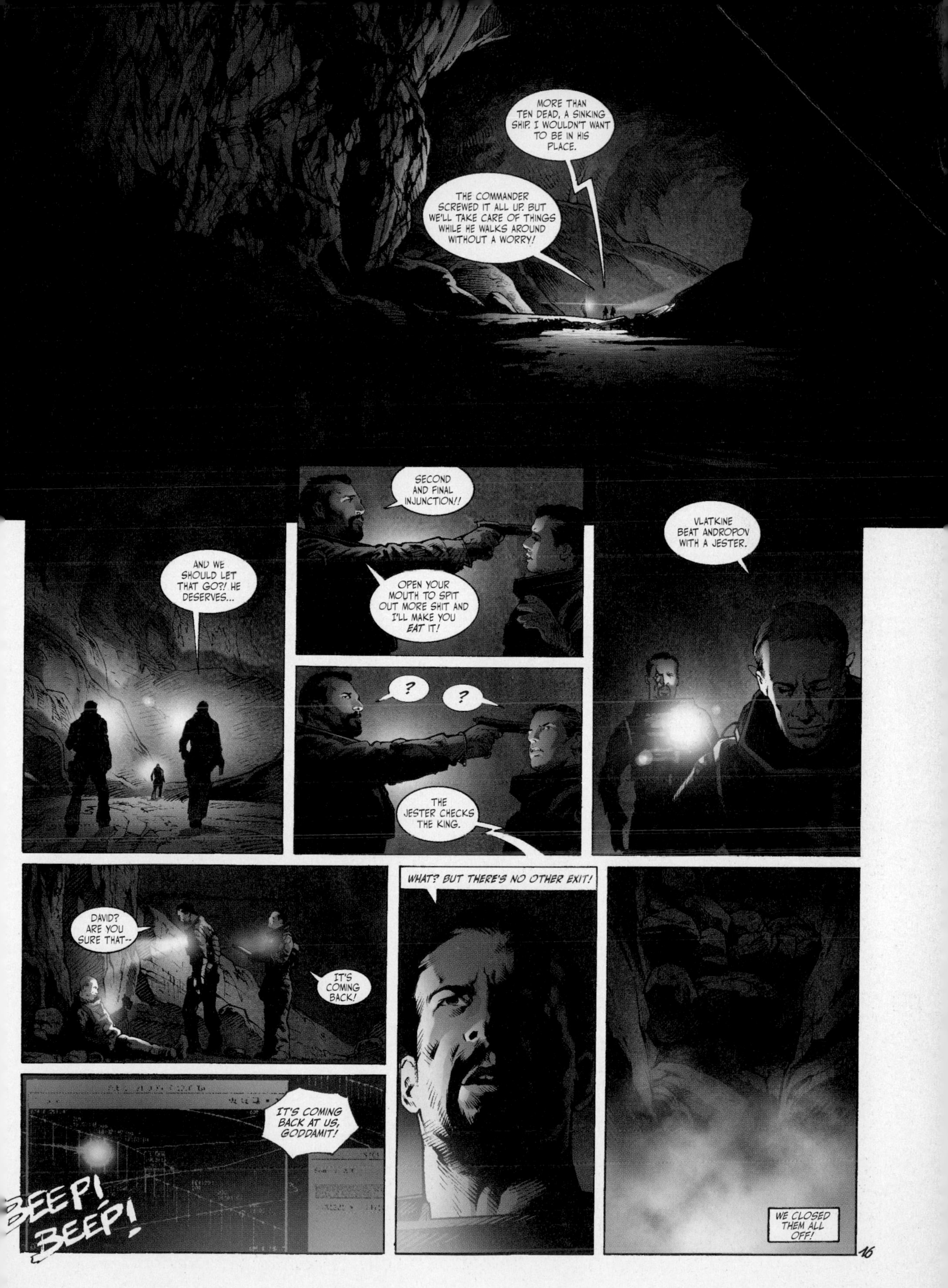

MORE THAN TEN DEAD, A SINKING SHIP. I WOULDN'T WANT TO BE IN HIS PLACE.
THE COMMANDER SCREWED IT ALL UP. BUT WE'LL TAKE CARE OF THINGS WHILE HE WALKS AROUND WITHOUT A WORRY!
AND WE SHOULD LET THAT GO?! HE DESERVES...
SECOND AND FINAL INJUNCTION!!
OPEN YOUR MOUTH TO SPIT OUT MORE SHIT AND I'LL MAKE YOU EAT IT!
?
?
THE JESTER CHECKS THE KING.
VLATKINE BEAT ANDROPOV WITH A JESTER.
DAVID? ARE YOU SURE THAT--
IT'S COMING BACK!
IT'S COMING BACK AT US, GODDAMIT!
BEEP! BEEP!
WHAT? BUT THERE'S NO OTHER EXIT!
WE CLOSED THEM ALL OFF!
16

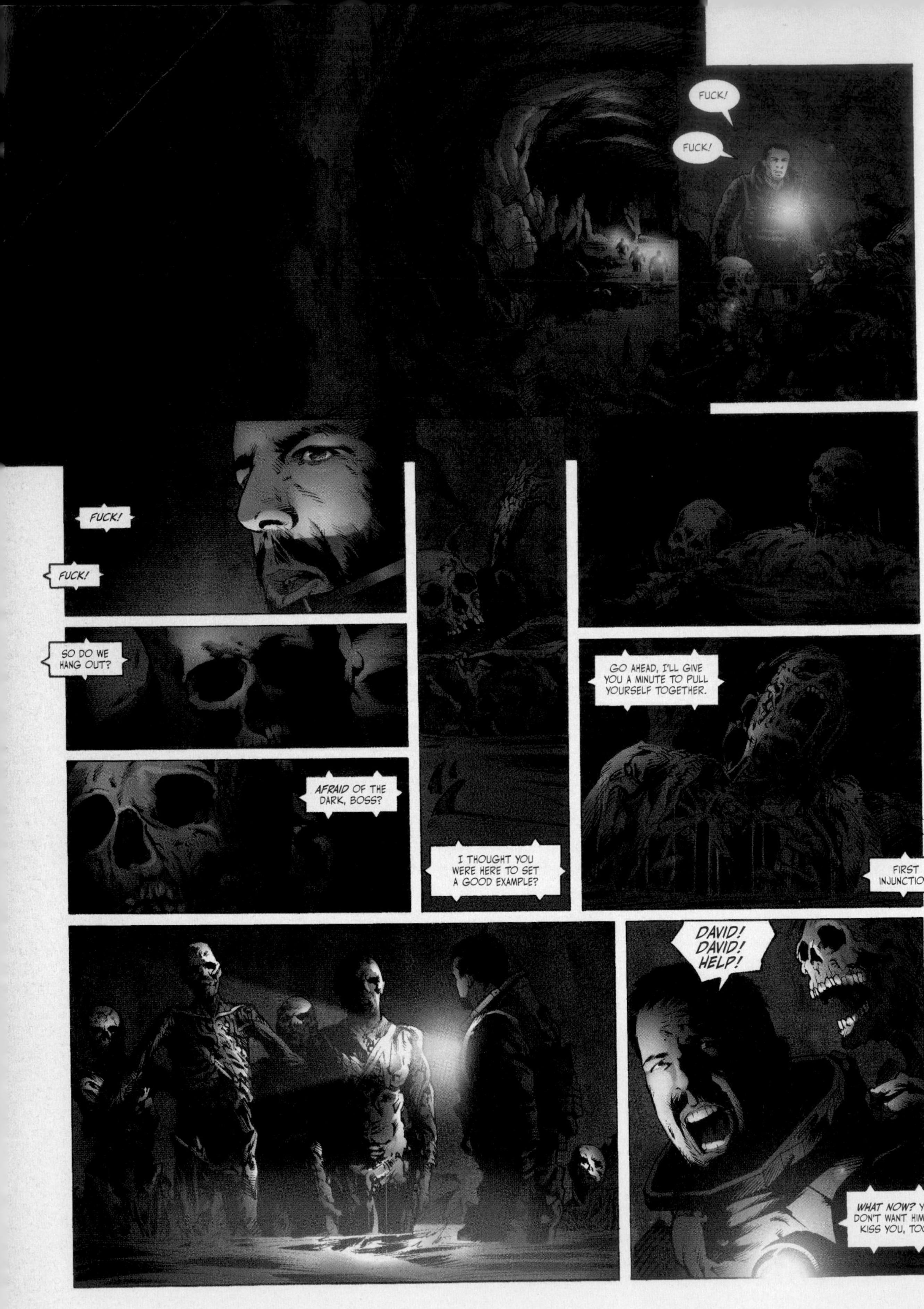
FUCK!
FUCK!
FUCK!
FUCK!
SO DO WE HANG OUT?
AFRAID OF THE DARK, BOSS?
I THOUGHT YOU WERE HERE TO SET A GOOD EXAMPLE?
GO AHEAD, I'LL GIVE YOU A MINUTE TO PULL YOURSELF TOGETHER.
FIRST INJUNCTION!
DAVID! DAVID! HELP!
WHAT NOW? YOU DON'T WANT HIM TO KISS YOU, TOO?

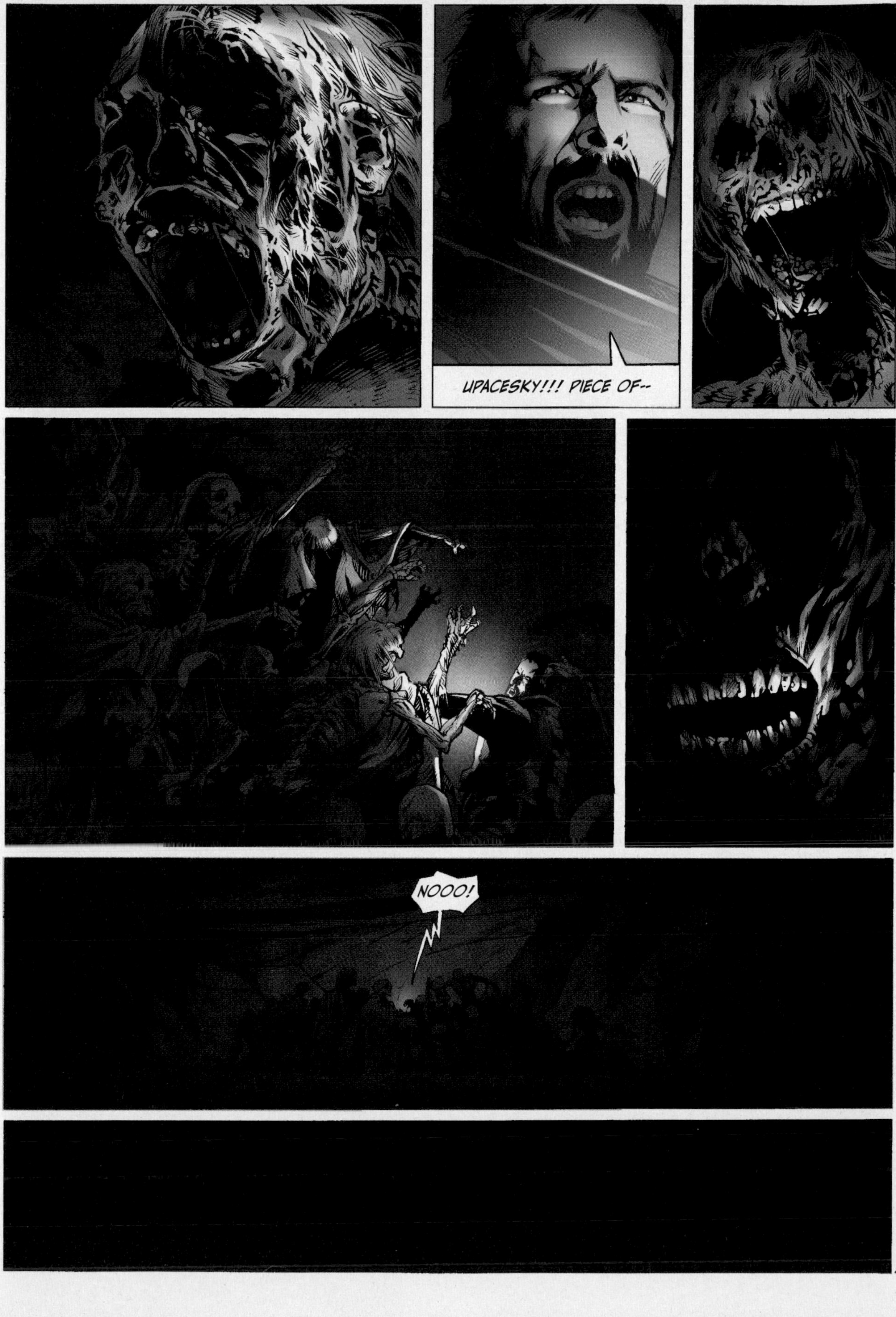
UPACESKY!!! PIECE OF--
NOOO!

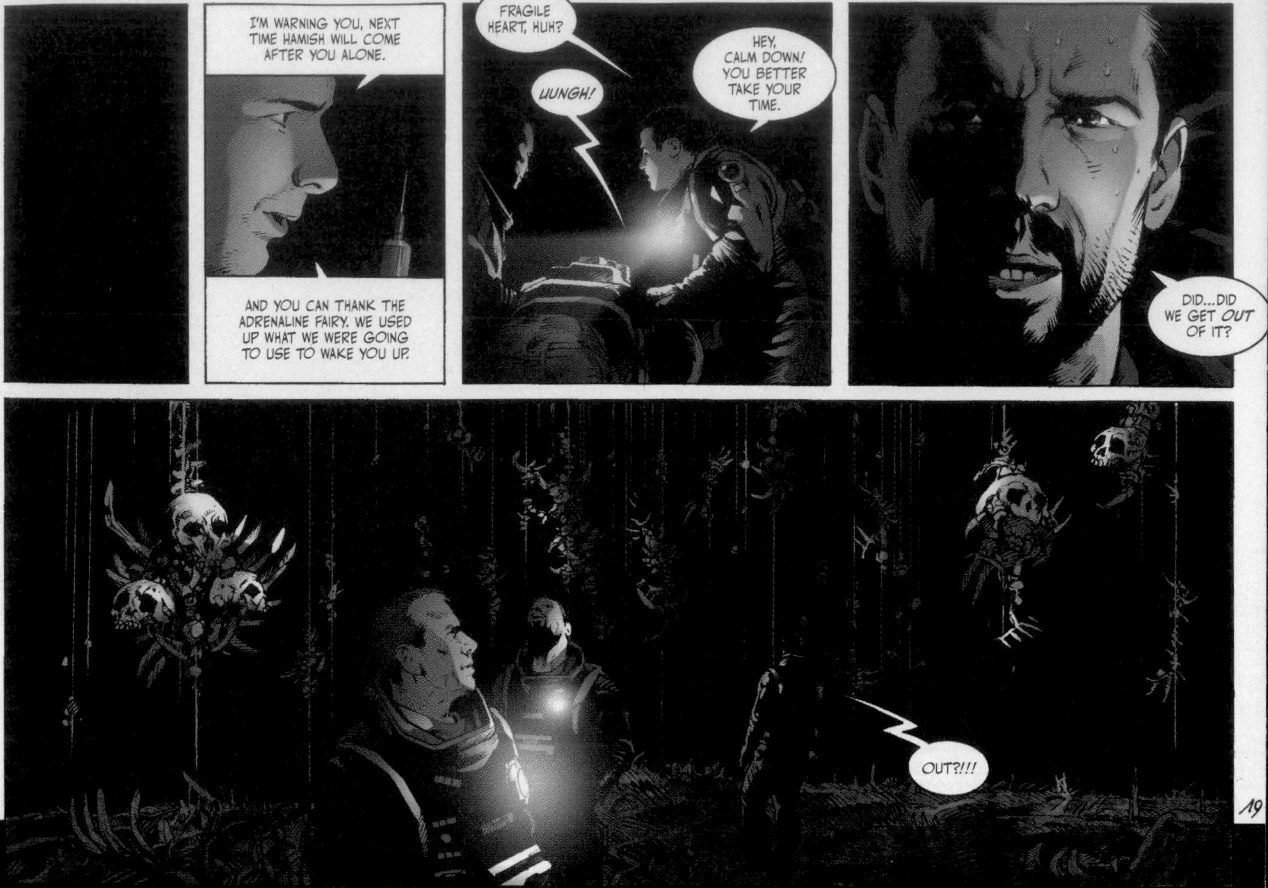
I'M WARNING YOU, NEXT TIME HAMISH WILL COME AFTER YOU ALONE.
AND YOU CAN THANK THE ADRENALINE FAIRY. WE USED UP WHAT WE WERE GOING TO USE TO WAKE YOU UP.
FRAGILE HEART, HUH?
UUNGH!
HEY, CALM DOWN! YOU BETTER TAKE YOUR TIME.
DID...DID WE GET *OUT* OF IT?
OUT?!!!

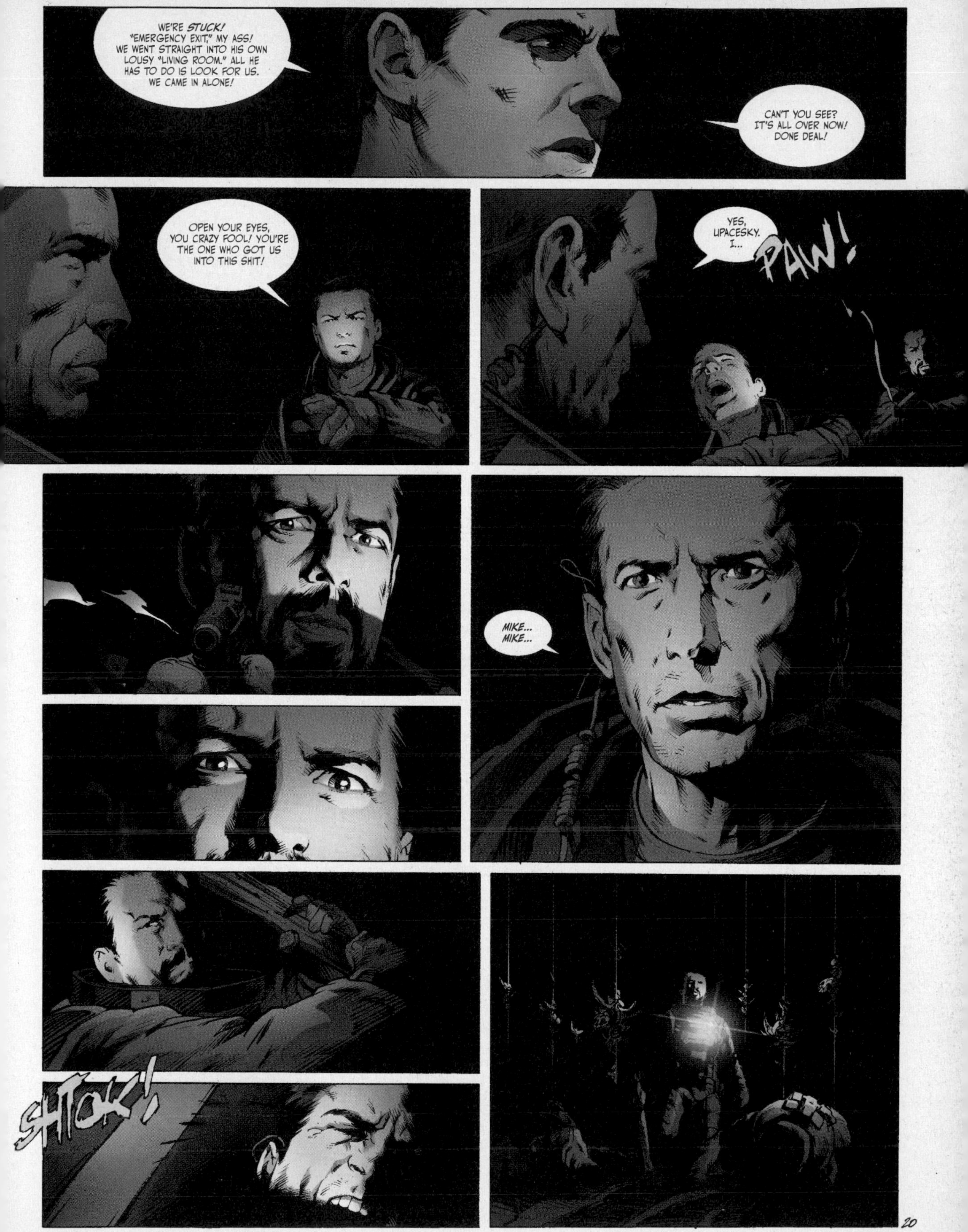
WE'RE STUCK! "EMERGENCY EXIT," MY ASS! WE WENT STRAIGHT INTO HIS OWN LOUSY "LIVING ROOM." ALL HE HAS TO DO IS LOOK FOR US. WE CAME IN ALONE!
CAN'T YOU SEE? IT'S ALL OVER NOW! DONE DEAL!
OPEN YOUR EYES, YOU CRAZY FOOL! YOU'RE THE ONE WHO GOT US INTO THIS SHIT!
YES, UPACESKY. I...
PAW!
MIKE... MIKE...
SHTOK!

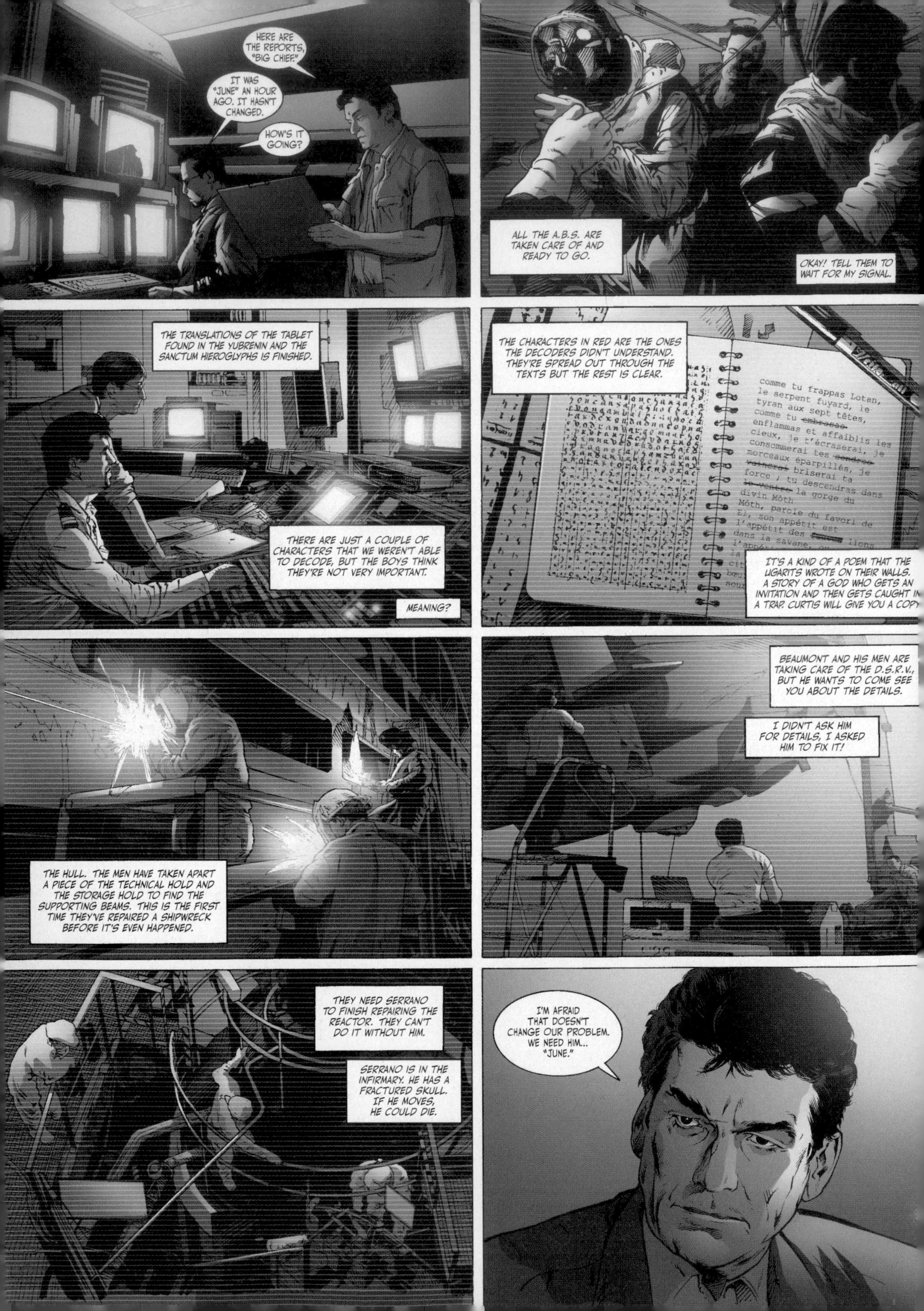
HERE ARE THE REPORTS, "BIG CHIEF."
IT WAS "JUNE" AN HOUR AGO. IT HASN'T CHANGED.
HOW'S IT GOING?
ALL THE A.B.S. ARE TAKEN CARE OF AND READY TO GO.
OKAY! TELL THEM TO WAIT FOR MY SIGNAL.
THE TRANSLATIONS OF THE TABLET FOUND IN THE YUBRENIN AND THE SANCTUM HIEROGLYPHS IS FINISHED.
THERE ARE JUST A COUPLE OF CHARACTERS THAT WE WEREN'T ABLE TO DECODE, BUT THE BOYS THINK THEY'RE NOT VERY IMPORTANT.
MEANING?
THE CHARACTERS IN RED ARE THE ONES THE DECODERS DIDN'T UNDERSTAND. THEY'RE SPREAD OUT THROUGH THE TEXTS BUT THE REST IS CLEAR.
comme tu frappas Lotan,
le serpent fuyard, le
tyran aux sept têtes,
comme tu
enflammas et affaiblis les
cieux, je t'écraserai, je
consommerai tes
morceaux éparpillés, je
briserai ta
force ; tu descendras dans
la gorge du
divin Môth
Môth, parole du favori de
El, son appétit est
l'appétit des lions
dans la savane,
IT'S A KIND OF A POEM THAT THE UGARITS WROTE ON THEIR WALLS. A STORY OF A GOD WHO GETS AN INVITATION AND THEN GETS CAUGHT IN A TRAP. CURTIS WILL GIVE YOU A COPY
THE HULL. THE MEN HAVE TAKEN APART A PIECE OF THE TECHNICAL HOLD AND THE STORAGE HOLD TO FIND THE SUPPORTING BEAMS. THIS IS THE FIRST TIME THEY'VE REPAIRED A SHIPWRECK BEFORE IT'S EVEN HAPPENED.
BEAUMONT AND HIS MEN ARE TAKING CARE OF THE D.S.R.V., BUT HE WANTS TO COME SEE YOU ABOUT THE DETAILS.
I DIDN'T ASK HIM FOR DETAILS, I ASKED HIM TO FIX IT!
THEY NEED SERRANO TO FINISH REPAIRING THE REACTOR. THEY CAN'T DO IT WITHOUT HIM.
SERRANO IS IN THE INFIRMARY. HE HAS A FRACTURED SKULL. IF HE MOVES, HE COULD DIE.
I'M AFRAID THAT DOESN'T CHANGE OUR PROBLEM. WE NEED HIM... "JUNE."

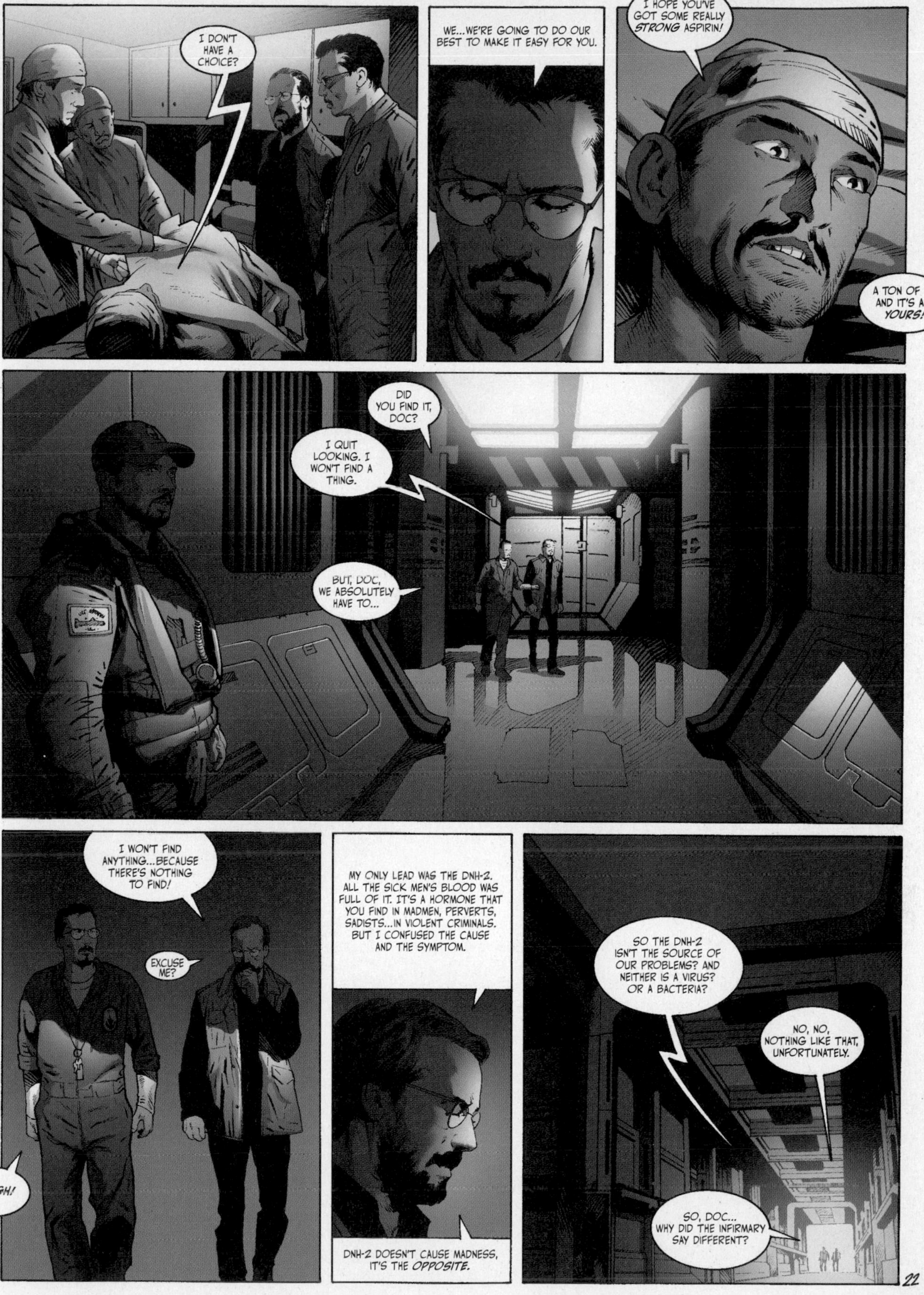
I DON'T HAVE A CHOICE?
WE...WE'RE GOING TO DO OUR BEST TO MAKE IT EASY FOR YOU.
I HOPE YOU'VE GOT SOME REALLY *STRONG* ASPIRIN!
A TON OF IT! AND IT'S ALL *YOURS!*
DID YOU FIND IT, DOC?
I QUIT LOOKING. I WON'T FIND A THING.
BUT, DOC, WE ABSOLUTELY HAVE TO...
I WON'T FIND ANYTHING...BECAUSE THERE'S NOTHING TO FIND!
EXCUSE ME?
COUGH!
MY ONLY LEAD WAS THE DNH-2. ALL THE SICK MEN'S BLOOD WAS FULL OF IT. IT'S A HORMONE THAT YOU FIND IN MADMEN, PERVERTS, SADISTS...IN VIOLENT CRIMINALS. BUT I CONFUSED THE CAUSE AND THE SYMPTOM.
DNH-2 DOESN'T CAUSE MADNESS, IT'S THE *OPPOSITE.*
SO THE DNH-2 ISN'T THE SOURCE OF OUR PROBLEMS? AND NEITHER IS A VIRUS? OR A BACTERIA?
NO, NO, NOTHING LIKE THAT, UNFORTUNATELY.
SO, DOC... WHY DID THE INFIRMARY SAY DIFFERENT?
22

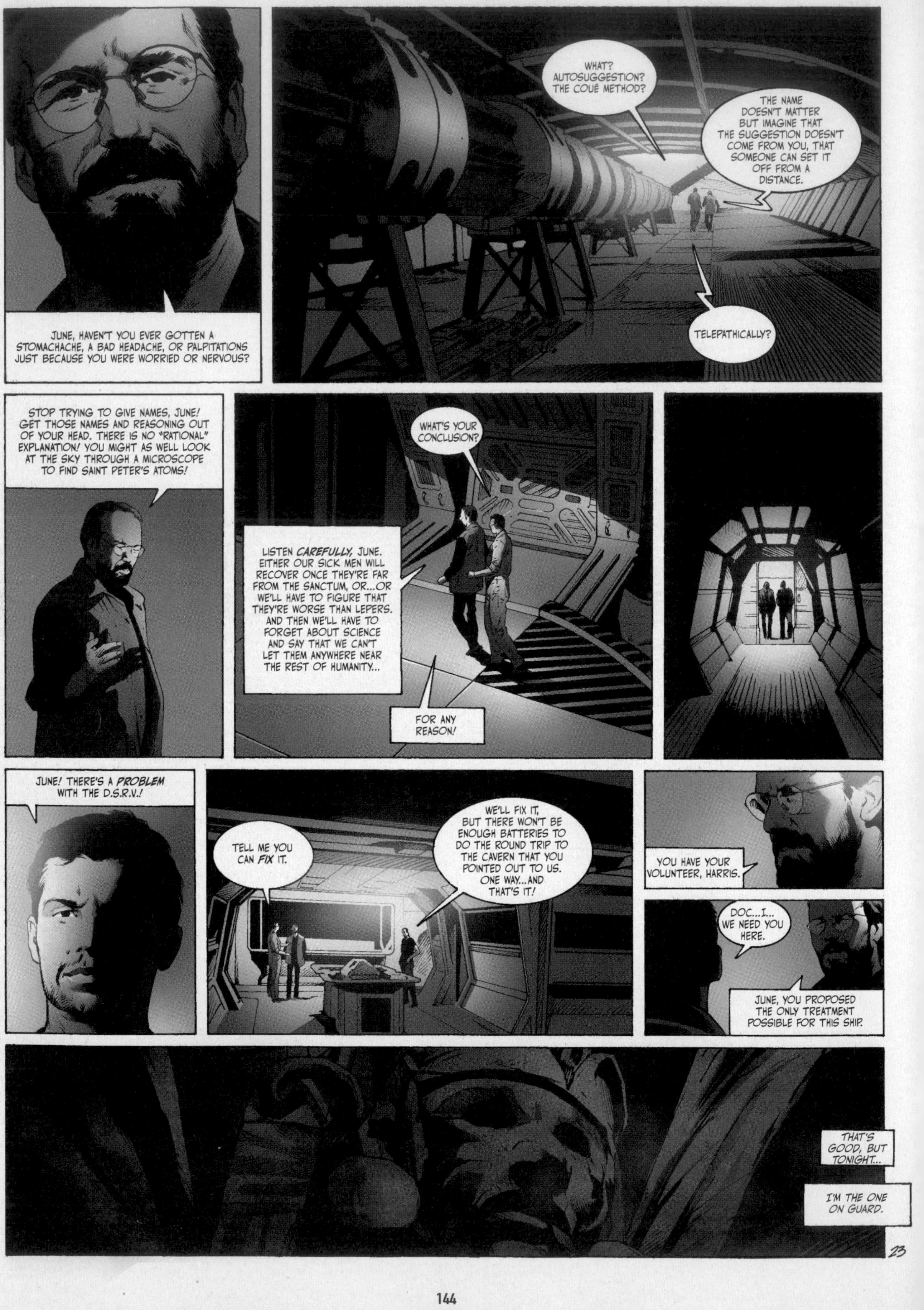
JUNE, HAVEN'T YOU EVER GOTTEN A STOMACHACHE, A BAD HEADACHE, OR PALPITATIONS JUST BECAUSE YOU WERE WORRIED OR NERVOUS?
WHAT? AUTOSUGGESTION? THE COUÉ METHOD?
THE NAME DOESN'T MATTER BUT IMAGINE THAT THE SUGGESTION DOESN'T COME FROM YOU, THAT SOMEONE CAN SET IT OFF FROM A DISTANCE.
TELEPATHICALLY?
STOP TRYING TO GIVE NAMES, JUNE! GET THOSE NAMES AND REASONING OUT OF YOUR HEAD. THERE IS NO "RATIONAL" EXPLANATION! YOU MIGHT AS WELL LOOK AT THE SKY THROUGH A MICROSCOPE TO FIND SAINT PETER'S ATOMS!
WHAT'S YOUR CONCLUSION?
LISTEN CAREFULLY, JUNE. EITHER OUR SICK MEN WILL RECOVER ONCE THEY'RE FAR FROM THE SANCTUM, OR...OR WE'LL HAVE TO FIGURE THAT THEY'RE WORSE THAN LEPERS. AND THEN WE'LL HAVE TO FORGET ABOUT SCIENCE AND SAY THAT WE CAN'T LET THEM ANYWHERE NEAR THE REST OF HUMANITY...
FOR ANY REASON!
JUNE! THERE'S A PROBLEM WITH THE D.S.R.V.!
TELL ME YOU CAN FIX IT.
WE'LL FIX IT, BUT THERE WON'T BE ENOUGH BATTERIES TO DO THE ROUND TRIP TO THE CAVERN THAT YOU POINTED OUT TO US. ONE WAY...AND THAT'S IT!
YOU HAVE YOUR VOLUNTEER, HARRIS.
DOC...I... WE NEED YOU HERE.
JUNE, YOU PROPOSED THE ONLY TREATMENT POSSIBLE FOR THIS SHIP.
THAT'S GOOD, BUT TONIGHT...
I'M THE ONE ON GUARD.
23

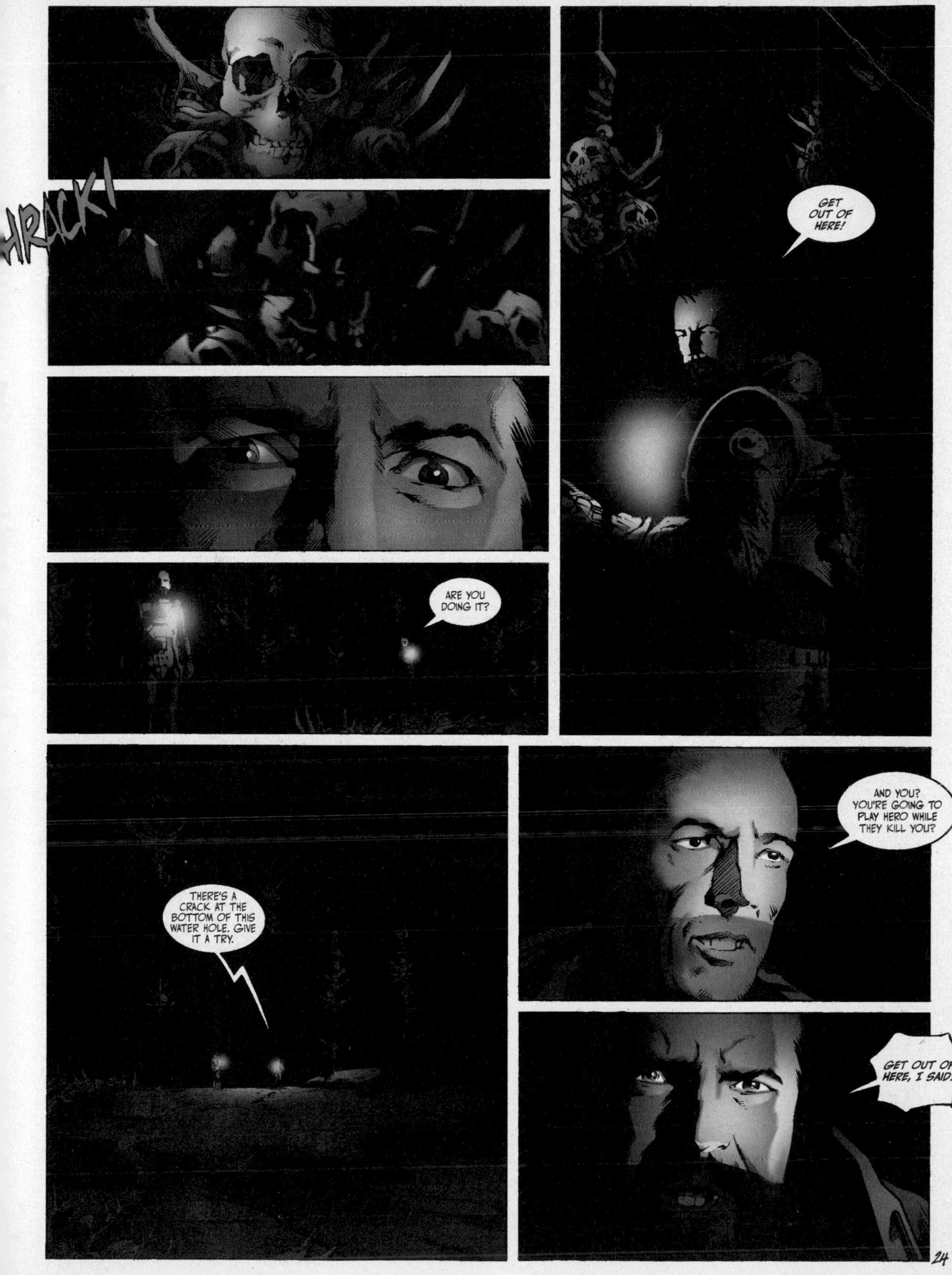
HRACK!
GET OUT OF HERE!
ARE YOU DOING IT?
AND YOU? YOU'RE GOING TO PLAY HERO WHILE THEY KILL YOU?
THERE'S A CRACK AT THE BOTTOM OF THIS WATER HOLE. GIVE IT A TRY.
GET OUT OF HERE, I SAID!
24

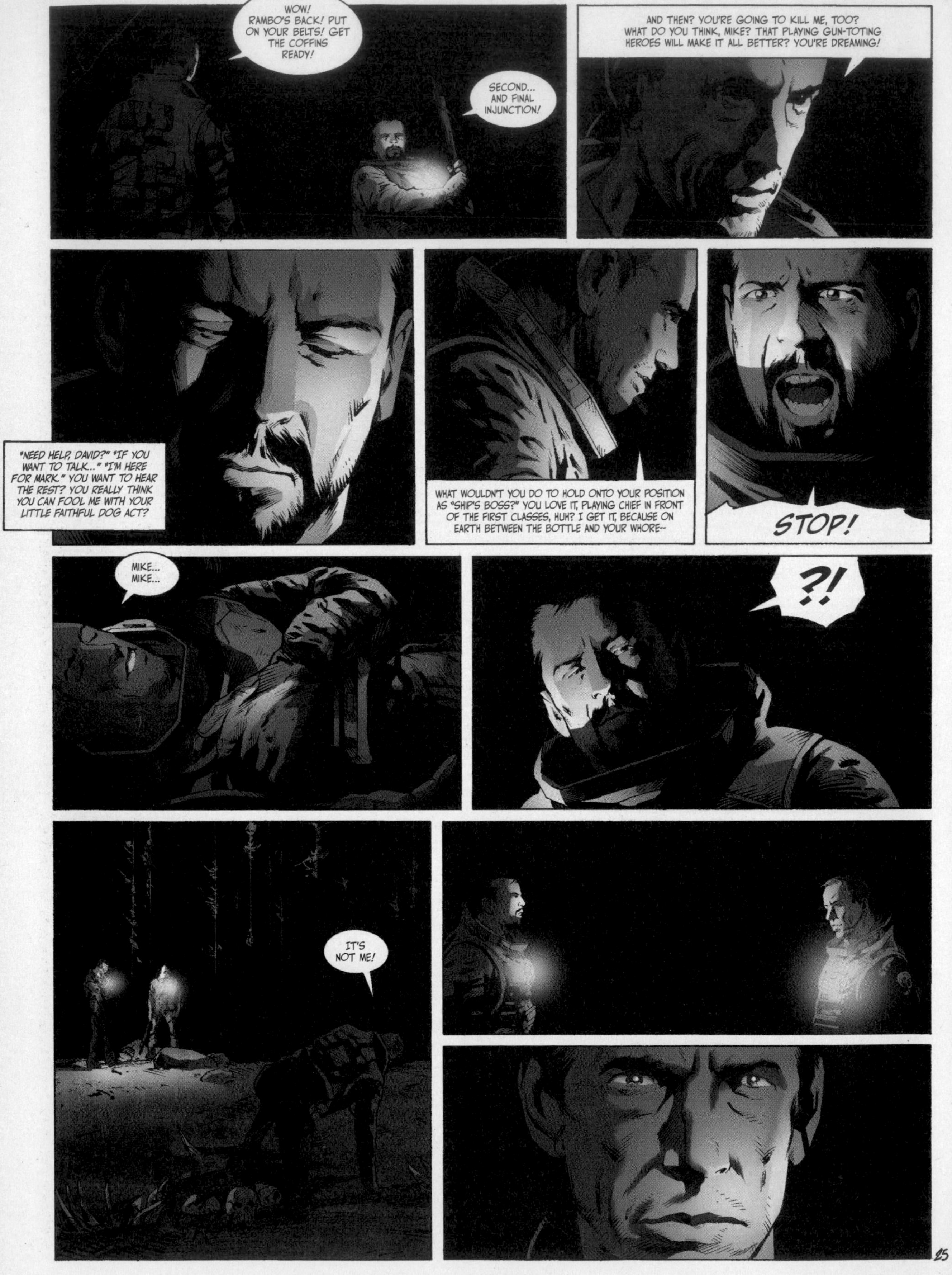
WOW! RAMBO'S BACK! PUT ON YOUR BELTS! GET THE COFFINS READY!
SECOND... AND FINAL INJUNCTION!
AND THEN? YOU'RE GOING TO KILL ME, TOO? WHAT DO YOU THINK, MIKE? THAT PLAYING GUN-TOTING HEROES WILL MAKE IT ALL BETTER? YOU'RE DREAMING!
"NEED HELP, DAVID?" "IF YOU WANT TO TALK..." "I'M HERE FOR MARK." YOU WANT TO HEAR THE REST? YOU REALLY THINK YOU CAN FOOL ME WITH YOUR LITTLE FAITHFUL DOG ACT?
WHAT WOULDN'T YOU DO TO HOLD ONTO YOUR POSITION AS "SHIP'S BOSS?" YOU LOVE IT, PLAYING CHIEF IN FRONT OF THE FIRST CLASSES, HUH? I GET IT, BECAUSE ON EARTH BETWEEN THE BOTTLE AND YOUR WHORE--
STOP!
MIKE... MIKE...
?!
IT'S NOT ME!
25

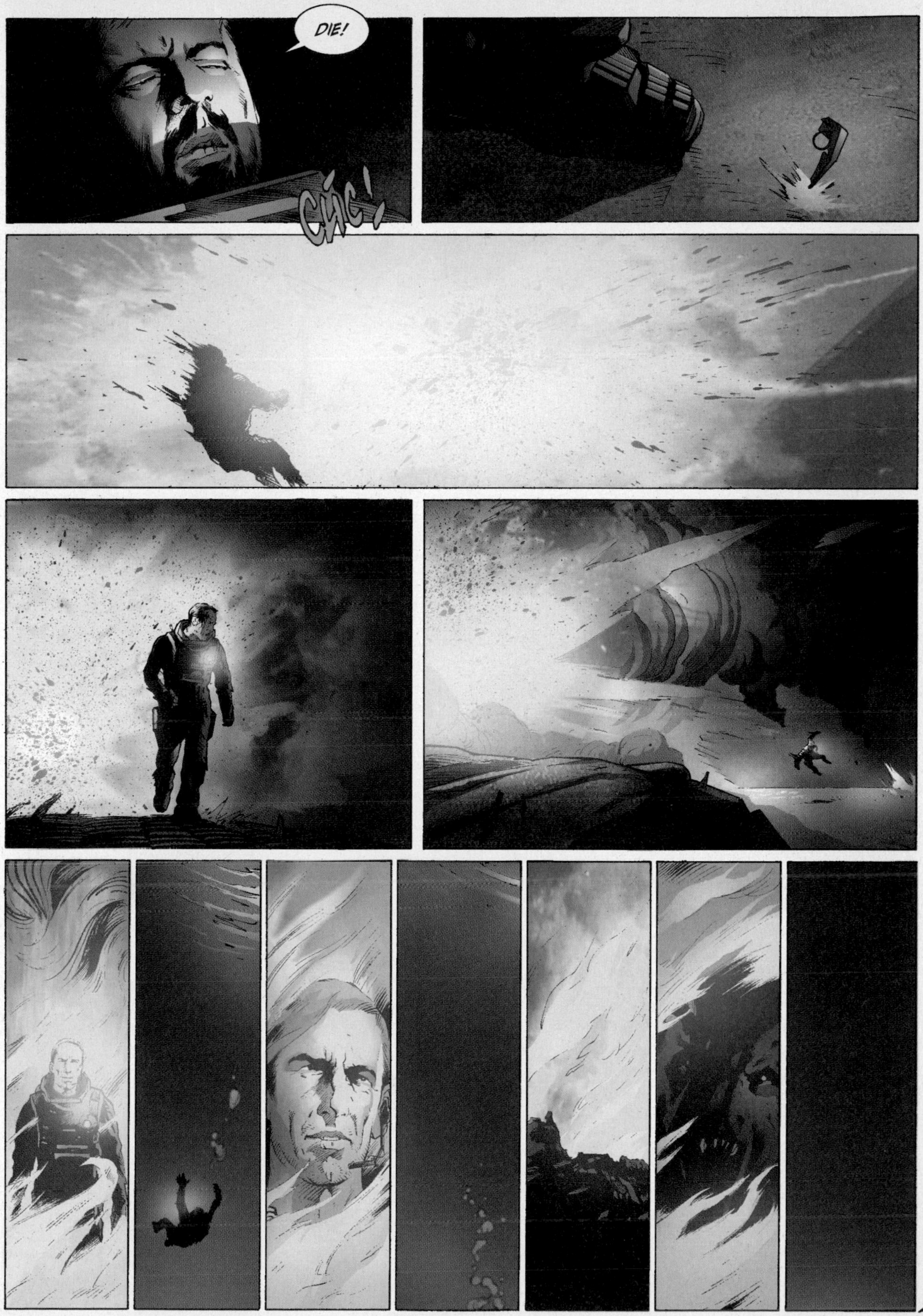
DIE!
CLIC!
26

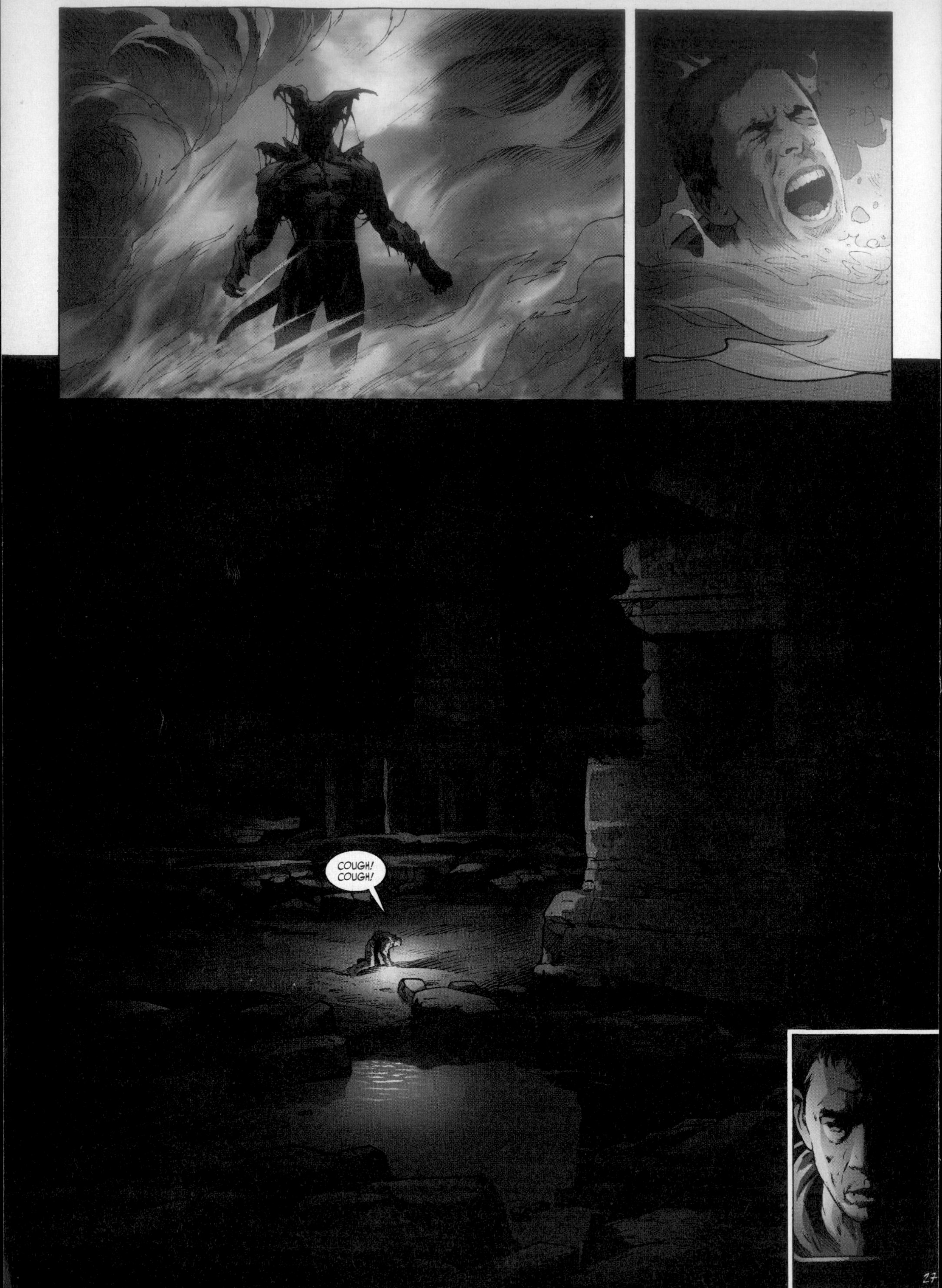
COUGH!
COUGH!

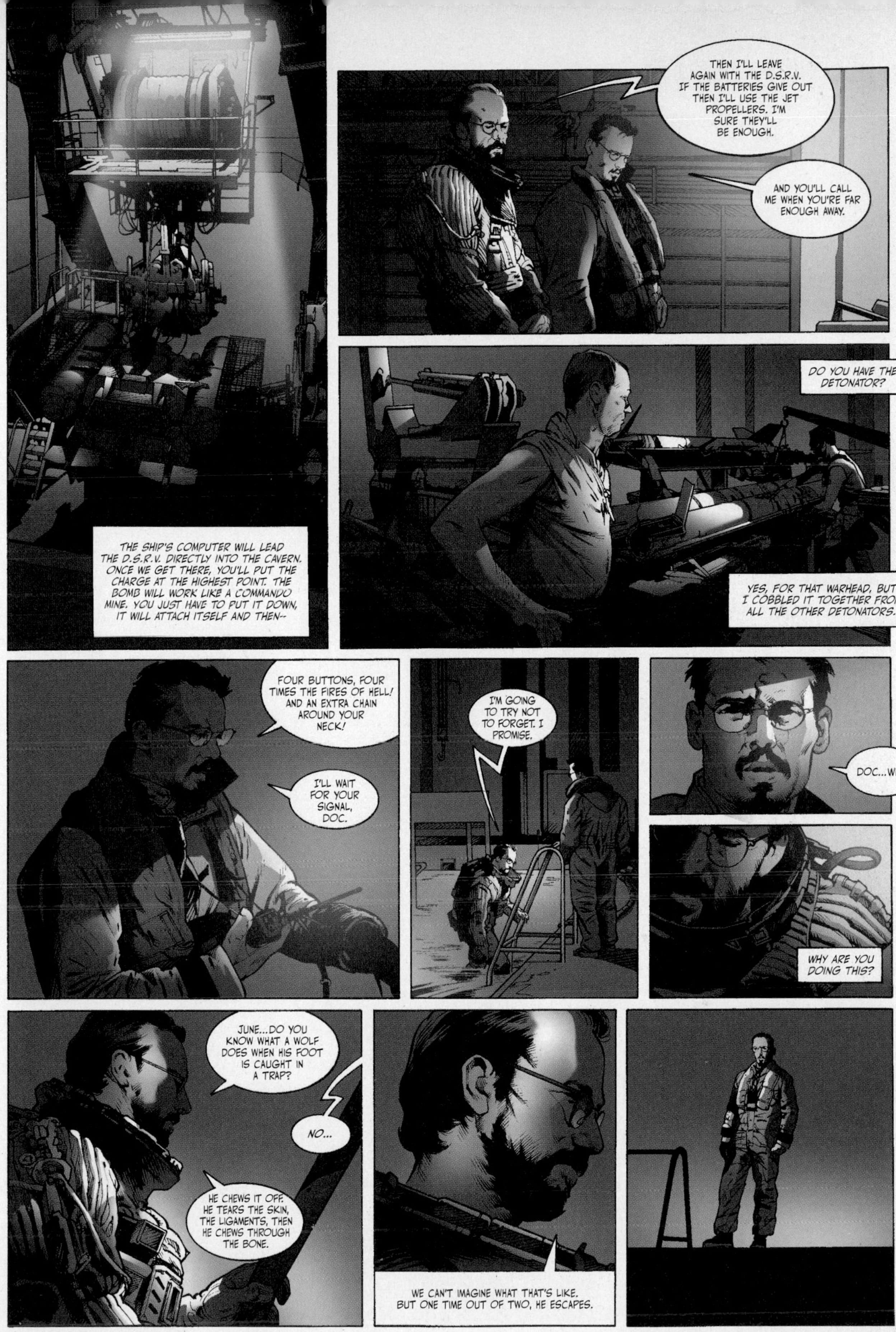
THEN I'LL LEAVE AGAIN WITH THE D.S.R.V. IF THE BATTERIES GIVE OUT THEN I'LL USE THE JET PROPELLERS. I'M SURE THEY'LL BE ENOUGH.
AND YOU'LL CALL ME WHEN YOU'RE FAR ENOUGH AWAY.
THE SHIP'S COMPUTER WILL LEAD THE D.S.R.V. DIRECTLY INTO THE CAVERN. ONCE WE GET THERE, YOU'LL PUT THE CHARGE AT THE HIGHEST POINT. THE BOMB WILL WORK LIKE A COMMANDO MINE. YOU JUST HAVE TO PUT IT DOWN, IT WILL ATTACH ITSELF AND THEN--
DO YOU HAVE THE DETONATOR?
YES, FOR THAT WARHEAD, BUT I COBBLED IT TOGETHER FROM ALL THE OTHER DETONATORS.
FOUR BUTTONS, FOUR TIMES THE FIRES OF HELL! AND AN EXTRA CHAIN AROUND YOUR NECK!
I'LL WAIT FOR YOUR SIGNAL, DOC.
I'M GOING TO TRY NOT TO FORGET. I PROMISE.
DOC...WHY?
WHY ARE YOU DOING THIS?
JUNE...DO YOU KNOW WHAT A WOLF DOES WHEN HIS FOOT IS CAUGHT IN A TRAP?
NO...
HE CHEWS IT OFF. HE TEARS THE SKIN, THE LIGAMENTS, THEN HE CHEWS THROUGH THE BONE.
WE CAN'T IMAGINE WHAT THAT'S LIKE. BUT ONE TIME OUT OF TWO, HE ESCAPES.
28

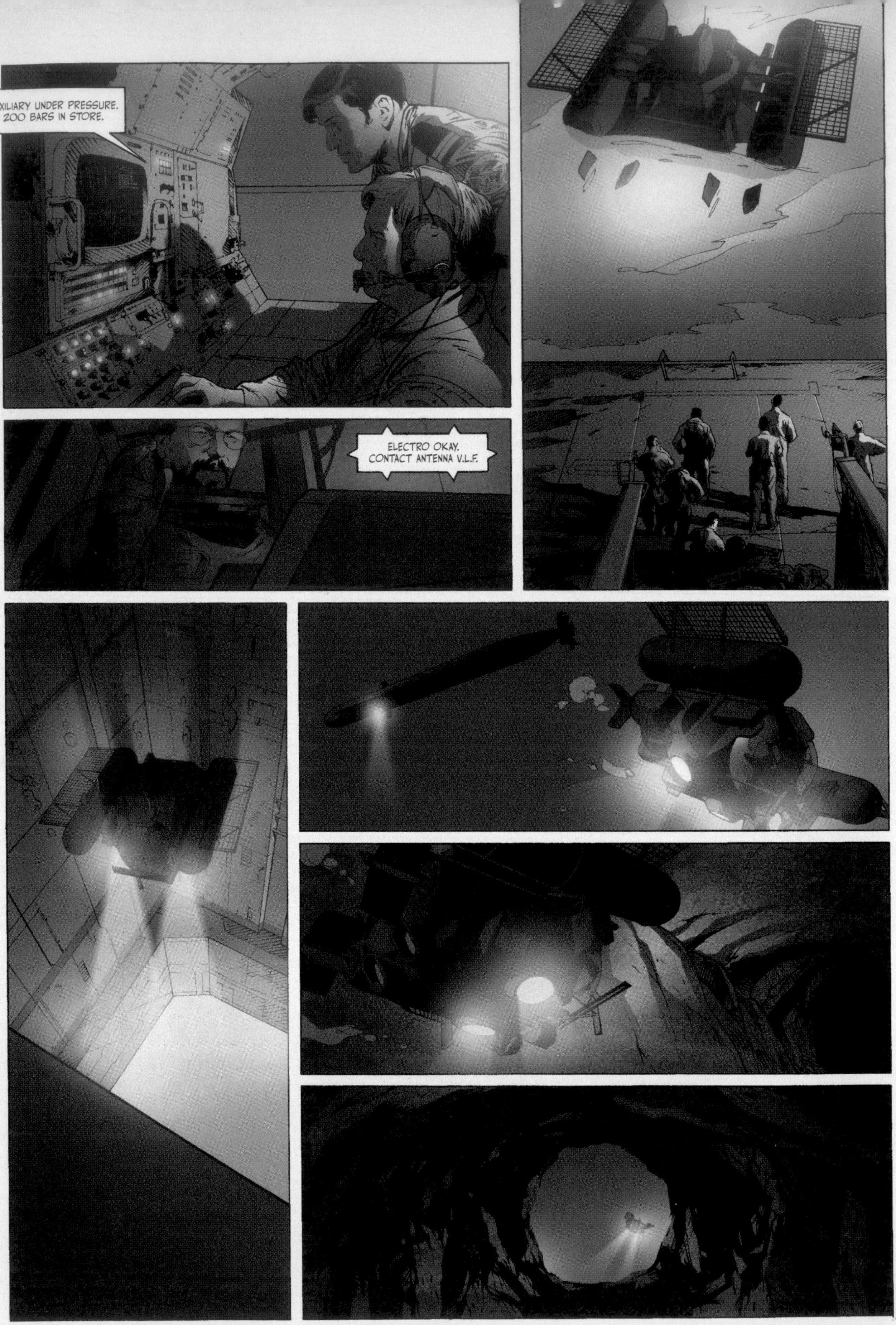

AUXILIARY UNDER PRESSURE. 200 BARS IN STORE.
ELECTRO OKAY. CONTACT ANTENNA V.L.F.

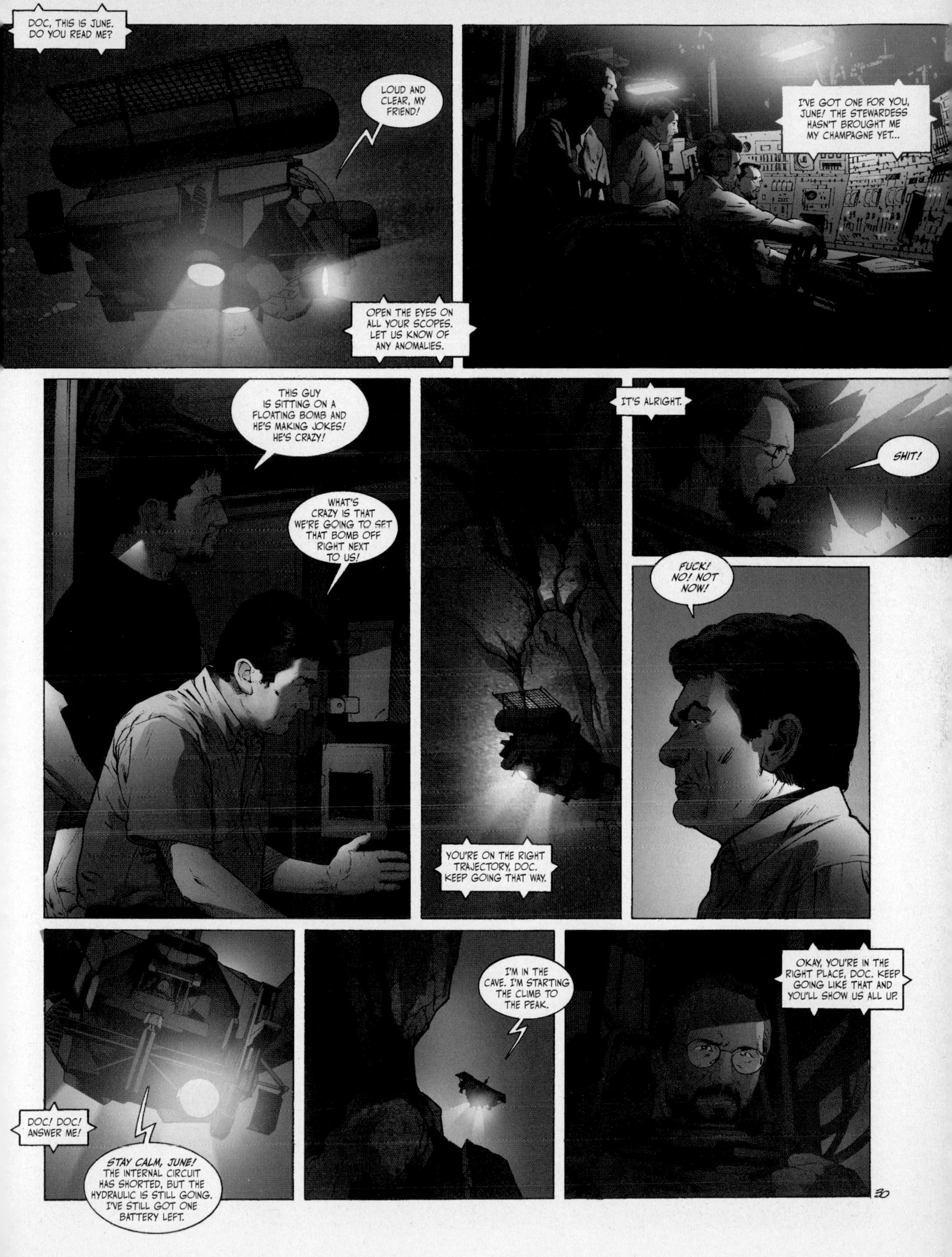
DOC, THIS IS JUNE. DO YOU READ ME?
LOUD AND CLEAR, MY FRIEND!
OPEN THE EYES ON ALL YOUR SCOPES. LET US KNOW OF ANY ANOMALIES.
I'VE GOT ONE FOR YOU, JUNE! THE STEWARDESS HASN'T BROUGHT ME MY CHAMPAGNE YET...
THIS GUY IS SITTING ON A FLOATING BOMB AND HE'S MAKING JOKES! HE'S CRAZY!
WHAT'S CRAZY IS THAT WE'RE GOING TO SET THAT BOMB OFF RIGHT NEXT TO US!
YOU'RE ON THE RIGHT TRAJECTORY, DOC. KEEP GOING THAT WAY.
IT'S ALRIGHT.
SHIT!
FUCK! NO! NOT NOW!
DOC! DOC! ANSWER ME!
STAY CALM, JUNE! THE INTERNAL CIRCUIT HAS SHORTED, BUT THE HYDRAULIC IS STILL GOING. I'VE STILL GOT ONE BATTERY LEFT.
I'M IN THE CAVE. I'M STARTING THE CLIMB TO THE PEAK.
OKAY, YOU'RE IN THE RIGHT PLACE, DOC. KEEP GOING LIKE THAT AND YOU'LL SHOW US ALL UP.

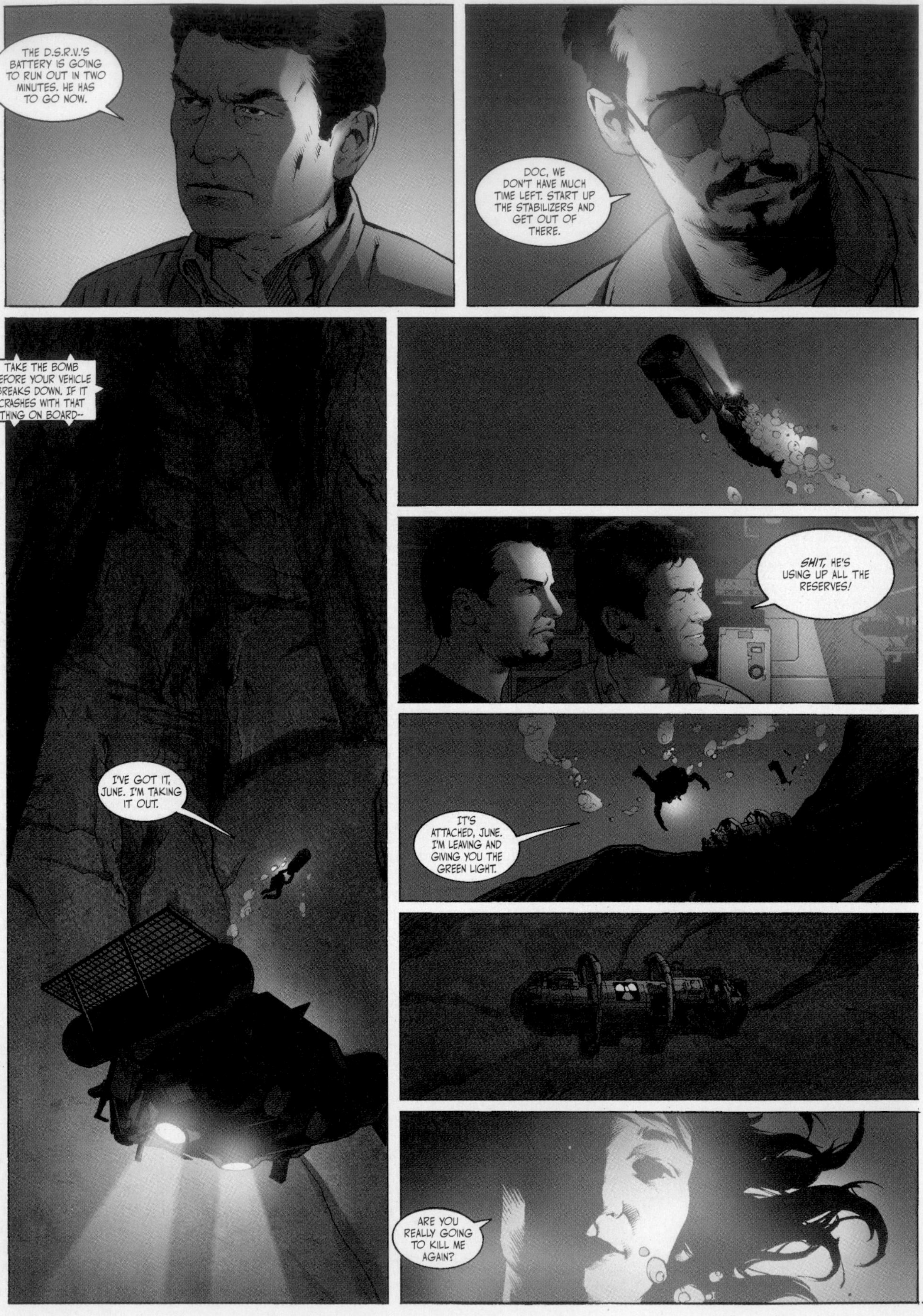
THE D.S.R.V.'S BATTERY IS GOING TO RUN OUT IN TWO MINUTES. HE HAS TO GO NOW.
DOC, WE DON'T HAVE MUCH TIME LEFT. START UP THE STABILIZERS AND GET OUT OF THERE.
TAKE THE BOMB BEFORE YOUR VEHICLE BREAKS DOWN. IF IT CRASHES WITH THAT THING ON BOARD--
I'VE GOT IT, JUNE. I'M TAKING IT OUT.
SHIT, HE'S USING UP ALL THE RESERVES!
IT'S ATTACHED, JUNE. I'M LEAVING AND GIVING YOU THE GREEN LIGHT.
ARE YOU REALLY GOING TO KILL ME AGAIN?
31

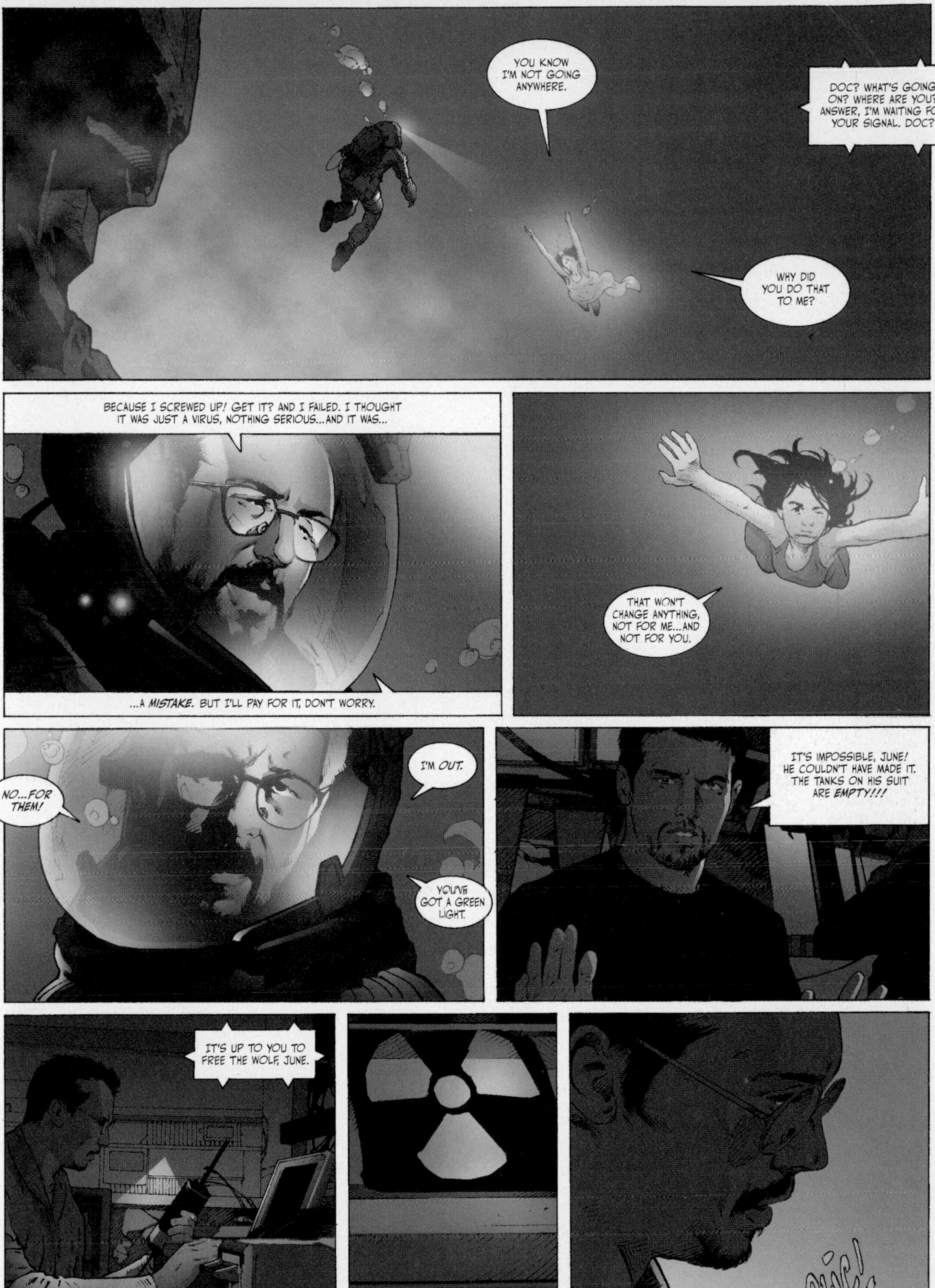
YOU KNOW I'M NOT GOING ANYWHERE.
DOC? WHAT'S GOING ON? WHERE ARE YOU? ANSWER, I'M WAITING FOR YOUR SIGNAL. DOC?
WHY DID YOU DO THAT TO ME?
BECAUSE I SCREWED UP! GET IT? AND I FAILED. I THOUGHT IT WAS JUST A VIRUS, NOTHING SERIOUS...AND IT WAS...
...A MISTAKE. BUT I'LL PAY FOR IT, DON'T WORRY.
THAT WON'T CHANGE ANYTHING, NOT FOR ME...AND NOT FOR YOU.
NO...FOR THEM!
I'M OUT.
YOU'VE GOT A GREEN LIGHT.
IT'S IMPOSSIBLE, JUNE! HE COULDN'T HAVE MADE IT. THE TANKS ON HIS SUIT ARE EMPTY!!!
IT'S UP TO YOU TO FREE THE WOLF, JUNE.
CLIC!
32

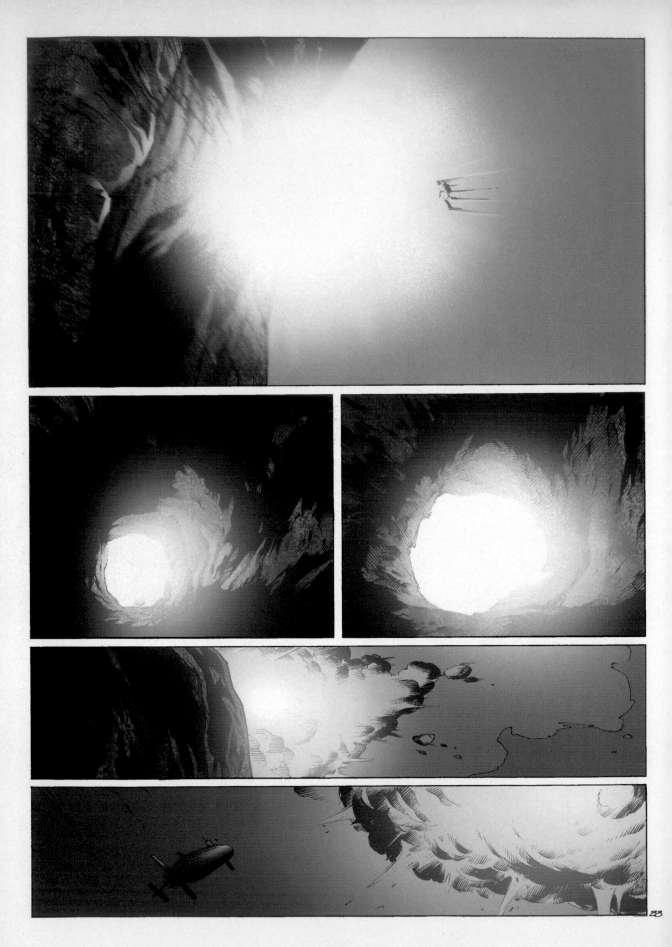

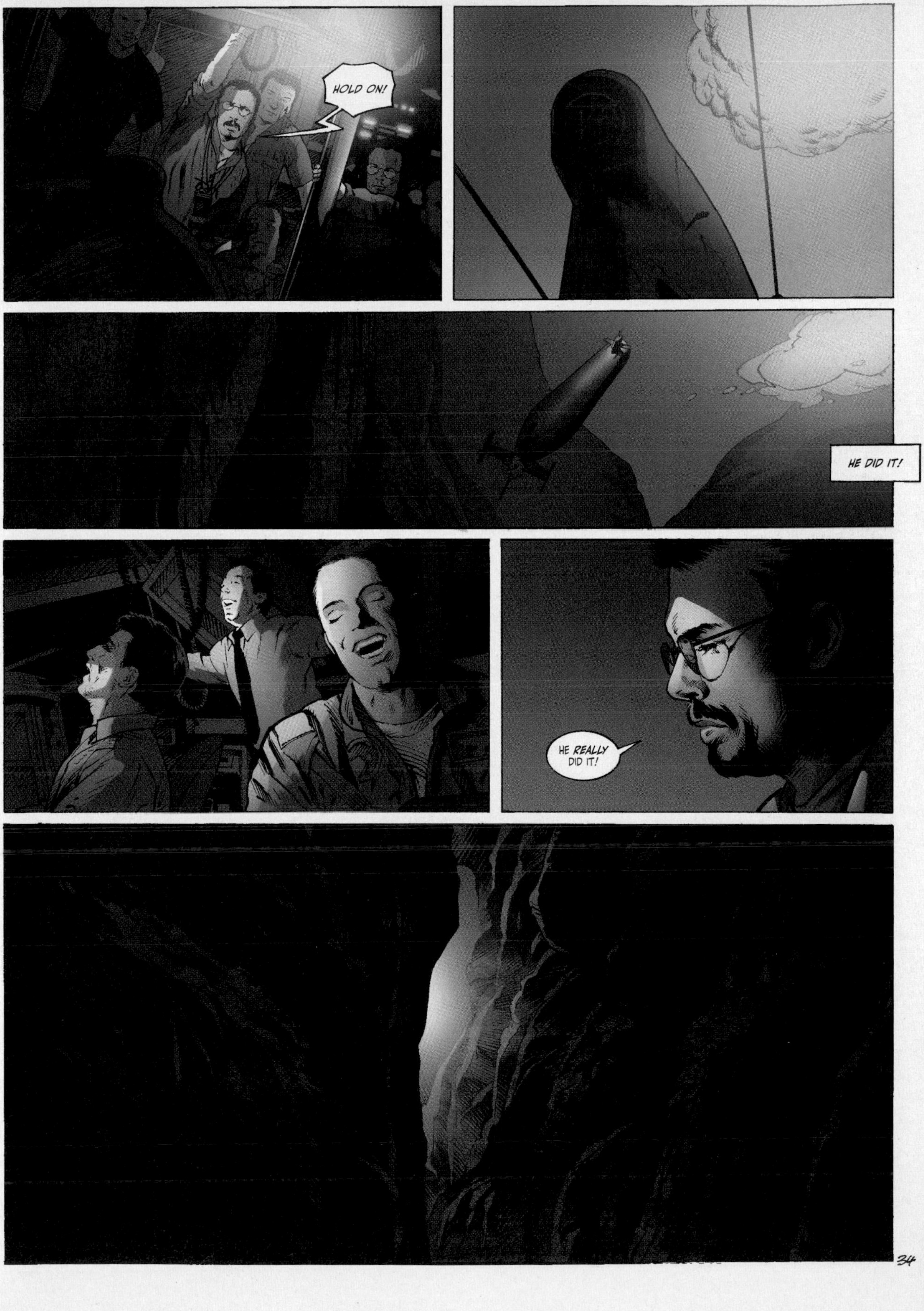
HOLD ON!
HE DID IT!
HE REALLY DID IT!
34

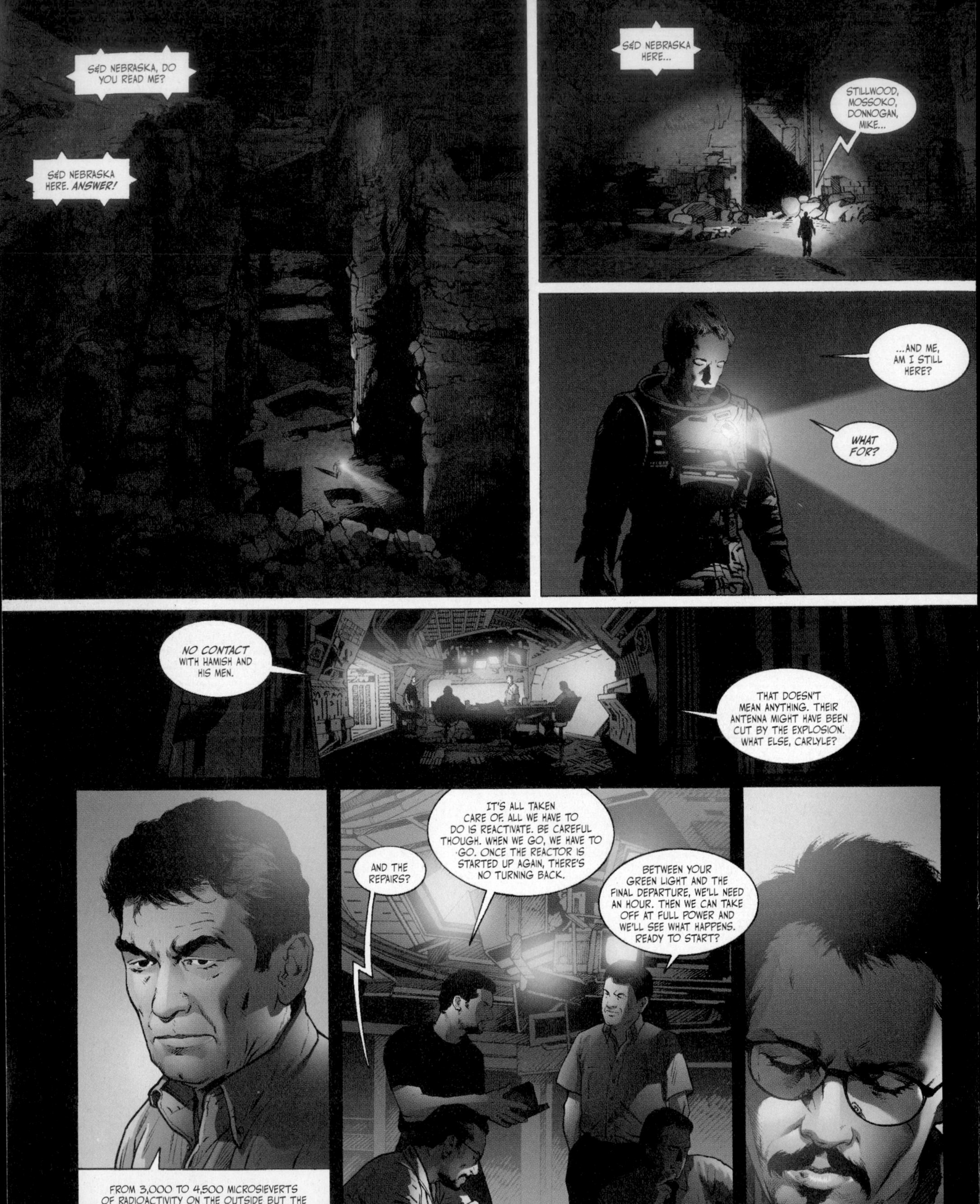
S&D NEBRASKA, DO YOU READ ME?
S&D NEBRASKA HERE. ANSWER!
S&D NEBRASKA HERE...
STILLWOOD, MOSSOKO, DONNOGAN, MIKE...
...AND ME, AM I STILL HERE?
WHAT FOR?
NO CONTACT WITH HAMISH AND HIS MEN.
THAT DOESN'T MEAN ANYTHING. THEIR ANTENNA MIGHT HAVE BEEN CUT BY THE EXPLOSION. WHAT ELSE, CARLYLE?
FROM 3,000 TO 4,500 MICROSIEVERTS OF RADIOACTIVITY ON THE OUTSIDE BUT THE HULL MIGHT HOLD IT OFF. THE SCANNERS ARE RECORDING VARIATIONS IN PRESSURE AT THE EXPLOSION POINT. WE MIGHT HAVE MANAGED TO BREACH THE STONE CEILING. AS FOR NEBRASKA, NO SIGNIFICANT DAMAGE BUT WE HAVE SEVEN NEW CLIENTS IN THE INFIRMARY.
AND THE REPAIRS?
IT'S ALL TAKEN CARE OF. ALL WE HAVE TO DO IS REACTIVATE. BE CAREFUL THOUGH. WHEN WE GO, WE HAVE TO GO. ONCE THE REACTOR IS STARTED UP AGAIN, THERE'S NO TURNING BACK.
BETWEEN YOUR GREEN LIGHT AND THE FINAL DEPARTURE, WE'LL NEED AN HOUR. THEN WE CAN TAKE OFF AT FULL POWER AND WE'LL SEE WHAT HAPPENS. READY TO START?
35

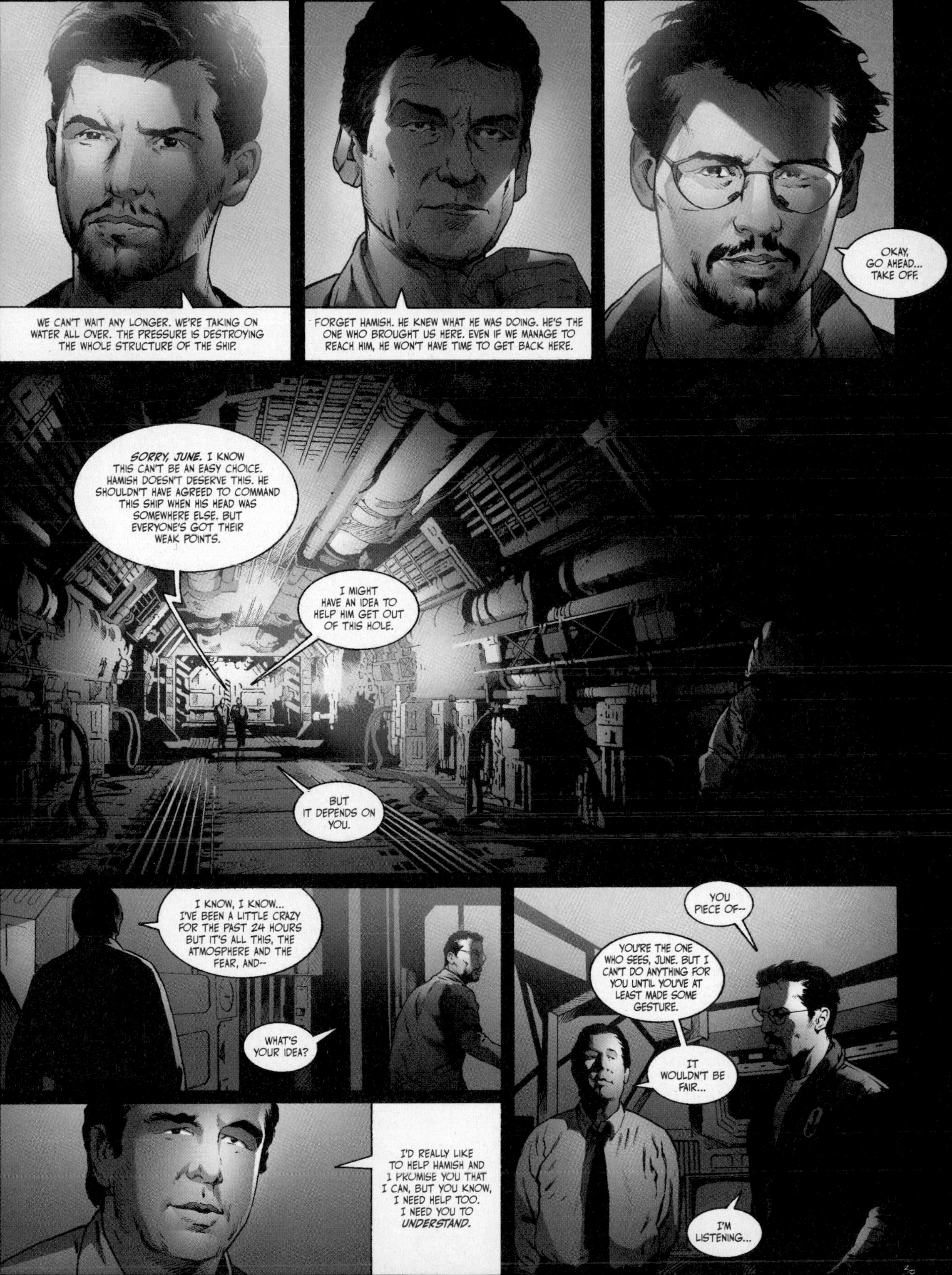
WE CAN'T WAIT ANY LONGER. WE'RE TAKING ON WATER ALL OVER. THE PRESSURE IS DESTROYING THE WHOLE STRUCTURE OF THE SHIP.
FORGET HAMISH. HE KNEW WHAT HE WAS DOING. HE'S THE ONE WHO BROUGHT US HERE. EVEN IF WE MANAGE TO REACH HIM, HE WON'T HAVE TIME TO GET BACK HERE.
OKAY, GO AHEAD... TAKE OFF.
SORRY, JUNE. I KNOW THIS CAN'T BE AN EASY CHOICE. HAMISH DOESN'T DESERVE THIS. HE SHOULDN'T HAVE AGREED TO COMMAND THIS SHIP WHEN HIS HEAD WAS SOMEWHERE ELSE. BUT EVERYONE'S GOT THEIR WEAK POINTS.
I MIGHT HAVE AN IDEA TO HELP HIM GET OUT OF THIS HOLE.
BUT IT DEPENDS ON YOU.
I KNOW, I KNOW... I'VE BEEN A LITTLE CRAZY FOR THE PAST 24 HOURS BUT IT'S ALL THIS, THE ATMOSPHERE AND THE FEAR, AND--
WHAT'S YOUR IDEA?
I'D REALLY LIKE TO HELP HAMISH AND I PROMISE YOU THAT I CAN, BUT YOU KNOW, I NEED HELP TOO. I NEED YOU TO UNDERSTAND.
YOU PIECE OF--
YOU'RE THE ONE WHO SEES, JUNE. BUT I CAN'T DO ANYTHING FOR YOU UNTIL YOU'VE AT LEAST MADE SOME GESTURE.
IT WOULDN'T BE FAIR...
I'M LISTENING...

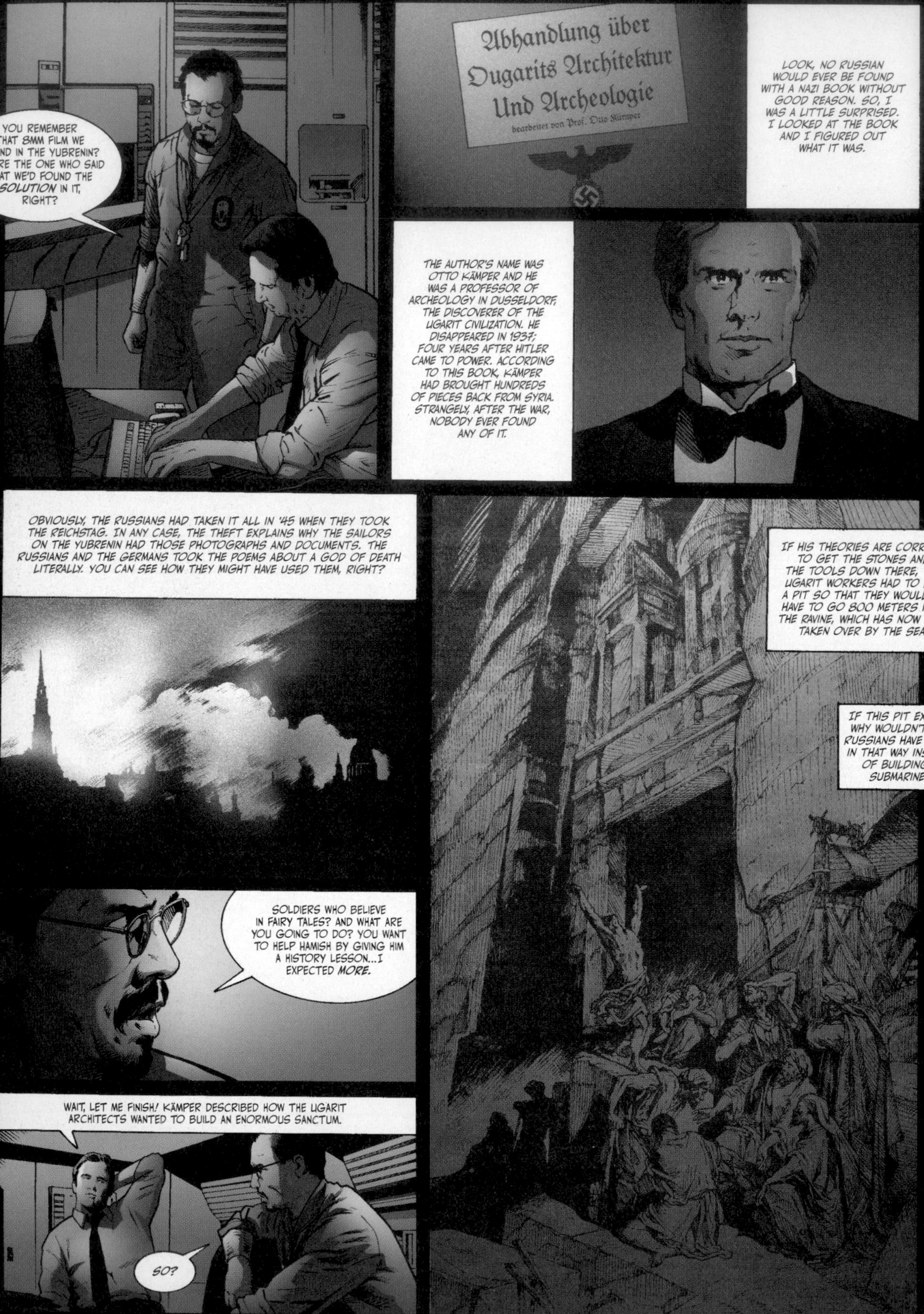

YOU REMEMBER THAT 8MM FILM WE FOUND IN THE YUBRENIN? YOU'RE THE ONE WHO SAID THAT WE'D FOUND THE SOLUTION IN IT, RIGHT?
Abhandlung über Ougarits Architektur Und Archeologie
bearbeitet von Prof. Otto Kämper
LOOK, NO RUSSIAN WOULD EVER BE FOUND WITH A NAZI BOOK WITHOUT GOOD REASON. SO, I WAS A LITTLE SURPRISED. I LOOKED AT THE BOOK AND I FIGURED OUT WHAT IT WAS.
THE AUTHOR'S NAME WAS OTTO KÄMPER AND HE WAS A PROFESSOR OF ARCHEOLOGY IN DUSSELDORF, THE DISCOVERER OF THE UGARIT CIVILIZATION. HE DISAPPEARED IN 1937; FOUR YEARS AFTER HITLER CAME TO POWER. ACCORDING TO THIS BOOK, KÄMPER HAD BROUGHT HUNDREDS OF PIECES BACK FROM SYRIA. STRANGELY, AFTER THE WAR, NOBODY EVER FOUND ANY OF IT.
OBVIOUSLY, THE RUSSIANS HAD TAKEN IT ALL IN '45 WHEN THEY TOOK THE REICHSTAG. IN ANY CASE, THE THEFT EXPLAINS WHY THE SAILORS ON THE YUBRENIN HAD THOSE PHOTOGRAPHS AND DOCUMENTS. THE RUSSIANS AND THE GERMANS TOOK THE POEMS ABOUT A GOD OF DEATH LITERALLY. YOU CAN SEE HOW THEY MIGHT HAVE USED THEM, RIGHT?
SOLDIERS WHO BELIEVE IN FAIRY TALES? AND WHAT ARE YOU GOING TO DO? YOU WANT TO HELP HAMISH BY GIVING HIM A HISTORY LESSON...I EXPECTED MORE.
WAIT, LET ME FINISH! KÄMPER DESCRIBED HOW THE UGARIT ARCHITECTS WANTED TO BUILD AN ENORMOUS SANCTUM.
SO?
IF HIS THEORIES ARE CORRECT, TO GET THE STONES AND THE TOOLS DOWN THERE, THE UGARIT WORKERS HAD TO DIG A PIT SO THAT THEY WOULDN'T HAVE TO GO 800 METERS INTO THE RAVINE, WHICH HAS NOW BEEN TAKEN OVER BY THE SEA.
IF THIS PIT EXISTS, WHY WOULDN'T THE RUSSIANS HAVE GONE IN THAT WAY INSTEAD OF BUILDING A SUBMARINE?

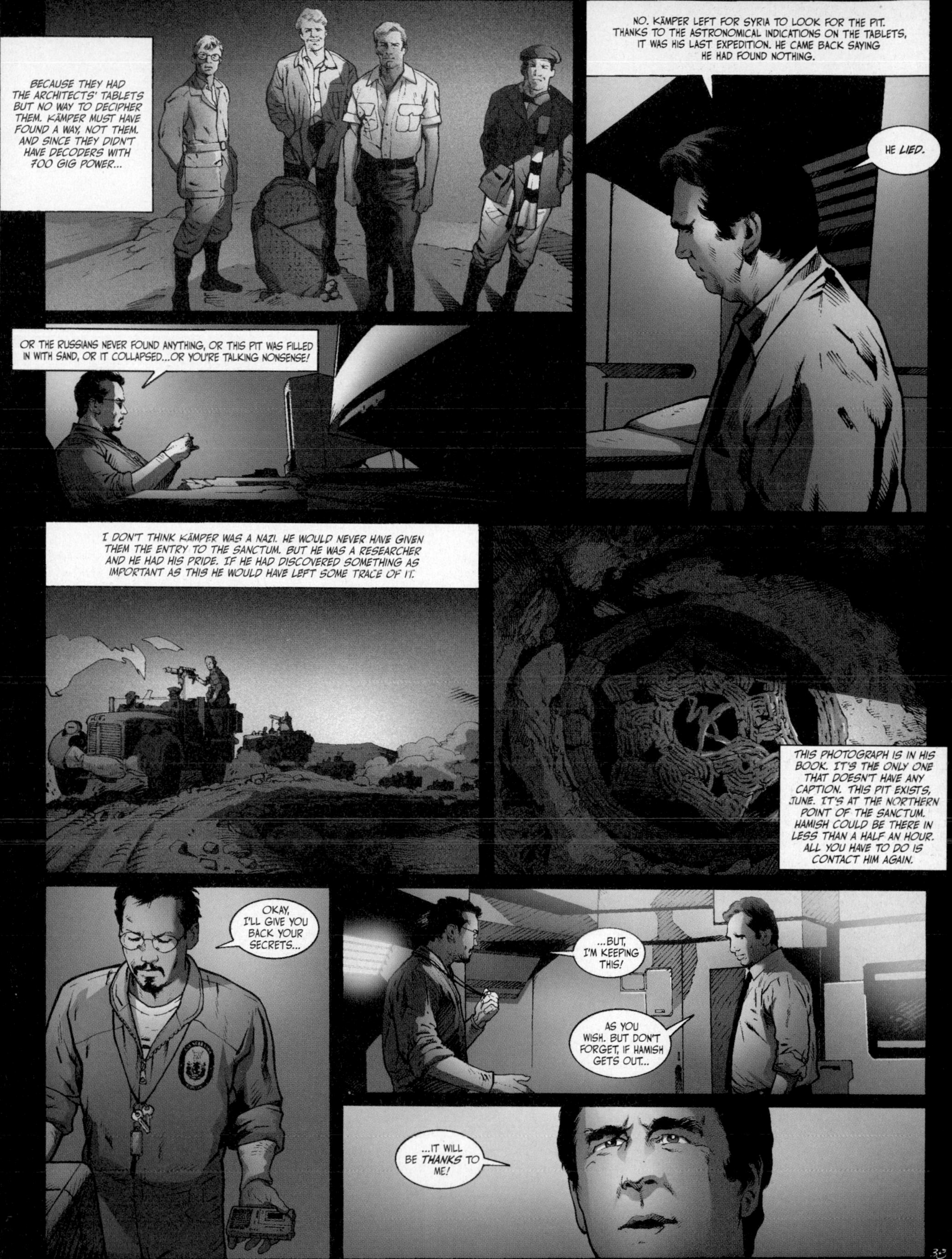
BECAUSE THEY HAD THE ARCHITECTS' TABLETS BUT NO WAY TO DECIPHER THEM. KÄMPER MUST HAVE FOUND A WAY, NOT THEM. AND SINCE THEY DIDN'T HAVE DECODERS WITH 700 GIG POWER...
NO. KÄMPER LEFT FOR SYRIA TO LOOK FOR THE PIT. THANKS TO THE ASTRONOMICAL INDICATIONS ON THE TABLETS, IT WAS HIS LAST EXPEDITION. HE CAME BACK SAYING HE HAD FOUND NOTHING.
HE LIED.
OR THE RUSSIANS NEVER FOUND ANYTHING, OR THIS PIT WAS FILLED IN WITH SAND, OR IT COLLAPSED...OR YOU'RE TALKING NONSENSE!
I DON'T THINK KÄMPER WAS A NAZI. HE WOULD NEVER HAVE GIVEN THEM THE ENTRY TO THE SANCTUM. BUT HE WAS A RESEARCHER AND HE HAD HIS PRIDE. IF HE HAD DISCOVERED SOMETHING AS IMPORTANT AS THIS HE WOULD HAVE LEFT SOME TRACE OF IT.
THIS PHOTOGRAPH IS IN HIS BOOK. IT'S THE ONLY ONE THAT DOESN'T HAVE ANY CAPTION. THIS PIT EXISTS, JUNE. IT'S AT THE NORTHERN POINT OF THE SANCTUM. HAMISH COULD BE THERE IN LESS THAN A HALF AN HOUR. ALL YOU HAVE TO DO IS CONTACT HIM AGAIN.
OKAY, I'LL GIVE YOU BACK YOUR SECRETS...
...BUT, I'M KEEPING THIS!
AS YOU WISH. BUT DON'T FORGET, IF HAMISH GETS OUT...
...IT WILL BE THANKS TO ME!

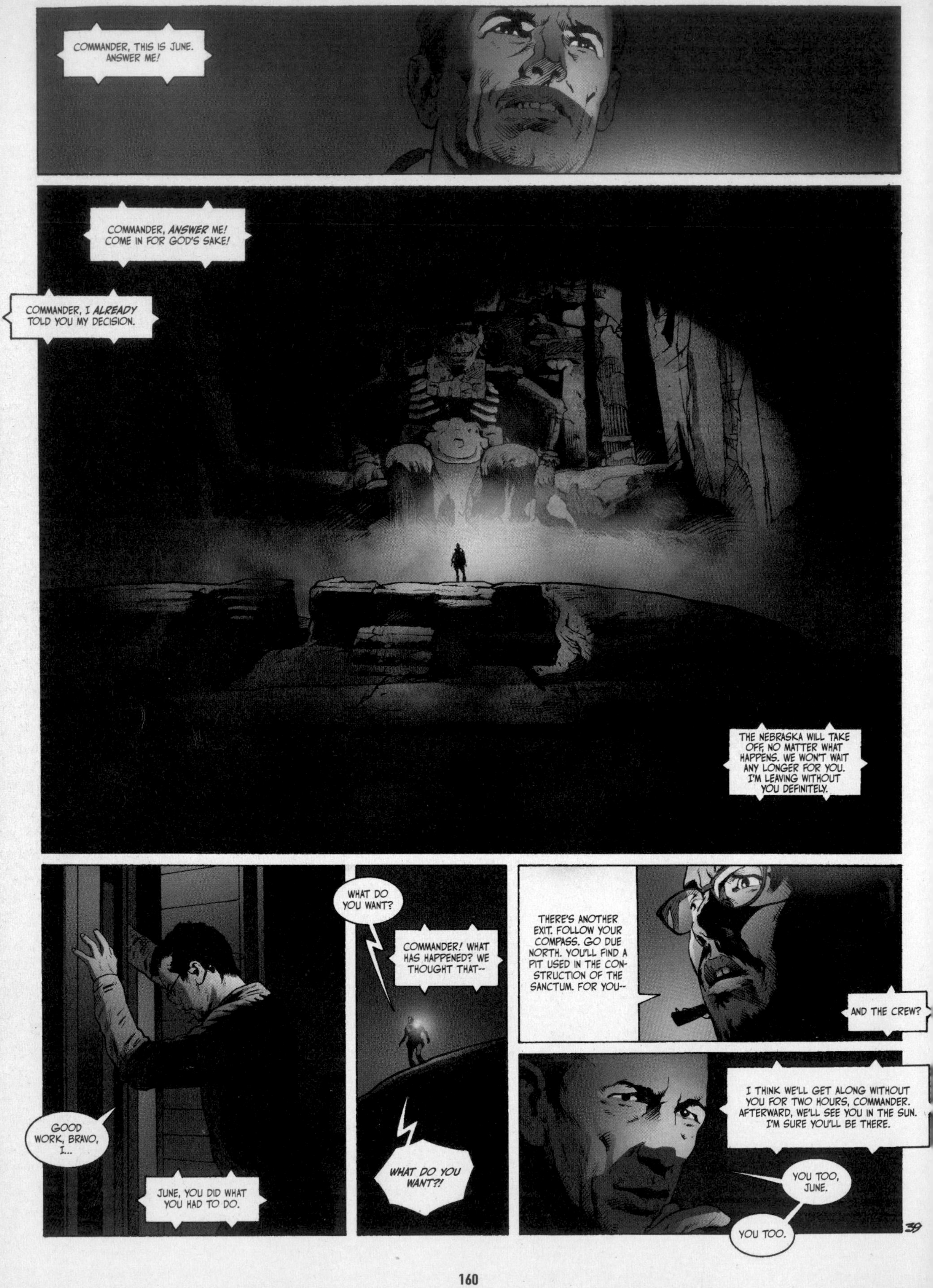
COMMANDER, THIS IS JUNE. ANSWER ME!
COMMANDER, ANSWER ME! COME IN FOR GOD'S SAKE!
COMMANDER, I ALREADY TOLD YOU MY DECISION.
THE NEBRASKA WILL TAKE OFF, NO MATTER WHAT HAPPENS. WE WON'T WAIT ANY LONGER FOR YOU. I'M LEAVING WITHOUT YOU DEFINITELY.
GOOD WORK, BRAVO, I...
JUNE, YOU DID WHAT YOU HAD TO DO.
WHAT DO YOU WANT?
COMMANDER! WHAT HAS HAPPENED? WE THOUGHT THAT--
WHAT DO YOU WANT?!
THERE'S ANOTHER EXIT. FOLLOW YOUR COMPASS. GO DUE NORTH. YOU'LL FIND A PIT USED IN THE CONSTRUCTION OF THE SANCTUM. FOR YOU--
AND THE CREW?
I THINK WE'LL GET ALONG WITHOUT YOU FOR TWO HOURS, COMMANDER. AFTERWARD, WE'LL SEE YOU IN THE SUN. I'M SURE YOU'LL BE THERE.
YOU TOO, JUNE.
YOU TOO.
39

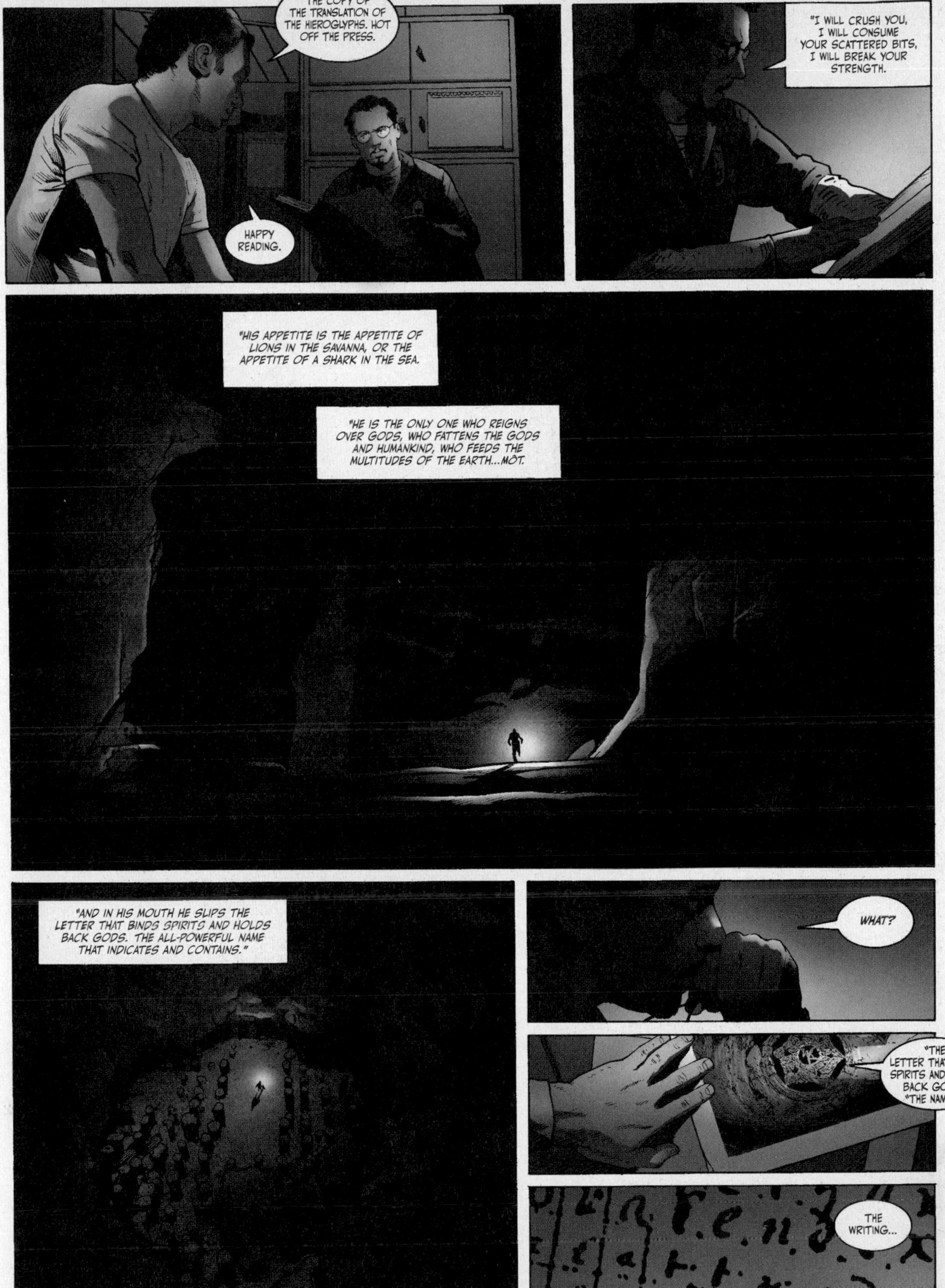
THE COPY OF THE TRANSLATION OF THE HIEROGLYPHS. HOT OFF THE PRESS.
HAPPY READING.
"I WILL CRUSH YOU, I WILL CONSUME YOUR SCATTERED BITS, I WILL BREAK YOUR STRENGTH.
"HIS APPETITE IS THE APPETITE OF LIONS IN THE SAVANNA, OR THE APPETITE OF A SHARK IN THE SEA.
"HE IS THE ONLY ONE WHO REIGNS OVER GODS, WHO FATTENS THE GODS AND HUMANKIND, WHO FEEDS THE MULTITUDES OF THE EARTH...MÔT.
"AND IN HIS MOUTH HE SLIPS THE LETTER THAT BINDS SPIRITS AND HOLDS BACK GODS. THE ALL-POWERFUL NAME THAT INDICATES AND CONTAINS."
WHAT?
"THE LETTER THAT BINDS SPIRITS AND HOLDS BACK GODS." "THE NAME..."
THE WRITING...
40

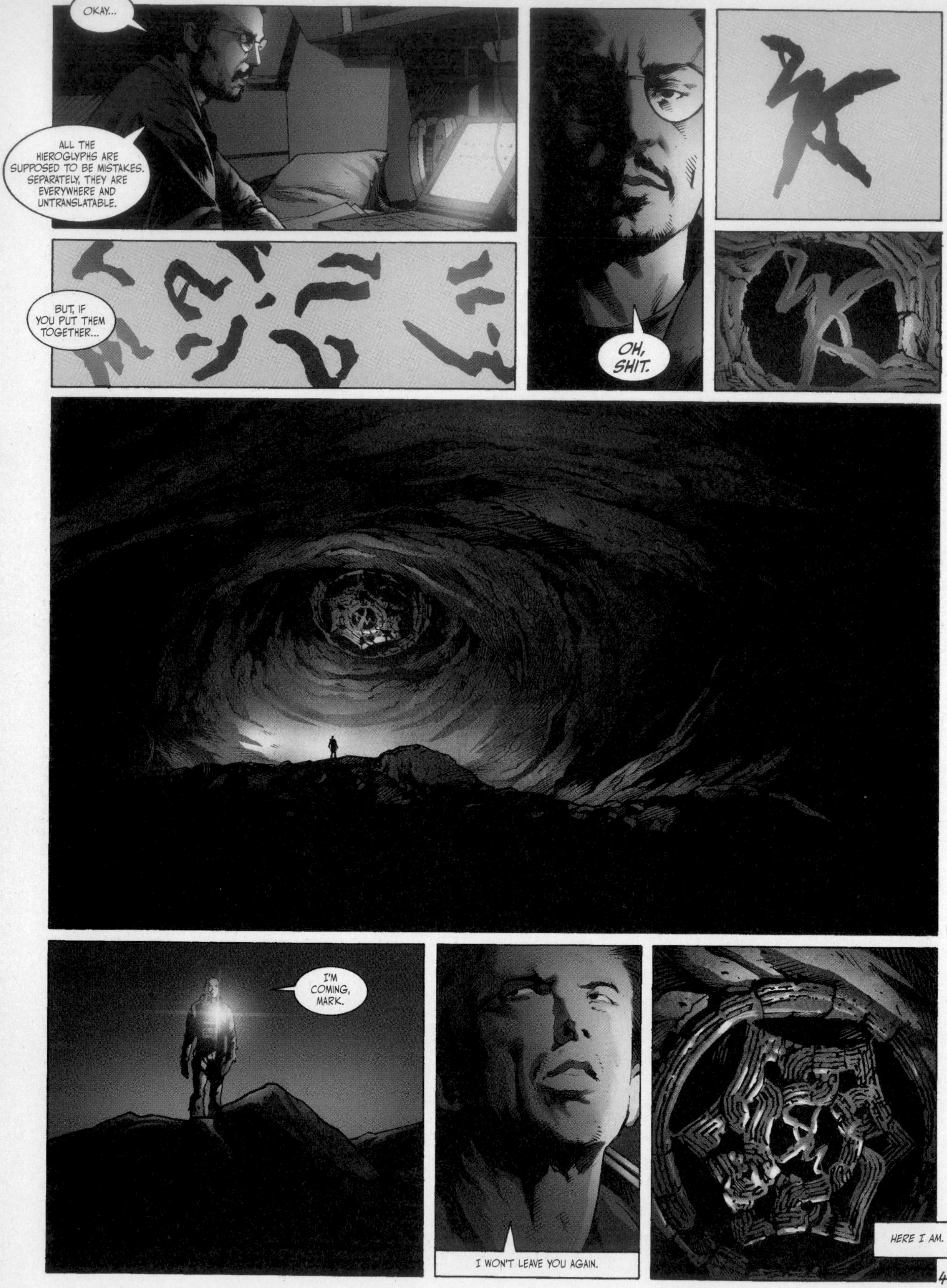
OKAY...
ALL THE HIEROGLYPHS ARE SUPPOSED TO BE MISTAKES. SEPARATELY, THEY ARE EVERYWHERE AND UNTRANSLATABLE.
BUT, IF YOU PUT THEM TOGETHER...
OH, SHIT.
I'M COMING, MARK.
I WON'T LEAVE YOU AGAIN.
HERE I AM.
41

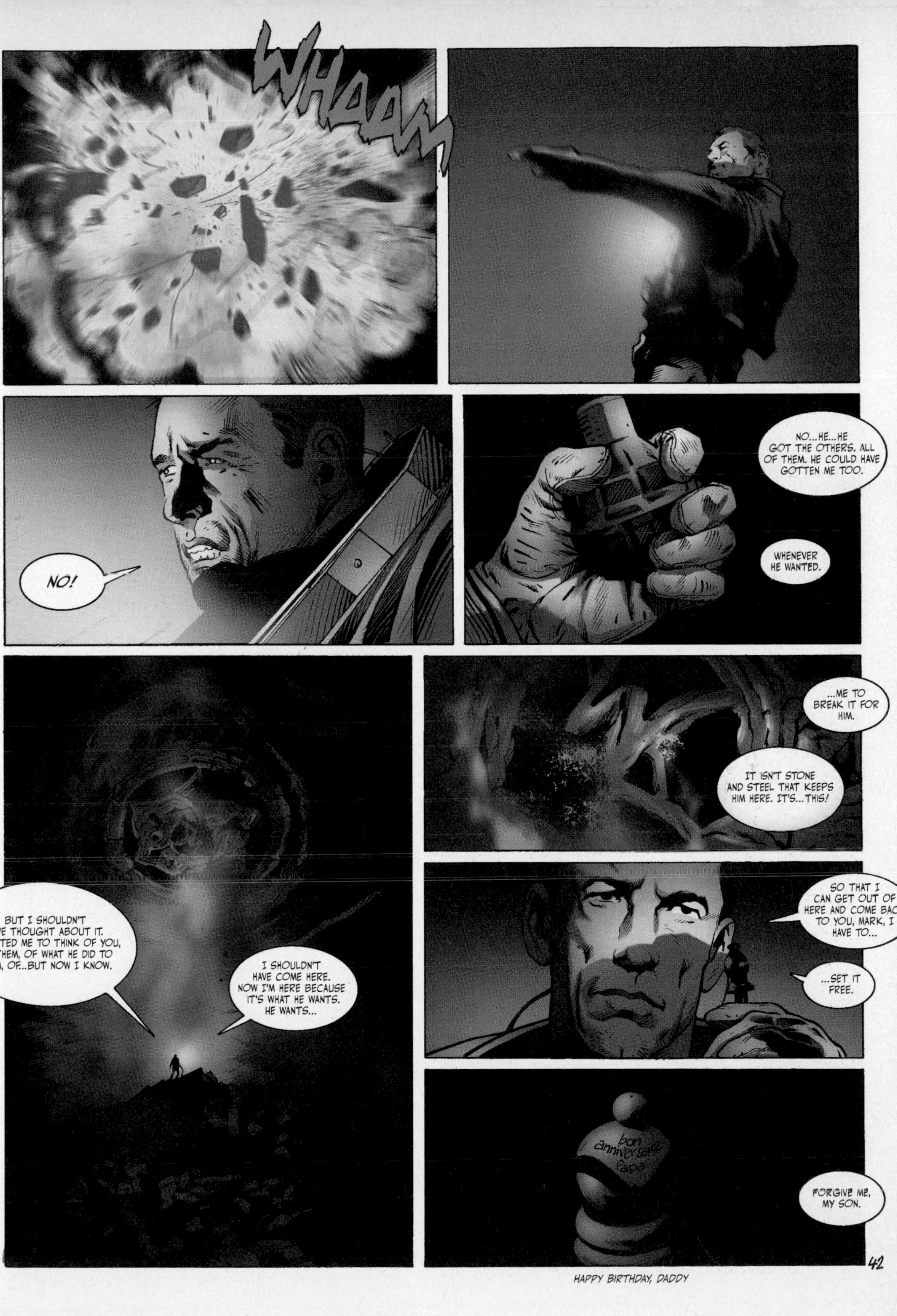
WHAAM
NO!
NO...HE...HE GOT THE OTHERS. ALL OF THEM. HE COULD HAVE GOTTEN ME TOO.
WHENEVER HE WANTED.
BUT I SHOULDN'T HAVE THOUGHT ABOUT IT. HE WANTED ME TO THINK OF YOU, OF THEM, OF WHAT HE DID TO THEM, OF...BUT NOW I KNOW.
I SHOULDN'T HAVE COME HERE. NOW I'M HERE BECAUSE IT'S WHAT HE WANTS. HE WANTS...
...ME TO BREAK IT FOR HIM.
IT ISN'T STONE AND STEEL THAT KEEPS HIM HERE. IT'S...THIS!
SO THAT I CAN GET OUT OF HERE AND COME BACK TO YOU, MARK, I HAVE TO...
...SET IT FREE.
bon anniversaire papa
FORGIVE ME, MY SON.
42
HAPPY BIRTHDAY, DADDY

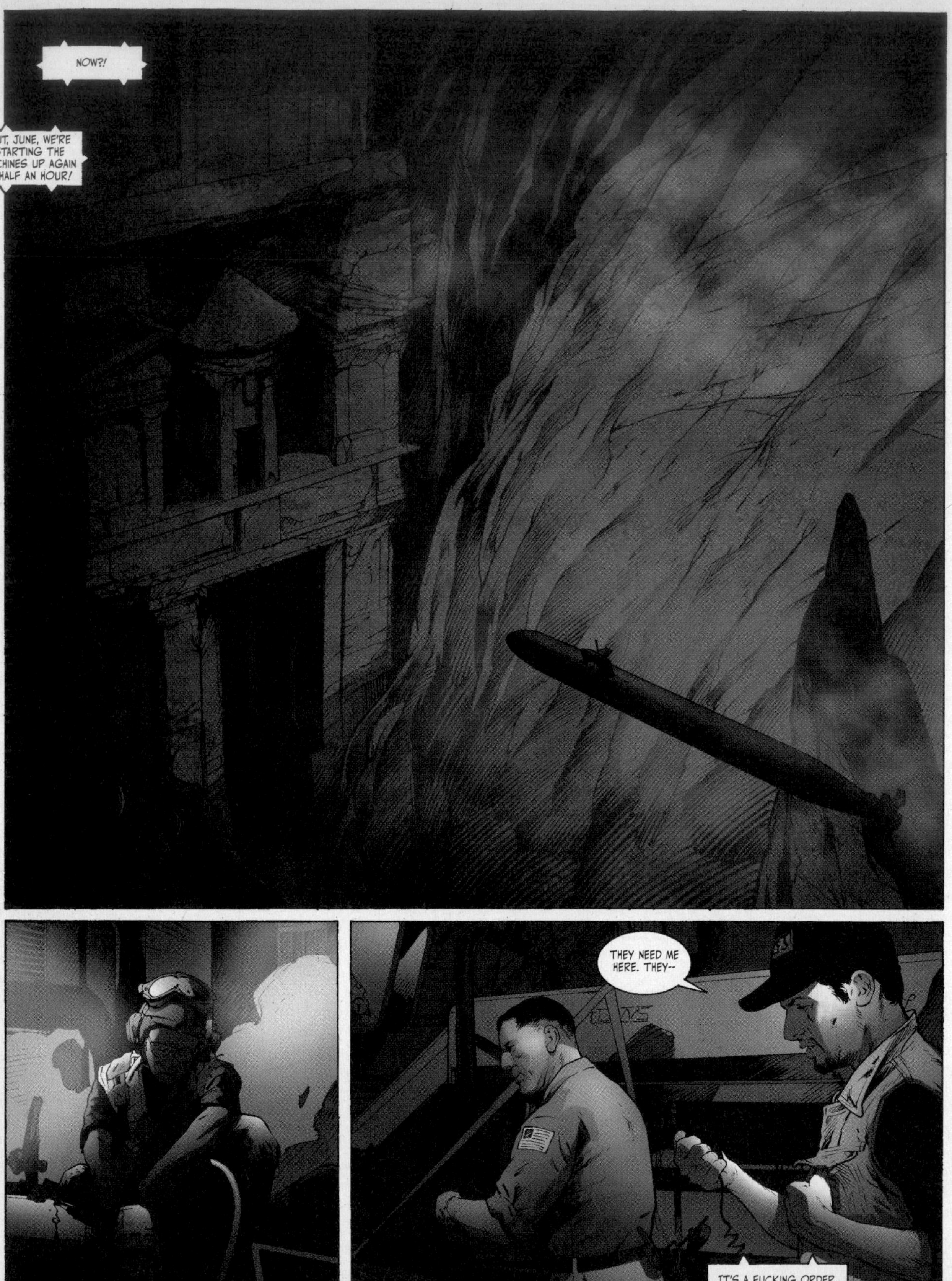
NOW?!
BUT, JUNE, WE'RE STARTING THE MACHINES UP AGAIN IN HALF AN HOUR!
THEY NEED ME HERE. THEY--
IT'S A FUCKING ORDER, BEAUMONT! GET OUT OF HERE NOW!
43

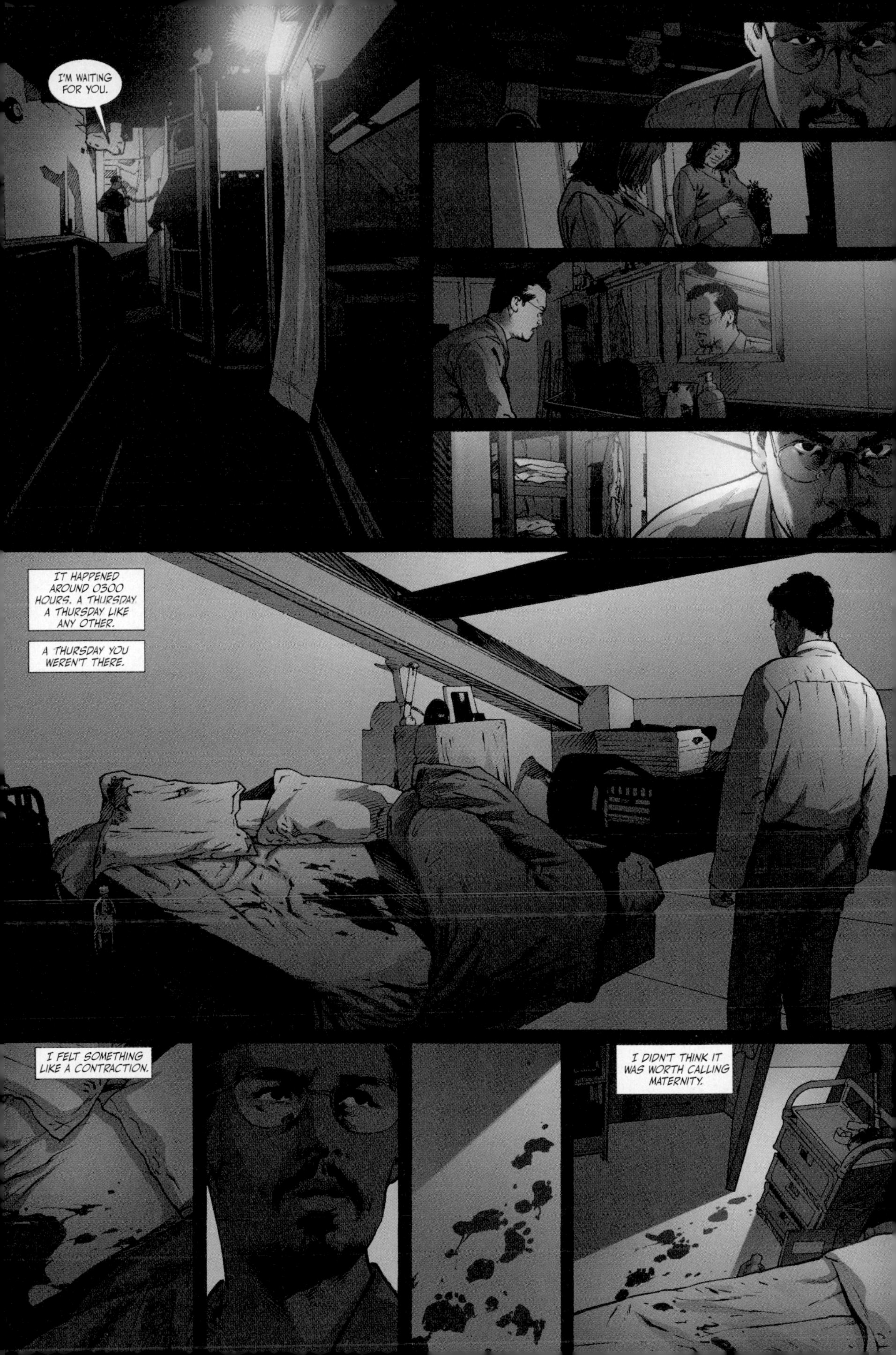
I'M WAITING FOR YOU.
IT HAPPENED AROUND 0300 HOURS. A THURSDAY. A THURSDAY LIKE ANY OTHER.
A THURSDAY YOU WEREN'T THERE.
I FELT SOMETHING LIKE A CONTRACTION.
I DIDN'T THINK IT WAS WORTH CALLING MATERNITY.

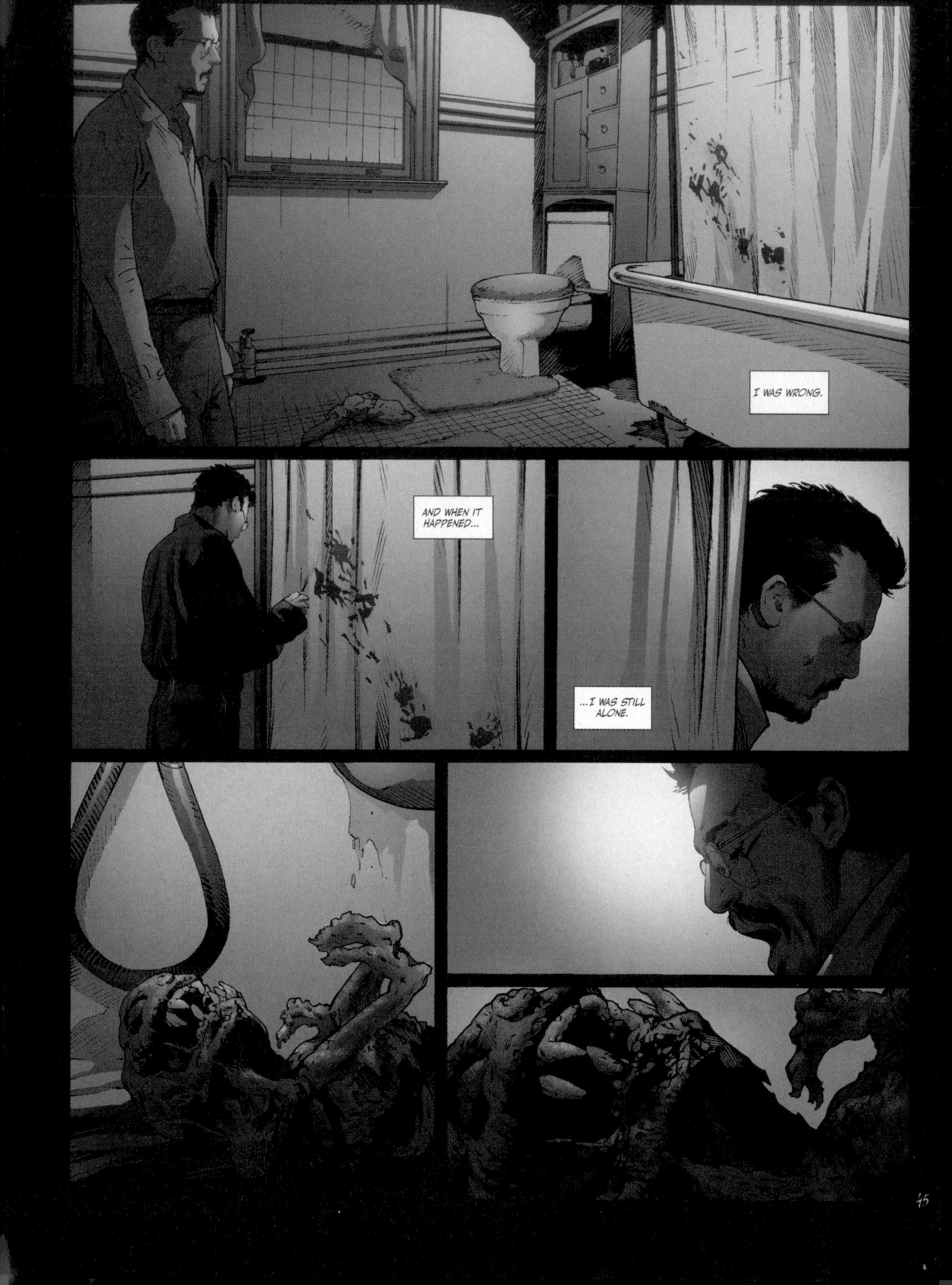
I WAS WRONG.
AND WHEN IT HAPPENED...
...I WAS STILL ALONE.

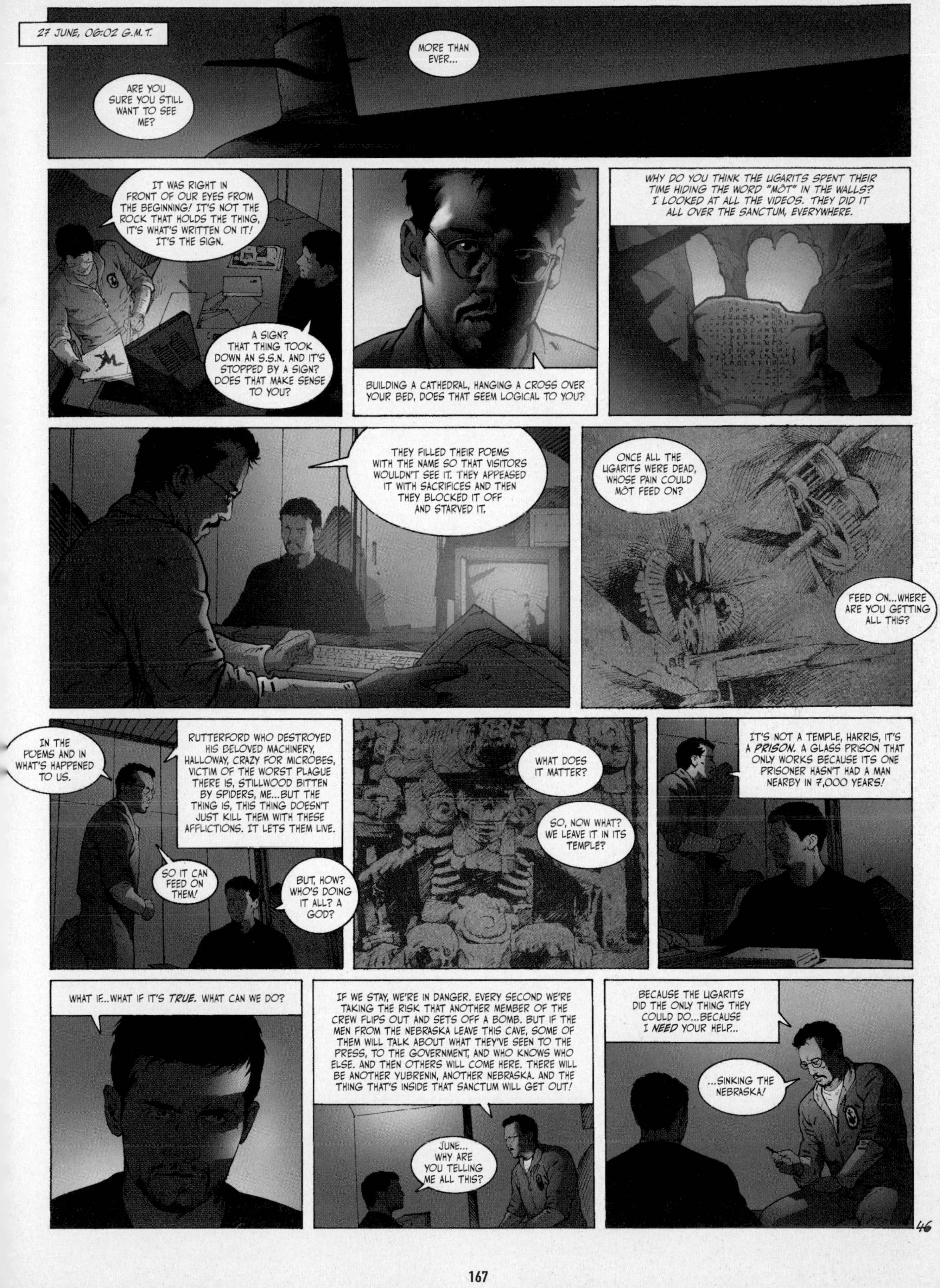

27 JUNE, 06:02 G.M.T.
ARE YOU SURE YOU STILL WANT TO SEE ME?
MORE THAN EVER...
IT WAS RIGHT IN FRONT OF OUR EYES FROM THE BEGINNING! IT'S NOT THE ROCK THAT HOLDS THE THING, IT'S WHAT'S WRITTEN ON IT! IT'S THE SIGN.
A SIGN? THAT THING TOOK DOWN AN S.S.N. AND IT'S STOPPED BY A SIGN? DOES THAT MAKE SENSE TO YOU?
BUILDING A CATHEDRAL, HANGING A CROSS OVER YOUR BED, DOES THAT SEEM LOGICAL TO YOU?
WHY DO YOU THINK THE UGARITS SPENT THEIR TIME HIDING THE WORD "MÔT" IN THE WALLS? I LOOKED AT ALL THE VIDEOS. THEY DID IT ALL OVER THE SANCTUM, EVERYWHERE.
THEY FILLED THEIR POEMS WITH THE NAME SO THAT VISITORS WOULDN'T SEE IT. THEY APPEASED IT WITH SACRIFICES AND THEN THEY BLOCKED IT OFF AND STARVED IT.
ONCE ALL THE UGARITS WERE DEAD, WHOSE PAIN COULD MÔT FEED ON?
FEED ON...WHERE ARE YOU GETTING ALL THIS?
IN THE POEMS AND IN WHAT'S HAPPENED TO US.
RUTTERFORD WHO DESTROYED HIS BELOVED MACHINERY, HALLOWAY, CRAZY FOR MICROBES, VICTIM OF THE WORST PLAGUE THERE IS, STILLWOOD BITTEN BY SPIDERS, ME...BUT THE THING IS, THIS THING DOESN'T JUST KILL THEM WITH THESE AFFLICTIONS. IT LETS THEM LIVE.
SO IT CAN FEED ON THEM!
BUT, HOW? WHO'S DOING IT ALL? A GOD?
WHAT DOES IT MATTER?
SO, NOW WHAT? WE LEAVE IT IN ITS TEMPLE?
IT'S NOT A TEMPLE, HARRIS, IT'S A PRISON. A GLASS PRISON THAT ONLY WORKS BECAUSE ITS ONE PRISONER HASN'T HAD A MAN NEARBY IN 7,000 YEARS!
WHAT IF...WHAT IF IT'S TRUE. WHAT CAN WE DO?
IF WE STAY, WE'RE IN DANGER. EVERY SECOND WE'RE TAKING THE RISK THAT ANOTHER MEMBER OF THE CREW FLIPS OUT AND SETS OFF A BOMB. BUT IF THE MEN FROM THE NEBRASKA LEAVE THIS CAVE, SOME OF THEM WILL TALK ABOUT WHAT THEY'VE SEEN TO THE PRESS, TO THE GOVERNMENT, AND WHO KNOWS WHO ELSE. AND THEN OTHERS WILL COME HERE. THERE WILL BE ANOTHER YUBRENIN, ANOTHER NEBRASKA. AND THE THING THAT'S INSIDE THAT SANCTUM WILL GET OUT!
JUNE... WHY ARE YOU TELLING ME ALL THIS?
BECAUSE THE UGARITS DID THE ONLY THING THEY COULD DO...BECAUSE I NEED YOUR HELP...
...SINKING THE NEBRASKA!
46

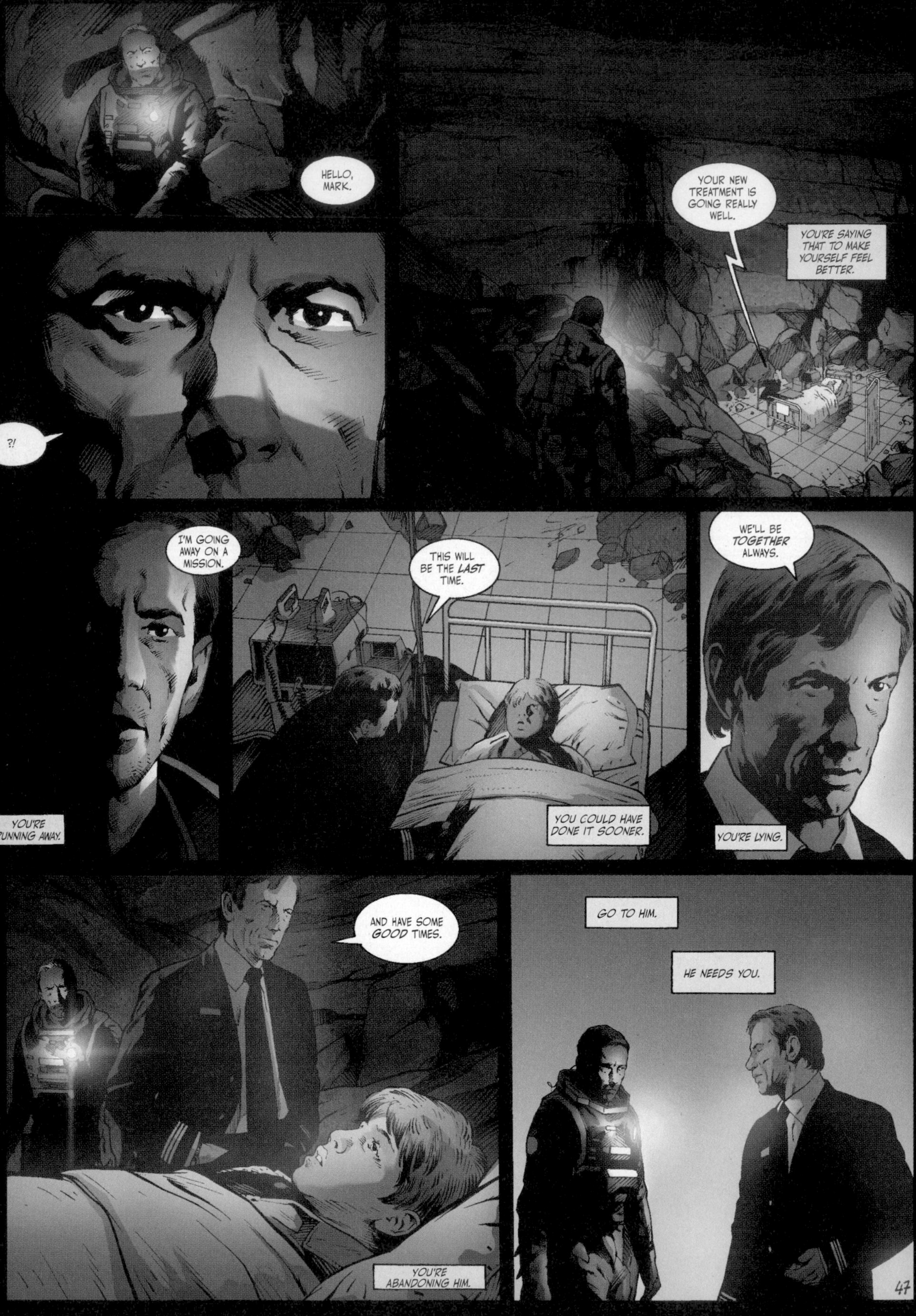

HELLO, MARK.
YOUR NEW TREATMENT IS GOING REALLY WELL.
YOU'RE SAYING THAT TO MAKE YOURSELF FEEL BETTER.
?!
I'M GOING AWAY ON A MISSION.
YOU'RE RUNNING AWAY.
THIS WILL BE THE LAST TIME.
YOU COULD HAVE DONE IT SOONER.
WE'LL BE TOGETHER ALWAYS.
YOU'RE LYING.
AND HAVE SOME GOOD TIMES.
YOU'RE ABANDONING HIM.
GO TO HIM.
HE NEEDS YOU.

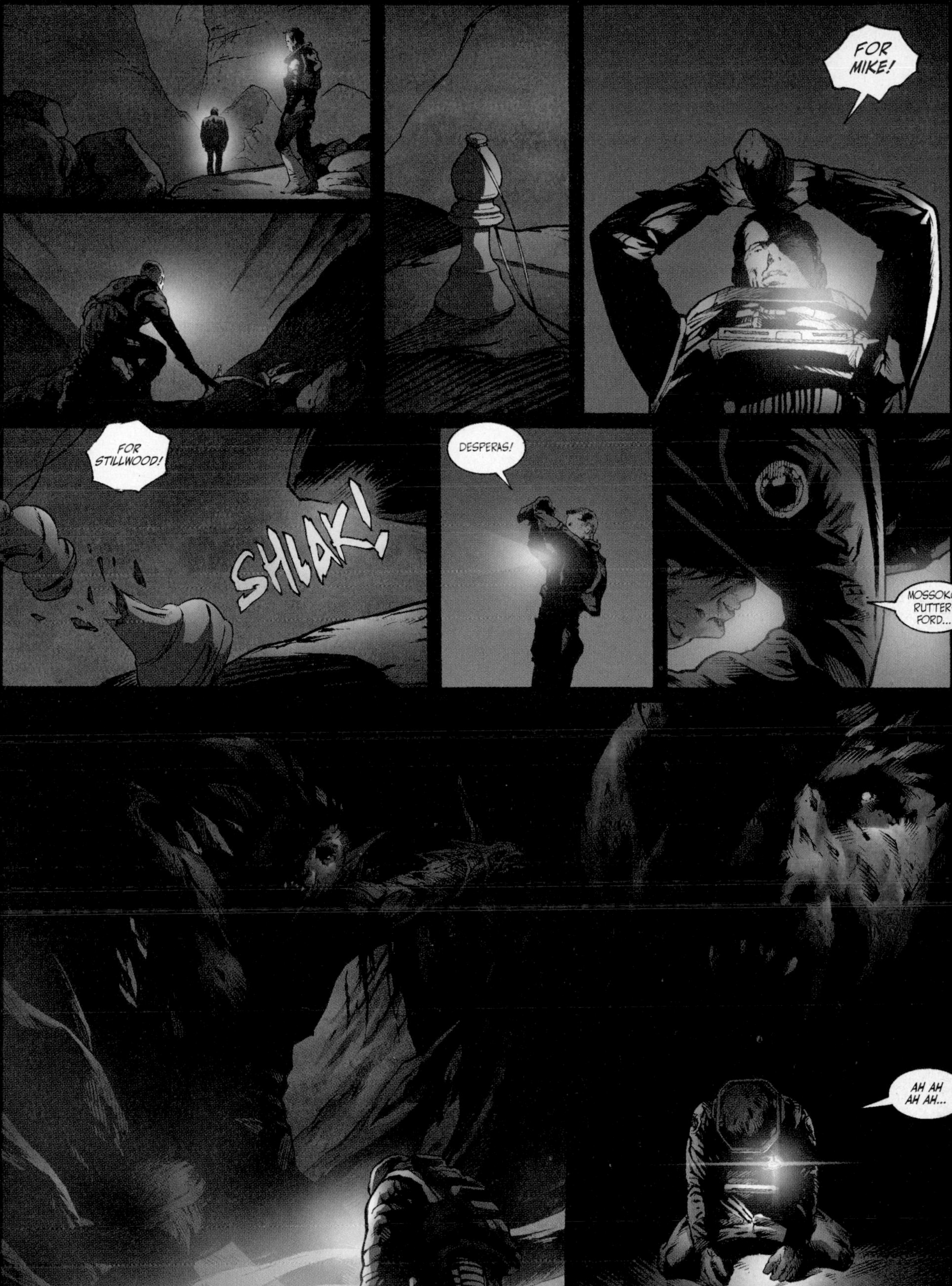
FOR MIKE!
FOR STILLWOOD!
SHLAK!
DESPERAS!
MOSSOKO, RUTTER-FORD...
AH AH AH AH...

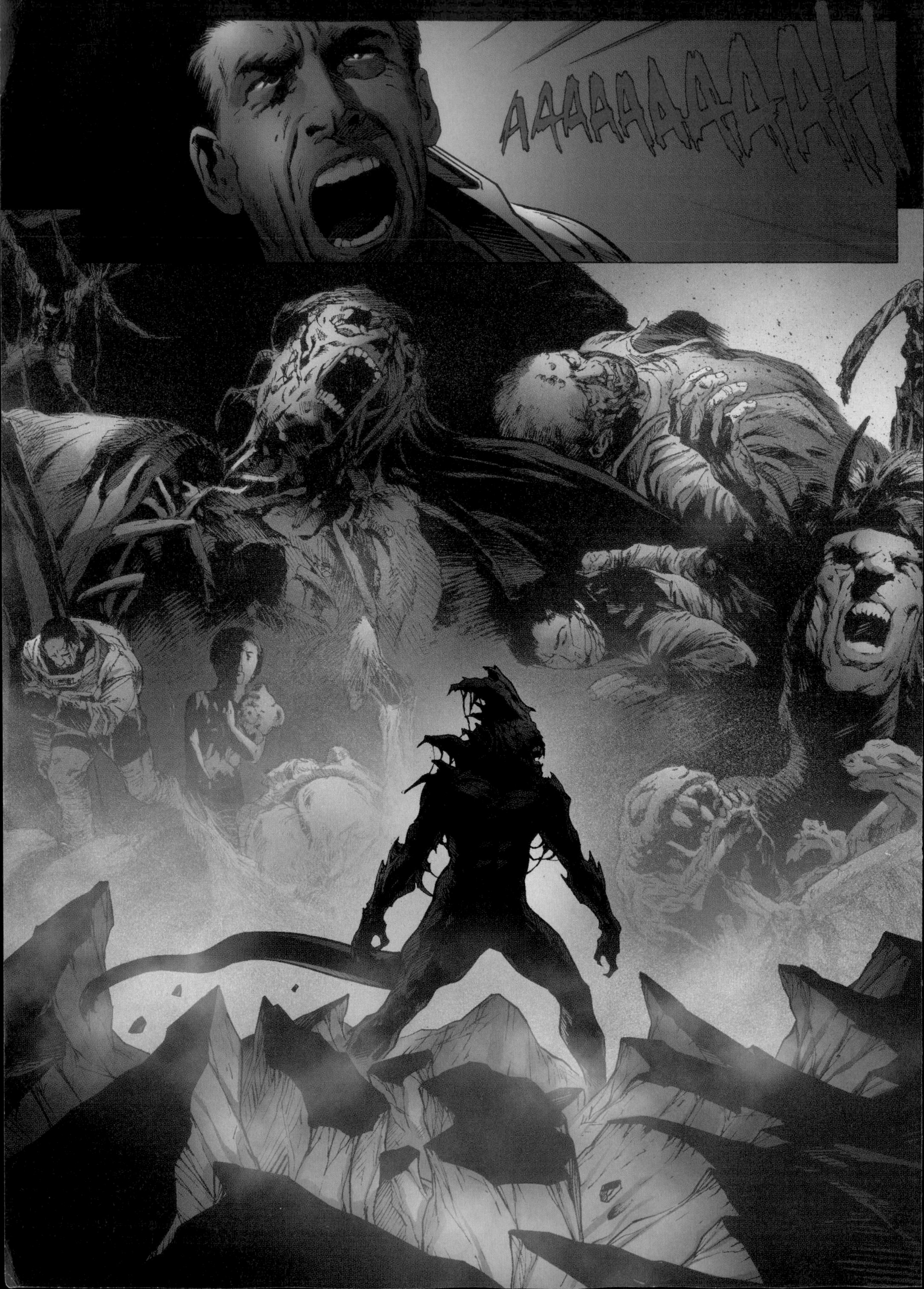
AAAAAAAAAAH

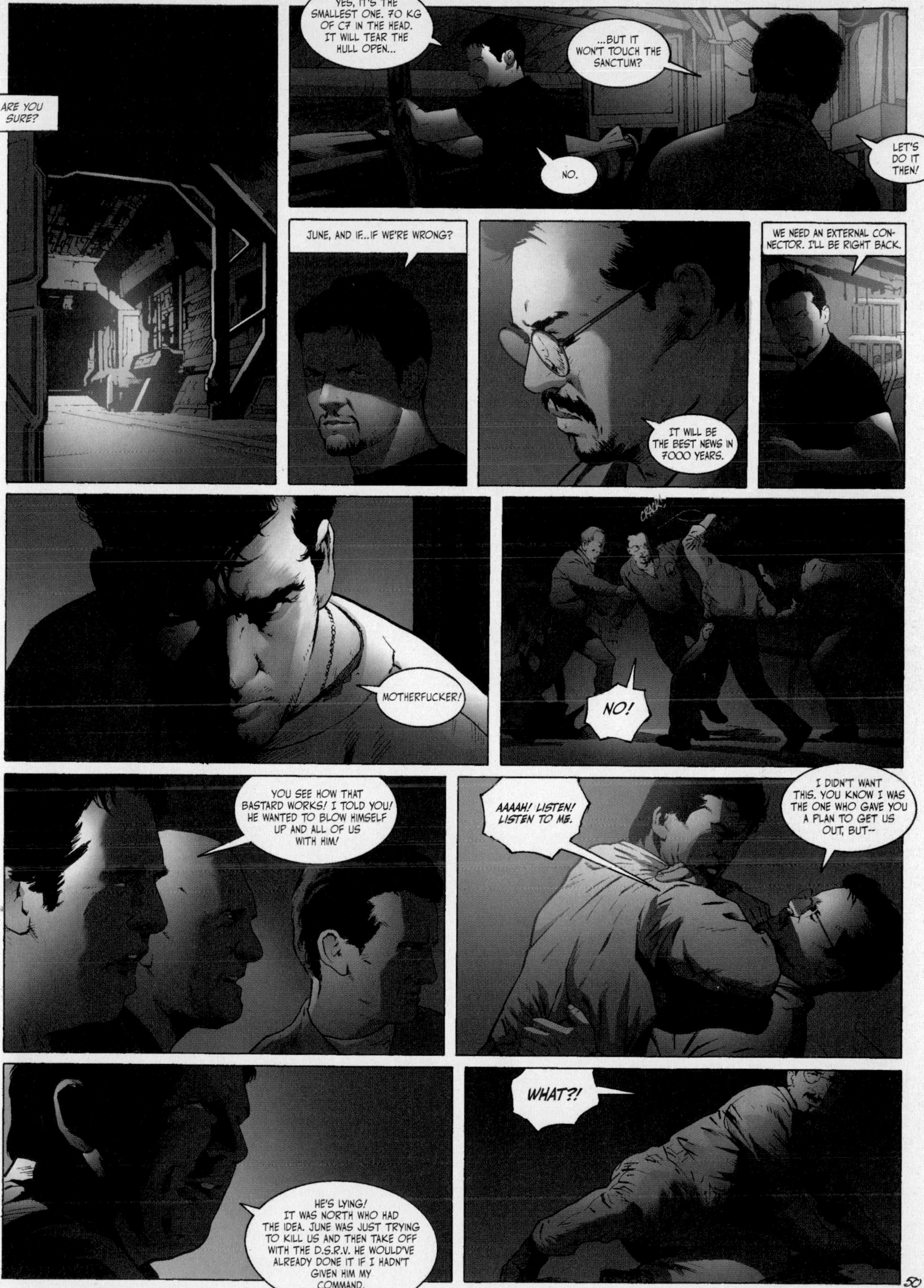
ARE YOU SURE?
YES, IT'S THE SMALLEST ONE. 70 KG OF C7 IN THE HEAD. IT WILL TEAR THE HULL OPEN...
...BUT IT WON'T TOUCH THE SANCTUM?
NO.
LET'S DO IT THEN!
JUNE, AND IF...IF WE'RE WRONG?
IT WILL BE THE BEST NEWS IN 7000 YEARS.
WE NEED AN EXTERNAL CONNECTOR. I'LL BE RIGHT BACK.
MOTHERFUCKER!
CRACK!
NO!
YOU SEE HOW THAT BASTARD WORKS! I TOLD YOU! HE WANTED TO BLOW HIMSELF UP AND ALL OF US WITH HIM!
AAAAH! LISTEN! LISTEN TO ME.
I DIDN'T WANT THIS. YOU KNOW I WAS THE ONE WHO GAVE YOU A PLAN TO GET US OUT, BUT--
HE'S LYING! IT WAS NORTH WHO HAD THE IDEA. JUNE WAS JUST TRYING TO KILL US AND THEN TAKE OFF WITH THE D.S.R.V. HE WOULD'VE ALREADY DONE IT IF I HADN'T GIVEN HIM MY COMMAND.
WHAT?!
50

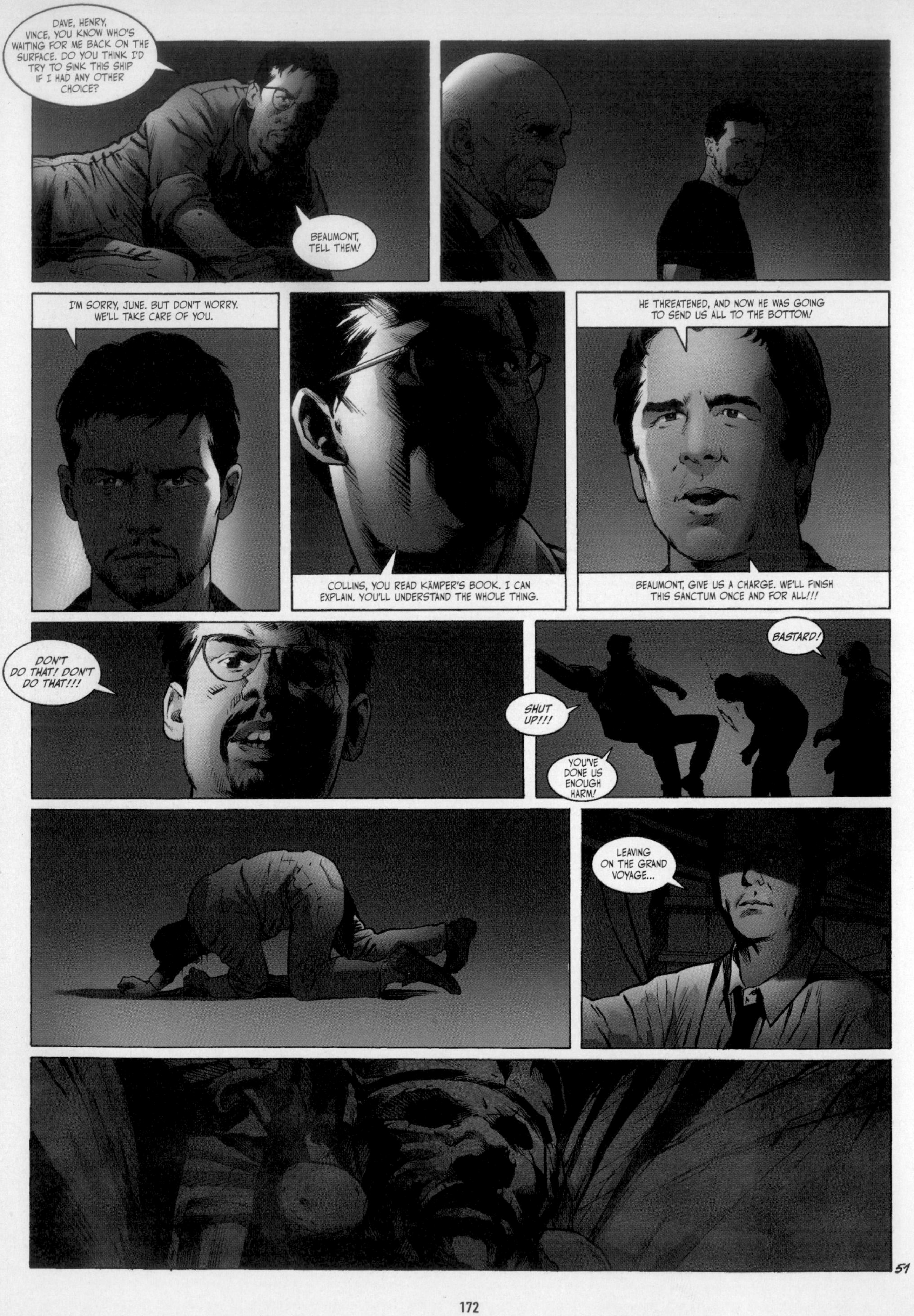
DAVE, HENRY, VINCE, YOU KNOW WHO'S WAITING FOR ME BACK ON THE SURFACE. DO YOU THINK I'D TRY TO SINK THIS SHIP IF I HAD ANY OTHER CHOICE?
BEAUMONT, TELL THEM!
I'M SORRY, JUNE. BUT DON'T WORRY. WE'LL TAKE CARE OF YOU.
COLLINS, YOU READ KÄMPER'S BOOK. I CAN EXPLAIN. YOU'LL UNDERSTAND THE WHOLE THING.
HE THREATENED, AND NOW HE WAS GOING TO SEND US ALL TO THE BOTTOM!
BEAUMONT, GIVE US A CHARGE. WE'LL FINISH THIS SANCTUM ONCE AND FOR ALL!!!
DON'T DO THAT! DON'T DO THAT!!!
BASTARD!
SHUT UP!!!
YOU'VE DONE US ENOUGH HARM!
LEAVING ON THE GRAND VOYAGE...
51

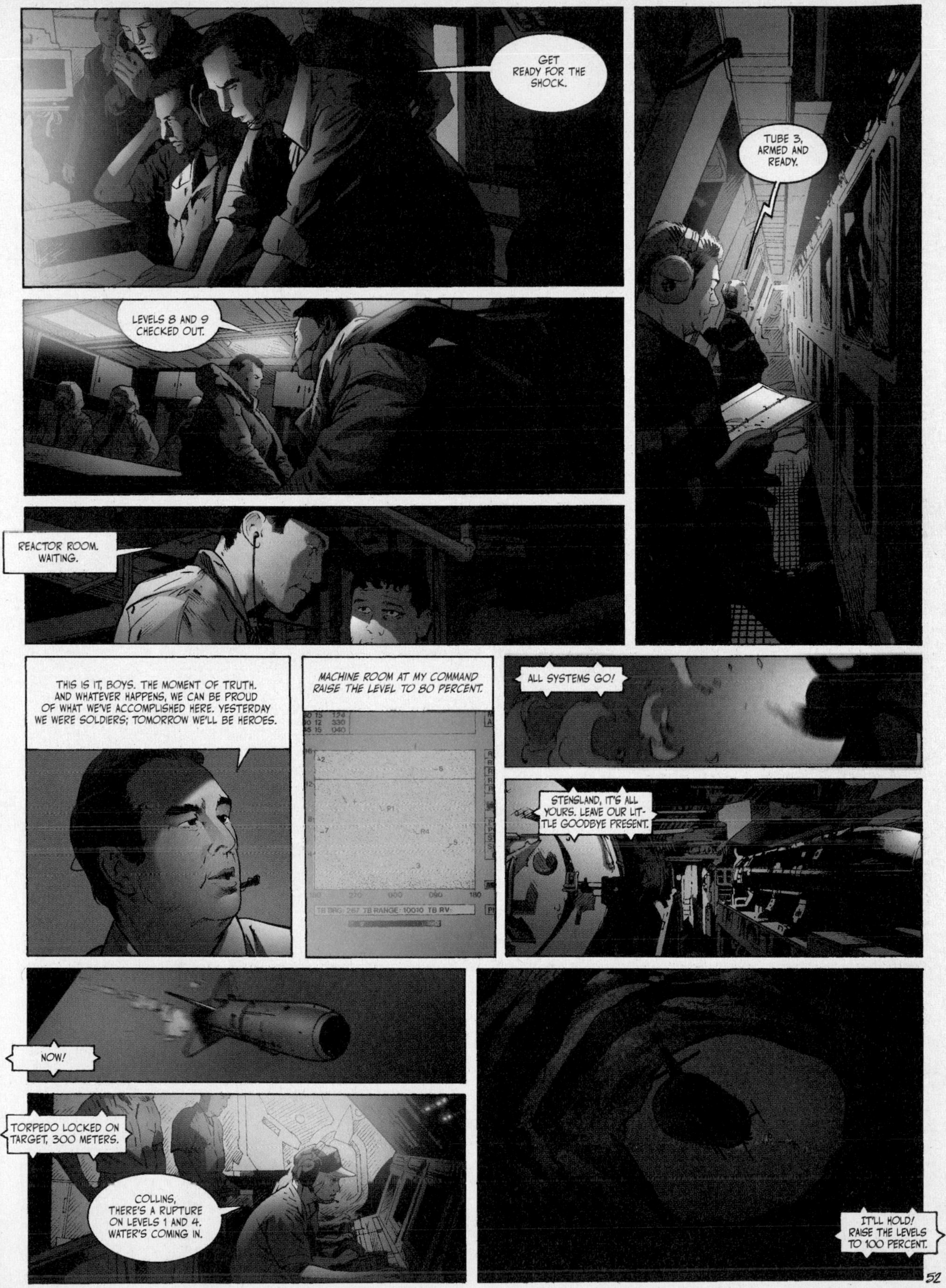
GET READY FOR THE SHOCK.
TUBE 3, ARMED AND READY.
LEVELS 8 AND 9 CHECKED OUT.
REACTOR ROOM. WAITING.
THIS IS IT, BOYS. THE MOMENT OF TRUTH. AND WHATEVER HAPPENS, WE CAN BE PROUD OF WHAT WE'VE ACCOMPLISHED HERE. YESTERDAY WE WERE SOLDIERS; TOMORROW WE'LL BE HEROES.
MACHINE ROOM AT MY COMMAND RAISE THE LEVEL TO 80 PERCENT.
ALL SYSTEMS GO!
STENSLAND, IT'S ALL YOURS. LEAVE OUR LITTLE GOODBYE PRESENT.
NOW!
TORPEDO LOCKED ON TARGET, 300 METERS.
COLLINS, THERE'S A RUPTURE ON LEVELS 1 AND 4. WATER'S COMING IN.
IT'LL HOLD! RAISE THE LEVELS TO 100 PERCENT.
52

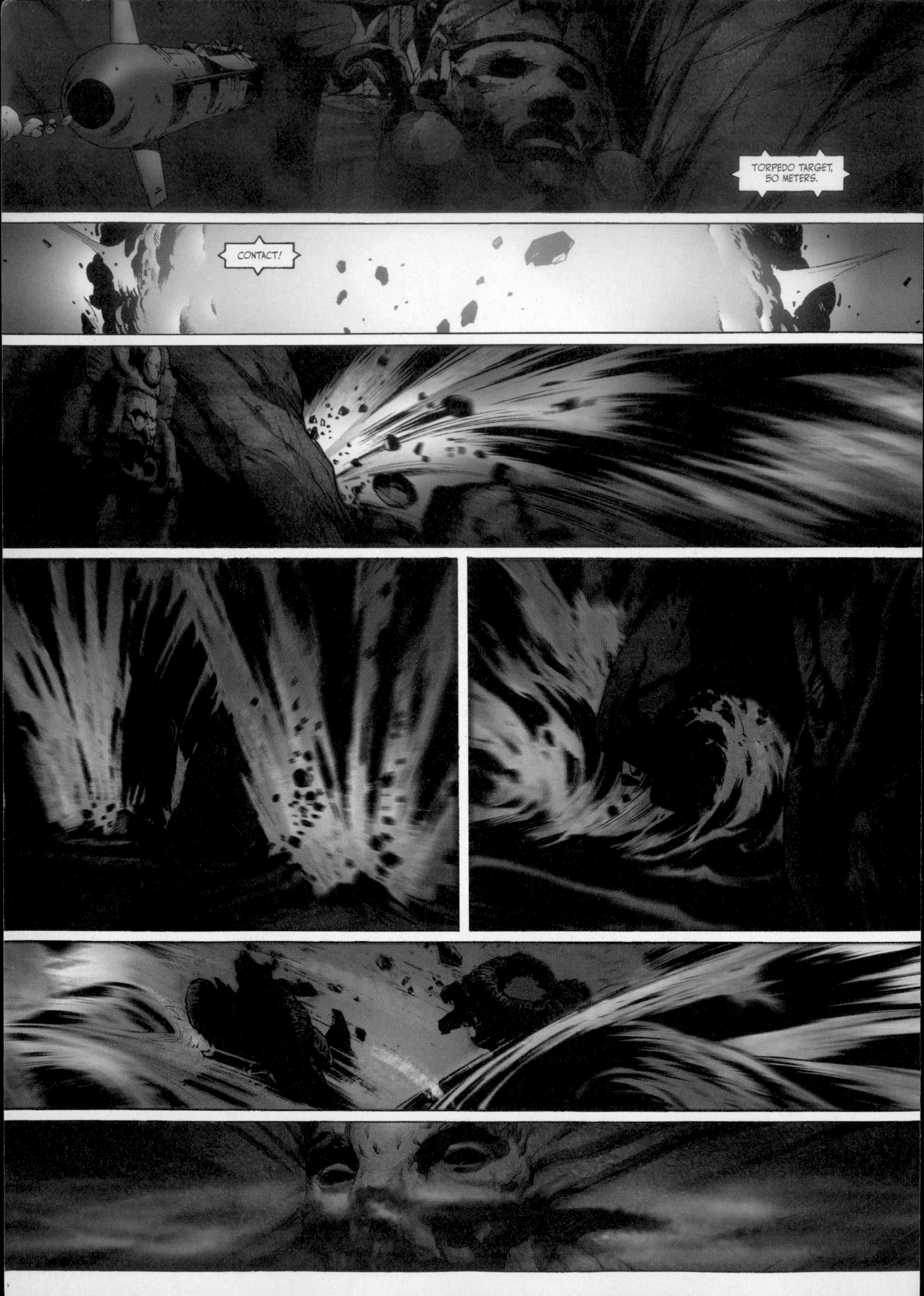
TORPEDO TARGET, 50 METERS.
CONTACT!

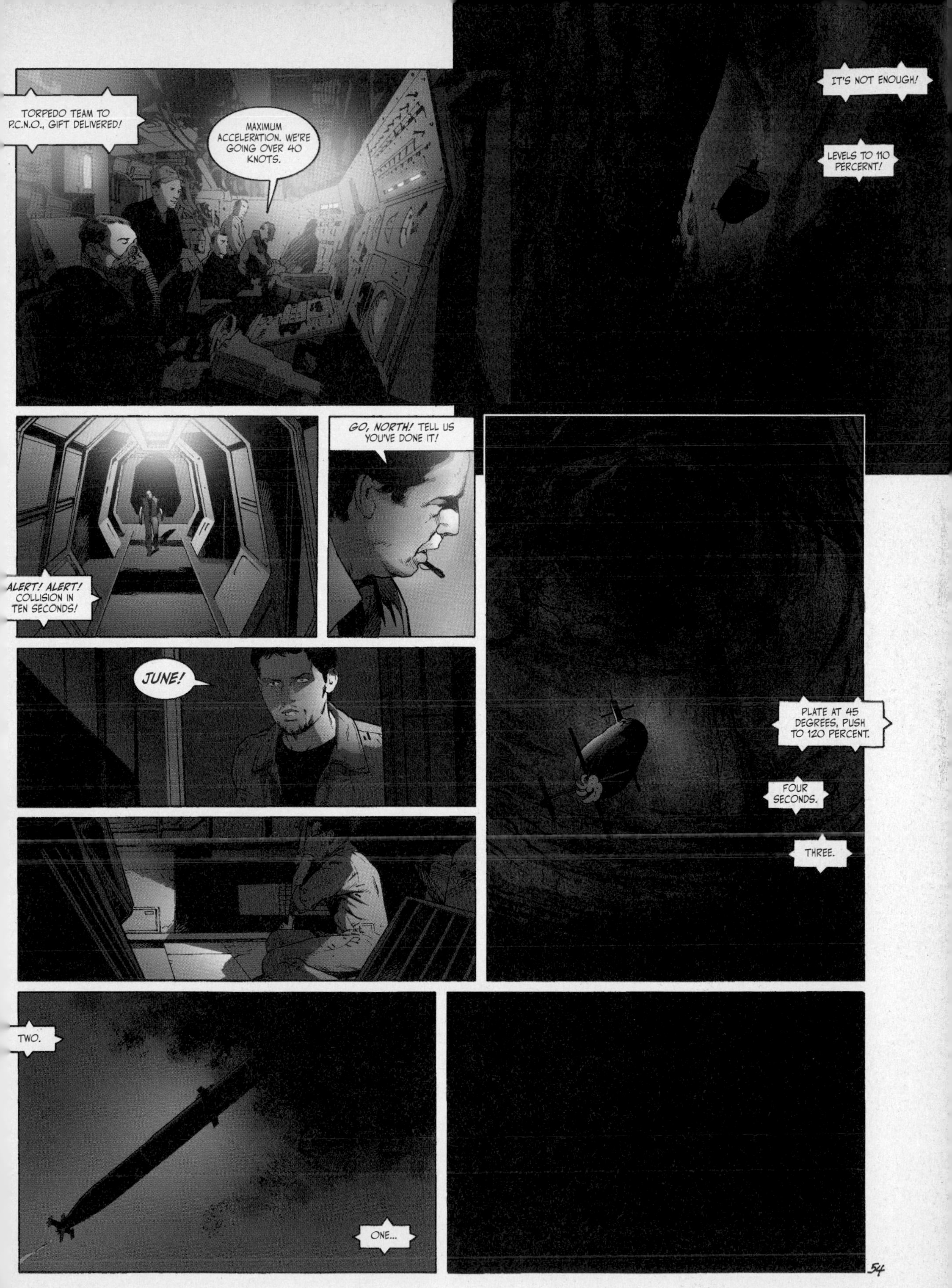

TORPEDO TEAM TO P.C.N.O., GIFT DELIVERED!
MAXIMUM ACCELERATION. WE'RE GOING OVER 40 KNOTS.
IT'S NOT ENOUGH!
LEVELS TO 110 PERCERNT!
ALERT! ALERT! COLLISION IN TEN SECONDS!
GO, NORTH! TELL US YOU'VE DONE IT!
JUNE!
PLATE AT 45 DEGREES, PUSH TO 120 PERCENT.
FOUR SECONDS.
THREE.
TWO.
ONE...
54

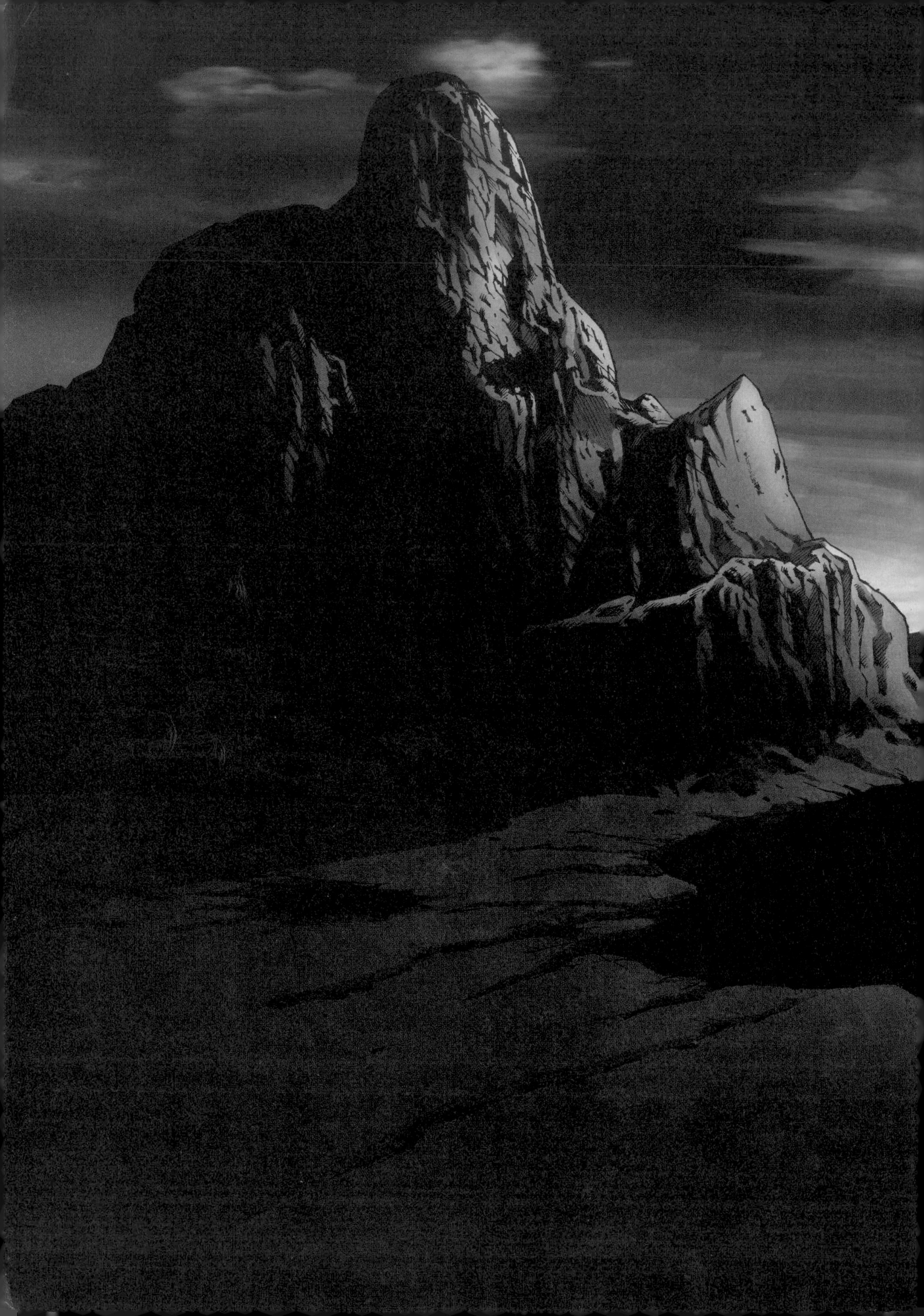

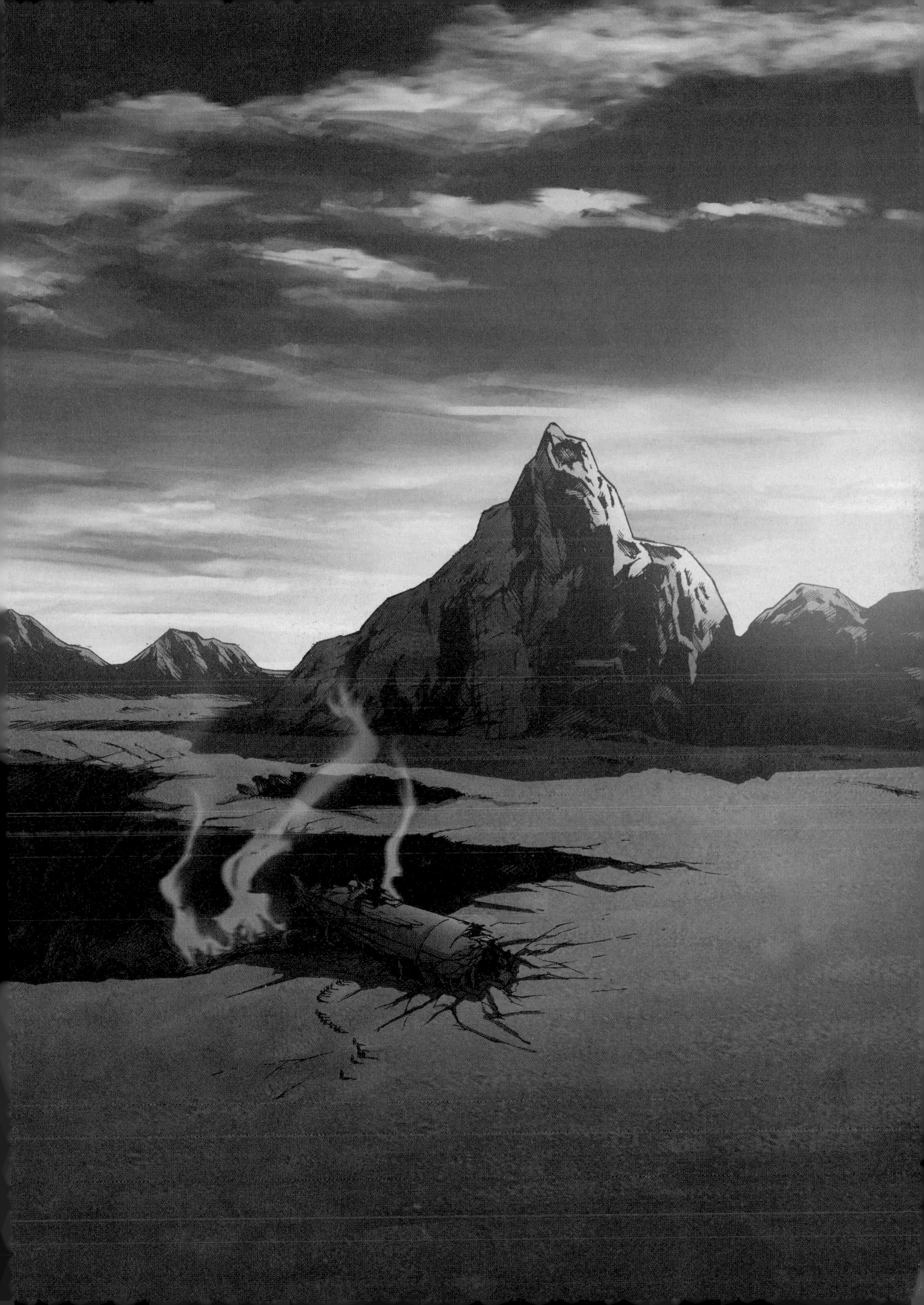

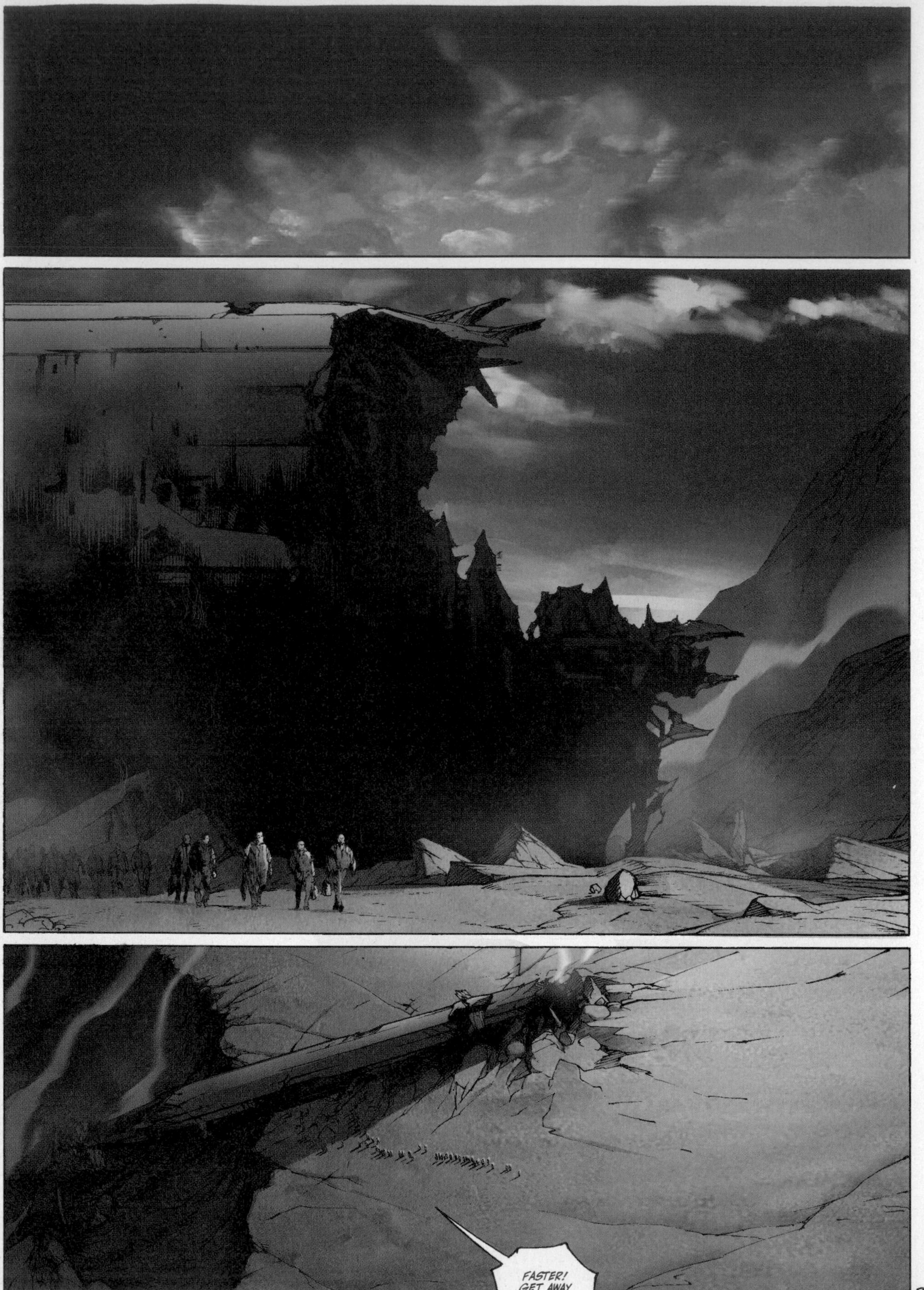
FASTER! GET AWAY FROM IT!
57

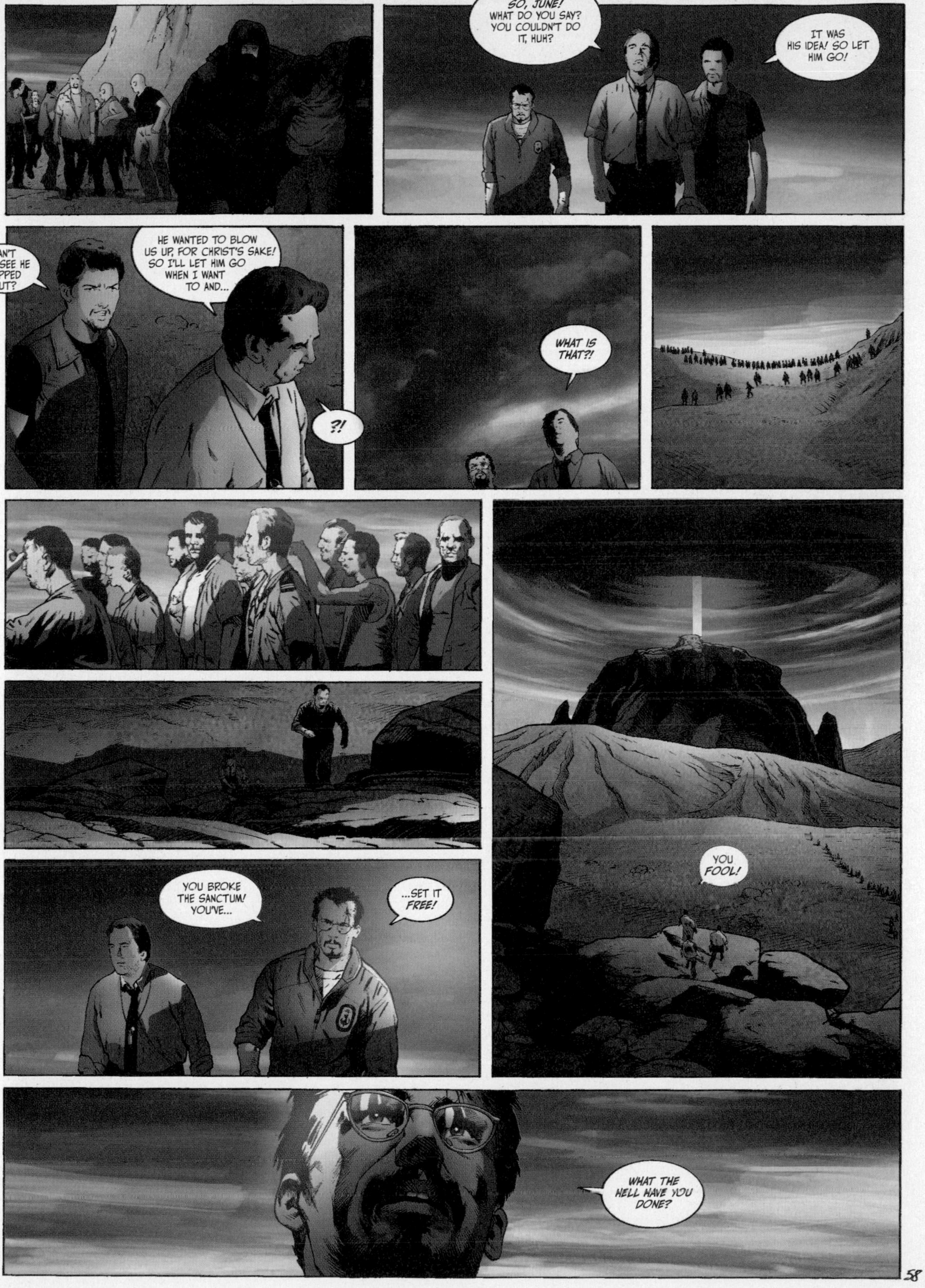
SO, JUNE! WHAT DO YOU SAY? YOU COULDN'T DO IT, HUH?
IT WAS HIS IDEA! SO LET HIM GO!
CAN'T YOU SEE HE FLIPPED OUT?
HE WANTED TO BLOW US UP, FOR CHRIST'S SAKE! SO I'LL LET HIM GO WHEN I WANT TO AND...
?!
WHAT IS THAT?!
YOU BROKE THE SANCTUM! YOU'VE...
...SET IT FREE!
YOU FOOL!
WHAT THE HELL HAVE YOU DONE?
58

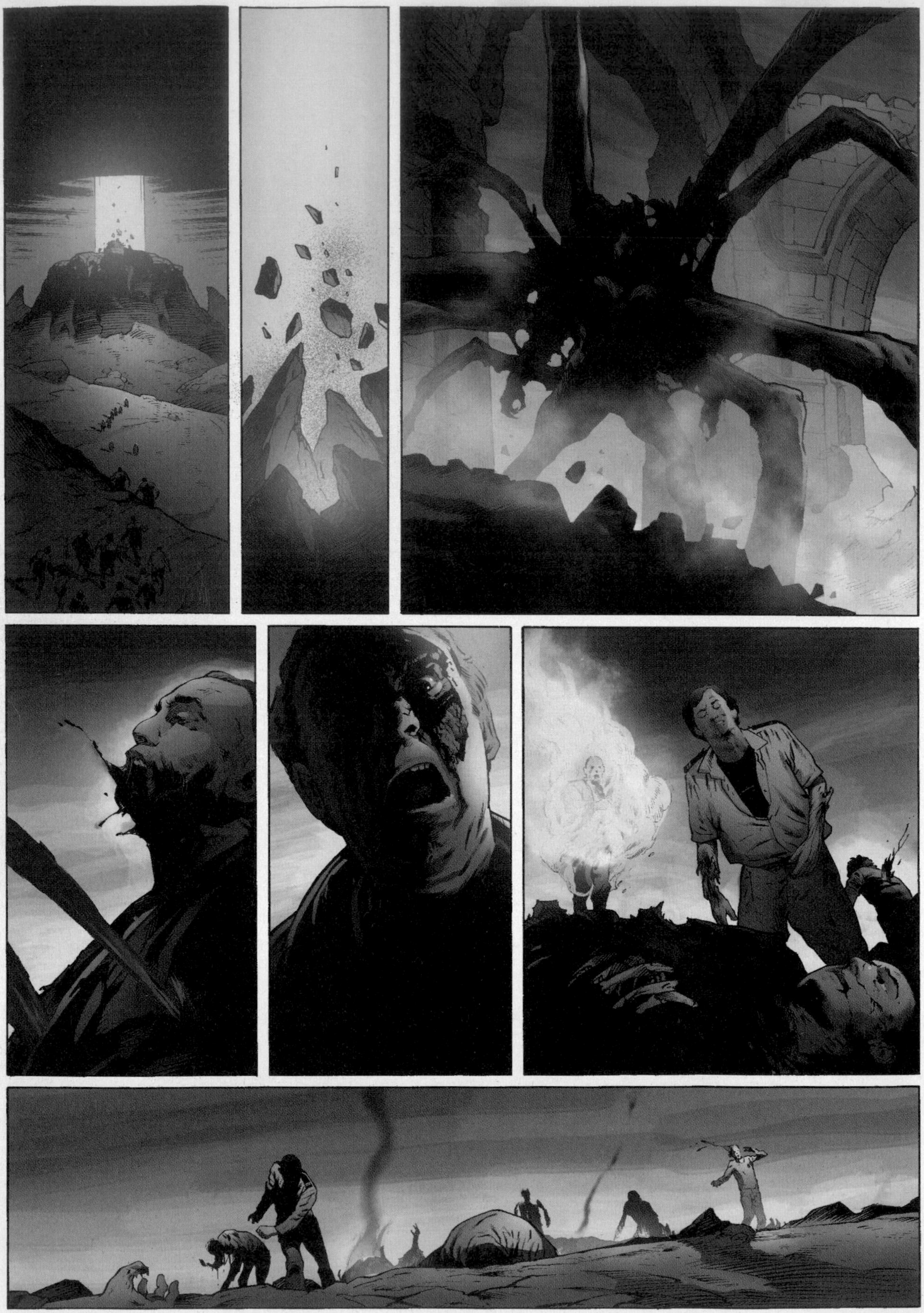

59

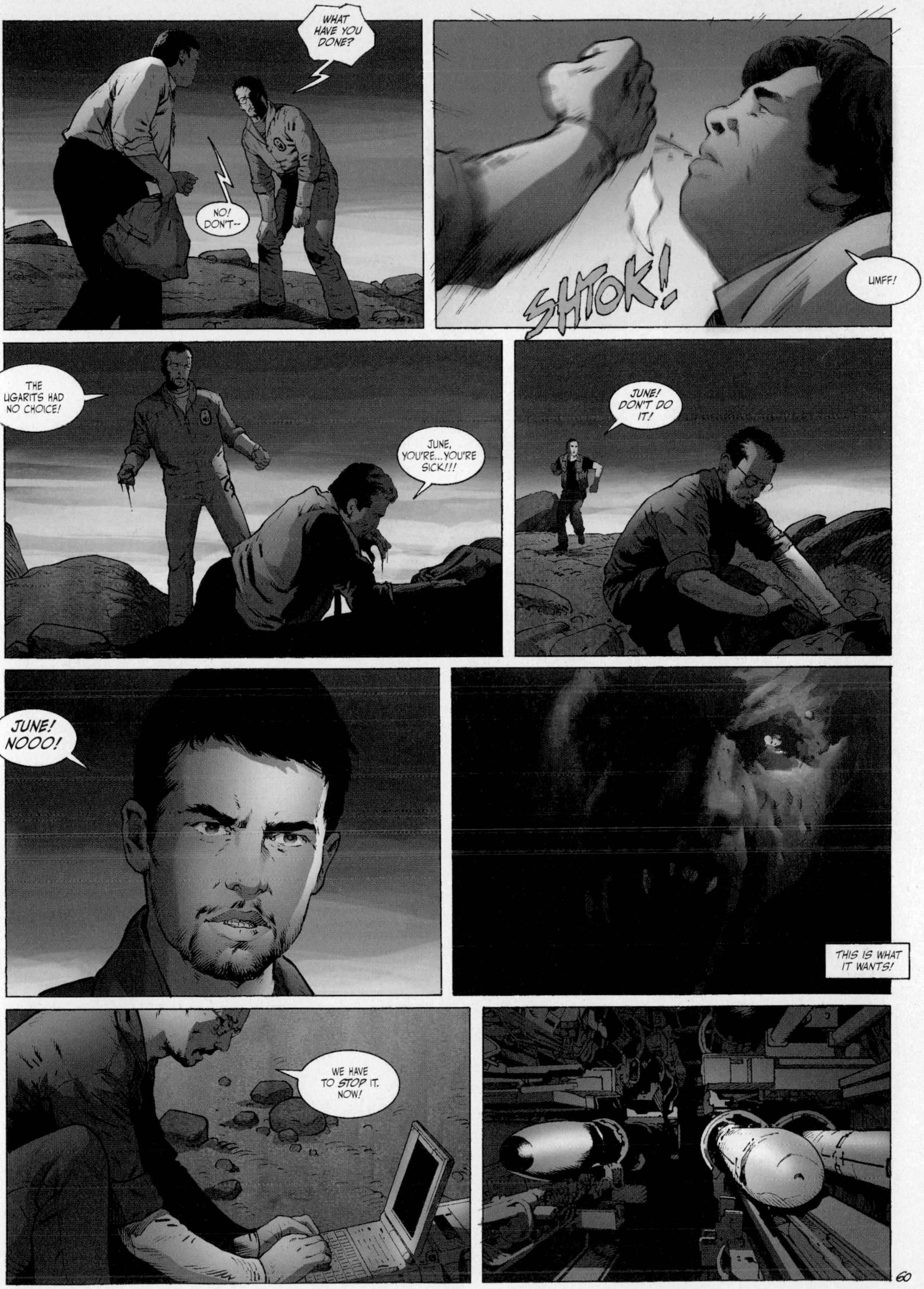
WHAT HAVE YOU DONE?
NO! DON'T--
SHTOK!
UMFF!
THE UGARITS HAD NO CHOICE!
JUNE, YOU'RE...YOU'RE SICK!!!
JUNE! DON'T DO IT!
JUNE! NOOO!
THIS IS WHAT IT WANTS!
WE HAVE TO STOP IT. NOW!
60

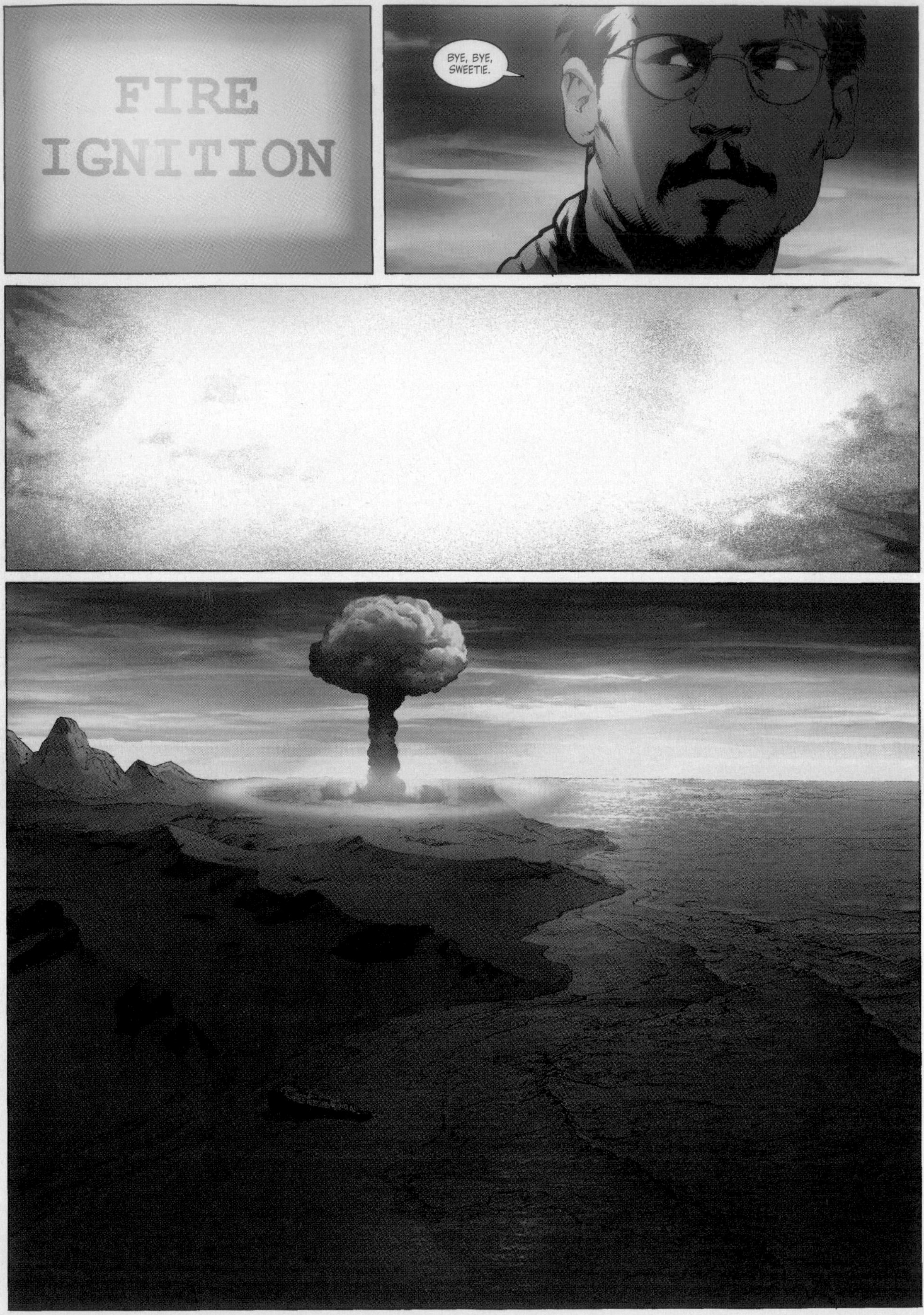
FIRE
IGNITION
BYE, BYE, SWEETIE.

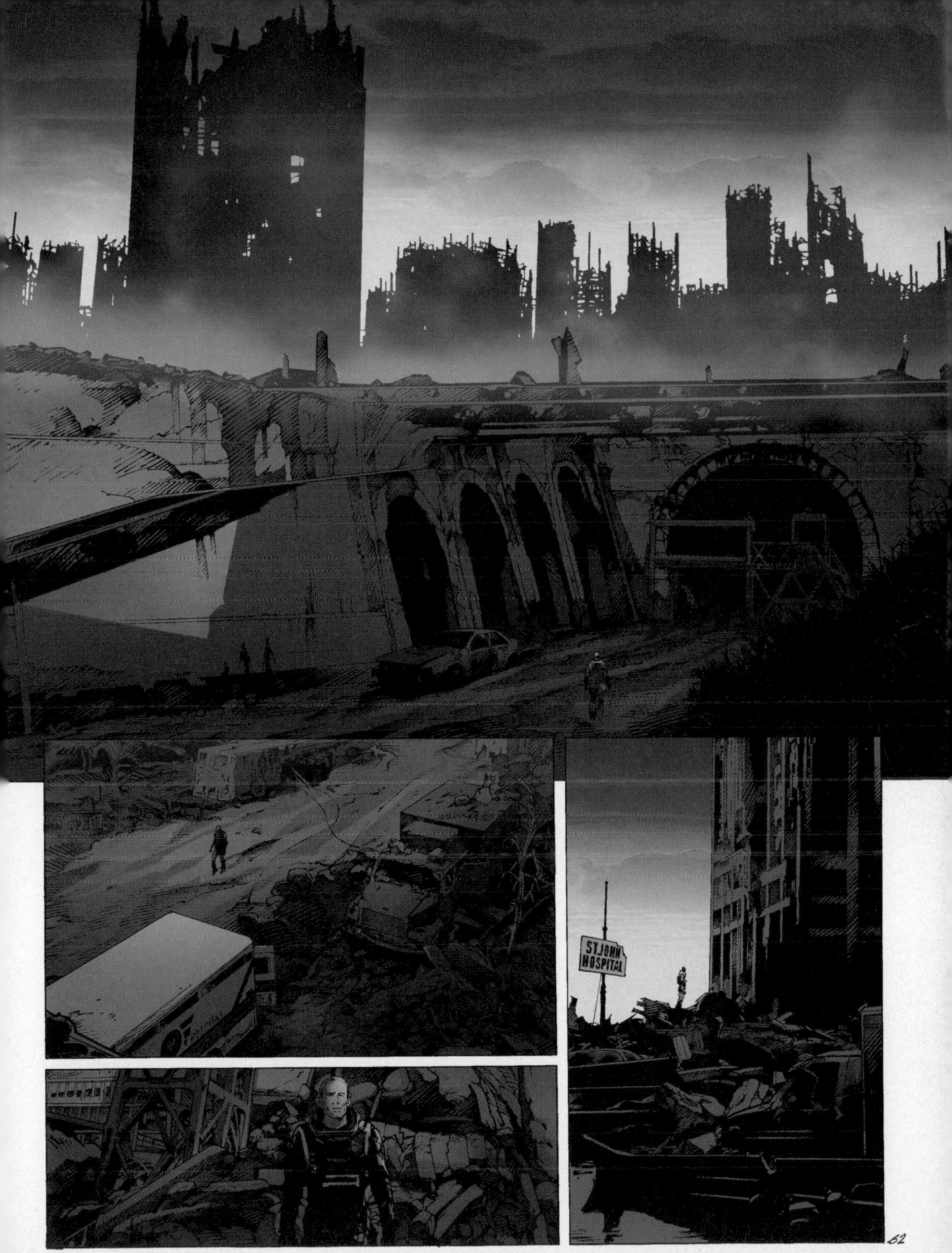
ST JOHN
HOSPITAL

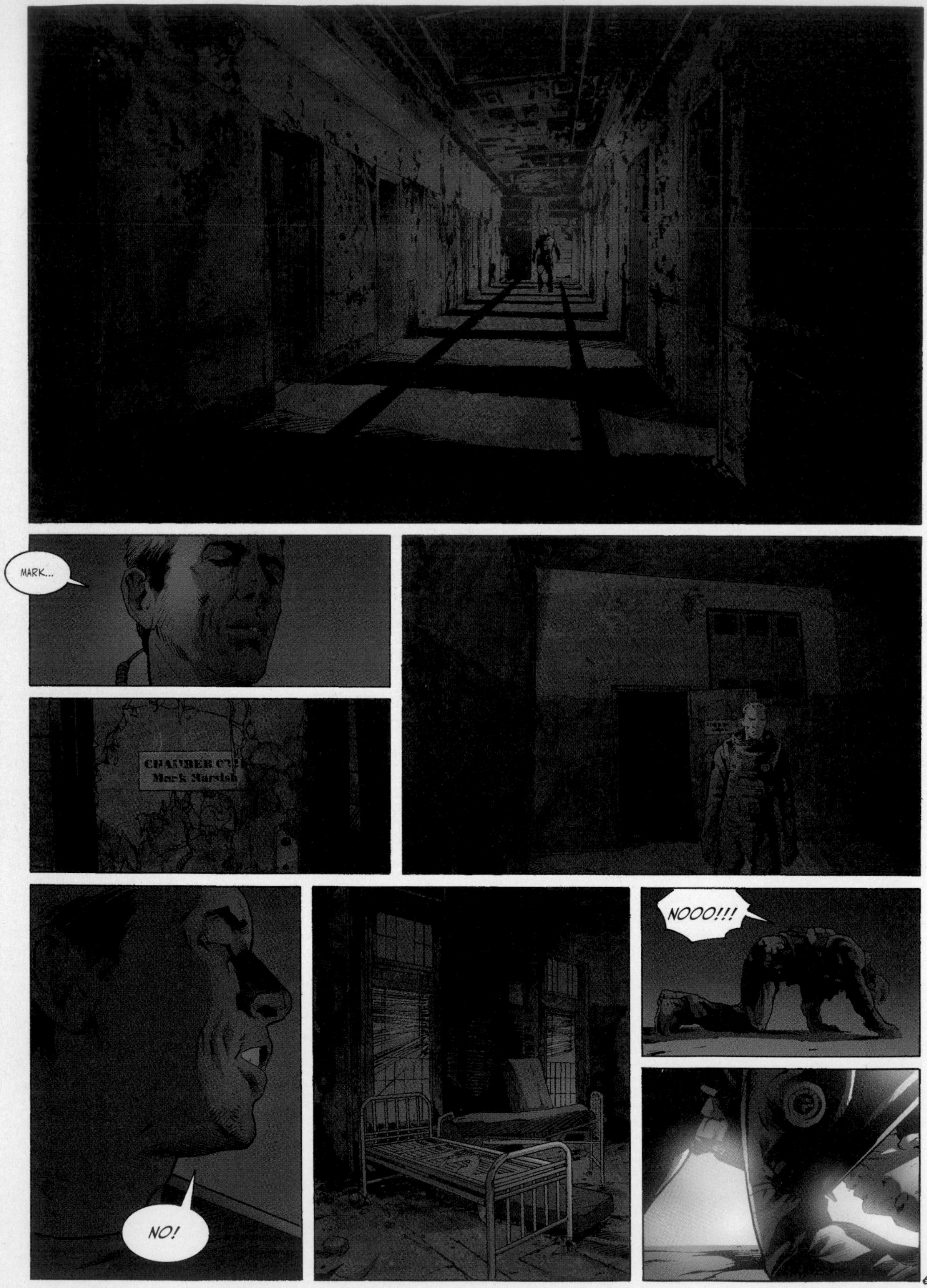
MARK...
NO!
NOOO!!!

63

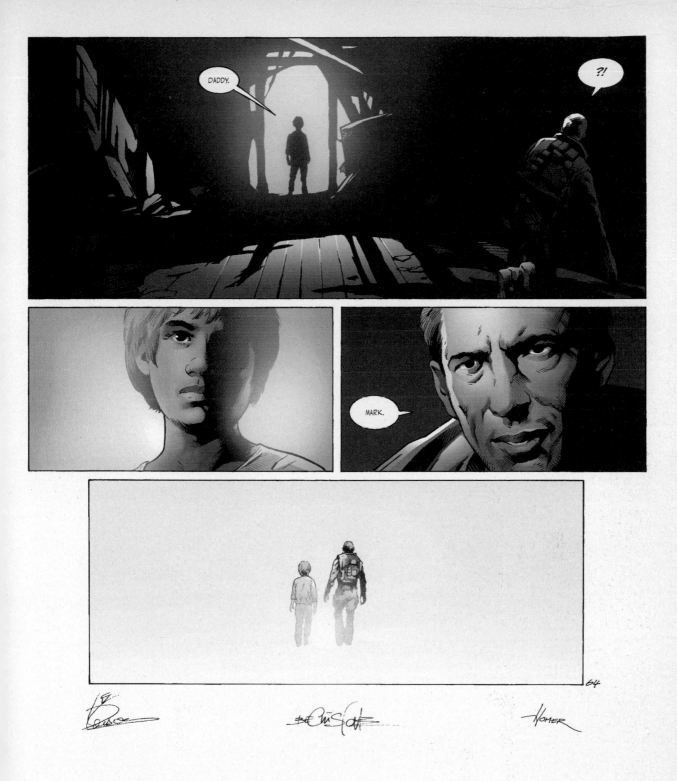

FOR MAXIME......YOUR LITTLE SMILE
IS THE LIGHT IN MY SANCTUM.
XAVIER DORISON

The light of the gods, Shapash,
the burning strength of the skies was in the hands of the divine word.
One day, days pass, days into months, the virgin Anat
seeks as the cow seeks her calf
as the sheep seeks her lamb,
so Anat's heart seeks Ba'al.
She takes the divine word, with sword she slices it,
with winnow she winnows it, with fire she burns it,
with the grindstone she crushes it, on the steppe she disperses it
that birds might devour her flesh,
her limbs consumed by sparrows.
Her flesh crying out to flesh...

- Ugarit poem

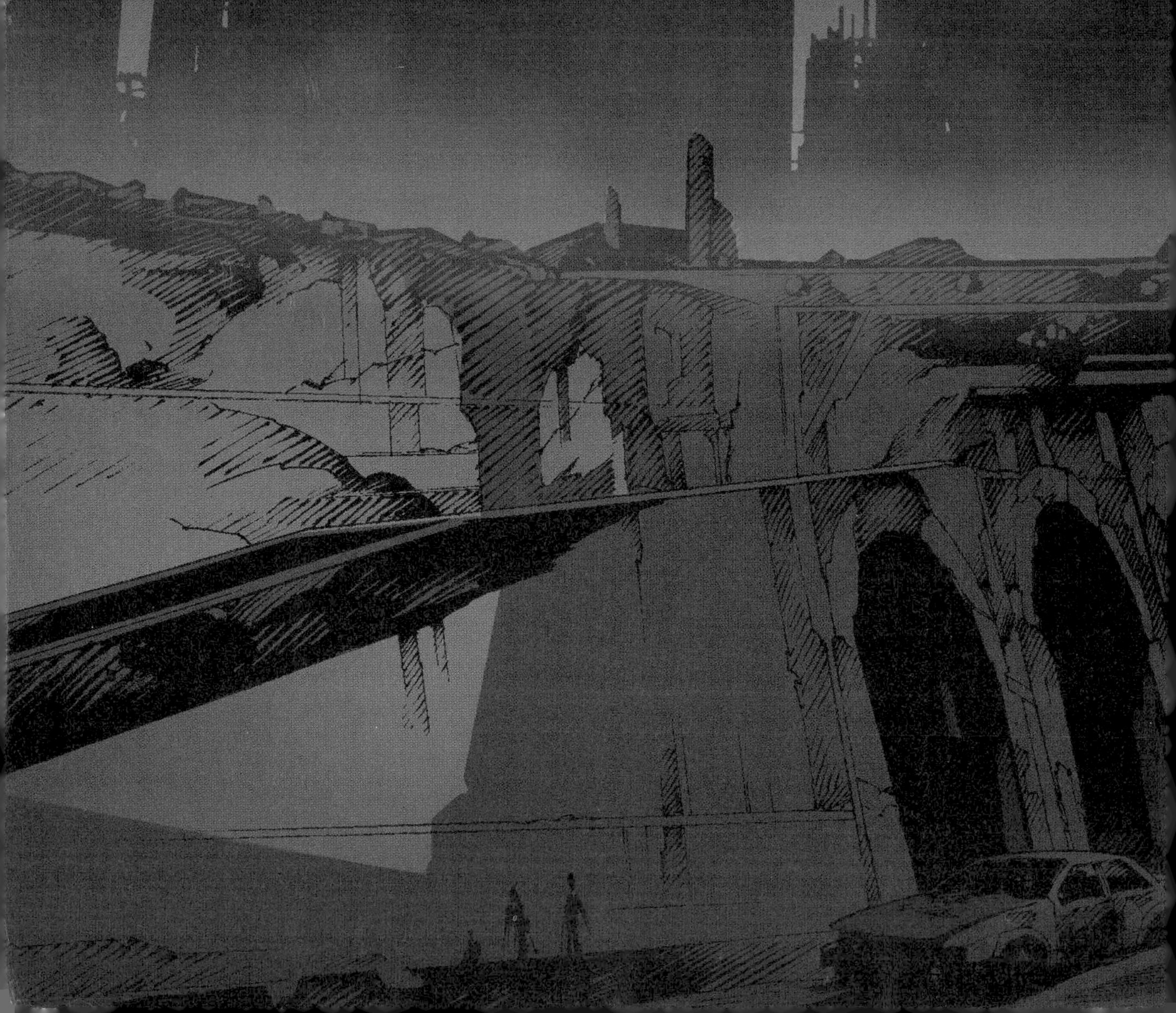

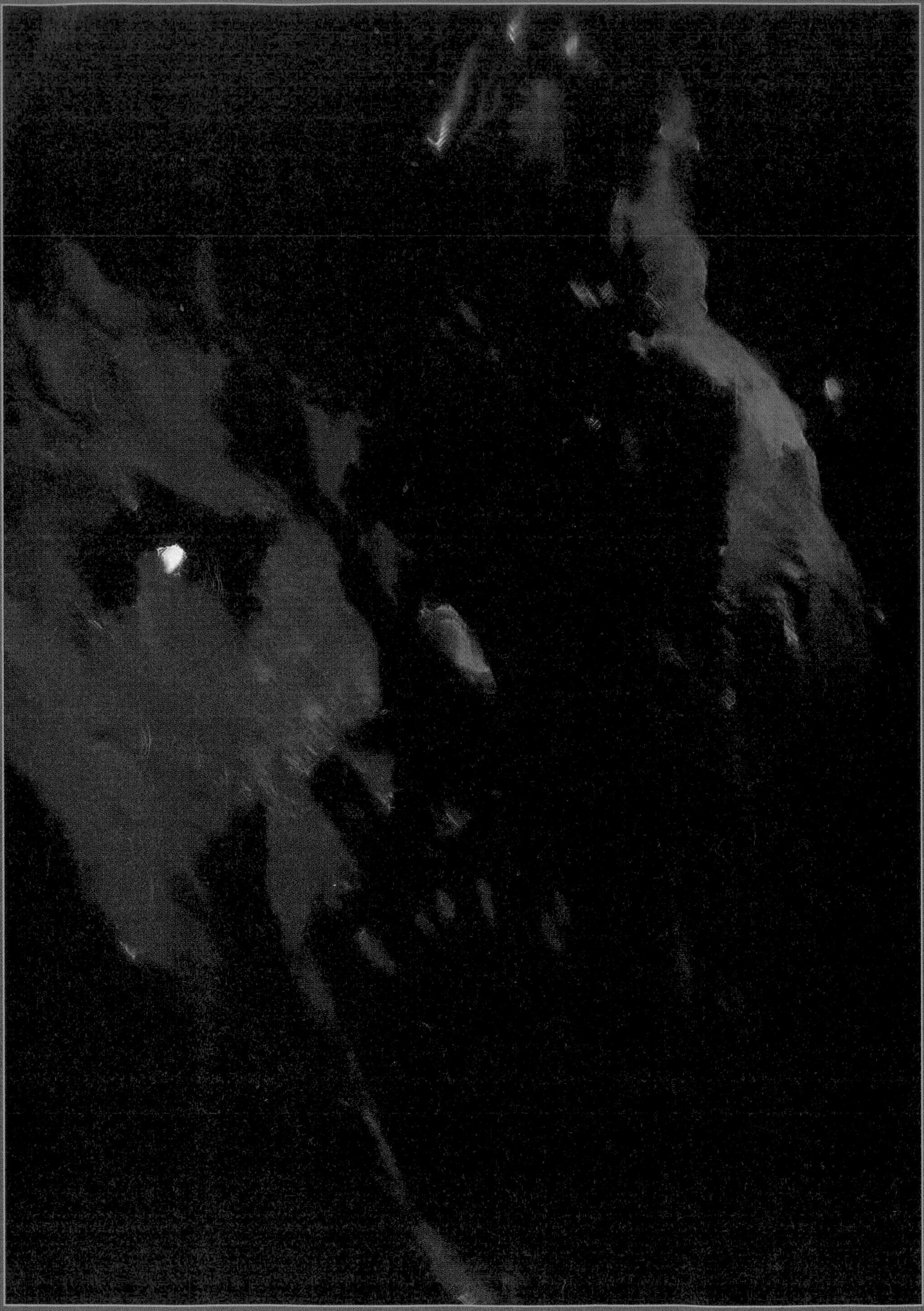

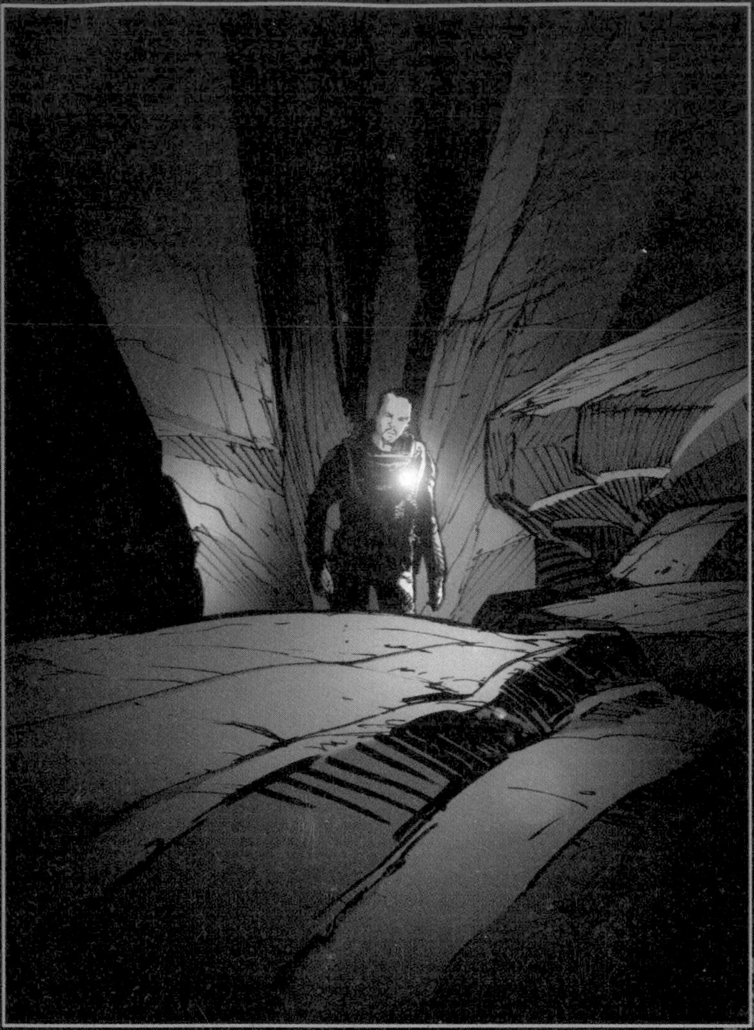

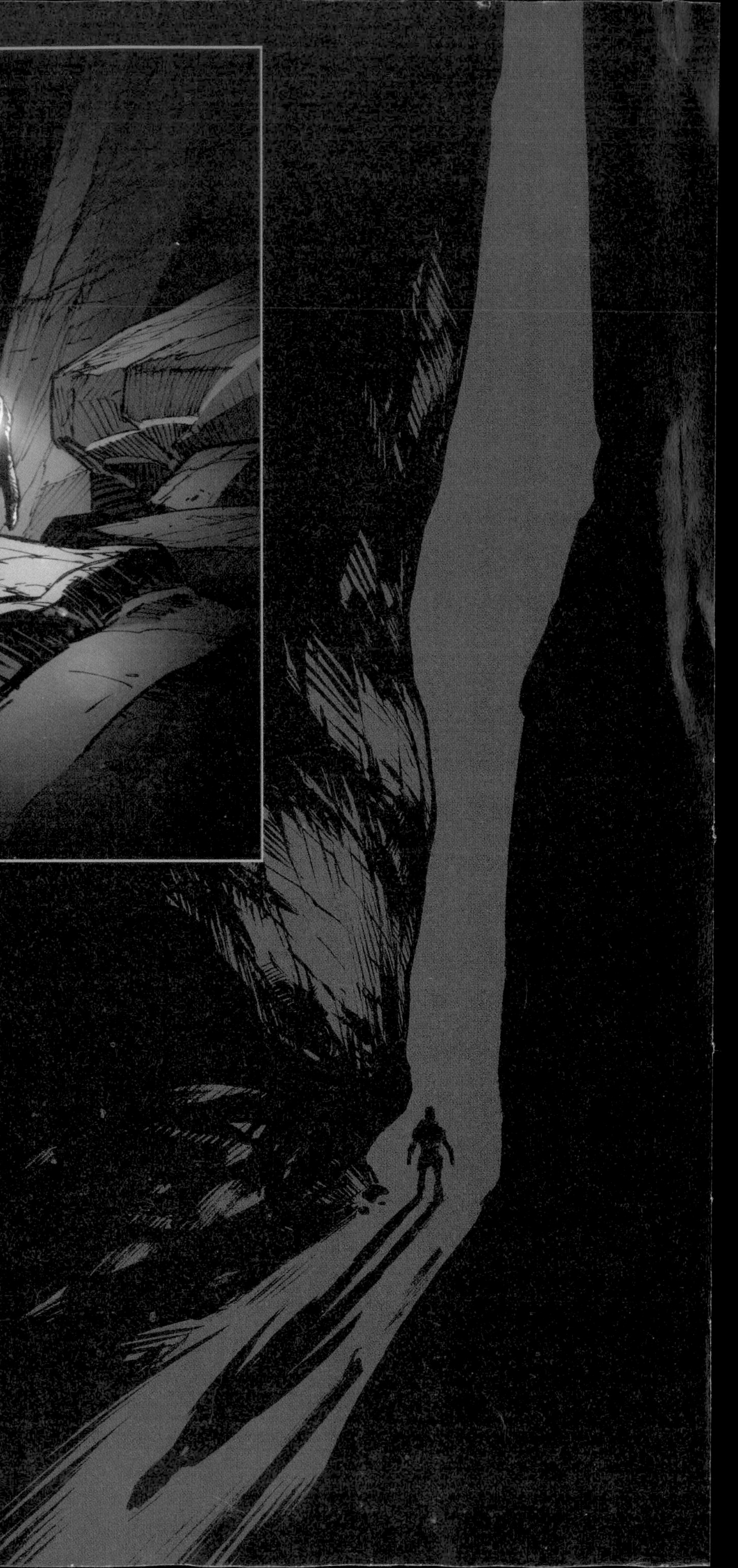

This page:
Promotional illustration

Opposite page:
Unused cover for the French graphic album, SANCTUAIRE #3: MÔT